St Antony's Series
General Editor: **Eugene Rogan** (1997–), Fellow of St Antony's College, Oxford

Recent titles include:

Carl Aaron
THE POLITICAL ECONOMY OF JAPANESE FOREIGN DIRECT INVESTMENT
IN THE UK AND THE US

Uri Bialer
OIL AND THE ARAB–ISRAELI CONFLICT, 1948–63

Craig Brandist and Galin Tihanov (*editors*)
MATERIALIZING BAKHTIN

Mark Brzezinski
THE STRUGGLE FOR CONSTITUTIONALISM IN POLAND

Reinhard Drifte
JAPAN'S QUEST FOR A PERMANENT SECURITY COUNCIL SEAT

Simon Duke
THE ELUSIVE QUEST FOR EUROPEAN SECURITY

Tim Dunne
INVENTING INTERNATIONAL SOCIETY

Marta Dyczok
THE GRAND ALLIANCE AND UKRAINIAN REFUGEES

Ken Endo
THE PRESIDENCY OF THE EUROPEAN COMMISSION UNDER
JACQUES DELORS

M. K. Flynn
IDEOLOGY, MOBILIZATION AND THE NATION

Anthony Forster
BRITAIN AND THE MAASTRICHT NEGOTIATIONS

Ricardo Ffrench-Davis
REFORMING THE REFORMS IN LATIN AMERICA

Fernando Guirao
SPAIN AND THE RECONSTRUCTION OF WESTERN EUROPE, 1945–57

Anthony Kirk-Greene
BRITAIN'S IMPERIAL ADMINISTRATORS, 1858–1966

Bernardo Kosacoff
CORPORATE STRATEGIES UNDER STRUCTURAL ADJUSTMENT IN ARGENTINA

Huck-ju Kwon
THE WELFARE STATE IN KOREA

Cécile Laborde
PLURALIST THOUGHT AND THE STATE IN BRITAIN AND FRANCE, 1900–25

Eiichi Motono
CONFLICT AND COOPERATION IN SINO–BRITISH BUSINESS, 1860–1911

C. S. Nicholls
THE HISTORY OF ST ANTONY'S COLLEGE, OXFORD, 1950–2000

Laila Parsons
THE DRUZE BETWEEN PALESTINE AND ISRAEL, 1947–49

Shane O'Rourke
WARRIORS AND PEASANTS

Patricia Sloane
ISLAM, MODERNITY AND ENTREPRENEURSHIP AMONG THE MALAYS

Karina Sonnenberg-Stern
EMANCIPATION AND POVERTY

Miguel Székely
THE ECONOMICS OF POVERTY AND WEALTH ACCUMULATION IN MEXICO

Ray Takeyh
THE ORIGINS OF THE EISENHOWER DOCTRINE

Steve Tsang and Hung-mao Tien (editors)
DEMOCRATIZATION IN TAIWAN

Yongjin Zhang
CHINA IN INTERNATIONAL SOCIETY SINCE 1949

Jan Zielonka
EXPLAINING EURO-PARALYSIS

St Antony's Series
Series Standing Order ISBN 0–333–71109–2
(*outside North America only*)

You can receive future titles in this series as they are published by placing a standing order. Please contact your bookseller or, in case of difficulty, write to us at the address below with your name and address, the title of the series and the ISBN quoted above.

Customer Services Department, Macmillan Distribution Ltd, Houndmills, Basingstoke, Hampshire RG21 6XS, England

The Politics of Telecommunications in Mexico

Privatization and State–Labour Relations, 1982–95

Judith Clifton
Lecturer in Political Communications
Institute of Communications Studies
University of Leeds

in association with
ST ANTONY'S COLLEGE, OXFORD

First published in Great Britain 2000 by
MACMILLAN PRESS LTD
Houndmills, Basingstoke, Hampshire RG21 6XS and London
Companies and representatives throughout the world

A catalogue record for this book is available from the British Library.

ISBN 0–333–75148–5

First published in the United States of America 2000 by
ST. MARTIN'S PRESS, INC.,
Scholarly and Reference Division,
175 Fifth Avenue, New York, N.Y. 10010

ISBN 0–312–23019–2

Library of Congress Cataloging-in-Publication Data
Clifton, Judith, 1967
The politics of telecommunications in Mexico : privatization and state–labour rela-
tions, 1982–95 / Judith Clifton
p.   cm. — (St. Antony's series)
Includes bibliographical references and index.
ISBN 0–312–23019–2 (cloth)
1. Teláfonos de Máxico, S.A.   2. Sindicato de Telefonistas de la Repàblica
Mexicana.   3. Telephone companies—Mexico.   4. Privatization—Mexico.
5. Telephone companies—Employees—Labor unions—Mexico.   I. Title.
II. Series.

HE8880.T435 C58   1999
384'.0972—dc21

99–049938

This book is printed on paper suitable for recycling and made from fully managed and sustained
forest sources.

10   9   8   7   6   5   4   3   2   1
09   08   07   06   05   04   03   02   01   00

Printed and bound in Great Britain by
Antony Rowe Ltd, Chippenham, Wiltshire

To my parents, for all their many kinds of support
and to Daniel, for everything

Contents

List of Tables and Figures

Preface

The origins of this book are my research interests in the process of democratization in general and my particular fascination with the case of Mexico. I was especially interested to enquire how the political system in Mexico had managed to remain so stable in marked contrast to many other developing countries, including those in Latin America.

My research started out as a DPhil candidate at St Antony's into one of the most important trade unions in Mexico during the 1980s and 1990s, the telephone workers' union. I wanted to analyse whether its project of representing a kind of 'new unionism' actually offered more union democracy and autonomy, and what consequences this might have for the stability of the political system and prospects for democracy. It was necessary to analyse the rise of this 'new unionism' movement within the context of the political, economic and social climate during the Salinas administration (1988–94) and, in particular, the privatization programme at the heart of which was the sale of Mexico's national telephone company, Teléfonos de México (TELMEX).

In my analysis of the evolving relationship between the Mexican government and the telephone workers' union contrast is made with the experiences of other Mexican trade unions in the same period, such as the unions of petroleum workers, teachers, electricity workers, miners and so on. However, there were reasons which made the telephone workers' union a special case. The telecommunications industry is at the heart of a transformation towards an increasingly information-dependent age. The convergence of computer, telephone and audio-visual technology means that the telecommunications sector is undergoing dramatic structural change, making it one of the most dynamic industries, as well as one increasingly subject to international competition. Telecommunications played a crucial role in both the economic and political policies of the Mexican government after the 1982 debt crisis. The sale of TELMEX was by far the most important single instance of privatization executed by Salinas both in financial and strategic terms. I argue in this book that the rise of 'new unionism' in Mexico is inseparable from these developments. The complexity of the telecommunications sector, the difficulties in researching such a sensitive topic, the key role of telecommunications in economic policy and politics during this period, justify a study which concentrates almost solely on this sector, though some comparisons are drawn with tele-communications policy in other Latin American countries. The lack of detailed work on how Mexican trade unions operate from within – a gap which was pointed out by Roxborough more than a decade ago and which continues to exist – provides another important reason for analysing one sector in detail. This helps avoid generalizations about state–labour relations and the dynamics of organized labour within the political system.

I would like to thank my supervisor, Alan Knight, for his guidance, sharp comments and careful reading of my work throughout the years that I was researching and writing this thesis at St Antony's. I am also grateful to Francisco Zapata at El Colegio de México for his help and support while I was conducting my fieldwork in Mexico from October 1994 to July 1995. I have also had many useful conversations and comments on various draft chapters of this work and must thank Daniel Díaz Fuentes, Nikki Craske, Laurence Whitehead, Kevin Middlebrook, Barbara Harriss-White, Mike Heller and Ngaire Woods.

JUDITH CLIFTON

List of Abbreviations

AHMSA	*Altos Hornos de México*
ASPA	*Asociación Sindical de Pilotos Aviadores* (Union Association of Pilots)
ASSA	*Asociación Sindical de Sobrecargos de Aviación* (Union Association for Airport Cargo Handlers)
ATM	*Alianza de Tranviarios de México* (Alliance of Mexican Tram Workers)
CANACINTRA	*Cámara Nacional de la Industria de Transformación* (National Chamber of Transformation Industry)
CEL	*Comité ejecutivo local* (Local union executive committee)
CEN	*Comité ejecutivo nacional* (National executive committee)
CEPAL	*Comisión Económica para América Latina* (Economic Commission for Latin America)
CFE	*Compañía Federal de Electricidad* (National Electricity Company)
CGOCM	*Confederación General de Obreros y Campesinos de México* (General Confederation of Mexican Workers and Peasants)
CGT	*Confederación General de Trabajadores* (General Confederation of Workers)
CNC	*Confederación Nacional Campesina* (National Peasants Confederation)
CNV	*Comité nacional de vigilancia* (National vigilance committee)
CNOP	*Confederación Nacional de Organizaciones Populares* (National Confederation of Popular Organizations)
CNTE	*Coordinadora Nacional de Trabajadores de la Educación* (National Coordination of Education Workers)
COM	*Casa del Obrero Mundial* (House of the World Worker)
CONASUPO	*Compañia Nacional de Subsistencias Populares* (National Campaign for Popular Subsistence)
CONCAMIN	*Confederación de Cámaras Industriales* (Confederation of Industrial Chambers)

COOC	*Coalición de Organizaciones Obreros y Campesinos* (Coalition of Worker and Peasant Organizations)
COPARMEX	*Confederación Patronal de la República Mexicana* (Confederation of Management of the Mexican Republic)
CROC	*Confederación Regional de Obreros y Campesinos* (Regional Confederation of Workers and Peasants)
CROM	*Confederación Regional Obrera Mexicana* (Confederation of Regional Mexican Workers)
CT	*Congreso de Trabajo* (Labour Congress)
CTAL	*Confederación de Trabajadores de América Latina* (Confederation of Latin American Workers)
CTM	*Confederación de Trabajadores de México* (Confederation of Mexican Workers)
CUT	*Confederación Única de Trabajadores* (Unified Workers' Confederation)
FDN	*Frente Democrática Nacional* (National Democratic Front)
FESEBES	*Federación de Sindicatos de Empresas de Bienes y Servicios* (Federation of Unions of Companies of Goods and Services)
FNOC	*Frente Nacional de Obreros y Campesinos* (National Front of Workers and Peasants)
GATT	General Agreement on Trade and Tariffs
IMF	International Monetary Fund
ISDN	Integrated Services Digital Network
ISI	Import Substitution Industrialisation
JCA	*Juntas de Conciliación Arbitraje* (Boards of Arbritration)
JFAC	*Junta Federal de Arbitraje y Conciliación* (Federal Board of Arbitration and Conciliation)
LFT	*Ley Federal de Trabajo* (Federal Labour Law)
MSF	*Movimiento Sindical Ferrocarrilero* (Railway Workers Union Movement)
MT	*Movimiento Popular Urbano Territorial* (Popular Movement of Urban Areas)
NAFTA	North American Free Trade Agreement
OECD	Organisation for Economic Co-operation and Development
PAN	*Partido de Acción Nacional* (National Action Party)
PECE	*Pacto para la Estabilidad y el Crecimiento Económico* (Pact for Stability and Economic Growth)

PEMEX	*Petróleos Mexicanos* (Mexican Petroleum)
PIMES	*Programa para la Inmediata Mejoramiento del Servicio* (Programme for the Immediate Improvement of Service)
PIRE	*Programa para Inmediata Recuperación Económica* (Programme for Immediate Economic Recovery)
PNR	*Partido Nacional Revolucionario* (National Revolutionary Party)
PRD	*Partido de la Revolución Democrático* (Party of the Democratic Revolution)
PRI	*Partido Revolucionario Institucional* (Party of the Institutionalized Revolution)
PRM	*Partido de la Revolución Mexicana* (Party of the Mexican Revolution)
PRONASOL	*Programa Nacional de Solidaridad* (National Solidarity Programme)
PSE	*Pacto de Solidaridad Económica* (Pact of Economic Solidarity)
SCT	*Secretaría de Comunicaciones y Transportes* (Ministry of Communications and Transport)
SHCP	*Secretaría de Hacienda y Crédito Público* (Ministry of Finance and Public Credit)
SICARTSA	*Siderúrgica Lázaro Cárdenas-Las Truchas* (Lázaro Cárdenas-Las Truchas Steel Plant)
SITIAVW	*Sindicato Independiente de Trabajadores de la Industria Automotriz de Volkswagen* (Independent Union of Workers of Volkswagen Automobiles)
SME	*Sindicato Mexicano de Electricistas* (Mexican Union of Electricity Workers)
SNTE	*Sindicato Nacional de Trabajadores de la Educación* (National Union of Education Workers)
SNTMMSRM	*Sindicato Nacional de Trabajadores Mineros, Metalúrgicos y Similares de la República Mexicana* (National Union of Mining, Metallurgical and Related Workers of the Mexican Republic)
SPP	*Secretaría de Programación y Presupuesto* (Ministry of Planning and Budgeting)
STERM	*Sindicato de Trabajadores Electricistas de la República Mexicana* (Union of Electricity Workers of the Mexican Republic)

STFRM	*Sindicato de Trabajadores Ferrocarrileros de la República Mexicana* (Union of Railway Workers of the Mexican Republic)
STIC	*Sindicato de Técnicos y Manuales de la Industria Cinematográfica* (Union of Technicians and Manual Workers of the Cinematography Industry)
STPRM	*Sindicato de Trabajadores Petroleros de la República Mexicana* (Union of Petroleum Workers of the Mexican Republic)
STPS	*Secretaría del Trabajo y Previsión Social* (Ministry of Labour and Social Security)
STRM	*Sindicato de Telefonistas de la República Mexicana* (Union of Telephone Workers of the Mexican Republic)
SUTERM	*Sindicato Unico de Trabajadores Electricistas de la República Mexicana* (Unified Union of Electricity Workers of the Mexican Republic)
TELMEX	*Teléfonos de México* (Mexican Telephone Company)
UOI	*Unidad Obrera Independiente* (United Independent Workers)
VAM	*Vehículos Automotores Mexicanos* (Mexican Motor Vehicles)

Introduction

During the 1980s, many social scientists expressed a renewed optimism about the prospects for democratic growth across the world.[1] This optimism was triggered by key events including the collapse of dictatorships in Southern Europe during the 1970s, in the Southern Cone Latin American countries and also in East Asian countries.[2] The year 1989 in particular marked a 'watershed' in world politics with the fall of the Berlin Wall which signalled the beginning of the end of Communism in the Soviet Union. Huntington, among the more extreme analysts, claimed that a 'third wave' of democracy was sweeping across the globe.[3] In the same period, an economic debate which had been growing in importance during the previous decade became yet more influential. The central issue concerned the limits of the postwar model of a mixed economy which was increasingly questioned in the industrialized countries.[4] The efficiency and performance of the public sector were deemed to be constraints on economic growth. A reconsideration of the nature and role of the state in developed and developing market economies led to the view that government involvement had been excessive.[5] Attempts were made in the former Soviet Union to replace the old model of central planning with one that was more market-oriented and export-led. In the aftermath of the 1982 debt crisis, most Latin American governments decided to pursue dramatically different economic policies and abandoned the former model of import substitution industrialization (ISI) for a neoliberal model which had at its heart a reduction of the role of the state in the economy.

The concurrence of dramatic political and economic change in this period inspired some observers to produce a particular *genre* of literature on the subject of democracy which resurrected a classic question with origins in the Enlightenment, and even, in Ancient Greece, namely, the relationship between political and economic change.[6] This body of literature was by no means homogeneous: certain analysts were influenced by modernization theory; others by rent-seeking theory; and still others – perhaps the majority – by a cocktail of both. These analysts reasoned that, since recent political democratization had evolved at the same time as economic liberalization during the 1980s, there was a causal connection between them.[7] Assuming this was true, the question of 'sequencing' became fashionable – should political or economic reform lead the changes – and Gorbachev's policies of *glasnost* and *perestroika* were used as critical reference points since the reformer finally lost control over his reforms.

This trend had a profound impact on the analysis of the Mexican political system. Notwithstanding the fact that the political system in Mexico had exhibited a high degree of stability, continuity and capacity to adapt to different circumstances since the 1930s – in marked contrast to the more volatile systems of other Latin American countries such as Argentina, Brazil and Chile in the same period – many analysts such as Delal Baer, Morici, Roett, Rubio and Weintraub[8] were convinced that the force of economic reforms meant that democratization trends could not be resisted.[9] The outcome of the 1988 presidential elections whereby the presidential candidate of the *Partido Revolucionario Institucional* (PRI) gained only fractionally more than 50 per cent of the votes, in contrast to the usual result of at least 70 per cent, was taken by many observers as proof of society's discontent with the party. This dissatisfaction was only partly caused by the negative impact of the debt crisis and subsequent austerity measures. Many analysts and Mexican politicians believed that political reform was urgent if the party was to stay in power, since they increasingly perceived that the party's traditional mechanisms of mustering support had dramatically declined.[10] Since the PRI was losing support from its traditional corporate stalwarts, such as organized labour, and had decreasing financial resources with which to bring them back to the fold, some claimed that the party was losing its grip on the corporate pact, which had entered an advanced state of disintegration. Certain analysts took the argument further and utilized normative and futuristic speculations when they claimed that democratization was *bound* to happen in Mexico.[11]

Nevertheless, by the end of the Salinas administration in 1994, relatively few of the democratizing reforms anticipated by these authors had been realized. Indeed, this administration ended in a dramatic display of the inadequacy of the political reforms implemented. Events such as the peasant uprisings in Chiapas and Guerrero, the former exploding symbolically on the day after the signing of the NAFTA treaty on 1 January 1994, allowed these Mexicans to voice their discontent at having been neglected by the government and abandoned to live in poverty and social exclusion. Moreover, the assassinations of top-level PRI politicians, including Colosio, the PRI's presidential candidate, pointed to the severity of intra-élite conflicts over the future political and economic trajectory which the country should follow. The subsequent president, Ernesto Zedillo, was charged with defusing this political situation. He took steps to accomplish this partly by opening up more political space for the opposition parties, for example by increasing the main opposition parties' presence in Congress to the extent that the PRI lost its traditional dominance, and by holding elections for a Mayor in Mexico City which the PRD candidate, Cuauhtémoc Cárdenas, won.

Most of the analyses published about the Salinas administration shared, as a general consensus, that, while economic reform had been far-reaching, political reform was modest. Interestingly, most analysts explained the lack of political reform by pointing to specific features of the political system itself, rather than considering why economic liberalization had not brought about the predicted political changes. Centeno explained that economic reform had been implemented in a top–down authoritarian style by an élite isolated from political pressure in an 'inner cabinet'.[12] Other analysts claimed that in some instances political change had been resisted by different sectors within society, including local government[13] or organized labour.[14]

Unfortunately, analysts did not return to the question of the relationship between political and economic change when trying to unravel why it was that economic liberalization flourished while political reform was seriously lacking in the period. The omission was 'unfortunate' because the concerns at the heart of a significant body of analysis were left inconclusive. Moreover, *prima facie*, since Mexico exemplified such an extreme asymmetry in the success of its economic reforms but failure in its political reforms, it offered a rebuttal of the claims of those who insisted that democratization would inevitably follow economic liberalization. Thus, an analysis of the situation in Mexico would shed light on the general question of the relation between economic and political change.

The principal aim of this work is to establish what can be learned from the Mexican experience with regard to the relationship between political and economic reform. In order to do this it was first necessary to define and limit the topic of research. The bulk of my analysis is focused on the administration of President Salinas (1988–94) since it was during this period that there was a high degree of asymmetry between economic and political reform: while dramatic programmes of economic liberalization were implemented, so much so that the president earned the nickname of Latin America's 'Thatcher', political reform was much less forthcoming. I chose to reject attempting to link the broad concept, 'economic liberalization', with another vast topic, 'democracy', on a macro scale at the national level, which was a tendency exhibited in much of the literature written by the authors mentioned earlier.[15] Instead, I decided to study one element of the complex and diverse policies which are generally understood as 'economic liberalization', namely, privatization. Furthermore, I limited my study of the possible democratizing impact that this component of economic liberalization had upon society to examining those actors most directly affected, namely, the government, business and the union. The most important case of privatization in Mexico, in both financial and strategic terms, was chosen, that is, the privatization of *Teléfonos de México* (TELMEX) in 1990.[16] The conclusions derived from this work are thus limited to an observation about the dynamic relations between political and economic change in the case of this huge privatization exercise and its impact on the main actors involved. This is an important case not only because of the significance which TELMEX played during the privatization process. The study of this case of privatization sheds light on the way in which the nature of the state–labour corporatist relationship changed. Hernández Juárez, the leader of the telephone workers' union, became the major spokesman for a reputedly 'new' kind of unionism in Mexico, and he increasingly fought to carve out a place for this 'new' unionism alongside the CTM and other traditional labour confederations. Thus I was interested to analyse whether this 'new unionism' actually brought about a democratizating effect upon the traditional state–labour pact.

It is sustained in this work that the processes of economic and political change are tightly interlinked, if not inseparable, processes. One of the most straightforward and fundamental defences of their interconnection is that a government's decision to implement a particular economic measure – whether privatization or nationalization – is also a political decision. However, I repudiate the argument that the policies of economic liberalization and privatization *inevitably* bring about a democratization of the relationship between the actors involved. In particular, I show that, in the case of the privatization of

TELMEX, the claim that the corporate political system based on clientelism, patronage and corruption, would be eroded by the logic of neoliberal economic reform made by analysts including Delal Baer, Roett, Rubio and Weintraub, proved inaccurate. Political decisions played an immensely important role throughout the implementation of the privatization programme in Mexico, and this has been largely underestimated in the literature. My research shows that the privatization of TELMEX generated new resources and opportunities which helped to lubricate a relationship between the state, management and the union that bore many similarities to previous examples of this kind of corporatist relationship. Accordingly, the results concur with a newly emerging body of criticism which returns to the question of the link between political and economic reform, using as evidence the multiple experiences of developing countries in experiencing reform.[17] These writers claim that, in their analyses of the processes of economic and political liberalization in developing countries (including countries in Latin America, Asia and Africa), new resources and opportunities were produced which were used to corrupt ends, and, often, helped to continue clientelist political arrangements such as corporatism which had previously been endangered by a lack of resources with which to facilitate them. The conclusions derived from analysis of the case study of the privatization of TELMEX coincide with their fundamental conclusions. In direct contradiction to the arguments explicit in the New Political Economy,[18] it is argued that corporatist political systems based on clientelism and sometimes corruption can be equally as comfortable with neoliberalism as they were with protectionism.

In order to research this topic I spent one year in Mexico, mostly in Mexico City, where the majority of the telephone network is concentrated, and also in Puebla, where the third largest telephone network system in the republic is located.[19] During the year I consulted primary documents obtained from TELMEX, the relevant government agencies – in particular the Labour Ministry and the Communications and Transport Ministry – and the telephone workers' union. I interviewed ex-members of the Salinas administration including the Secretary of Labour Farrell, the Secretary of Communications and Transport Caso Lombardo and functionaries of both agencies. I also interviewed top- and middle-level TELMEX management executives. A great deal of my time was spent with STRM leaders and I interviewed key union characters including most of the non-elected 'comisionados'. Towards the end of the year, I also conducted a survey with a representative sample of telephone operators, the results of which are included in the Appendix. In addition, I was able to interview many opposition telephone workers or ex-workers who had been fired for their dissidence. I also interviewed journalists, academics and intellectuals who were interested in this field.

One of the main difficulties of working on labour topics in Mexico,[20] in contrast to certain other Latin American countries such as Chile, is gaining access to the union, both at the national level – interviewing leaders and attending national conferences – and at the shop-floor level, observing work practices. During the course of this research it proved much simpler to persuade former cabinet members and busy top-level TELMEX executives to be interviewed than union leaders! Moreover, it was impossible to speak with workers on the shop-floor without the leaders' permission.[21] The problem of inaccessibility to unions has been reflected in much of the literature on organized labour in Mexico[22] and the result is that most unions are categorized as being of type 'A' or 'B' on the basis of a few superficial observations such as whether or not they belong to an 'official' labour confederation.[23] In this literature, union democracy and autonomy are analysed only in terms of the relations between the 'state' and 'labour'. Often, categories such as 'democratic' or 'official' are used without an analysis of the union's internal practices.[24] Furthermore, the state is usually treated as if it were a homogeneous entity without being disaggregated into different state agencies. There were three main reasons why it proved possible to observe, from close range, the internal workings of the STRM in this research. First, the union leaders boasted that the STRM was the most democratic and progressive union in Mexico and was, moreover, at the vanguard of technological change. For these reasons, the leaders seemed to be relatively proud of the fact that they were an object of a study. Second, I was introduced to top union leaders through a contact with an academic from El Colegio de Mexico, and was an outsider, moreover, a '*guerita*', so I probably enjoyed access to the union that many Mexican researchers might be denied.[25] Many of the union members were fascinated that I was fascinated by them. Third, after meeting top union leaders and gaining their confidence, I persuaded them to cooperate with my research project. Over the course of a year, I slowly, but firmly, insisted that I should be allowed to interview union leaders, and finally, conduct a survey at the shop-floor level. I started pressuring union leaders in November, and I had my results by July.

Publications on privatization to date are dominated largely by international institutions, particularly the World Bank and the ECLAC, and, although certain volumes are extremely useful, both tend to have an ideological leaning.[26] Even among works written by individuals, it often remains difficult for the analyst to refrain from taking a pro- or anti-privatization stance. Another characteristic of the majority of privatization literature is that it is circumscribed by a financial or business approach. Rarely is the impact of privatization upon the union or the workforce considered in detail. Moreover, works on contemporary labour relations in Mexico tend not to analyse examples of privatization in any great detail. This means that there was almost no overlap between the two bodies of publications, and this work aims to situate itself within the gap.

The organization of this work is as follows. In the first two chapters I present a synthesis of the 'state-of-the-art' of the literature on the two main topics that concern us. The first chapter contains an analysis of the way in which the Mexican political system has been presented in the literature and the contemporary problems with this analysis. In the second chapter, I critically analyse the way in which state–labour relations in Mexico have been treated in the literature, and, in particular, point to the limitations in some of the concepts used to describe organized labour. I follow this by suggesting an alternative perspective which rejects an analysis of the union as a 'black box' and much of the dichotomous terminology used by many analysts of organized labour such as '*charro*' or 'democratic'. My approach instead concentrates on analysing union practice from the inside. I present a brief history of the STRM which adopts this method of analysis. In Chapters 3 and 4, I account for the key economic changes undertaken by the Mexican government from the mid-1980s, including telecommunications policy and its reform. I also analyse the reasons that the STRM, unlike most other unions, chose to accept the government's project of economic restructuring and, later, privatization. The final chapter analyses in detail the politics of the privatization of TELMEX in 1990, and, in particular, argues that the project of '*nuevo sindicalismo*' evolved in direct parallel to the government's privatization project. Thus, in this case study, the dynamic links between political and economic change are highlighted. Finally, in my conclusion, I explain what I have learned about the links between economic and political change in this case study, and what is the significance of this '*nuevo sindicalismo*' for organized labour generally in Mexico. My survey and interviews, which were used to analyse, from a 'bottom–up' perspective the way in which privatization affected telephone workers at the shop-floor level, are included in the Appendix.

1
Continuity and Rupture in the Mexican Political System

The way in which the *Partido Revolucionario Institucional* (PRI)[1] has monopolized power in Mexico for the bulk of the twentieth century continues to be a point of fascination for analysts of Latin American politics. The ruling party's stability, durability and longevity are remarkable, and these characteristics have set it apart from other governments in Latin America. Even on an international scale, the PRI has outlived all other revolutionary governments this century. During the 1950s and 1960s, visiting scholars to Mexico returned optimistic about the direction in which Mexican politics were heading, and they praised the social and economic progress being made.[2] However, after 1968, when the Mexican army massacred hundreds of protesting students at Tlatelolco in Mexico City, there was a growing revulsion against this former optimism. From around the late 1960s to the present, many analysts agree that the best classification is an 'inclusionary authoritarian' system.[3] Vargas Llosa's oft-quoted description of the PRI as the 'perfect dictatorship', due to its ability to adapt to new situations and to maintain control over society through a façade of tolerance, remains one of the most apt clichés used by observers to describe the PRI.[4]

Many reasons have been put forward to explain the longevity of the party and the relative political stability which it has enjoyed since its creation in 1929. To provide a comprehensive explanation is a complex task, partly because of the longevity and omnipresence that characterize the party. However, there is a high degree of consensus in the literature concerning the aspects which underpin the PRI's power.[5]

8

The Mexican political system

The Mexican political system is often analysed as if it were a human pyramid, given the importance of hierarchical and vertical networks of power and patronage. At the top of this pyramid sits the incumbent president in whom an enormous amount of power is concentrated. Cosío Villegas compared him to an absolute, but temporary, monarch since he is required to step down after six years have passed and must refrain from being involved overtly in politics thereafter.[6] While in power, the president enjoys a great deal of discretion and he may intervene personally in the decision-making processes of the institutional branches of government, including judicial and legislative matters. Presidential succession, which has occurred like clockwork every six years since the administration of Lázaro Cárdenas (1934–40), has been accomplished by the *dedazo*, which refers to selection by the incumbent of his successor. Secrecy still surrounds the *dedazo* and the criteria used by the president to hand-pick his successor. This process, which may disappear from 2000, was probably the most potent informal ritual embedded in the Mexican political system, and the 'linchpin' of authoritarianism in Mexico.[7]

The constitutional clause of no re-election of the president and state governors ensures a high degree of élite circulation and helps to prevent blockages in the system.[8] This mobility has placated rivalry which could lead to division within the party: since there is regular élite turnover, politicians understand that they have a greater chance of success if they remain patiently within the system waiting for a turn at power rather than if they were to splinter off and attempt to form their own party.[9] While positions of power are circulated among the élite, surnames belonging to members of the 'Revolutionary Family' appear repeatedly, fulfilling their pact to share power in post-revolutionary Mexico.[10]

The oxymoronic title of the party – the party of the institutionalized revolution – provides a clue as to how the regime claims legitimacy. First, it states that it is the legitimate party of the Mexican Revolution and, while successive administrations have utilized different styles, policies and rhetorics, all have defended their various policies by using a legitimating discourse which claims they are revitalizing and renewing the spirit of the revolution. Second, the party argues that it promotes national peace and stability through guaranteeing the continuity of the post-revolutionary institutions. The logic is that a vote for the party is a vote for Mexico – a vote against the party amounts to anti-patriotism. One of the ways in which the party attacks its enemies is by accusing them of being anti-Mexican or of being influenced by other countries (which amounts to the same thing).[11]

The PRI has proved highly capable of surviving through reform and renewal, although these measures have always been limited. In part, the party's survival has been achieved by its capacity to respond to the 'climate' in society, among workers, peasants, industrialists and other capitalists, by moving from the left to the right side of the political spectrum and back again. The party has tended to open up the political system incrementally, via limited liberalization measures, such as electoral reform in 1977 and 1990, through a relaxing of rules like the *apertura democrática* during the Echeverría administration. Many analysts claim that the party implements liberalization reforms only when it feels its legitimacy is seriously challenged. These reforms are thought to act as 'safety valves' to release steam preventing society from becoming too 'hot'. The PRI has no fixed or rigid ideology: explanations have been employed ingeniously to justify both protectionism and liberalization in defence of the Revolution.

In terms of coping with its enemies, the regime has tended to avoid the excessive, systematic and visible violence characteristic of other Latin American authoritarian governments. Usually, the PRI's strategy has been to try to defuse potential conflict before it breaks out. Talented would-be opposition leaders are often 'co-opted', which means that they are attracted by party members and brought into the fold of the PRI having succumbed to a series of temptations.[12] Whenever strong, organized opposition has reared its head, the party has proved itself a master at 'divide and rule' tactics. For instance, it has demonstrated fickle favouritism of diverse labour organizations in order to provoke rivalry and jealousy, and prevent any one of them from becoming too powerful.[13] For these reasons, overt violence in Mexico generates massive outcries from the public, such as the response of anger and outrage when the Mexican army opened fire on students in 1968 and, more recently, when it repressed peasant guerillas in Chiapas. Often, violence is avoided in the major, visible, cities but it does take place in rural areas which are out of the public spotlight. Moreover, the federal government tries to avoid responsibility for the violence in comparison to other South and Central American governments. Executive violence is constrained by attention from the international media, all the more important after Mexico joined the North American Free Trade Agreement (NAFTA) and the Organisation for Economic Cooperation and Development (OECD), the recent internal assassinations of top-ranking PRI politicians being a sore and worrying exception for the party.[14] Finally, since the media in

Mexico is subject to censorship, the extent of violence exercised by the regime during the 1990s is difficult to ascertain.

The regime's top–down organization of society into blocks bound together by a relationship based on bossism, clientelism and sometimes force, is seen as being partly, if not largely, responsible for the unity and stability that have come to be the hallmark of the Mexican political system.[15] During the administration of Lázaro Cárdenas, party organizations to represent workers in the *Confederación de Trabajadores de México* (CTM), the peasants in the *Confederación Nacional Campesina* (CNC) and the military were founded. In 1943 the *Confederación Nacional de Organizaciones Populares* (CNOP) was established to provide an organization for industrialists, professionals and members of other middle-class organizations. These mass-based institutions are often said to be the 'pillars' upon which the party rests.[16] The legitimacy of the PRI was partly based on the acceptance and participation of the leaders of these mass organizations. Though the military originally constituted one arm of the corporate system, its budget was reduced gradually over various *sexenios* and dominated by civilians, making Mexico distinct from many other Latin American countries.[17] The control of the military is another reason given for political stability since the chance of military coups has been greatly curtailed. There is a debate in the literature as to whether the corporatist system was originally created during the Lázaro Cárdenas administration with the genuine intention of enabling citizens effectively to organize and participate in politics, or whether they were part of a cynical government scheme to divide and control mass society.[18] However, there is greater consensus that with the onset of the Alemán administration, and the ensuing policy of the *'charrazo'*,[19] the corporatist system was used increasingly by the government in order to contain and control society.

Finally, many analysts consider that the backbone of stability in Mexico was the so-called 'Mexican Miracle' which refers to the steady annual economic growth of around 6 per cent from the end of the 1930s to around 1970. Hansen claimed that the government was able to fund the continual absorption of new groups and members into the corporate political system by using these financial resources. However, he observed that the economic growth model was 'miraculous' only for some: distribution was skewed, and the fact that government incorporated sectors of society into the party did not mean that these diverse sectors were enjoying effective representation.[20] On the contrary, the unequal distribution of economic growth was a direct result of the top–down organization of society and the fact that each sector was controlled by a leader who was offered concessions by the government in return for limiting and controlling the demands made on the state[21] by workers and peasants.[22] In other words, unequal allocation of the fruits of economic growth and an inclusionary authoritarian corporatist political system were mutually reinforcing in Mexico.

Political rupture or ruptured politics?

As mentioned above, there is a relatively high degree of consensus in the literature about the roots, principal characteristics and mechanisms of the Mexican political system. However, there is disagreement on the trajectory and dynamics of the system particularly since the 1940s. The debate comes into play when analysts attempt to characterize the way in which the political system is evolving, particularly the extent to which it is exhibiting changes and continuities. The problem is evident in the literature on organized labour, social movements, electoral reform, government policy, and among more recent themes, reform of the state.[23]

The debate can be summarized as follows. Some analysts, who assume that the political system can be adequately explained by the set of rules described in the first section, have painted a simplistic and rosy picture of the PRI in its 'golden age' which they claim dated from the 1940s to the end of the 1960s. In this period, the rules of the political game remained intact, and the regime encountered relatively few challenges and thus underwent few changes for over two decades. This literature reflected the 'glacial pace at which the Mexican system seemed to be evolving'.[24] For these analysts, the heyday of the PRI came to a dramatic end in 1968 in Tlatelolco, when the Mexican army opened fire killing hundreds of demonstrating students. The party had shown limits in its ability to represent a growing, changing population: it had failed to incorporate an important section of society, an increasingly urbanized, educated youth. The use of repressive and visible violence marked the party's desperation to reassert control in the face of its loss of legitimacy.[25] Newell and Rubio labelled the post-1968 period an 'era of political decay'[26] and an increasing number of publications on Mexico contained the word 'crisis' or 'transition' in their title. Many of these authors tended to try to predict – in retrospect, prematurely – the imminent downfall of the regime.

Other commentators, including historians, geographers, anthropologists and political scientists, rejected this 'rupture' argument and claimed that it was over-simplistic and misleading.[27] Their concern was that a 'PRI hegemony' had been constructed by the analysts who assumed that the PRI had been able to control with equal success all citizens, from workers to capitalists, across a vast geographically diverse terrain. Moreover, they claimed that the argument that economic growth fed and lubricated a smooth political trajectory until economic crisis, followed by an economic crisis which throws the system in jeopardy, was oversimplistic and two-dimensional. They argued that the PRI was never a wholly homogeneous or hegemonic power: it was historically ramshackle and unevenly spread throughout the territory of Mexico. Through detailed regional and individual case studies, analysts have traced what some have described as a 'new' aspect of the political system to show that it was not necessarily new at all. Pansters demanded that the politicians' and academics' claim of the 'new' must be more firmly located in its historical context.[28]

Many analysts in this group stressed the issue of geographical diversity, and insisted that the party's influence across the country was unevenly spread, lumpy and thin in parts. Far from being a perfect dictatorship, the PRI's domination over society could be compared more accurately, if surprisingly, to a swiss cheese.[29] Other analysts focused on the state's relationship with a sector of society (whether this be through a formal corporatist arrangement or not) and argued that the effectiveness of state control over diverse groups has been grossly exaggerated.[30] Rubin denied that popular movements of the last 20 years were new, since they were a continuation – albeit with important variations – of political practice in Mexico over the entire twentieth century.[31] Roxborough showed that there were considerable levels of conflict in industrial relations that had been underestimated in the literature. Moreover, he pointed to the diversity among organized labour which should be recognized, since some unions in certain labour markets were more militant and combative than others, and generalized statements about organized labour over-looked important differences.[32]

These analysts insisted that instead of there being a 'rupture' in the Mexican political system in 1968, the trajectory of the political system had been 'ruptured' in the literature by those who were responsible for oversimplifying an interpretation of Mexican history. Too often, assumptions were made by social scientists without solid foundation, and this helped to feed beliefs about a 'PRI golden age'. One of the roots of this problem was pointed out by Knight.[33] Much of the historical work on Mexico had a cut-off date in the 1940s. Political scientists tended to start writing about the 1960s and continued to the present (or to the future), so that there was a huge gap in the research on politics and history in

Mexico between 1940 and the 1960s – the very period which has been referred to as the 'golden age' of the PRI – and to merely fill in these two crucial decades with a broad brush sketch was clearly unsatisfactory. Smith made the important point that the assumption that 'nothing much has changed' in Mexican politics since the 1930s had been exacerbated by the 'systems analysis' trend in political science which focuses more on the maintenance of the political system than on the sources and causes of transformation.[34] One of the ways forward is the application of more quantitative methodology such as the use of statistical analysis within the fields of history and social science which requires a more interdisciplinary approach. Indeed, the increased use of quantitative research methodology within the field of political science in recent years is revealing some interesting results in studies on Mexico which force traditional assumptions to be reconsidered.[35]

The importance of this debate is not limited to a disciplinary bickering between political scientists, historians and economists. Its importance is crucial. If the gritty, complex nature of politics in Mexico is glossed over, and the degree and characteristic of political stability in Mexico are exaggerated between 1930 and 1970, an inaccurate '*pax priista*' is reified. This presents real problems for the analyst who wishes to interpret the contemporary situation in Mexico. If, in analysing contemporary Mexican politics, we assume a PRI 'golden age' from the 1940s to the end of the 1960s as a backdrop, we are likely to make many mistakes, since we are assuming a PRI peace that did not actually exist. For instance, we could interpret a certain event, such as the peasant rebellion in Chiapas in January 1994 as a wholly new phenomenon, due to a lack of understanding or knowledge about the history of peasants in Mexico, and therefore go on to interpret its significance in an ahistorical way without carefully considering what aspects are new and which are a repetition of the past. In this way, a political analyst seeking signs of an emerging political liberalization or political democratization in Mexico might be confounded. Since the debate regarding the extent to which the system is changing or staying the same is at the heart of much contemporary writing on Mexico further examination of this question is important for a more accurate account of politics in Mexico. This debate came to the forefront of political analysis in Mexico during the Salinas *sexenio*. During this period, government rhetoric included promises that there would be many novelties and changes between 1988 and 1994. The 1988 election results were disastrous for the PRI, and Salinas claimed that they signalled the end of one-party rule. The party, recognizing the need to adjust to the new challenges, would disentangle itself from archaic corporatist mechanisms and adapt to a more autonomous society comprising individuals. The policy of economic liberalization started cautiously by the De la Madrid administration would be pursued aggressively and relentlessly by the Salinas cabinet. Mexico would unshackle itself from the chains of the third world and propel itself upwards through greater linkage with the first world by agreeing to such trade pacts as the NAFTA and OECD membership. Indeed, the administration of Salinas oversaw genuine and dramatic changes in economic policy though limited political reform.

The political analyst was therefore challenged to attempt to characterize the nature and extent of the reform undertaken in the *sexenio*; in particular, to distinguish what constituted new, meaningful, potentially democratizing reform, and which reforms were cosmetic, or variations on old themes. It is difficult to account for the changes in Mexican politics in the late 1980s and 1990s unless we have a firm foundation for and an accurate understanding of that system prior to the contemporary period. This problem is complex and has wide-ranging implications, and this research attempts to tackle the analysis of politics in contemporary Mexico with this line of enquiry in mind. This simplistic 'rupture' model of Mexican politics is rejected here and a more complex, geographically diverse, unevenly spread political trajectory is assumed. One of the problems in assuming this position is to resurrect the over-quoted aphorism that is so often used in the Mexican case: that, chameleon-like, the party has had to change in order to stay the same. However, I argue that it is more accurate to say that the party has had to change in order to stay in power; sometimes this has meant it has undergone real and substantive change, other times the change may be purely cosmetic. In all cases, the party has tried to ensure that the changes made are the minimum necessary for its survival. It is the political analyst's task to characterize the nature and implications of those changes. Without being more specific about the kind, degree and consequences of change, the Lampedusa aphorism is almost as guilty of over simplification as the 'golden age to crisis' argument.

Changing paradigms in the 1980s – a threat to stability?

In many countries, the 1980s were characterized by a return to economic liberalization. The virtues of Adam Smith's invisible hand were resurrected and consensus emerged that promoted the liberalization and privatization of the economy, particularly in the UK and the

United States. However, the decision to implement a privatization programme was not only based on an economic evaluation of the market versus the state. Each government also had political motivations. In the UK these motivations included reducing government involvement in industry, diminishing the public sector borrowing requirement, and easing problems of public sector pay determination by weakening the public sector unions.[36]

In the case of Latin America, the model of import substitution industrialization (ISI) which had been pursued in the major countries since the 1950s came under attack for having produced serious market distortions and was even blamed for having led the countries into financial crisis.[37] A new consensus regarding the reduced role of the state in Latin America emerged which had been diffused through the economics departments of universities and also through international financial agencies. Between 1988 and 1992 Latin America and the Caribbean pursued privatization policies with such speed that the region accounted for two-thirds of the revenue raised (in total US$60 billion) through such programmes in the developing world.[38]

Concurrently, dramatic events were taking place in the political arena around the globe. The former Soviet Union was crumbling and its leaders admitted Communism's defeat. Attempts were made to replace the Soviet model of central planning with a more market-oriented economic model. Nearer home, many military dictatorships in Latin America were handing over power to civilian governments. Globally, political and economic change was dramatic, as the postwar world seemed to be taking on a new economic and political world order.[39]

In the aftermath of the 1982 debt crisis, the Mexican government decided to follow this new direction in economic policy making. Neoliberal economic reforms were introduced, at first gradually by the De la Madrid administration, and then dramatically by the Salinas administration. This change in direction has been interpreted as one of the most important policy reforms for Mexico, and for many other countries in Latin America in the twentieth century, marking a move away from postwar ISI policies.

One of the ways in which these profound changes were reflected in the academic and journalistic worlds was to generate a renewed interest in the analysis of the possibilities for democratization across the third world. Already at the beginning of the 1980s, observers claimed that the government's austerity measures to obtain economic stabilization might result in mass discontent on the part of workers and peasants, which in turn could cause a significant challenge to the party. They argued that the results of the 1988 presidential elections were disastrous for the PRI. The 'official' counts showed that the party had gained only fractionally more than 50 per cent of the votes, whereas historically the PRI has usually enjoyed at least 70 per cent of the votes. The worst electoral performance in its history seemed to be a proof of society's discontent with the party. This was not only because of economic reasons. Many analysts and Mexican politicians believed that political reform was urgent if the party was to stay in power, since it was becoming increasingly apparent that its traditional mechanisms of mustering support were declining.[40] Since the PRI had lost support from its traditional corporate stalwarts, such as organized labour, some claimed that the PRI was losing its grip on the corporate pact, which had entered an advanced state of disintegration.

It might not seem wholly appropriate to mix vague, impressionistic and at the time still unproven, statements about global changes with specific issues regarding politics in Mexico, but this is exactly what happened in the literature. However, events were by no means interpreted in the same way by all analysts. Responses to these dramatic changes could be classified into three main groups: (1) The 'optimists' who claimed that there was a 'wave' of democracy sweeping across the globe, and they reasoned that, since political democratization had come at about the same time as economic liberalization, there was a causal connection between them. Assuming this was true, the questioning of 'sequencing' became fashionable: how should change be brought about – should political or economic reform lead the changes? (2) The 'agnostics' who denied there was any connection between political democratization and economic liberalization and (3) the 'pessimists' who, reacting against the 'optimists', claimed that economic reform might lead to the consolidation of authoritarian rule in Mexico. In this last category the analysts did not necessarily claim that there was a necessary relationship between economic liberalization and authoritarianism;[41] the connection posited was more circumstantial and conjunctural.

The 'optimists'

The most important group among the 'optimists' for the Mexican population at large was the Salinas administration, which adopted in its official rhetoric an upbeat optimism about the impact that economic reform would have on society at large. This discourse will be examined in more detail in the following chapters. Salinas promised he would push through economic liberalization and by so doing, Mexico would become a candidate to enter the first world. He also promised that there would be political reforms, particularly democratization and modernization of the party, which would come about as an inevitable consequence of the economic reforms.[42] Journalists and other commentators drew contrasts between the former Soviet Union and Mexico: while Gorbachev had insisted that *glasnost* must accompany *perestroika*,[43] Lorenzo Meyer had famously quipped that Salinas wanted *perestroika* without the *glasnost*.[44] Salinas protested:

> Freedoms of what you call the glasnost kind have existed for decades in Mexico. What hasn't existed is the freedom of productive activity because the government owned so many enterprises. So actually, we have been more rapidly transforming the economic structure while striving along many paths of reform on the political side. But, let me tell you something. When you are introducing such a strong economic reform, you must make sure that you build the political consensus around it. If you are at the same time introducing additional drastic political reform, you may end up with no reform at all. And we want to have reform, not a disintegrated country ... as we move along the path toward consolidating our economic reforms, political reform will continue to evolve in Mexico.[45]

Observers of Mexico who asserted that there was a positive linkage between economic liberalization and political democratization in the 1980s were influenced by two main strands of belief, and usually their arguments contain a cocktail of influences from both. One posited an absolute, causal, even mechanical logic – between economic growth and democracy. In doing so, they were partially resurrecting the logic of modernization theory of the 1950s. This theory contended that economic growth and liberalization created social forces – in particular a more educated, urbanized, autonomous and 'diamond-shaped' society fat with middle class[46] – that would seek political democratization. Applying this logic to Mexico, the analysts stated that once neoliberal economic reforms were set in motion, the political system would, logically, become more open too. Trade liberalization, which would mean a greater consumer choice, would also imply that citizens would expect to enjoy correspondingly greater political choice. The events which had led to an unravelling of the Soviet Union led some analysts to claim that once policies had been set in motion it could be difficult to contain the consequences. However, some parts of this analysis that echo modernization theory smack of ideology and wishful thinking more than showing signs of a rigorous methodology:

> The first intimations of structural political change are appearing. They must. It is foolhardy to introduce massive economic and financial liberalisation, foster the integration of the economy into North America and the new global marketplace, and begin the modernisation of Mexican society while ignoring political change.[47]

The precise way in which economic and political change were interconnected was left vague:

> Open economies ... tend to promote broader political participation and generate multiple sources of political power. This is not dogma; case after case confirms the pattern, and for a simple reason. In closed economies, the government (regardless of its electoral nature or democratic quality) and special-interest groups have the last word in all, or most, decisions that are critical for development. Closed economies generate lucrative monopolies that make a few private groups very wealthy and most people very poor. Power tends to be concentrated, forcing the majority of the population to live on the fringes. An open economy decentralises decisions and, therefore, political power.[48]

Rubio was being selective in this 'case after case' analysis; for instance, he used the case of the fall of Pinochet in Chile to argue that economic reforms had brought about democratization, but ignored the case of China. Other analysts borrowed from the theory of rent-seeking, some more loosely than others. These argued that rent-seeking occurs when efforts and resources are diverted from productive activities into non-productive ones, and they blamed the wasted resources on the creation of market restrictions and state intervention into markets. In Krueger's classic article she argued that limiting the amount of licences to import only created wasted efforts of bribes, corruption in the struggle to obtain a licence.[49]

For these writers, the liberalization of the economy in Mexico would require the withdrawal of the state from economic management. They considered that this would be a good thing, since it would give opportunity for a role to be played by other actors including business entrepreneurs, trade unions and foreigner and domestic capitalists.[50] Decision-making, once highly centralized and concentrated in the state, would become decentralized, or, as some put it, privatized. Trade liberalization and integration enshrined in the GATT and NAFTA agreements respectively would mean a shift from discretionary import licensing to one based on tariffs so that the government would intervene less.[51] Transferring firms which once comprised the *parastatal* sector to private hands would also, they argued, reduce opportunities for patronage, bribery and corruption. Clearly, the writers welcomed the proposition of neoliberalism and slimming down the role of the state in its management of the economy of the presumably attractive 'emerging market'.

A great many of these writers were primarily interested in the economic and not the political consequences of reform in Mexico. However, there were some analysts, influenced by the 'rent-seeking' model, who also had an interest in the political consequences of economic change. Among them, Delal Baer argued that, once competition was introduced by opening the economy, corruption would be eroded, and the 'oil' which had been used to lubricate the complex system of patronage would run out. The analogy ends with the political machine running completely out of steam. The decades-old corporatist system formed in the 1930s could not survive 'neoliberal' reform. Delal Baer's message was explicit: a market economy was 'fundamentally incompatible with corporatism'. Corporatism had been maintained while Mexico's economy was closed and protected. State patronage, in the form of giving favours to leaders of business, industry and agricultural corporations, in return for loyalty at the ballot box, had resulted in a widespread system of corruption and inefficiency. Isolated from competition, union leaders had enjoyed a monopoly on contracts from industry, the bureaucracy worked best when it was bribed, and property rights were enforced only selectively. Competition would erode this corruption.[52] Qadir *et al.* equated societies prone to rent-seeking with low prospects for a budding of democracy, since they created patronage systems depending on the control of state power, but those societies which could clean themselves up with competition in the economic arena might also become more competitive politically.[53]

Writers influenced by rent-seeking theory believed that corruption was the cement of the corporate system, and that this could all be broken down simply by introducing international competition. In short, competition broke down the institutionalization of corruption.[54] In this discussion of corruption, no precise definition was offered, but superior overtones prevailed that claim corruption was a problem of developing economies based on a corporatist system, but that corruption did not exist in advanced capitalist countries.[55] In the worst case, the notion of corporatism was used almost synonymously with that of corruption.[56] Morici called the reform in Mexico the privatization of decision-making. New economic openness would, if not put an end to corruption, at least provide less opportunities for it to fester.[57]

Specialists in organized labour who assumed this logic, including Berins Collier and Bizberg, claimed that trade unions would be affected by these changes. In their opinion, the logic of a state-managed economy favoured a corporatist system, but economic liberalization was contrary to that logic.[58] The state–labour alliance which had rested on the control and provision of wages, benefits, housing and food subsidies would break down. Bizberg argued that political rationality, which had characterized state–labour relations through decades of growth, would have to give way to economic reason. By this he meant that many of the inefficiencies inherent in the traditional corporatist system such as worker protectionism would be removed by competition and open markets. Moreover, he claimed that economic liberalization clashed fundamentally with the centralized, hierarchical and rigid forms of decision-making upon which corporatism was founded.[59] Corporatism had an 'homogenizing' effect on wages, but economic liberalization would force greater differences between wages of workers of different sectors to emerge, thus reducing the role of corporatism. Economic liberalization would mean reducing the power of union leaders since they would receive less economic rewards from the state. Union power would thus become decentralized rapidly, and this in turn would bring about a decentralization of decision-making, so that there would be more opportunities for workers to be involved in deciding the best forms of action. He also claimed that the introduction of modern labour techniques would encourage greater worker participation.[60]

Rubio wrote along the same lines and claimed that collective bargaining would be transformed. Greater worker participation on the shop-floor would somehow lead to increased participation at the city, state or national level:[61]

> labour relations will largely cease to be negotiated at the highest corporatist levels (among the heads of labour confederations and the heads of business organisations, brokered by the government) but negotiated directly by the firm and the union. The individual unions will strengthen while the federations, confederations, and other traditional corporatist structures will weaken. This will be a transcen-

dental political change, one that will dismantle the strongholds of the old PRI boss. The question is what will replace them.[62]

Delal Baer claimed that once the unions were less dependent on the state for patronage, they would be driven increasingly by market forces and would negotiate their collective contract directly with management, without the intervention of the Secretary of Labour, and therefore avoiding the favours and hand-outs which accompanied this traditional style of collective bargaining. Since the government was signing international trade agreements which locked it into these neoliberal policies, he argued that the reforms were here to stay, and the party had lost its traditional ability to swing from left- to-right wing policies (the so-called 'pendulum-effect') which for many years had given it significant ideological and political flexibility.

The 'pessimists' and the 'agnostics'

By no means all commentators were carried away by the 'optimistic' arguments outlined above. It is easy to find strong criticism of the assumptions of both the theories of modernization and rent-seeking in general, as well as the way in which these theories were applied to Mexico. Modernization theory has been criticized since the 1950s for many reasons, among other things, for being too lineal, for failing to distinguish between political liberalism and democratization, and for assuming that processes under way in countries with a 'developing democracy' in the late twentieth century can be compared with experiences of industrializing nations in the nineteenth century.[63] It has also been criticized for its tendency to subordinate politics to economics by stressing that economic growth and liberalization are the key driving forces which bring about change in social and political relations in society. Politics is thus shaped essentially by economics, and the notion that politics has a dynamism and energy of its own is not considered.

The contribution of the rent-seeking literature was that it added a new element to the traditional *laissez-faire critique* of state intervention since it emphasized the additional distortions created by unproductive profit-seeking activities which were brought about in response to government intervention. The assumption was that rent-seeking activities resulted from public action, so a privately run enterprise must be more efficient than one in which the state plays a role. The logical conclusion of this assumption was that the only way in which rent-seeking can be reduced was to reduce government intervention.

Fishlow criticized the rent-seeking literature by arguing that it did not take into account the existence of externalities and imperfections in the market that justified the intervention of the government in the economy in the first place.[64] Moreover, it only considered the costs of public action without also calculating the benefits.[65] Streeten criticized rent-seeking theorists on the grounds that they assumed that the efforts 'lost' in non-productive activities could have been channelled into a more useful productive activity, but it was not clear that activities such as lobbying could be put to productive ends. He pointed out that it was not clear that rent-seeking activities were not equally common in the private sector as in the public sector.[66]

The policy implications of the rent-seeking analyses are that corruption can be reduced when the state's role in the economy is cut back through privatization and deregulation.[67] Unproductive bargaining (at worst, bribes) between agencies including government representatives, unions and management representatives which the theory claims are rampant when the government intervenes in the economy would be phased out when market liberalization and competition are introduced.

A common criticism of both schools was that the connection made between economic growth and democracy was too deterministic and unilinear. O'Donnell's connection of an 'elective affinity' between the difficult stages in ISI and bureaucratic authoritarian regimes had the same weakness as Lipset's – both could be proved wrong by case studies in other countries.[68] To claim that there was a simple correlation between economic and political liberalization or democratization seemed obviously incorrect given that there were empirical examples from around the world that confirmed one hypothesis and denied the next, showing that the world was clearly too complex a place to reflect such simplistic deterministic rules. Gourevitch showed that of the four 'grand theories': (democracy requires markets; markets require democracy; democracy requires central planning and markets require authoritarianism) there were examples from around the world that would confirm one and deny the other.[69]

Both modernization and rent-seeking analysis used the terms economic and political liberalization and democratization in vague ways. All of these terms indicate a process, not an overnight transformation, with distinct stages. If there is more than one definition of a term there will almost certainly be more than one view about how these processes might interact.[70] Often, 'economic liberalization' was employed as if it was one thing, and was rarely broken down into its component policies. These policies might include reducing import tariffs, adjusting the exchange rate, selling off, merging or liquidizing state enterprises and removing subsidies to make production internationally competitive. Each aspect is distinct and has different consequences upon society at large. Economic reform can last many years or decades, and each country applies different policies using various methods, approaches and at variable speeds. An individual country's effort to pursue economic liberalization is influenced by various factors including: its insertion into the world economy (labour market and primary resources), the degree and nature of its dependence on trade and its foreign exchange position.[71] It is therefore important to aim for greater precision in the discussion of economic reform by breaking down and carefully defining which aspect of economic reform is under consideration.[72] For the purposes of this book, privatization will be isolated from other elements of economic reform.

It is also important to distinguish between political liberalization and democratization. Political liberalism is defined here as a step towards opening up the political system which might include reforms to allow an opposition party to win a state governorship, measures to control the funding of all parties and permission for opposition parties to present their manifestos on the television. However, the complex question is the relationship between the two: political liberalization and democratization.[73] If political liberalization is implemented effectively and parties compete genuinely in terms of resources and media coverage, it might be possible for democratization to increase. On the other hand, if these measures are taken, yet electoral fraud is finally used to prevent the opposition from winning, then political liberalization provides only a hollow façade which hides the fact that there has been scant democratization.[74] In the discussion about the process of democratization, it is important to have a model of democracy in mind, a goal to which a country is hopefully moving. But what kind of democracy is envisaged? A stable and effective democracy ('just like us')[75] or a kind of democracy which is understood in the national context?[76] Moreover, since the subject of this book is the changing relationship between the state and organized labour, it is necessary to focus on a subset of the broad topic of democracy which is union democracy and industrial democracy.

Those analysts (whether 'pessimists' or 'agnostics') writing on Mexico who rejected the assertion that economic reform would lead to political democratization in Mexico also tended to avoid making any kind of direct and causal links between economic and political change. 'Pessimists' proposed that economic liberalization in Mexico might in fact help the PRI in its consolidation of authoritarian rule, though not in a deterministic way but, rather, due to a number of conjunctural factors, including US foreign policy preferences and policies implemented by the government in order to revitalize its support from the base. Cuauhtémoc Cárdenas, leader of the PRD, was among them. He argued that by joining NAFTA and opening up the economy, the PRI was placating the US government. With future access to a liberalized trading zone, the US government would seek to continue supporting the political system it knew well, the PRI, regardless of whether or not it was a democratic party.[77] Dresser claimed that the regime was using neopopulist measures, principally the *Programa Nacional de Solidaridad* (PRONASOL), to accompany economic liberalization in order to reconstruct state–society links, maintain social peace and recapture PRI votes lost in 1988 and thus was also a 'pessimist' about the possibilities of democratization.[78]

Most 'agnostics' did not consider that there were determining links between economic and political liberalization and also veered away from futuristic speculations. In their prognosis for the future of Mexico, Cornelius *et al.* stated that they preferred not to make an inevitable connection between political and economic change.[79] Camp claimed that while economic reform required a political consensus if it was to be implemented successfully, the kind of political reform being proposed by the government such as the modernization of the corporate system would not necessarily follow, since that would be tantamount to removing support from beneath the PRI's foundations. He believed that in Mexico economic reforms were being put into place in an authoritarian fashion.[80] Coppedge claimed that there was no necessary relation between economic and political liberalization in the short term, since the arguments showing a positive correlation were as strong as those arguing for a negative correlation. However, this did not mean that there were not causal connections in the long term. He argued that when the state reduced its patronage within society, this would not fundamentally change state–society relations. Even if material benefits designed to lubricate the corporate system were cut severely, 'selective distribution of a small pie is just as effective as selective distribution of a large one, as long as it is the only pie in town'.[81]

Smith pointed to the fact that many of the writers analysing economic reform in Mexico had vested interests in the outcome. He noted that pro-NAFTA supporters tended to claim that it would bring more democracy, but that anti-NAFTA writers said that it would diminish it.[82] He pointed out that many of these pro-NAFTA authors were North Americans, and their claim that political democratization would follow on from economic liberalization was largely an 'article of faith' which lacked foundations.[83] He further stated that their interest was that Mexico would become a modern, liberal neighbour, while remaining politically stable, so that it would be a useful trade partner along with Canada. In the political arena, as Whitehead noted, the North American government probably promoted the political status quo, more than a contingent change, especially after the scares of 1988 when the left-wing party mounted a serious challenge to the PRI.[84] He concluded that the influence of NAFTA could open up possible spaces for democratization, but whether greater democracy was actually achieved would be dependent upon whether the government took steps to bring about an increase of democracy within society.[85]

In the examination of economic and political change in Mexico, many analysts made a leap between the economic reforms and political change in terms of election results. The evidence that economic opening was bringing about political reform was directly linked to the results at the ballot box. Weintraub and Delal Baer claimed that the PRI was sharing more power with the *Partido Acción Nacional* (PAN) in accepting the loss of four senatorial seats in 1988 and one governorship in 1989; they therefore jumped to the conclusion that market reforms in Mexico were breaking down authoritarianism.[86] When the PRI did well in the 1991 mid-term elections 'without excessive resource to manipulation' this was used as further proof that the PRI was becoming more democratic.[87] The election results were taken very much at face value, and the authors did not query why, for instance, the results of the *Partido de la Revolución Democrático* (PRD) were dismal after 1988.[88] Morici also assumed that economic opening was making Mexico more democratic, and argued this by pointing to the fact that the PAN won governorships in Baja California Norte in 1991 and Chihuahua state 1992.[89] Moreover, the authors did not make a serious or detailed connection between the impact of market reforms and votes. They showed no clear evidence that economic reform had any direct influence on the electoral results, and indeed, any attempt to directly connect these two processes would have to be much more methodical. The fact that both processes occurred roughly at the same time is not adequate evidence. Neither did the authors distinguish clearly between political liberalization and political democratization, and it could be argued that the PRI's allowing a handful of PAN victories is another move towards political liberalization. The connection between the liberalization and democratization is indirect, and usually not convincing. An approach is thus required that examines the impact of an element of economic reform in isolation from economic liberalization in general focusing specifically on how the relationships change between those actors most directly affected.

Contemporary interpretations of politics in Mexico

The first analyses published towards the end of and after the Salinas administration have attempted primarily to answer the general questions: *how* and *why* was it possible that dramatic economic reforms were put into place during that *sexenio* while the political reforms implemented by the government were minimal?[90] Although the Mexican economy has been fraught with uncertainties since the devaluation of the peso in 1994, it cannot be denied that qualitative, dramatic steps were taken during the *sexenio* such as signing the NAFTA agreement and the privatization programme, neither of which is easily reversible. However, in contrast to the persistent government rhetoric which stressed individual, autonomous citizenship and democratization and modernization of the corporate bases of the party, political changes were slow to emerge. Admittedly, new reforms were implemented, such as modifications to electoral and human rights issues. However, the addition of a handful of opposition state governors, and greater opposition pressure in municipal governments, coupled with an increase in organizations being charged with regulating human rights, were the limits of these reforms during this period. Furthermore, it is not clear to what extent they have led to a democratization.[91] Apart from these changes, it seemed that much of the political reform undertaken by the government had finally been reversed or blocked towards the end of the *sexenio*.

Given that much of the analysis in the 1980s had as its central thrust the question of the possible links between democracy and markets, and that the experience of Mexico has been dramatic economic reform but limited political change, the Salinas administration would appear to be a highly relevant and interesting case study which could be used to try to redress the original questions. Indeed, many of the recent analyses written at the end of the Salinas *sexenio* start out with this inquiry.[92] Unfortunately, however, the question of economic reform and its impact on political change tends to be dropped quickly, and most of the authors turn to the political system itself, and government policies in particular, to seek for answers.[93] In most of the new literature, therefore, there is little explicit analysis of the ways in which economic and political reforms interacted. The new literature published so far can be divided into two main approaches: those which in general limit their analysis to the state; and those which consider the problem from a state-centred and society-centred point of view.[94]

State-centred approaches

Through a rigorous analysis of changes in élite recruitment patterns and institutional reforms within the PRI over the last two decades, Centeno argued that a core technocratic bureaucracy was able to put into place wide-reaching economic reforms during the Salinas *sexenio*.[95] The power of the president was reasserted and decision-making was concentrated in a loyal élite of talented economists whom the president had hand-picked to surround him. This team closed off decision-making procedures to other influences and pressures from society, excluding them from their policy-making decisions. For Centeno, therefore, economic reform was imposed top–down in an authoritarian fashion (he labelled it '*Salinastroika*' – *perestroika* without much *glasnost)* by an exclusive and isolated ruling élite. While changes in the élite recruitment patterns help to explain the single-mindedness of economic policy-makers during this period, the central weakness of Centeno's argument is that he only explains how the policies came to be agreed upon. However, there is a large gap between the process of decision-making and policy implementation. Moreover, rarely does policy implementation produce the exact results expected. Compromises, U-turns and failures are common.

Other analysts attempted to fill in this gap between the making and the implementation of policy by analysing the changing relationship between the state and society. In general, these authors claimed that the state tried to strengthen itself and facilitate neoliberal reforms by changing the coalition upon which it rested. Following along the lines of Centeno, Teichman concurred that the decision-making process in Mexico became more authoritarian and concentrated in the economic 'superélite', in isolation from political pressures of political bureaucrats and trade unions, and used this as a major reason to explain how economic liberalization and privatization went ahead swiftly in Mexico.[96] In order to explain the implementation of neoliberal policies, principally privatization, she stated that the party decided to redefine its political coalition by shedding labour and small and medium sized industries while at the same time, rekindling its relationship with big business.[97] By the decision to 'shed labor', Teichman referred to the government's harsh policies of repressing strikes, imposing modified labour contracts, dramatically reducing wages and removing powerful union leaders who were against government policy and replacing them with others who supported the government. In her view, state–society relations became less controlled by a centralized clientelism, and more represented by a new kind of increasingly segmented clientelism. She argued that corporatist and clientelist relations between the state and society were still at play, but that state–society relations were more fragmented, and clientelism operated within traditional and newer structures as well and became linked more directly to the presidency.

In my opinion, Teichman's bold explanation that neoliberal reform was facilitated by narrowing down the state's coalitional base is too sweeping. One of my main criticisms is that the author limited her analysis to a 'state-centred' one, and considered how the policy decisions emanating from the cabinet were conceived and implemented, but she did not analyse how society managed to resist these decisions, unlike other analysts including Craske, Middlebrook and Heredia (see below). By so doing, Teichman tended to treat organized labour as if it were a homogeneous bloc, rather than as being made up of diverse unions which represent different economic sectors. She did not disaggregate the government's policies towards organized labour in an attempt to highlight the various strategies employed nor did she treat Salinas' project of '*nuevo sindicalismo*' which he nurtured from 1989. Organized labour undoubtedly became less important as a government ally during the 1980s, as evidenced by falling wages and a decline in its political power.[98] However, it managed to avoid the modification of the *Ley Federal de Trabajo* (LFT), the central labour legislation in Mexico, and it insisted on the continued renewing of an economic pact throughout the Salinas *sexenio*. If the government wanted rid of labour, as Teichman claimed, it proved extremely difficult to shake off. The 1988 presidential elections briefly offered unions a glimmer of hope of alternative sources of political power in the form of the *Frente Democrática Nacional* (FDN). However, due to internal differences of the FDN coalition as well as external intimidation from the PRI, this alternative source of political power quickly started to fade.[99]

My argument is not that there was no change in the state–labour relationship, nor that, in the government's reorganization of the coalition base, it simply decided to 'get rid' of labour. In my opinion, the government's policy towards organized labour was contradictory and differed dramatically depending on the sector in question. Most importantly, my research on the emergence of a so-called '*nuevo sindicalismo*' showed that the government's efforts to renew links with certain sectors of labour – principally unions of the most dynamic areas of the economy – was a key factor in the project to carry out a relatively conflict-free privatization programme with which the Salinas administration has been credited.

Dresser argued that PRONASOL, ostensibly a government project to redress some of the economic inequalities that neoliberal reforms would create, had a political as well as an economic purpose. She claimed that it was a top–down political strategy, emanating from the technocratic core of government, designed precisely to facilitate the implementation of economic liberalization. At the beginning of the Salinas administration, the president announced the launch of this new self-help programme which would channel government funds to the poorest in Mexico in order to partially fund a variety of projects, providing a 'safety-net' to those who would be negatively impacted by the effects of neoliberalism. He claimed that its intended recipients were the 48 per cent of the population that was living below the official poverty line and especially the 19 per cent who were considered to be living in extreme poverty.[100] He tried to convince Mexicans that PRONASOL was apolitical since members of other political parties were allowed to be involved and a point was made of avoiding PRI logos on Solidarity open days.[101] Dresser was unconvinced of the government rhetoric that claimed it was seeking, disinterestedly, to help the poor, and stated that the government actually wanted to use the programme as a means of re-tying large segments of the population to the PRI in a new clientelistic relationship.[102]

At the end of the *sexenio*, many commentators argued that Dresser had been right.[103] Horcasitas and Weldon used quantitative methods based on regional studies to show that PRONASOL spending had been specifically targeted towards areas where it was believed the money would inspire a return to electoral loyalty to the PRI, rather than to the poorest areas of the country.[104] PRONASOL was supposed to bring about decentralization, since it was 'demand-driven', and the demands should emerge from the grass roots and be directed to central government. Moreover, the bureaucratic obstacles were supposed to be lifted, so that there would be a fluid channel between the base and the political apex. However, Cornelius *et al.* argued that one result of presidential leap-frogging over his middle-men in order to implement PRONASOL was that the president undermined local politicians' authority, while at the same time boosting his own popularity.[105] Bailey argued that the effect of PRONASOL was in fact to modernize presidential centralism, and to recover from the loss of respect for the president evident in the presidential elections in 1988.[106] Knight pointed out that Salinas reconstructed an image of a powerful and popular president by taking a few tips from Lázaro Cárdenas, such as travelling around the country to meet 'normal' Mexican people and listening to their problems.[107] The assumption that PRONASOL could bring about greater democratization was naive: instead, it was designed to provide the political conditions necessary to sustain the economic model.[108]

State/society-centred approaches

Knight reminded us that, in the case of post-revolutionary Mexico, it is insufficient to merely consider 'high', or élite politics and ignore 'low' politics. The revolution brought about a rupture in the link between political élites and the oligarchy and established a regime which planted deep vertical roots in a society which it partially ordered and controlled.[109] Brachet-Marquez made a valid point in her claim that 'top–down' decision-making in Mexico has often been shaped by pressures from below.[110]

Other authors such as Middlebrook, Craske and Heredia integrated a state-centred analysis with a society-centred perspective when attempting to account for political and economic change in Mexico. The meaning of society-centred varies according to the different authors' understanding of the term, but in general, this approach tackles questions on a horizontal plane, in contrast with the state-centred approach, which could be described as being of a more vertical nature and which focuses its analysis on the top ranks of the party. The 'society-centred' approach might consider the make-up of a corporate bloc such as its heterogeneity, history and strength, the ideology of its leaders and how the bloc is integrated into the economic and political structure of the country.

Craske provided a good example of a state and society-centred approach in her analysis of the Salinas administration's efforts to reform the popular sector, the CNOP, by examining the obstacles to party reform both within the higher echelons of the party apparatus, and also at the level of local politicians and at the grass roots. While

Centeno showed that Salinas elected a core, specialized technocratic team in order to push through economic reform, Craske pointed to the fact that the reform of the popular sector involved a mixed team of traditionalists (the so-called *'dinosauros'*) and modernizers from the PRI headquarters in Mexico City and many regions in the country. There was no common accepted programme of reform, which meant that any attempt to implement reform proposed by the modernizers had first to battle against the traditionalists if it was to see the light of day.

The reform of the CNOP was chaotic. The newly constituted *Frente Nacional de Obreros y Campesinos* (FNOC) (which was a revamped version of the CNOP) tended to have overlapping functions with newly intro-duced schemes including PRONASOL and the *Movimiento Popular Urbano Territorial* (MT). Both of these were created to reabsorb independent local groups and organizations which had strayed from the PRI fold. This meant that the leaders responsible for the FNOC, PRONASOL and MT tended to fight over duties and power. The reform therefore generated rivalry between the different leaders, and in retrospect this may have been the purpose of government, since it facilitated their pushing out middle-men who were no longer considered efficient.[111]

In particular, the new projects introduced by the new leaders threatened to reduce or phase out powers of the established ones, along with their *camarillas*. Open and democratic elections were perceived by incumbent leaders as threatening their own position as well as offering opportunities to others with no track record, experience or party loyalty. As one official put it: 'democracy shows no respect for leaders'.[112] In the face of non-cooperation or outright resistance, the FNOC became what the CNOP had been at the beginning of the *sexenio*.

Heredia concurred with Centeno in stating that economic liberaliza-tion was made possible due to the 'unprecedented degree of élite cohesion' that characterized those implementing economic policy during the administrations of De la Madrid and Salinas.[113] She also argued that the policies were implemented without eliciting an organized response or resistance from society due to 'the nature of the Mexican political system'. By that, she referred to the structure of political authority 'based on hierarchical patronage networks that cut across classes and sectors'. In her argument, Heredia argued for the 'primacy of the political' in reaction against those analysts who claimed that economic change would bring about political change.[114] Heredia argued that collective action organized around common economic interests has been frustrated historically in Mexico by the problem of clientelism, which has been responsible for easing the way for governance and top–down control. However, in my view this explanation is unconvincing since it assumes that collective action can only take place in a perfect world where clientelism does not exist. In general, she argued that labour leaders remained loyal to the government or remained part of the channel of the patronage system, because union–government relations operate on a long-term basis. They might be prepared to pay for the short-term costs needed to support the government through difficult times, expecting at the end some kind of compensation when conditions improve.[115]

Within the corporate system, organized labour has been blamed for being particularly resistant to political change. Cornelius labelled it the 'most conservative sector' in society.[116] In Zapata's opinion, the alliance between the state and organized labour remained intact throughout the 1980s and first half of the 1990s, since the main actors continued to work together albeit in a climate of greater turbulence.[117] He claimed that economic crisis and consequent restructuring meant that the state was changing the nature of the former relationship and was seeking new labour allies. One of the fullest accounts of labour's resistance to change is provided by Middlebrook, whose most recent contribution rests on historical sources, which give particular weight to the significance of the revolutionary heritage of Mexico, and also to quantitative methodology.[118] This book will be analysed in more detail in the next chapter; here I will present Middlebrook's explanation of how and why organized labour resisted political reforms over the last decade.[119] Initially, he argued that the terms under which organized labour entered national politics after the revolution conditioned its future.[120] From then on, labour would be controlled top–down by government policies which limited its ability to organize (by controlling the registering of unions, and preventing a single peasant-worker alliance), to make demands and to act (particularly to strike). Moreover, legal institutions such as the *Ley Federal de Trabajo* (LFT) and the *Juntas de Conciliación y Arbitraje* (JCA) framed the boundaries within which labour could act or make demands. However, state-centred explanations are not adequate as they do not account for the diversity of responses from the various segments of the labour market nor the different responses from unions within a similar industry. A careful account also needs to be taken of the internal weakness within organized labour and the ideology of some labour leaders, particularly of Fidel Velázquez who continued to be loyal to the revolution until his death in 1997.[121]

Middlebrook claimed that the CTM successfully managed to block potentially important government proposals including the reform of the LFT and the reorganization of the *Congreso de Trabajo* (CT).[122] It did so because it feared democratization or liberalization of the pact between labour and the state could reduce mobility for labour leaders in politics and threaten labour's opportunities to enjoy power within the government apparatus. He concluded that the possibility that labour could contribute to a democratization of politics in Mexico is low. The relationship between labour and the state had always been highly unequal but in the 1980s it became even more one-sided.[123] Nonetheless, labour leaders insisted on continuing with the traditional negotiating styles. Finally the government accepted labour persistence, since the Salinas administration required the support of labour in its economic policies, and was determined to achieve an oderly presidential succession.

The lessons so far?

For many analysts, the 1988 presidential election results were the watershed which prompted the party to recognize the urgency of reforming the party by revitalizing mass support.[124] The PRI made something of a 'come-back' in the 1991 mid-term elections, particularly in areas where the FDN had been strong in 1988, while the PAN's victories improved steadily but gradually, so it seemed clear that the PRI recovered from the depths of its situation in 1988.[125] Moreover, while the results of the August 1994 elections showed that Zedillo received around the same number of votes as had Salinas, the PRI did recover some of its lost ground in Mexico City and Chihuahua.[126] However, President Zedillo has been forced to make concessions to the opposition parties and in 1997 the Mexico City election for the Mayor was won by the PRD candidate while the PRI's presence in Congress has shrunk to an unprecedentedly low 39 per cent.

During the Salinas administration, reform of the structure of the party was not pushed through with anything like the determination or conviction that reforms in the economic arena had been. Analyses of political reform during the Salinas *sexenio* have tended to locate the reasons for political inertia as emanating either from the party at the highest level, and/or they have stressed the internal conflict within the party, between top politicians and regional *caciques*. Some argued that it was never really the government's intention to open up or liberalize the structure of the party.[127] Instead of seeking to dismantle corporatism, the government was afraid of the consequences of possible political fallout, so government reform was introduced aimed at renewing the corporate system by devising new methods to reabsorb those who had fallen from the PRI fold.[128] PRONASOL was one example of a project designed to reorient mass support for the PRI away from a vertical, hierarchical and class-based structure to one aligned more on geographical issues of community. This would not represent anything new, since attempts to revamp corporatism form a fundamental characteristic which keeps the system alive.[129]

Craske claimed that while the government may have lacked the political will to reform corporatism, change was also blocked by those within the party apparatus. First, resistance was apparent due to the conflicting ideas among members in the higher ranks of the party. Craske and Jones pointed to a lack of real political will on the part of the PRI to put into practice its proclaimed reforms of the popular sector, and of the *ejido* respectively, due to internal division between top politicians over the proposals. One of the ways round this problem was to implement confused and contradictory reforms, some of which started and were halted quickly, others which, when scrutinized, reveal the confusion and indecision behind the scenes.[130] Second, political reform was blocked by middle or low-level PRI bureaucrats or by leaders of the various corporatist blocks. One of the main reasons that the PRONASOL project was perceived to be one of the most effective reforms was because the president chose to 'leapfrog' over the bureaucracy of his own system, so that he could manage it personally for the first few years from Los Pinos. If it is assumed that *caciques* were responsible for blocking political reform during the Salinas administration, the corporatist system could be compared to a Frankenstein for the PRI; it created a monster which the master no longer knew how to control. This is not a sudden problem, visible only in recent years. As Knight wrote, 'Mexican history is littered with examples of political and economic reforms wrecked on the flinty rocks of *caciquismo*'.[131] Since the formation of the PNR, certain federal attempts to reform the party have been blocked by inertia or opposition from its members from lower down the party system.[132] Literature on the De la Madrid administration also points out how members of the party obstructed reform.[133] However true this is, the *cacique* argument has its limits. The fact that Fidel Velazquez, *cacique par excellence*, who monopolized power at the head of the CTM and the CT for decades until his death in July 1997, was an important factor in explaining organized labour's docility, but it could not constitute the only reason. Though his permanence, experience and authority were a key explanation, it is also important to recognize the way in which labour policies could continue unaltered after his death since labour practices are deeply engrained and institutionalized from labour leaders down to rank and file.

Middlebrook's account of the reasons for labour's resistance to reform introduces other elements into the analysis in addition to considering the obstacles of party bureaucrats and labour leaders. He stressed the heterogeneity of the labour sector and integrated his account with other factors including levels of industrial growth and dynamism which affect unionization patterns. This is extremely important when trying to account for the diversity of responses from a vast, heterogeneous body of workers, unions and confederations.

Framing the question

Since the predictions of the 'optimists' were wrong, the question of dramatic economic reform, and the impact this might have on political reform, has largely been dropped in the analysis of Mexican politics in the 1980s and 1990s. However, the fact that political reforms tended to stagnate in Mexico during the Salinas *sexenio* should not be taken to demonstrate that economic and political reform should be considered separate and isolated phenomena. One of the reasons for the mistakes of the 'optimists' was the imposition of rigid, deterministic and unilineal links between economic and political change. Even when North advanced his 'new institutional economics', he recognized that economic reform may change the formal political rules almost overnight, but the informal political rules were much more difficult to erase.[134] Another problem was the 'optimists'' preference for using grand theories in order to arrive at macro-conclusions. Many of the authors tried to explain the totality of (different) experiences while they overlooked crucial regional differences and sectoral differences in the case of labour. Organized labour was treated as one bloc instead of as players, of different sizes with diverse interests and powers which would be affected in dramatically different ways by reforms. An over-mechanical association was made between ISI policies and a corporatist system lubricated top-down by the government in the 'golden age' and by competitive open markets with the breakdown of corporatism. The corporate bloc was depicted as a rigid structure which would break down under economic duress. Moreover, it was considered as a homogeneous bloc, instead of a body of diverse labour organizations representing different sized unions, from various geographical regions, from different manufacturing and service sectors.

As some of the results of economic and political reform undertaken by governments of developing countries become visible, a body of analysts have argued that economic liberalization, which, according to the 'rent-seeking' school would clean away corruption, actually did the opposite.[135] In their view, privatization, economic liberalization and sometimes democratization in many Latin American countries and India generated resources and opportunities which led to new possibilities for corruption to occur. In the specific cases of Argentina, Brazil and Venezuela, other authors showed how many neoliberal reforms such as tariff reforms and privatization opened up new ways in which presidential graft, misuses of money for personal gain and abuses of public office abound.[136]

I argue that economic and political reform were almost inseparable in Mexico during this period, but that the links between them were flexible, creative and even opportunistic rather than rigid, conjunctural rather than deterministic, and confused and reversible rather than unilineal. I agree that economic austerity measures, the cuts made to employment and wages as a result of economic reform severely weakened the labour movement. However, I reject the determinism of the rent-seeker analysts who claimed that economic liberalization would wash away the corruption endemic in corporatist arrangements. There is evidence from many developing countries that privatization actually generated more opportunities for clientelistic practices and corruption.[137] I argue that Mexico was not immune to this trend, and that, in some instances, such as the case of the privatization of TELMEX, corporatist arrangements between the government, management and trade unions were lubricated as never before by new resources freed up by privatization. In this case, corporatism was as comfortable with protectionist policies as with neoliberal ones. Thus, the exchange between the government, the union and management withered or blossomed under the effects of economic liberalism depending on the sector and unions involved, but there was no absolute deterministic rule.

In order to arrive at my conclusions, it will be necessary to dis-aggregate some of the concepts and phenomena taken as a whole by the 'optimists'. First, in order to avoid the problem of making vague macro-connections between political and economic reform, such as between electoral results and economic liberalization, I transfer the analysis from a macro to a micro scale. My analysis of the interplay between economic and political change will focus on one particular, though important, case study, and will show state–society relations in action while under the impact of economic restructuring.

When considering organized labour, it is important to analyse the heterogeneous characteristics which make up the whole movement in order to explain the diverse responses from unions and organizations. In so doing, it is crucial to examine economic factors such as the insertion of a particular industry into the economy according to its dynamism, the potential for growth in that industry in the face of integration and liberalization, and the repercussions that technological change might have for that industry.

Privatization is one of the many elements which comprise economic liberalizing policies, and it will be singled out as the specific process under examination. At its most primitive level, privatization can be interpreted as meaning the change of ownership of a company or industry from public to private hands. However, privatization can take different forms and have various effects depending on the industry/ firm privatized and whether it is a monopoly or operates in a competitive environment. The privatization of a mine, a *Compañia Nacional de Subsistencias Populares* (CONASUPO) store, and a national telephone company have fundamentally different consequences. It is important to stress that although privatization, or the passing of a firm from public to private hands, is part of the package of liberalizing reforms, the fact that a firm has been privatized does not necessarily mean that it has been liberalized. In the case of eradicating monopolies, liberalization can occur only if competition is given a genuine chance to enter the market, or if effective regulation is put into place. Governments obviously have the choice whether to accompany privatization with openings to competition or regulation, or to privatize a monopoly. Vickers and Yarrow have stressed that the change in ownership of a company may be much less important on its rates of efficiency than the fact that it operates in a competitive or non-competitive market.[138] It is argued in this book, therefore, that when the way in which economic and political reforms were woven together during privatization is understood, a clearer picture can be built up of the consequences of economic liberalization on state–labour relations in Mexico.

2
State–Labour Relations in Mexico: Opening up the Black Box

Since telephone worker union dissidents ousted their unpopular *charro* leader and set up a new, elected, leadership in 1976, the final year of an administration which had been characterized by 'independent' union breakaway movements, the *Sindicato de Telefonistas de la República Mexicana* (STRM) has prided itself on being one of the most open, democratic and progressive of Mexico's leading unions. This assertion was fortified during the Salinas *sexenio* since the president promoted the STRM as the exemplary model which should be emulated by all other unions. The STRM opted to cooperate with the policy of privatization, unlike many other unions. One of the most infamous and important cases was that of the oilworkers' union PEMEX whose leader, La Quina, openly opposed the privatization of the oil company. Other unions organized strikes in an attempt to oppose privatization of their company such as those of the airline union, Aeroméxico.[1]

Throughout and after the privatization of TELMEX, the STRM was praised by the government for having successfully negotiated the privatization terms while remaining a 'democratic' union responsive to workers' demands. STRM leaders claimed that privatization of TELMEX had resulted in a stronger and more autonomous union, and that one of the consequences was that union members had increased their participation in union affairs. The STRM secretary-general, Francisco Hernández Juárez, was selected to travel abroad with President Salinas to represent Mexican unions during the NAFTA negotiations. The union leader lectured throughout Latin America to promote union cooperation with privatization programmes and was asked by the president to publish a book outlining the ways in which unions could strengthen their autonomy and democracy during economic restructuring.[2] The privatization of TELMEX and its consequences for democracy was presented as the prototype model in Mexico during the Salinas *sexenio* and it is therefore pertinent to examine this case. The privatization of TELMEX merits study for two other main reasons. First, for its financial contribution of US$6 billion to the Mexican Treasury, which represented 30 per cent of the entire profits generated by the privatization programme during the Salinas administration.[3] Second, since it was one of the first large companies to be privatized by Salinas, it constituted the launching-pad of a privatization programme which was successful by Latin American standards.[4]

In order to examine the interplay between economic and political reform and, in particular, to consider whether the privatization of TELMEX had an impact on democratization, it is necessary to define the relevant units of analysis. The focus will be on the players most directly involved in the privatization process: the state, TELMEX management, and the leaders and members of the STRM.[5] The study of relations·between labour and the state is particularly important since the state has historically controlled and put limits upon organized labour. As Manuel Camacho wrote:

> The fundamental political function of the union apparatus which constitutes a corner-stone of the Mexican political system is the regulation of worker mobilization and participation, and to minimize cross-class alliances between workers' subordinate classes thus impeding popular mobilization.[6]

One of the manifestations of increased democracy due to privatization would be that the state would relax its control over the STRM, or, put the other way round, that the union would be able to find more autonomy vis-à-vis the state to conduct union affairs as its members wished and not as the state instructed. A second, related, indicator of greater democracy would be that the STRM would find more autonomy within the body of organized labour. However, union autonomy from the state and labour federations does not necessarily translate into a greater democracy for union members if their leaders rule over them in an oligarchic fashion. Thus, a third signal of the growth of democracy would be if the government and organization of the union became more democratic. Since organized labour has been considered to be one of the main pillars upholding the regime, a fourth indicator of greater democracy would be that the change in the relationship between the STRM and the state brought about a dismantling of the state–labour pact which might herald the weakening of inclusionary authoritarianism in Mexico.

Before investigating these points it is necessary to analyse the way that state–labour relations in Mexico have been understood in the literature. The first section of this chapter analyses briefly the creation of labour legislation and institutions in the post-revolutionary era, state tutelage and repression of the labour movement and the significance of breakaway union movements. In my opinion, there are two major problems with this literature. First, there is a tendency in this literature for the state to be understood as the key influence in the evolution, growth and character of the labour movement without considering other factors. Thus the rise of 'independent' unionism in the 1970s is explained largely by the Echeverría administration's decision to relax labour policy in order to regain legitimacy for the government after the student massacre of 1968, while the fall of 'independent' unionism is connected to the state's withdrawal of its support.[7] Some of the most recent publications on organized labour in Mexico rightly criticize the overly state-centred explanation of labour relations in Mexico in the mainstream literature.[8] The second major problem, in my view, is the vague and misleading use of terms to describe unions in the literature which Roxborough pointed out nearly two decades ago, but which still has not been overcome as an obstacle to the analysis of state–labour relations.[9] The main problem is that unions and labour confederations are analysed as if they were single and monolithic entities or 'black boxes'. Unions and labour confederations are characterized largely by their external behaviour in relation to the state and their internal union practices are rarely considered. The second section of this chapter analyses the reasons for these limitations and presents a way of overcoming them in the analyses of the relationship between the STRM and the state.

The third and final section examines the relationship between the STRM and the state using primary and secondary sources in the light of the critical analysis of the literature on organized labour in Mexico as well as mainstream works on industrial relations and union democracy. One of the main findings is that the terms used to describe unions such as *charro* or democratic and 'independent' or 'official' have contributed to obscuring rather than shedding light on the character and trajectory of the STRM union and its relationship with the state and the labour movement. Another important conclusion is that state policy was highly significant in influencing the STRM but it was not the only factor, and a more complete analysis is needed if we are to consider the influence of a growing labour force, transformations in the service, and the impact of technology.

The state–labour pact in Mexico

Establishment

Between the end of the phase of armed uprising of the Mexican Revolution and the 1940s, key labour legislation was established. This included in particular Article 123 of the Mexican Constitution and the LFT, and labour institutions such as the JCA, which codify the circumstances under which workers can form a union, bargain collectively, hold workers' meetings, go on strike and many other aspects of labour laws. This legislation and institutional organization constitutes a framework which defines and shapes the relationship between labour and the state. It is important, therefore, to examine the conditions in which this framework was first constructed in order to analyse the legacy of the way in which the state–labour relationship evolved.

As workers intensified their organizing activities at the beginning of the twentieth century, the frequent intervention of revolutionary governments contributed towards the shape that this burgeoning labour movement was beginning to take. When one of the first labour organizations, the *Casa del Obrero Mundial* (COM), which was founded in 1912, agreed in 1915 to make a pact to support Carranza to fight against Zapata and Villa in the final years of the revolution, labour was rewarded for its support with the inclusion of Article 123 in the Constitution. This article, which detailed many aspects of labour law, was favourable to workers, and granted them rights to organize, strike, and defined their working conditions.[10] However, Ashby pointed out that although this was the longest article in the Constitution, and an advanced labour law in international terms, this did not mean that labour had necessarily gained it due to its own strength alone. Organized labour was small and weak during the revolutionary years and workers engaged in industry comprised only 15 per cent of the country's working population.[11] The total workforce fell after 1910 and this level was not regained until the 1930s. At the beginning of the 1930s, there were around 1.5 million urban workers, half of whom were employed in the industrial sector and the other half in the service sector. During the period 1910–30 employment in these sectors declined and statistics suggest evidence of a reverse pattern of migration to rural areas.[12] Knight notes that the radical content of the article was not, however, a serious threat, since labour lacked the muscle to attempt to enforce it.[13] Moreover, the article had been written by the constitutionalists and handed down from on high to the workers who had not participated in its drafting. There was a lack of correspondence, therefore, between gains made by labour and their real power. One of the most important consequences of Article 123 is that the state became an arbiter between capital and workers, or, in other words, the conciliator of classes.[14]

The enactment of the LFT in 1931 bolstered the state's legitimacy as interlocutor between management and labour.[15] Article 123 had not allowed exclusive federal jurisdiction over labour affairs, so individual states enacted many different laws and had varying labour institutions. The LFT was a milestone in the centralization of state administrative authority over labour. The JCA were tripartite boards comprising representatives of government, business and labour, and they functioned at the national and regional level in order to resolve labour disputes, decide whether a strike would be recognized legally (or rejected and thus made 'inexistent') as well as legally accepting collective labour contracts.

A contemporary observer, Ernst Gruening, wrote in 1928 that it was government backing, not labour strength, that determined the outcome of labour conflicts and strikes in that period.[16] Perceiving that labour was one of the easiest sectors in society to mobilize, government leaders strove to align with organized labour in order to bolster the regime. A pattern was developed whereby the government favoured openly one confederation over the others, and awarded its leaders privileges with government posts and financial incentives in return for their unflinching support and their control over rank and file. President Calles struck a close relationship with a small élite in the *Confederación Regional Obrera Mexicana* (CROM) known as *Grupo Acción* led by Luis Morones. This group, funded by the government, negotiated issues of union strategy in secret.[17] In return for CROM loyalty, most of the members of the *Grupo Acción* were given positions in the Senate or the House of Deputies. Furthermore, when Calles became president (1924–8), he promoted Morones to Secretary of the Department of Industry, Commerce and Labour. The CROM repaid the government for this preferential treatment by supporting it in its fight against the Church and foreign interests.[18]

Since subservience to the government meant avoiding labour conflict and strikes, and the union élite discussed union strategy in closed meetings, workers' demands and participation were hardly high on the leaders' list of priorities. Pro-government behaviour was rewarded with benefits which leaders could deliver to workers. This personalistic style of labour dominance contained the seeds of a more brutal form of union control known as '*charrismo*' which occurred in the 1940s and 1950s. While a confederation enjoyed government support it could expect privileged treatment, but the moment that the government withdrew that support, the union's power started to disintegrate quickly. Once the government stopped supporting the CROM in the late 1920s, the confederation's power quickly disintegrated, and union members started to leave.

The administration of Lázaro Cárdenas (1934–40) is interpreted as a positive one for workers by many analysts[19] though there is considerable debate about how radical Cárdenas' policies were in reality.[20] During this *sexenio* some of the more radical, pro-labour policies were implemented and, as the labour force tripled between 1930 and 1940,[21] workers became increasingly organized. National unions were established in the 1930s including the *Sindicato de Trabajadores Ferrocarrileros de la República Mexicana* (STFRM) in 1933, the *Sindicato Nacional de Trabajadores Mineros, Metalúrgicos y Similares de la República Mexicana* (SNTMMSRM) in 1934 and the *Sindicato de Trabajadores Petroleros de la República Mexicana* (STPRM) in 1935.[22] Of particular importance was the creation in 1936 of the *Confederación de Trabajadores Mexicanos* (CTM) with the aim of unifying urban workers in a confederation which would form part of the reorganized party, the *Partido de la Revolución Mexicana* (PRM). The nationalization of the railroad system in June 1937 and the oil industry in March 1938 were also regarded as victories for labour since foreign owners were excluded and, in the case of the railroad workers' union, workers were allowed to participate in management. Workers enjoyed wage increases and benefits during this period, as well as improved working conditions.[23]

Ashby claimed that the era of *Cardenismo* differed from the past. He wrote that prior to 1934:

> there only appeared to exist the freedom to strike and other syndical liberties; labor tribunals and the speeches of government officials were always favorable to the interests of labor, but the most important strikes were transformed into failures for the working class. The unions were overpowered by the political influence of the corrupt leaders, and the labor courts decided in favor of private interests against the worker. Beginning in 1935, there were worker conflicts that were decided in favor of the workers, due to the inauguration of a new system of statecraft.[24]

During 1934–40, the relationship between labour and the state became increasingly intimate. The Cárdenas administration required labour's support in order to bolster the power of the state as the arbiter of the nation's economy while reducing the power of private industry. It therefore supported the CTM, by helping it financially and by persecuting its enemies. The CTM was at this time led by Lombardo Toledano who enjoyed a close relationship with Cárdenas, and both shared the objectives of presenting a popular front in the face of the outbreak of the Spanish Civil War.[25] In 1939, the CTM backed Avila Camacho as the presidential candidate in the elections. Once Avila Camacho's victory was assured, eight labour representatives were appointed as senators and 24 were given deputy posts in reward for labour support.[26]

Ashby argued that the long-term consequences of labour's cooperation with the state was damaging since labour was increasing its dependency on the state.[27] Hamilton claimed that, as the state increased its legitimacy as an interlocutor in labour affairs during the Cárdenas administration, labour lost any autonomy it might otherwise have had.[28]

In the aftermath of the revolution then, the state–labour pact emerged as a lopsided, uneven trade-off in which the labour movement, usually headed by the 'favourite' confederation, provided unheroic but pragmatic support for the government. The government, on the other hand, in search of regime stability, legitimacy and support, rewarded labour for its loyalty by designating selected labour leaders with political posts while granting leaders concessions which they could hand down to their members. Since government leaders required loyal labour support and rewarded union leaders in return for this, the system did not provide incentives for union leaders to consider worker demands. Workers' demands were thus only seriously considered if they became so urgent that they amounted to a serious threat to the leader's control over the union. Labour's cooperation with the state and its incorporation into the PRM was interpreted as being synonymous with its loss of independent political power.[29] Thus, the state–labour relationship was in fact a poisoned chalice. On the one hand, labour leaders that managed to control their rank and file could find, through the state, access to political power (which they could use to improve the workers' lot) and financial rewards (which they could use to distribute to union members). On the other hand, these benefits came at a high cost which was the integrity, autonomy and independence of the movement which had not in any case existed previously to any great degree.

Consolidation

During the late 1940s and early 1950s, the state–labour relationship underwent a shift to the right. Labour specialists such as Bethell and Roxborough, Middlebrook and Zapata have associated this with the parallel change in economic policy pursued by the Mexican government.[30] Mexico, like other Latin American countries, pursued an outward-oriented economic model from the nineteenth century which had been relatively successful until the outbreak of the First World War. The shocks of the two World Wars and the Great Depression caused a severe economic crisis in the region.[31] As Latin American countries could no longer sell sufficient exports they were unable to earn the income necessary to purchase former levels of imports. The result of isolation from world markets and international economic depression was the emergence of a new strategy of inward-looking growth.[32]

ISI policies included the application of a variety of protectionist measures including tariffs on imports which restrained foreign competition, and devaluation of the peso (1948–9, and again in 1954) which would make Mexican goods more competitive internationally. National manufacturing was stimulated, a new body of prominent industrialists was established, and the industrial labour force expanded.[33] ISI proved to be a successful policy in Mexico in terms of GDP which grew at an annual average rate of around 6.4 per cent from the 1950s to the late 1960s. However, economic growth was highly skewed, and was accompanied by mass poverty, regional imbalances, social tensions and injustice.[34]

During the last years of the Second World War, strike activity reached an all-time high of 766 strikes in 1943 and 887 in 1944.[35] Although the government, representatives of industry and the CTM had signed the *Pacto Obrero Industrial*, in which organized labour committed itself to support the official strategy of the national industry project, this agreement did not put an end to the strikes. It became clear that divisions and problems of ungovernability within the labour movement were increasing.[36] In the face of the possibility of losing control over labour, the government took dramatic steps to reassert discipline.

The period from 1947 to 1951 was a defining one for the state–labour relationship. In particular, there were two key developments. First, the labour movement as a whole began to be structurally dominated by the CTM. Second, rivalry between diverse factions within the CTM were quashed and the more conservative faction gradually increased its control over the leadership. In 1947 there was rivalry for the election of the next CTM secretary-general between three main groups headed by the conservative Fidel Velázquez, the left-wing labour intellectual Lombardo Toledano, and the more radical leader of the railroad workers' union, Luis Gómez.[37] Lombardo Toledano was marginalized within the CTM and expelled finally in January 1948.[38] Furthermore, the radicals were ousted as noted below, so Fidel Velázquez and his supporters started to dominate the organization.[39]

Radical unionists, led by Luis Gómez, secretary-general of the railroad workers' union and Valentin Campa, left the CTM in the same year in protest at the new conservative leadership and formed the *Confederación Única de Trabajadores* (CUT) which, albeit briefly, provided a serious challenge to the CTM.[40] By February 1948 a larger coalition, including the CUT and many other national industrial unions, formed the *Coalición de Organizaciones Obreros y Campesinos* (COOC). Talavara and Leal calculated their share of total union membership to be 22.4 per cent in comparison with 21 per cent in the CTM and the 4.7 per cent share in the CROM.[41] Together, the CTM and CUT accounted for nearly one-half of all unionized workers, and they were the two giant bodies fighting for dominance over the labour movement. Many of the remaining unions either belonged to a minor federation or did not belong to a labour federation at all. The government, recognizing the potential power of the combined forces of the railway, mining and petroleum workers at the centre of CUT, took dramatic action which effectively purged the unions of militant and left-wing members. This action was known as the *charrazo*.[42] The first *charrazo* took place in 1948 when the government intervened when the railroad workers called a strike in protest against wage cuts. The elected leader was removed by force from his position and a pro-government representative was imposed in his place.[43] During the next three years state authorities exacerbated internal divisions within the miners' union (SNTMMSRM) and petroleum workers' union (STPRM) by continually showing preferential treatment to pro-government union representatives and, by the beginning of the 1950s, all three formerly troublesome unions were controlled by government-allied leaders.[44] The STPRM rejoined the CTM in 1951.

According to Roxborough, it was primarily because of this repressive government intervention that a new phase in state–labour relations was born:

> By 1948 a serious challenge to the Mexican political system had been beaten off. The next two years were devoted to mopping up,

and by the early fifties the Mexican economy was in a position to embark on a sustained period of rapid growth. The political underpinning of this growth-model were, on the one hand, the political stability enshrined in the unchallenged rule of the revolutionary party and, on the other hand, the smooth functioning of Mexico's brand of corporatist industrial relations, which came to be known as *charrismo*.[45]

Mexico's relatively tranquil industrial relations in the period from the 1950s to the beginning of the 1970s, achieved largely by ensuring top–down control over workers by the *charrazos*, and the structural dominance of the CTM, provided a foundation for the rapid economic growth and political stability that accompanied the Mexican 'miracle'.[46] Though the government and pro-government unionists, such as CTM leaders, used anti-communist rhetoric to justify the repression of left-wing unionists and other militants, it was the domestic requirements of a docile labour force which were more important.[47] By 1954, the CTM boasted a membership of 32.3 per cent of unionized workers, and the second and third largest confederations lagged far behind, the *Confederación Regional de Obreros y Campesinos* (CROC) having 4.7 per cent of workers and the CROM 4.6 per cent.[48] In 1960 CTM membership share increased further to 38.5 per cent.[49] The CTM had a fundamental role in the process of capital accumulation. It curbed workers' demands in an attempt to maintain wages at a level acceptable to the government, it supported the government at critical times such as the period between the president's *dedazo* and presidential succession, and it controlled rank and file through clientelistic means using corrupt union officials. The government pursued a policy of encouraging diversity in the labour movement from the 1950s, by allowing and supporting the formation of rival confederations, aimed at limiting the CTM's power.[50]

The overall annual decrease in the number of strikes, and the fall in the average number of workers on strike from the 1940s onwards is attributed to the increasingly strict control exercised by the state over organized labour, and the alliance made between labour bosses, management and the state.[51] Middlebrook showed that there was a definite shift in state policy towards strikes at the federal level.[52] Between 1938 and 1945 an average 32 per cent of the strike petitions filed by the JCA were recognized as valid and 'official'. There was considerable diversity in this period, the lowest percentage of recognized strikes was in 1940 at 8 per cent and the highest figures reached were 66.3 per cent, 66.5

per cent and 40.7 per cent in 1943, 1944 and 1945 respectively. However, between 1963 and 1993, the situation had changed dramatically with on average only 2.2 per cent of strike petitions filed being recognized as official. These figures were less volatile and ranged from 1 per cent in 1973 to 4.2 per cent in 1982. Unfortunately Middlebrook has not been able to produce a comprehensive set of figures (in particular, data are missing for the number of strike petitions made between 1946 and 1962) so, although it is clear there was a turning point in the government's labour policy it is not possible to pinpoint exactly when this occurred.

The alliance between the government and organized labour was lubricated by the relative success of import-substitution industrialization from the late 1950s to the early 1970s.[53] The government had resources which it could distribute to union *charros* for their personal gain (the richest *charros* were renowned for extravagant and luxurious lifestyles) and also for redistribution to their union members. Between 1952 and 1974 the real wage of workers in the manufacturing sector in Mexico City increased annually (apart from in 1957 and 1970).[54] In addition, the number of government health and welfare programmes (particularly those directed towards unionized employees in the formal sector) grew dramatically from the 1940s to the 1970s,[55] and there was also the benefit of economic growth which produced new sources of employment.

In the period from the 1950s to the beginning of the 1970s then, most of the unions and labour confederations in Mexico were headed by *charro* leaders who were charged with keeping wages in line with levels acceptable to the government, maintaining the unions within one of the PRI-affiliated labour confederations and cooperating generally with government policies. Collective bargaining was largely a formality which was conducted between the *charro* and management, or between the individual union *charro* leaders and the confederation *charro* leader.

Charro leadership did not go uncontested and many movements emerged from unions throughout the period to oust them. This trend could be seen as the precursor of the 'independent union' movement of the 1960s and 1970s. The most important of these movements was the railroad workers' union during 1958 and 1959.[56] Other important movements took place within the STRM, the *Sindicato Mexicano de Electricistas* (SME), the *Sindicato de Trabajadores Electricistas de la República Mexicana* (STERM) and the *Sindicato Nacional de Trabajadores de la Educación* (SNTE) in an attempt to oust their *charro* leaders.[57]

However, each movement met with severe government repression. The 1948 railroad workers' strike which was held to demand wage increases and the removal of the *charro* Díaz de León as secretary-general was broken within weeks by military intervention, and the leaders of the dissident union were accused of sabotage and jailed. The severity of the suppression of the strike and the subsequent purges of dissidents in other unions, including the SNTE and STRM, gave way to a period of relative political tranquillity among unions from the industrial sectors in the 1960s.[58]

Breaking away: 'independent unionism'

In the late 1960s and 1970s, labour insurgence from diverse unions in the manufacturing, commercial and service sectors increased, and the *charro* leader was ousted and replaced by an elected leader in a number of unions including the SNTE (1972), some of the automobile unions including DINA (1962) and Volkswagen (1972), and the STRM (1976). Important dissident movements, which used the tactic of remaining within the national industrial unions, emerged, such as the *Tendencia Democrática* led by Rafael Galván in the *Sindicato Único de Trabajadores Electricistas de la República Mexicana* (SUTERM), and the *Movimiento Sindical Ferrocarrilero* (MSF), an opposition group of railroad workers led by Demetrio Vallejo. The *Comité Nacional de Trabajadores de la Educación* (CNTE) grew within the SNTE in the late 1970s and transformed the union by ensuring that executive leaders had been elected democratically.[59]

One of the reasons for this swell in labour insurgency was Echeverría's attempt to re-establish legitimacy for the regime by adopting a dual policy of 'democratic opening' and 'shared development' in the aftermath of the bloody repression of students in 1968.[60] 'Democratic opening' entailed an increasingly tolerant attitude towards political dissidence; some political prisoners were freed (including Demetrio Vallejo, the former leader of the railroad workers' union, who had been jailed for his promotion of radical and autonomous unionism) and by 1977 the electoral system had been reformed. From the economic viewpoint, Echeverría announced his new policy of 'shared development'. This policy brought about a dramatic expansion of the parastatal sector, which swelled from 86 state-owned corporations in 1970 to 740 by the end of his administration.[61] In 1972, TELMEX was nationalized, or 'mexicanized', which meant that the government had acquired 51 per cent of its shares. Public spending was poured into housing, schooling and other development programmes.

Both political and economic projects had important consequences for organized labour since greater pluralism was permitted to develop within the labour movement. The regime tolerated the action of dissident groups to oust the *charro* leaders and replace them with elected leaders. This weakened the CTM since often one of the first actions of these new leaders was to remove the union from the CTM and, therefore, the PRI, and in many cases joining another confederation that was not aligned with the party. Moreover, the government actually extended legal recognition to the *Unidad Obrera Independiente* (UOI), one such independent confederation. Smith argued that, as the presidential elections of 1976 approached, Echeverría recognized that he needed support from Velázquez to control the rank and file prior to the *destape* and presidential succession.[62] Thus, the author claimed that once the state threw its weight behind the CTM, the independent movement tended to wither away. While the government's tolerance of 'independent' unionism was crucial for the movement's success, I argue that a 'top–down' explanation is not adequate alone to explain the emergence or the demise of breakaway unionism. It cannot clarify, for instance, why Echeverría's 'democratic opening' sparked off democratizing movements in some unions but not in others.

Unions in the automobile sector have attracted more attention from scholars than others because this sector contains an array of unions which behaved in a different way throughout the period enabling inter-sectoral contrasts and comparisons to be drawn.[63] Middlebrook argued that one of the consequences of economic development on this sector was that the traditional mechanisms of labour control were eroded due to rapid industrial expansion and change, specifically in the transformation of the automobile industry from an assembly-based one to a manufacturing one during the 1960s. This change involved dramatic increases in the number of workers employed by automobile companies such as Auto-Mex/Chrysler, Diesel Nacional, Ford and General Motors, which increased their 1960 workforce of between 10 000 and 15 000 by at least a four-fold factor by 1975.[64] Volkswagen grew at the fastest rate with 250 workers in 1960 and 9515 by 1975. Many of these unions had been members of confederations such as the CTM during the 1950s, and their collective contracts had been negotiated on their behalf by the CTM. However, as workers' wages rose, the industry became increasingly capital intensive with large and growing worker concentrations per firm and rising worker productivity. Traditional mechanisms of collective bargaining proved unable to deal with many of these newly emerging problems, and from the 1960s to the mid-1970s roughly three-quarters of the largest automobile unions broke away from the CTM.[65] Middlebrook argued that it was possible to determine whether a specific automobile union broke away from or remained in the 'official' labour confederation in which they were a member by considering the degree to which that union already enjoyed democratic practices. He argued that General Motors, for instance, underwent a huge transformation but its trade union members did not need to break away from the labour confederation to which they belonged since their union already enjoyed a high degree of autonomy. The *Vehículos Automotores Mexicanos* (VAM) trade union did not break away from the CTM, but at the same time apparently it did not experience growth at the rate of the other main companies, and it remained in oligarchic hands.[66]

An appreciation of the significance of the state's influence on and control over labour is crucial if we are to understand the way in which the labour movement in Mexico has taken shape and under what constraints. The expansion of state apparatus to administer the labour movement profoundly shaped the way in which labour became organized, and the nature of the relationship cemented between labour and the state. State intervention in the late 1940s and early 1950s was a turning point which cleared the way for ISI and economic growth. However, a state-centred analysis is not the only perspective that can be used to understand the characteristics of organized labour, and it could be argued that as the Mexican economy is increasingly integrated with the rest of North America, a state-centred analysis is increasingly inadequate as the main explanation for the nature of the state–labour relationship. Industrialization profoundly affected union sizes and work practices, which in turn had an effect on transforming labour relations.[67] A state-centred approach would suggest that there was no legacy of 'independent' unionism since it could not survive once the state withdrew its support. However, this argument does not consider inherent tensions and forces within the labour movement which brought about a reorganization of the remaining unions once the state decided that 'independent' unionism would no longer be favoured.

Opening up the black box

Roxborough criticized what he called the 'standard account' of the development of the labour movement in Latin America for its overemphasis on the state's capacity to co-opt or repress rank and file insurgency, and for its assumption, in the specific case of Mexico, that 'trade unions are more or less passive instruments of an authoritarian state'.[68] He argued that rank and file insurgency has been a constant feature of industrial relations in Mexico and that the control of labour by the state has been 'far more fragile and subject to contest than appears at first sight'. The process of *charrismo* in the late 1940s was substantially more difficult, slow and problematic than the standard account suggests. One of the reasons for an over-homogenized picture, he argued, was the lack of detailed monographs on organized labour which existed until the 1970s.[69] With the benefit of these sources we can see that the relationship between the state and labour has been, and still is, more complex than was described in earlier analyses.[70] His observation forms one important strand of the criticism mentioned in the first chapter of this book that claims that the political stability in Mexico in the period between 1950 and 1980 has been exaggerated.

Roxborough pointed out some of the limitations of the terms used by analysts to describe unions. He noted that there is a trend to use a binary method of categorization for unions in the literature, and that unions are lumped into belonging to one or the other category. Furthermore, many of these terms were undefined and used loosely.[71] The term *charro* originated in government intervention in the railroad workers' union in 1958–9, but this particular kind of intervention was in fact rare, and the term *charro* is more often used to describe any unpopular labour leader.[72] This has further implications. The noun, *charro* (cowboy) is used with the suffix *charr-azo*, to refer to the act in which a 'democratic' union leader is ousted and replaced by a pro-government leader. On the other hand *charr-ismo* is used to describe many kinds of anti-labour government policies. Unions in Mexico are classified first and foremost by their relationship with the state. If they belong to the CTM or to another of the umbrella labour confederations associated with the PRI, they are called 'official' or 'bureaucratic'. If they belong to a labour confederation outside the PRI-affiliated labour umbrella, or simply do not belong to a confederation at all, they are labelled 'independent'. Many assumptions are made in the literature about the nature of a union on this basis. 'Official' unions are believed to be docile since they are controlled top–down by corrupt union leaders. 'Independent' unions are generally expected to be militant, since they are led by 'democratic' leaders who are perceived to be less corrupt than *charro* leaders, since they must act more 'autonomously' from the government due to pressure from rank and file.

In contrast to these ideal-types, Roxborough's study of the behaviour of nine automobile unions in the 1970s concluded that the variable which explained union insurgence in this sector was not whether it was 'official' or 'independent' but the degree of real autonomy it enjoyed from the official union structure.[73] Trade union militancy was not, however, confined to 'independent' unions since some of the 'official' unions were also militant. Thus, control over the rank and file by union leaders and the state was not as complete as suggested in the literature. Other related factors which were considered to make a union more militant were strong organizational abilities, with a high number of union members being paid to act as full-time union officials, and a democratic system of union government.[74]

Roxborough conducted his fieldwork in 1978 and stressed the levels of union dissidence apparent in the breakaway movements at that time, and thus his conclusion was that state control over labour had been exaggerated in the literature. In retrospect, his hopes for the future of 'independent' unionism appear to be over-optimistic. Most analysis of the Mexican labour movement in the 1980s and 1990s has attempted to explain the reasons for the lack of insurgence or union mobilization in the face of economic austerity measures.[75] Unfortunately, however, Roxborough's observations about the loose and misleading application of terms such as *charro* or 'democratic' leadership, and 'official' and 'independent' unions have not been integrated fully into the literature, and these terms continue to be used rather vaguely, while new terms such as neo-*charro* have also been introduced without further explanation in much of the more recent literature on state–labour relations.[76]

In my view, the principal reason for this vague classification of unions is that, too often, the literature on organized labour in Mexico treats unions as 'black boxes' which are analysed as single and monolithic entities. Rarely are internal divisions and tensions within a union highlighted, or changes in internal union practice analysed in detail.[77] A union is defined by its physical position vis-à-vis the state, and many union characteristics are categorized on the basis of this. In most of this literature it is considered satisfactory to label a union according to its external behaviour, which could be called its 'foreign policy', rather than its internal practices, or its 'domestic policy'. The label 'independent union' refers to the fact that it is not a member of the CTM or another 'official' labour confederation and does not necessarily infer that the union in question is 'independent' in terms of union practices, government or outlook. Gómez Tagle was aware of this problem when she referred to the STERM as containing a 'democratic current' but admitted that she used the term not because she believed that the current was 'democratic', but because she wanted to distinguish it from the bureaucratic leadership of the STERM and also because she wished to indicate that the union was trying to attain more union democracy.[78]

Part of the reason for the scarcity of literature which deals with the internal mechanisms of union politics in Mexico is the difficulty of obtaining inside information about how unions are run. For the researcher there is the problem of breaking through the barrier of secrecy which many unions erect, and, consequently, of not being able to witness its politics in practice or to access primary sources on union meetings, events and history. There is also a lack of analysis at the shop-floor where union practice can be seen at the day-to-day level. The STPRM has avoided cooperating with inquisitive researchers, including leading analysts of Mexican labour such as Middlebrook.[79] Other analysts such as Thompson and Roxborough have noted the difficulties of gaining information about union practices in Mexico.[80] Unions at times initially cooperate with a researcher but they may withdraw all access if a researcher writes negatively about them.[81] One indication of a union's monopoly over this kind of knowledge is that a researcher often needs to obtain permission from union leaders, at both local and national levels, and not from management, to conduct research on the shop-floor. Without inside access to the union, analysis based on 'cold' data on a union can lead researchers to erroneous conclusions based on the superficial appearance of union politics.

One of the main efforts in this research was to attempt to go beyond the typological problems of labelling unions in a dichotomous way in my study of the STRM. It would be necessary for me to delve into the internal as well as the external union policies practised by the STRM prior to and during privatization. This approach helped me to clarify the differences in practice between the so-called 'democratic' or 'insurgent' period of post-1976 STRM history with its *charro* and 'official' past. I decided to analyse both internal union practice at the national level and also at the shop-floor level.[82] STRM union leaders agreed to cooperate with this research, and to allow me access to union leaders and rank and file, partly because they genuinely consider themselves a democratic and progressive union, and partly because I was fortunate in being able to establish a key contact who could facilitate my access to the STRM at a high level.[83] My strategy was to gain the confidence of the national union leaders first, then obtain their permission to conduct surveys and interviews with telephone workers. The fieldwork was conducted over the period of a year, which provided sufficient time for the union leaders to develop confidence in the project. In addition, when explaining the subject of my research to the union leaders, I stressed those aspects which examined the effect of new technology upon the telephone workers, and this is an issue of which the union is proud. Also, I downplayed that part of my work which analyses the relationship between union democracy and government. Primary material on union democracy in the STRM was gathered from the STRM press office's archives of STRM pamphlets and union magazines, from attendance at union assemblies and workers' meetings in Mexico City, and from numerous interviews with union leaders and rank and file, including supporters and enemies of Hernández Juárez and union members who claimed to have no particular interest in union politics.

As mentioned earlier, most interpretations of labour in Mexico have been too heavily state-centred and the result is that the state is perceived as the sole shaping and intervening force in the labour movement.[84] For instance, the impositions of *charro* leaders in the late 1950s have been explained in the literature as being due directly to government policy to accelerate ISI.[85] The expulsion of the *charros* is, similarly, connected to the relaxation of state policy on labour by the Echeverría administration in order to regain government legitimacy. Thus, Smith argued that, once the Echeverría administration withdrew its support for 'independent' unionism, the latter simply 'withered away'.[86] However, other factors should also be considered as playing a role in shaping the labour movement. Middlebrook forcefully argued that it is essential to also consider the rapid growth of the unionized workforce and the transformations in the automobile industry (from one based only on assembly to one completing the manufacturing process) when analysing the reasons for the rise of 'independent' unionism.[87] His argument gains currency when it is put in context with the literature which claims that, as trade is increasingly globalized, and as countries enter regional integration pacts, it is increasingly important to consider factors beyond the state when explaining domestic policies.[88] Technological change and the globalization of world trade are seen as trends which are eroding the viability of state-centred models of explanation. Brachet-Marquez correctly made the point that too much attention has been placed upon the state in the literature on state–labour relations. Instead, she took a more 'bottom-up' approach by emphasizing the way that state labour policy was influenced by workers' demands. However, she did not introduce new factors such as technology or industrial restructuring into her argument.[89]

The STRM: union democracy and state relations

In the light of this critical analysis of the literature on state–labour relations in Mexico, the rest of this chapter attempts to characterize the relationship between the STRM and the state, concentrating on the differences in practice between *charro* (1950–76) and 'democratic' leadership (1976 onwards). Both internal and external union practice will be analysed. Mainstream works on union democracy will be used as a guide to internal union behaviour and consideration will be given to the following: union leader turnover, the existence of competitive elections and opposition parties, and the nature and extent of worker participation in union and work-related issues. The examination of external union behaviour will include: the position of the STRM vis-à-vis the state, the relationship of the STRM to 'independent' labour and strikes and mobilizations.

The main conclusions of a comparison of the way in which unions behave under *charro* and 'democratic' leadership are that the leaderships were not antithetical. Indeed, there were important changes as well as significant continuities in both union leader types. Attention is also drawn to the factors that influenced changes in leadership (from *charro* to 'democratic'). In addition to the importance of state policy, growth and changes in the composition of the union and the national importance of telecommunications are significant. Moreover, the analysis shows that internal factors also played an important role, since 'independent' unionism threw up contradictions for the practice of union politics and union democracy.

Theories of union government and democracy

The literature on union democracy has a long, rich tradition, and no single theory of what constitutes union democracy has been agreed, particularly at the international level, since the variations with union government in practice have complicated the elaboration of a general theory. One of the problems in trying to apply the general literature on union democracy to Mexico specifically is that a large portion of the theories in the literature have been derived from case studies of unions in the developed world, particularly the United States and Europe. Care must therefore be taken to ensure that the details from Mexican unions are not distorted to fit the model but rather that the model is adapted appropriately when analysing the peculiarities of Mexican unions.

Many analysts consider that the central feature of union democracy is the existence of at least two rival factions within a union who vie for leadership. All parties must have a chance of succeeding at the elections so that competition is 'effective'. A prototype of a two-party union model was the International Typographical Union studied by Lipset *et al.* in 1956. However, the authors claimed that this two-party union system was 'a rare, even unique phenomenon'.[90] Michels proposed that oligarchic rule was more the norm than democratic rule within any large organization. The 'iron law of oligarchy' was the inevitable outcome in a large-scale organization since power was controlled by a select few. This élite leadership possessed resources which gave it an almost insurmountable advantage over other members, including superior knowledge, control over the means of communication, and experience and skill in the art of politics.[91]

Handleman was influenced by the work on competing parties within unions in his analysis of union democracy in Mexico. For him, the proof of its existence was that incumbent leaders could be ousted by a rival faction through a contested election.[92] Moreover, when election results for different parties were narrow, this was also a positive sign of union democracy. According to this logic, the SME was democratic since incumbent leaders were ousted three times between 1952 and 1973, and the STERM was oligarchical since Rafael Galván had served as its secretary-general continually throughout the period 1952–73.[93] Moreover, the margin of votes for opposition parties in the SME was slim, whereas none of Galván's opponents ever won more than 35 per cent. Handelman (1977) and Lipset *et al.* (1956) concurred in their proposals that effective (as opposed to institutional or nominal) opposition within a union is one of the signs of union democracy.[94] This hypothesis was used as the first indicator of union democracy in this research.

Thompson and Roxborough developed a useful framework for the analysis of union democracy in Mexico. In addition to stressing Handleman's point that the removal of incumbent leaders and narrow margin achieved in elections suggested the union was democratic, they also claimed that it was important for union democracy that the opposition party was strong enough to influence the decision-making of the incumbent leadership.[95] In addition, they claimed that, in order for a union to be considered democratic, elections for all executive posts should be contested (hypothesis number two). All members of the union should be entitled to vote via a secret ballot, their votes should be accurately counted, and the outcome of the election should be respected. The election must be contested, that is, there must be choice for the voter. Where elections are not held, or are not contested, the system is not even termed democratic.[96] Finally, union democracy can be measured by examining the turnover of union leaders (hypothesis number three).[97] A high turnover of leaders is interpreted as indicating mobility within union politics and opportunities for change.

Pateman's interpretation of union democracy was much broader and her work on democracy and participation within a trade union remains a classic.[98] Her approach rejects studies which limit their consideration of union democracy or oligarchy to the analysis of union government and elections, such as Michels, Clegg and Lipset, Trow and Coleman.[99] Industrial democracy goes beyond a worker's right to vote since a high level, and broad degree, of penetration of worker participation is also important as a criterion of union democracy.[100] Pateman distinguished between democracy and participation in a union. She argued that worker participation, by which she meant workers' involvement in and influence over the outcome of decision-making on matters of industry and the workplace, was an important component of union democracy in general.[101] She defined participation within industry as falling into two categories, 'high' and 'low'. 'High' participation was seen as a significant level of interest or ability on the part of the rank and file to influence top-level management, government officials or union leaders on topics of national importance or business. Participation at the 'low' level referred to rank and file's attempts to influence or change things that affected them daily at the shop-floor level.[102] Pateman makes two important remarks about these 'low' and 'high' levels of participation. First, rank and file may be more motivated to participate at the daily, tangible level of their workplace than be involved in national matters which may seem more distant and less directly relevant to them. Second, she claimed that participation at the low level is useful 'training ground' for participation at the higher level, and is thus of extreme importance for developing union democracy and participation in the long term.

She also divided the notion of participation into three vertical categories. First, 'pseudo-participation' occurred if workers were informed about an issue and invited to discuss it, when in fact the decision had already been taken. Management or union leaders adopted this style of contrived leadership in order to encourage workers to feel they were participating when in fact they were not.[103] The opportunity to debate was used merely as a means of inducing acceptance of the goal. Second, she maintained that 'partial participation' transpired when there were two or more parties, usually management and the union, which had an unequal influence in the final decision-making process. For instance if management negotiated with the union, the union may have influenced management but management took the final decision alone.[104] Third, 'full participation', a rare privilege for workers, would be where management and the union had an equal influence in taking decisions.

So, in addition to examining aspects of union government and opposition, Pateman claimed it was also important to consider the nature and extent of worker participation in industrial and union affairs such as collective bargaining or joint management–union consultations.[105] For fruitful worker participation it was important that workers received information about planned strikes or changes in the company. Quality circles may increase the extent of worker participation at the shop-floor level. She maintained that union representatives should reflect the composition of the rank and file in terms of gender, geographic location and work skill. Her view was that profit-sharing schemes may also be evidence of worker participation but it was important to consider whether these were distributed in accordance with the workers' salary, reinforcing hierarchies, or whether they were egalitarian.[106] Pateman's hypotheses on worker participation and union democracy will also be interwoven into the account and will become particularly important in the discussion of democracy in the STRM during the privatization of TELMEX which is discussed in the final three chapters of this book.

Union practice: 1950–75

Most telephone workers would agree that the history of the STRM can be divided into two periods; from its foundation in 1950 to the ousting of the *charro* leadership in 1976, and from the 'democratic' leadership of Hernández Juárez from 1976 to the present. During many of the interviews conducted with telephone workers in Mexico City and in Puebla with supporters of Hernández Juárez (so-called *juaristas*), as well as with his enemies and those uninterested in union politics, workers use the words 'before' and 'after' when discussing union history without making it explicit that they are continually referring to 1976 and the arrival of Hernández Juárez as their new, young 'democratic' leader.

Since the STRM was formed in 1950, its organizational structure at the national level has remained fundamentally unchanged. The National Executive Committee (CEN) and the National Vigilance Committee (CNV) constitute the two superior bodies within its organizational structure. The CEN is headed by the secretary-general who presides over a team of union members who occupy positions such as Secretary for External Affairs, Treasury, Internal Affairs and Labour Conflicts. The CEN's official duty is to carry out all the decisions taken at the annual convention. The official function of the CNV, which comprises a president and two secretaries, is to ensure that the union statutes are not violated by any union member including those in the CEN.[107] Clearly, if the secretary-general hand-picks all other members of the executive, the CNV would pose no threat whatsoever to his autonomy.

From the establishment of the STRM in 1950, infighting among its members for the control of the union was intense. This was partly because the STRM had come into being as a result of the merger between the respective unions of Mexico's two largest telephone companies, *Teléfonos Ericsson*, a subsidiary of Ericsson of Sweden, and *Compañía Telefónica Mexicana*, a subsidiary of ITT, which came to form a monopoly.[108] President Alemán named the union representatives who would sit on the first CEN board in 1950 and he selected a former ITT worker as the secretary-general, and an ex-Ericsson worker as President of the CNV. It was agreed that every two years there would be a switch so that, in 1952, the CEN would be led by a former Ericsson worker, while the CNV by an ex-ITT member.

The original STRM statutes written in 1950 stipulated that the union would be run in a democratic way including the secret ballot, leader turnover (re-election was prohibited as it was in the 1917 Mexican Constitution), a limited time period of two years for the executive's time in office, and respect of the outcome of elections. However, from the beginning, there was a powerful and dominant force which overturned these potentially democratic principles. The promise that union posts would be rotated between former ITT and Ericsson workers was never fulfilled. Although the original union statutes required elections for the executive team to be held every two years, all but one of the secretary-generals in the period 1950–76 overruled any of the clauses which would have limited their power. It was typical that they extended indefinitely the period in which they could remain in office in order to monopolize their power for as long as possible. Elections were postponed permanently and leaders lost their position when they were ousted by their stronger rivals. Union practice was clearly a long way from fulfilling hypothesis two concerning the effectiveness of elections.

An analysis of the turnover of the union executive (hypothesis three) between 1970 and 1975 (during which time there was one election for the executive team) shows that the concept of leader turnover hardly existed. Nine of the ten members heading the executive team in 1970–4 reappeared in the 1974–8 team.[109] In general, executives were juggled around from one position to another, but the chosen few, who had presumably proved faithful to the secretary-general, were rewarded with reselection on the team. One way in which these secretary-generals assured their grip on the union was to personally select a small, faithful group during the union's National Convention who would dominate all significant union posts. Union leadership could be characterized as typically oligarchical, and the result was that the union was dominated in this period by three men: Ayala Ramírez (1952–9), Guzmán Reveles (1962–7) and Salustio Salgado (1967–76).[110] The ingredient of union democracy which was leadership turnover was not evident in the *charro*-led union.

There was one, brief, interruption to this pattern of *charro* control during 1950–75. In January 1959, a movement headed by Pedro García Zendejas, which sought to end the prolonged leadership of Ayala Ramírez, gained worker backing to form the 'Movement for the Restoration of Union Democracy', a daring move in the light of the *charrazo* in October 1958 of the railroad workers' union. These telephone worker dissidents decided to go on strike in demand of a 25 per cent pay rise and workers promised to return to work once the government had promised to call a union election for a new executive.[111]

The dissidents were elected by the overwhelming majority. Rapidly, this new team rewrote union statutes in order to introduce democratic clauses which included the use of secret ballots during union elections, a limitation on the time that union executives could remain in office and a total prohibition of their re-election, and a guarantee that National Conventions would be held annually. The next year, they took the STRM out of the CTM, and established a pact of mutual alliance with the SME. In this year, both unions attempted to support each other during the negotiation of their collective contracts, whose annual negotiation happened to coincide in March. The government responded harshly using a policy of 'divide and rule'. While the SME was granted its demands, those of the telephone workers were denied, and the strike launched by the telephone workers was met by army occupation of key TELMEX work centres, a so-called *requisa*.[112] Subsequently, the government altered the negotiation date for the STRM collective contract to April thus diluting the potential collaborative power of the two unions. This group did not have much opportunity to prove whether it offered a genuinely more democratic alternative to the *charros* since its leadership was short-lived. Although union elections again resulted in the victory of the dissident movement in 1961, one year later, during a strike, the Secretary of Labour, Salomon González Blanco, directly intervened and installed Manuel Guzmán Reveles, a government and management ally, in the position of secretary-general.[113] The new leader filled all posts of the executive with hand-picked candidates in a closed, three-hour convention.[114]

Apart from this brief interruption, during the period 1950–75, opposition to the incumbent leadership was deliberately confounded in its attempts to organize. Rank and file were starved of information since union assemblies and the few conventions that were held consisted of an arena to inform workers about decisions that had already been taken by union leaders. Worker participation in national union affairs was very low. Collective bargaining was a closed formality between union leaders, government officials and TELMEX executives. *Charro* leaders minimized the number of meetings which were open to workers and even the annual National Convention, the most important of all the meetings, became in some cases a mere formality.[115] The union magazine, *1o de Agosto*, published several times a year, consisted of editorials written by the incumbent secretary-general and extracts of speeches made by the CEN at union assemblies.[116] Hypothesis one, that the ousting of incumbent leaders is an indication of union democracy, had proved to be partially true, since there were two attempts to oust *charro* leaders (1959 and 1976) in 26 years. Pateman's hypotheses on worker participation are not applicable to this period of union history, since union leaders did not even attempt to present an image of 'pseudo' participation, their control was unabashed and overt.

The relationship between union leaders and the government, particularly officials in the Labour Department and among TELMEX executives, was intimate. Secretary-generals depended to a large extent on external support for their survival. Candidates seeking to occupy the position of secretary-general first sought experience as local union delegates, and worked to gain the approval of TELMEX management and government officials before expressing interest in being promoted to higher union posts.[117] Once in power, union leaders were rewarded for their support of the PRI (principally through their being a CTM member) and their ability to contain the rank and file with seats in the House of Deputies. Some leaders, including Salustio Salgado, served as the President of the CT. Even when union leaders were ousted, the government might offer them compensation, for instance, when Salgado was ousted in 1976 by union dissidents he was recruited by the government as a PRI Deputy in Ometepec, Guerrero.[118] Labour Secretaries considered it their right to intervene and reject the 'wrong' secretary-generals and replace them with their preferred candidate, as occurred in 1961.

From *charrismo* to insurgency

In 1976, the last year of the Echeverría administration, a dissident movement swelled within the STRM and succeeded in ousting the incumbent leader, Salustio Salgado, who had controlled the union over the last nine years. Though Salgado had been unpopular throughout the period, the last straw was his signing of the annual salary agreement with management in April 1976, agreeing, without consulting the workers, to a 15 per cent wage rise and not the 35 per cent rise that the telephone workers had demanded. On hearing this news, telephone operators in the two largest centres in the capital, San Juan and Victoria, called strikes.[119] Using their telephones, the operators called other operators in centres across the republic, and by the following day, the telephone network was severely jammed. There were two interrelated reasons for their actions: first, in protest at the low wage increase, and second, because workers were excluded continually from collective bargaining and participation in the union. The operators were joined by other telephone workers including technicians and maintenance workers, and they occupied the STRM headquarters in Mexico City, setting up an alternative Executive Committee in opposition to the Salgado-led executive.

This dissidence was not led by Hernández Juárez, who by this time was employed in a telephone maintenance centre in Mexico City, but, once the movement was unleashed, he emerged at its forefront.[120] He had been active in union politics, most recently in 1975 in the successful negotiation of a *convenio* for his centre with TELMEX.[121] The force of the movement in April 1976 came in particular from the operators of Mexico City, though the speed with which the movement spread would suggest that discontent shown by workers was widespread. The display from the female section of the Mexican telephone workers' union in the 1970s was comparable to the efforts by female operators to unionize and mobilize which occurred in the United States and

Canada during the first few decades of the twentieth century.[122] By 1976, the operators had become the largest and most important sub-group of the union. In 1976 there were 22 000 STRM members of which the operators comprised more than one-third.[123] All of the TELMEX operators were women, and their display of dissidence could be interpreted as an effort to improve their working conditions as women. In Latin America in the 1970s over 60 per cent of women were employed in the service sector. Despite this, in general, women were unable to obtain positions of power in national labour movements, and, as in the cases of women activists in the teachers' and textile workers' unions, they played an active role within the union but were led by male unionists.[124] Unlike maintenance workers (almost entirely made up of a male workforce), who composed the other large sub-group of the STRM, and who worked in different places every day repairing the network, the operators worked in the same centre in close contact with each other, and their behaviour may have been reinforced by the shared experiences of the night shift. By 1976, the operators had still not gained a *convenio* to regulate work practices.[125] The *convenio* was a specific agreement made between management and a specific department of workers (such as technicians, or maintenance workers) which outlined their work conditions, hierarchies and wages in addition to the global collective contract which was signed between the whole workforce and management every two years. Without a *convenio*, operators did not receive compensation for work-related problems such as those emanating from repeated use of the keyboard, problems with eyesight due to bad lighting and back complaints due to their uncomfortable seats. They had long complained about the severe rules governing their workplace, including the humiliating way in which the TELMEX management installed (non-unionized) staff to survey unionized workers.[126] These management representatives, who were installed in most TELMEX workplaces around the country, are called *personal de confianza*, because management feels it can trust them. More general complaints by dissident telephone workers related to the centralization of union power, administrative bureaucracy, absence of fair elections for the CEN, longevity of union positions in the CEN and some in the local executive committees (CELs), and constant violations of the statutes.[127] In their explanation of union insurgency, Lipset *et al.* argued that the ITU union developed a strong sense of occupational community based on the experience of night shifts.[128] This helps explain the dissidence of the TELMEX operators who worked on a shift basis. Moreover, in contrast to TELMEX's maintenance workers and technicians who work alone, in different places, usually outside of TELMEX offices, these large groups of operators work in the same operator centres particularly in the larger cities.

The 'democratic' committee which installed itself at the union head-quarters agreed with Labour Secretary Gálvez Betancourt that workers would return to work if he promised that a referendum would be held throughout the union to elect an executive committee. This referendum would be for all workers who would cast their vote directly and in secret. During the previous 20 years workers had rarely had a chance to use their voting power since union officials had been selected by an inner clique at closed assemblies. In this referendum, workers had three choices: to opt for the return of Salgado, to select the young leader who had emerged at the head of the 'democratic' committee, Hernández Juárez, or to start from scratch and hold an election for all union posts. The results of the referendum, according to available sources, were clear: 86.3 per cent favoured Hernández Juárez as the new leader, 10.5 per cent supported Salgado, and 3.2 per cent voted for new elections.[129] Hernández Juárez therefore came into power by means of a referendum and with the support of a coalition of different groups, including the operators, who were united in their desire to oust Salgado. However, his victory was not established on the basis of a union-wide democratic election.

Union practice: 1976–84

When the newly elected executive entered office in 1976, one of the first things they did was to rewrite the union statutes. They borrowed many of the ideas for their reforms from the 1959 'democratic' movement.[130] In an effort to reintroduce electoral democracy, the union statutes asserted that workers would be granted the right to a secret ballot which would be held at the local level for every union post.[131] Leader turnover would be ensured by enforcing a two-year limit on the period for which union executives could hold office.[132] Moreover, once a worker had served on the executive board he/she had to abstain for four years before being allowed formally to participate in union politics again.[133] These 'democratic' principles, which ensured workers' rights to vote and the 'no re-election' clause, reflected some of the democratic concerns of the Mexican Constitution. Additionally, a National Electoral Commission was established with the task of ensuring the legitimacy of elections.[134] On paper there was a return to greater electoral democracy. Most of the democratic reforms introduced in 1976 were not new since they were inspired by the 'democratic' movement that had been a continuous element within the union and which came to the forefront at the end of the 1950s. If words were to be put into practice, workers could expect to see the elimination of *charro*-type union leadership which had been typical between 1950 and 1975.

Workers' participation in union affairs increased dramatically after 1976 since, under *charro* leadership, assemblies had been avoided. The 'democratic' union leaders reintroduced union assemblies which at first took the form of chaotic, excited and prolonged meetings, held in overcrowded auditoriums.[135] Worker participation was formalized gradually, and, in the 1983 statutes, it was guaranteed that the STRM's annual National Democratic Convention would be open to all union delegates so that the union's strategy would be discussed openly and decided by union members. Statutes ruled that workplaces which contained between 21 and 500 staff could send one delegate to the Convention: those with between 501 and 1000 employees could send two; the ones with between 1001 and 1500 were allowed three, and those with over 1500 workers could have four or more delegates.[136] At the local level, the representatives of each local or plant-based union would hold monthly assemblies.

The union magazine, which was retitled *Restaurador: 22 de abril*, contained more informative and political articles than its predecessor *1o de Agosto*, though its editors despised pluralism and revealed their strong Maoist influences. *Restaurador* included details about the state of negotiations with management, wage increases and other agreements made, as well as the secretary-general's criticism of poverty and economic development in Mexico. Thus at the 'high' and 'low' level, worker participation increased dramatically after 1976. However, as explained below, this increase in worker participation must be considered alongside the evolution of a parallel undemocratic system in the union, which has the effect of making these advances seem like Pateman's definition of 'pseudo-participation'.[137]

In both external and internal union practice, the contradictions of 'independent' unionism started to rear their head. The issue dominating the first National Convention held by the new executive in 1976 was the STRM's position vis-à-vis organized labour and the state.[138] From the beginning, Hernández Juárez made clear his pragmatism when he claimed that he was not in favour of an 'irrationally left-wing project' since he wanted struggle, but not suicide.[139] His message was that although the STRM should leave the CTM, as it had done in 1959, it should not abandon the CT. The majority of delegates agreed and, at the end of the convention they voted to leave the CTM, but to remain in the CT.[140] Delegates also voted to leave the PRI, and each worker was given the right to vote for whatever political party he or she desired.[141]

Under *charro* control, the STRM had mounted only a few strikes between 1950 and 1976. These included the revision of the first collective contract in 1952 before Ayala Ramírez took control. Only during the brief, 'democratic' period (1959–62) were strikes mounted regularly, including, in 1959, one aimed at ousting the *charro* leader, and again, in 1961 and 1962, in protest at low wages.[142] From the moment that the new leaders took control of the STRM the union entered a period of militancy. In April 1978, it went on strike when its demand to lower the retirement age by one year was not granted.[143] The strike lasted 16 hours and their demand was finally granted. The operators remained disgruntled since they still had not been granted the *convenio* that had provoked them to strike in 1976. In March 1979, they started another strike which soon spread across the union in demand for their *convenio*, which again they were finally granted. Hernández Juárez claimed that he supported the operators' demand in March 1979, but two months later the telephone workers launched another strike in protest at the unsatisfactory management offer in the negotiation of the collective contract, and the union leader's support for this strike was more wavering. The strike lasted eight days and tensions were high when the strike was finally brought to a halt after a union-wide referendum. Two-thirds of workers agreed to return to work, but one-third, based in Puebla, Veracruz and other cities, voted to continue the strike.[144] The strike had been met with a harsh *requisa* which was a dramatic display of state pressure on Hernández Juárez to put a stop to the strike. However, the state-centred explanation is not the only reason that the leader was forced to control the strike. He also wanted to control the disobedient radical opposition group that had continued to strike in an effort to undermine the leader's power.

In terms of internal union practice the contradiction of 'independent' and 'democratic' unionism meant that incumbent leaders had to be prepared to hand over their power after their time in office expired. From the beginning, the new union leaders, particularly Hernández Juárez, showed their taste for power. In the Second National Convention in 1978, the CEN decided that, instead of handing over power through executive elections to a new team, the statutes should be amended so as to extend the period in office from two to four years. They justified this on the grounds that two years did not allow sufficient time for the gains of the new 'democratic' leadership to be consolidated.[145] Extending the executive's period of time in office had also been the trick of the *charros*.

At the end of this period, in 1978, the CEN, led by Hernández Juárez, did a U-turn on the clause which prohibited the re-election of the post of secretary-general. Union members and delegates alike took unkindly to Hernández Juárez's proposal to allow for his own possible re-election, as they feared it could lead to the return of another *charro* leadership.[146] The union's 1979 National Convention was converted into a two-week debate on the meaning of union democracy, which in reality comprised a virulent and ideological attack by the incumbent leadership on the *Línea Democrática*, its main opposition within the union that had challenged Hernández Juárez for abusing the occasion of union insurgency in order to grab power for himself. Union leaders ejected the ringleaders of this opposition from the union in 1979. Hernández Juárez defended their ejection on rather dubious grounds by stating: 'It isn't because they are against me, it is because they are against the democratic structure of the union...'.[147] Finally, in an Extraordinary Convention in January 1980, the majority of delegates conceded that a referendum could be held asking all STRM members whether they would accept a transitory modification of the statute clause which prohibited re-election so that the secretary-general would be permitted to stand again.[148]

Since this original referendum in 1980, the method of maintaining power has become one of the linch-pins of Hernández Juárez's longevity. Every four years, prior to the renewal of executive positions through elections, the union holds a referendum which asks whether workers accept a one-off, transitory modification to the statutes that would allow the incumbent secretary-general to stand again. This referendum is not conducted as a secret ballot.[149] Each worker must tick whether they do or do not accept the reappearance of the incumbent secretary-general as a candidate for forthcoming elections, then sign above the referendum slip which states their worker number and workplace number. Since the majority have ticked the 'Yes' box, Hernández Juárez has been able to stand for secretary-general on every occasion. Any worker that challenges the continuity of Hernández Juárez's leadership has to be prepared to face the consequent discrimination of union delegates or commissioners in their workplace. In a mild form, this might take the form of intolerance if that worker is late, wishes to change shift, or wants to take leave due to personal reasons. In the more severe cases, workers might be 'sent to Coventry' by all members of a workplace, be accused unjustly of working badly, or even having their union membership withdrawn and, therefore, lose their job.[150]

Apart from the post of secretary-general, which has been assumed by Hernández Juárez from 1976 to 1999, the turnover of union officials (hypothesis number three) is high. First, there was a complete turnover of leaders in 1976, since none of the members of the *charro* committee reappeared in Hernández Juárez's teams. Second, once the 'democratic' leadership took over, there was a much higher degree of leadership turnover than there had been under *charro* leadership. Comparing the first (1976–80) and second (1980–4) executive teams, only six of the original 18 members of the 1976 team reappeared in 1980. Thus the rate of re-election from 1976/1980 was 33 per cent compared to the 90 per cent re-elected in the *charro* executive in 1970/4.[151] The reform of the electoral system in 1983 is discussed below: afterwards, as shown in Table 2.1, there was a near 100 per cent turnover of posts – with the exception of secretary-general – so it would appear the system of leader turnover had been perfected.[152] To conclude the analysis of hypothesis three, it would appear that there was a dramatic improvement of union democracy in the STRM after 1976.

Given this high leadership turnover in the STRM, the permanence of Hernández Juárez at the helm of the union, which was a distinctive feature of union oligarchy, might seem at first glance a paradox. *Charro* secretary-generals had attempted to keep their power by surrounding themselves with a trusted team. Arnaut has shown how the *Vanguardia Revolucionaria* which emerged from the SNTE in the 1970s, gradually manoeuvred its way through the union, and diluted the power of key executive posts in order to isolate the role of the secretary-general while at the same time installed *caciques* in posts of national and regional union representatives.[153] However, Hernández Juárez was surrounded by an executive team that changed every four years whose representatives are elected democratically. This had advantages and disadvantages. One advantage was that no one unionist accumulated too much power or experience in union politics to put themselves in a position in which they could rival the leader. The other main advantage was that the union had the appearance of democracy to its members and to outside observers, and every worker who was interested in union politics justly believed that he/she can strive towards being elected to represent the union at the national level. The disadvantage was that, because the executive was elected democratically and the leader had no control over the team with which he must work, he could not necessarily depend on it to support him. One of the explana-

Table 2.1 Composition of the STRM's National Executive Committee (CEN) and National Vigilance Committee (CNV) 1976–96.

CEN	1976–80	1980–84	1984–88	1988–92	1992–96
SECRETARY GENERAL	F. Hernández Juárez	F. Hernández Juárez	F. Hernández Juárez	F. Hernández Juárez	F. Hernández Juárez
INTERIOR SECRETARY	V. García Ruiz	P. Alemán Villa	R. Elías Luna	T. Parra Carrola	A. Arellano
LABOUR SECRETARY	L. Rojas Chávez	J. Montero	M. Heredia Figueroa	J. Castillo Magaña	R. Gutierrez
LABOUR SECRETARY 1	J. Alvarado Delgado	C. Green Zamacona	A. Moreno Cruz	C. E. Bustos	E. Chong
LABOUR SECRETARY 2	R. Rendón B.	M. Rodriguez Castro	J. Powell Rioseco	H. Peñaranda Gutierrez	R. Joya Gonzalez
EXTERNAL CONFLICTS SECRETARY	J. Serret Raposo	G. Peinado Reyes	J. Reyes Pérez	J. López Sanchez	M. Alvarez Samble
EXTERNAL CONFLICTS SECRETARY 1	A. Morales Gtez	F. Orozco Calderón	G. Flores Morán	R. Medellin Saldierna	B. Carrillos Cavazos
EXTERNAL CONFLICTS SECRETARY 2	S. Morales	J. Ramirez León	Y. Rendón Lizáraga	M. Herrera Rochin	J. Becerra Martinez
EMPLOYMENT SECRETARY	E. Gonzalez C	A. Maldonado J. Arguello	G. Flores Sanchez	D. Garcia Gonzalez	
EMPLOYMENT SECRETARY 1		E. Negrete	I. Muñoz	J. De la Rosa Ovando	F. Orozco Calderon
TREASURER	E. Sandoval	P. Vargas	F. Fuentes López	P. Soto Edeza	R. Aguilar
ORGANIZATION SECRETARY	E. Franco Chávez	S. Marales	I. Rojas	C. Bonales Ponce	E. Rossainz
ORGANIZATION SECRETARY 1		J. Tapia	L. García Rodriguez	E. Rodgríguez Juárez	S. Madriga
SOCIAL SECURITY SECRETARY	A. Cerecedo	I. Monge	L. Alarón	A. Olivares Torres	F. Alvarado

Table 2.1   continued

CEN	1976–80	1980–84	1984–88	1988–92	1992–96
SOCIAL BENEFITS SECRETARY 1		R. Villareal Chávez	P. Navarro Muñoz	J. Osuna y Osuna	L. Ley Mendez
SPORTS SECRETARY	J. Montero	J. Flores Sámano	J. Galicia Martínez	M. Moreno Ruvalcaba	A. Santana Coronel
PUBLIC RELATIONS SECRETARY	A. Maldonaldo	J. Alvarado Delgado	J. Villareal Adriano	J. Ocampo Flores	A. Royas Reyes
PRESIDENT	R. Villareal Chávez	M. Villanueva Covarrubias	J. López Marín	J. Polanco Carrillo	J. Espinoza
FIRST SECRETARY	I. Hernández Hernández	F. Gómez Cortés	C. Díaz Garnica	J. Reyes Flores	A. Sanchez Cordero
SECOND SECRETARY	R. Pedraza Lucio	A. Rodríguez Juvera	V. Herrera	V. Davalos Estrada	J. D'Loera Piña
PRESIDENT OF JUSTICE		G. Benítez Flores		G. Gonzalez Alemán	L. Peña Torres
SPORTS PRESIDENT		L. Navarro González		L. Arellano Ramíez/ J. Azpilcueta	J. Gonzalez Ramirez/ S. Reyes/F. Cano Estrada/A. Gomez Mendez
FINANCE PRESIDENT		M. Sánchez Rubio		O. Escalona Díaz	L. Peña Torres
FIRST SECRETARY		A. Mata Macedo		S. Vera Hernandez/ L. Montemayor/ J. Romero Venegas	B. Sol Orea
ECONOMIC STUDIES PRESIDENT		G. Benítez Flores		J. Castro Razo	J. Rodriguez Ramirez
HOUSE OF CULTURE PRESIDENT		P. Velez Rodriguez		E. Olvera Bravo/ I. Monge/G. Alba Cisneros	M. Verdugo Godinez
PRESIDENT OF GRANTS		J. Pérez Díaz		R. Cancino Gomez	
DIRECTOR OF PRESS	S. López	R. Miranda Sotelo		J. Gonzalez Briones	A. Castro Ramírez

Sources: Restaurador (1977–96) and Xelhuantzi López (1988).

tions why union members allowed the union leader to be re-elected was that STRM representatives put pressure upon workers to comply at the shop-floor level.

'Camarillas' and power in the STRM

Power was monopolized by the 'democratic' leadership after 1976 in two main ways. First, an undemocratic system to support the secretary-general was installed *in parallel* with the other relatively democratic structure of the CEN and CNV. Second, opposition factions were destroyed between 1976 and 1984. Since the union's electoral process was reformed in 1983, Hernández Juárez formalized a practice which he had initiated when he first became secretary-general in 1976.[154] This reform had the disguised objective of ensuring Hernández Juárez's continuity as secretary-general. It included an addition to the union statutes stating his right to hand-pick a team of union members who would be designated *comisionados*.[155] *Comisionados* would have the same voting rights as the elected union delegates[156] and would have two main functions. The first was to work from different regions and workplaces to exact enthusiasm from workers to vote for the Green Plan, which was the plan led by Hernández Juárez (following the tradition of the 'democratic' movement in 1959) and quell the first signs of any disobedience to central union policy. In this way they were to behave as union *caciques*.[157] The second function was to carry out union policy when instructed to do so by the secretary-general at the national level. He would reserve the right to choose from either a *comisionado* or an elected delegate when a job had to be done. According to many bitter delegates,[158] and concurring with the conclusions of my research,[159] Hernández Juárez preferred to use his own *comisionados* than delegates in all important tasks.

There is no fixed number of *comisionados*, but, in practice, there seems to be approximately the same number of *comisionados* as there are delegates in the executive, which is about 36.[160] This is a strategic number because the *comisionados* have a counterbalancing effect on the power of the democratically elected delegates without totalling outweighing them. Presuming the *comisionados* are faithful, Hernández Juárez automatically has 50 per cent of the vote before it is cast, and he requires only a small degree of cooperation from the delegates in order to pass any motion. Within the group of *comisionados*, there are two main sub-groups. The most important group is the inner circle which has been effectively in control of the union from 1976 to the present. Camp wrote that '*camarillas* are the glue of Mexican politics', and he showed how contacts and friendships made by Mexicans while attending schools or colleges have, in the last few decades, provided the largest source of initial networking among the Mexican élite.[161] In colleges and universities, among teachers and students in the classroom and in campus politics, mentor–disciple relationships form. Once formed, the mentor may choose to guide and support his disciple, and if the mentor secures a government position, he/she will often try and promote the recruitment of their disciples for a junior post in the government bureaucracy.[162]

The study of the formation of *camarillas* in Mexico has tended to focus on politicians, intellectuals and other influential families. However, it is also possible to seek out *camarillas* in other areas such as trade unions. In this case, we are far from the glamour of 'Ivy League' North American Universities that Camp considered of increasing importance in the networking between the future leaders of the country. The *camarilla* under study in the STRM originated in the corridors of the Department of Electronic Engineering in the *Instituto Politécnico Nacional* where the young students Hernández Juárez, Mateo Lejarza and Rafael Marino met. They had basic points in common. They were male teenagers of working-class families, they had been brought up in the capital, they shared the same higher education, and they met in the radicalized student climate which was soon to explode.

During his involvement in campus politics, Hernández Juárez met and soon became a disciple of Enrique Ruíz García.[163] Under this influence, Hernández Juárez, Lejarza and Marino founded the *Ateneo Lázaro Cárdenas* which was strongly influenced by Maoism, in particular, by the *Línea Proletaria*.[164] The *Línea Proletaria* was one of the two more influential branches (the other being *Línea de Masas*) which had sprung from a revived interest in Maoism and Maoist populism particularly after 1968. Both ultra-radical ideologies sought to bridge the gap between workers and peasants, and promoted immediate objectives in the transformation of everyday life ('the future begins now') and the increase of autonomy and self-determination through mass mobilization.

This threesome provided the seed of the *camarilla* which has controlled the STRM over the last 20 years. Lejarza, more than Hernández Juárez, is known to be the 'brain' of the STRM.[165] Hernández Juárez abandoned the course without finishing it in 1966 when he secured a job in a TELMEX maintenance centre, and he soon became involved in union department politics.[166] Once he was voted secretary-general in 1976, Hernández Juárez called on his mentor, Ruíz García, to advise him on union strategies, and created a circle of unelected top-level posts for his colleagues Lejarza and Marino.[167] The Ministry of Labour and TELMEX management criticized Hernández Juárez for being influenced by Ruíz García, who they claimed was running the union, and in 1981 forced Hernández Juárez to break off links with him.[168] However, if ultra radical ideology inspired the leaders in 1976, this soon wore out and was replaced by pragmatism.

The monopoly of union power by the *camarilla* in the STRM did not totally destroy, but did nevertheless significantly undermine and complicate the democratic gains which had been made after 1976, such as greater worker participation in union assemblies, the democratic election of union representatives, executive turnover and increased availability of information to workers. During the period of *charro* rule, the *camarilla* held its head high and the secretary-generals personally selected their executive teams without shame. However, after 1976, the *camarilla* was forced to go 'underground' and an image of union democracy was tacked on to the surface of union politics.

The threesome which constituted the original *camarilla* has since extended the system of *comisionados* by recruiting other union members after they demonstrated their loyalty, capacity and popularity while serving in democratically elected positions. An examination of the *curriculum vitae* of some of the most important *comisionados* in 1995 shows that there is a particular bias to recruit members who have already served, after being democratically elected, in the teams of the Secretary of Labour or the Secretary of Conflicts over the last ten years.[169]

The other important category of *comisionados* are the 'intellectuals' and 'ideologues' who are employed to produce books, academic articles for public consumption, and the union magazine, *Restaurador*, and to meet with researchers and journalists. Though there is a small number of 'intellectual' *comisionados*, these are deemed important by a union which prides itself on presenting a progressive, democratic and educated image. The STRM 'intellectuals' are not usually former telephone workers and are often recruited from universities after publishing articles or books on the union.[170] On a lighter note, there is a family influence permeating the system of *comisionados*. Jesus and Rafael, two of the secretary-general's brothers, have been employed as *comisionados* on the STRM's Sports Committee.[171] Their marginal (but perhaps enjoyable!) positions highlight the seriousness of top *comisionado* posts which Hernández Juárez possibly did not believe his brothers could manage. The system of *comisionados* was a crucial means of ensuring the continuity of Hernández Juárez from 1976, but it became particularly useful during the privatization of TELMEX. In theory, there is a high level of union democracy in the STRM in terms of worker turnover, but the *camarilla* system, undetected by elections, is the dominating control.

Hypothesis one, that effective opposition groups should exist for a union to be democratic, soon became a threat to Hernández Juárez. Almost immediately after he took up the position of secretary-general, the coalition which had voted for him, which was anti-Salgado but not undividedly pro-Hernández Juárez, started to show their internal differences.[172] Hernández Juárez was first challenged by an operator delegate, Rosina Salinas, who had been one of the leaders of the operator strikes in 1976.[173] Salinas was expelled from the union swiftly, on the grounds of being an agent of TELMEX.[174] A few dozen others were also expelled from the union (using the *cláusula de exclusión*) for allegedly being supporters of Salinas.[175]

After the first round of expulsions, the new leadership tolerated the existence of opposition parties, and the executive elections in 1978, 1980 and 1982 were all contested. In each of these elections, Hernández Juárez's Green Plan was challenged by the Orange Plan, led by the *Línea Democrática* in alliance with communist and anarchist elements. Though the accuracy of the election results is highly questionable, information on the votes produced by both supporters and opposition of Hernández Juárez concur that, between 1978 and 1982, the Orange Plan had the sympathy of around one-third of the union.[176] The other main contender for power was the pro-management Violet Plan, which had less support.[177] However, pluralism within the union was never accepted by the 'democratic' leadership. The official STRM magazine not only excluded any opinion that was not pro-*juarista*, but also openly demonized its opposition, particularly the *Línea Democrática*, for being *bourgeois*, an enemy of the working class, and influenced by interests outside the union.[178] The *Línea Democrática* (or the *Línea Dura* as the CEN called them) were supported by some of the largest telephone centres in the provinces such as Puebla, Veracruz, Guadalajara, Monterrey, and also some TELMEX departments in the capital. They accused Hernández Juárez of abandoning the democratic struggle pursued in the 1950s and pressurized him to follow more radical policies such as leaving the CT, and breaking off relations with the 'enemy of workers', the state.

Opposition was tolerated up to the point where it looked as if it would seriously threaten the established leadership. Against the wish of the union executive during 1981, wildcat strikes were organized on a local basis in Puebla, Veracruz and Monterrey.[179] In an attempt to centralize union control and appease both government and management, Hernández Juárez secured an agreement from union representatives that there would be no more wildcat strikes in the approaching negotiation of the collective contract in April 1982, and made a truce with management to this effect. However, the opposition refused to accept this truce and continued to organize wildcat strikes across the country.

Opposition action culminated in March 1982, when, during a union assembly, the opposition took over violently the STRM headquarters and set up its own executive, which was effectively the local Monterrey CEN transposed to Mexico City, and led by its secretary-general, Serafín Pedraza Plata. This occupation lasted for three months, and had significant support from the rank and file in large cities such as Puebla, Veracruz and Monterrey. However, it was not supported by the operators, who continued to be Hernández Juárez's key pillar of stability within the union.[180] In 1982, operators still constituted over one-third of the union and without their support it was difficult for an opposition party to succeed in ousting Hernández Juárez.[181] As support for the dissidents faded, those from Monterrey abandoned their project. Throughout the conflict, management exacerbated the problem by, in particular, sacking around 500 workers[182] and temporarily suspending 3000 in the first half of 1982.[183] They also tried to dislodge Hernández Juárez and replace him with a *charro* since he was seen not to be in full control of the union. One of the main reasons for the survival of Hernández Juárez was the institutional support granted by the CT, which not only accommodated the ousted executives in its offices but refused to recognize the dissident movement and vocally emphasized its backing of Hernández Juárez.[184] This experience marked a crisis in the politics of the STRM leader, and after 1982 he displayed an increasingly conciliatory stance towards the state and the 'official' labour movement, and he took steps to reform the union internally in order to ensure that he would wield complete control.

In February 1983, during an STRM extraordinary National Convention, reforms were introduced which radically changed the system of elections by blocking the opportunities for opposition groups to organize.[185] Since 1976, union members who wanted to contest elections had been able to form a group, draw up a manifesto, and compete under a workers' plan with the Green Plan led by Hernández Juárez. After the reform, groups of workers were no longer allowed to form a plan together. Instead, the process of voting was made more complex and long-winded. Every plan to be presented at election had first to be advertised in every workcentre or department. Interested participants could put themselves forward to represent the plan, indicating the post they wished to stand for.[186] After the first round of elections at the local or plant level, a second and third round would be held on a regional basis to pick the most popular candidates to represent that plan in their region. The reform divided the republic into nine zones, one of which was Mexico City.

The Hernández Juárez-led Green Plan was extremely well organized and required the first round of elections to be held 18 months prior to the final ones.[187] It was specified that the plan would be represented by two union representatives from each of the eight zones and 20 representatives from the capital. The CEN would therefore comprise 36 members, one half of which would be from the capital, the rest from other states.[188] The electoral reform had two outcomes. First, it meant that there was a 100 per cent turnover of union leaders in the executive. Second, it meant that the gap between the winning party and its opposition was widened dramatically. In 1984, the Green Plan obtained 73 per cent of all votes with a total of 17 295 while its contender, the Black Plan, received only 6500.[189] This was the highest victory yet for the Green Plan.[190] Thus the result of reform was to damage significantly the organizational abilities of the opposition. Moreover, as had been agreed in the 1983 National Convention, the ringleaders who had attempted a 'coup' in 1982 were expelled from the union, and every department was obliged to put in writing their recognition of the executive.[191]

The year 1983 also marked a turning point in the STRM's external behaviour. Since the first strike in 1976, the new 'democratic' leadership had gone on strike in 1978, in March and again in April of 1979, and yet again in 1980. In 1983, however, negotiation of the collective contract was accomplished without a strike and Hernández Juárez, under pressure from the government, renounced his links with the *Línea Proletaria*.[192]

Conclusion

In the first few years after 1976, the new leadership exhibited a mixture of democratic and oligarchic leadership policies, which co-existed in a tense relationship. Their original Maoist ideology was gradually replaced by a pragmatic approach to union politics. However, since 1982, union leadership increasingly developed a democratic union practice and worker participation to exist in parallel with an ever-expanding system of control based on *camarillas* and *caciquismo*. The outcome was that the 'democratic' leader succeeded in remaining in power for over 20 years, longer than the combined office of the STRM's three great *charros*. In 1996 he was voted in as secretary-general for 1996–2000. This is a central indicator of the existence of union oligarchy.

However, it is important to avoid the facile conclusion of labelling him a neo-*charro* leader, since this signifies a return to the dual categorization of labelling him either 'democratic' or, if not, a *charro*. To revert to this method of categorization would result in preventing a more sophisticated understanding of the dynamics of union politics and how and why they changed and adapted over time. This chapter has highlighted the contradictions of 'independent' unionism, and indicated reasons other than state pressure which directed or influenced union policy. Finally, the 'democratic' leadership exhibited important *continuities* with *charro* rule, in particular, the desire to maintain control over the union. However, there were also important differences, in particular, the necessity to paint a layer of democratic unionism and greater worker participation on to the surface of union politics while forcing undemocratic methods of control to go underground. The STRM union could not accurately be described as either 'democratic' or *charro* during this period since a new system of control evolved which projected a 'democratic' image while retaining at its core an oligarchic heart. It is essential to understand how the dual structure of the STRM evolved and became established after 1976 when analysing the way in which union politics changed again during the process of the privatization of TELMEX.

3
Neoliberal Economic Reform, Unions and the Anomaly of the STRM

One of the major consequences of the 1982 debt crisis was that many Latin American governments, including that of Mexico, abandoned the economic model[1] which they had pursued after the Great Depression which was characterized by inward-oriented growth.[2] The new economic model pursued was underpinned by outward-looking growth.[3] This chapter analyses the economic policy pursued by the De la Madrid government throughout the *sexenio* (1982–8), and, in particular, focuses on the impact that this policy had on organized labour. At the same time, the main reasons which led the Mexican government in the mid-1980s to change their policies towards the telecommunications sector are examined. After providing this broad panorama, I then focus on the specific dilemmas facing the STRM including the modernization and privatization of TELMEX. I examine why the STRM leaders decided to cooperate with plans to 'modernize' their company, at a time when many other unions showed outright hostility and opposition to such 'modernization' plans.[4]

The debt crisis and neoliberal economic reform

As analysts have already documented, serious problems in the Mexican economy were apparent during the 1970s, but they were largely disguised by the country's oil exports which, by the mid-1980s, yielded 60 per cent of total export revenues.[5] Since the oil industry, PEMEX, was government owned, profits were used to finance subsidies, public works and social programmes. However, government spending rose more quickly than export earnings, and it became necessary to finance the excess spending by borrowing abroad and through seigniorage. Mexico enjoyed a high rate of economic growth and, since oil prices were high and continued to rise, private banks competed to lend the country money.

However, as the world-wide recession began in 1981, and oil prices fell, the government had to borrow more to make up for reduced revenues. The Banco de México's reserves fell as its customers, nervous about a possible peso devaluation, exchanged pesos for dollars. In 1982 the recession deepened; demand for Mexican exports dropped, and the peso was devalued. Foreign banks began to question the ability of Mexico to repay its debt and were increasingly reluctant to lend more. Fearing another devaluation, Mexicans withdrew nearly all of the Banco de México's dollar reserves and on 12 August 1982, the government announced that its central bank had nearly exhausted its reserves. The bank was consequently nationalized and the government requested a moratorium on its debt totalling $80 billion, which made Mexico the world's second largest debtor country after Brazil. This helped trigger a general debt crisis across Latin America.

Management of the debt crisis involved governments of the debtor and creditor countries, private banks, the World Bank and the International Monetary Fund (IMF). The IMF acquired a critical role in the evolution of the new economic model pursued by governments of developing countries, since it became responsible for implementing the policy known as 'conditionality', which involved IMF invigilation of the policies that governments had to follow before they could request further loans. The stabilization plans designed by the IMF in the aftermath of the debt crisis included elimination of subsidies, price adjustments and reduction of public sector wages. The World Bank's programme of proposed structural adjustment and the IMF's adjustment programme had certain requirements in common: trade liberalization, elimination of subsidies, privatization of public enterprises, fiscal reform and control of deficits.[6] Cooperation between the two institutions and with creditor governments increased and, gradually, the policy objectives for Latin America crystallized into a coherent vision, which is often referred as the 'Washington Consensus'.[7]

Between 1982 and 1985, the economic objectives of the De la Madrid administration concentrated on restoring macroeconomic equilibrium in order to resolve the crises of the public deficit and external debt. The government's *Programa para Inmediata Recuperación Económica* (PIRE) aimed to reduce public expenditure and rationalize public investment projects. The situation worsened, however, in 1985, when economic conditions deteriorated sharply, due to a further fall in petroleum prices coupled with an increase in interest rates on the public debt.[8] This was further exacerbated by the devastating earthquake which shook Mexico City in September 1985. By 1985, problems with the stabilization programmes were evident, since Latin America was continuing to transfer to the rest of the world more in interest and profit remittances than it was receiving in net capital inflows. This negative transfer reached $30 billion in 1985, equivalent to 4 per cent of GDP of the region.[9] In response, the US, the leading creditor nation, designed a new initiative, the Baker Plan.[10]

At the same time, the IMF declared that Mexico had failed to meet the terms of the 1983–5 extended fund facility which had been negotiated in 1982 and the government and its creditor banks were forced to accept a new long-term IMF-sponsored stabilization programme. The central features of this new programme were that Mexico obtain an adequate macroeconomic equilibrium, reschedule its debt, and accelerate its restructuring programme which would be accomplished through reducing the public deficit to 5.1 per cent of GDP, deepening trade liberalization and speeding up the programme of privatization.[11]

The Mexican government's decision to embark on profound structural reforms after 1985 can thus be explained partly by exogenous factors, principally the conditionality attached to the new loans offered by foreign creditors, the IMF and the World Bank.[12] However, external pressure to reform economic policy acted as a catalyst upon the team led by De la Madrid whose cabinet contained a majority which supported favoured neoliberal economics and a smaller state.[13] These technocrats started to propound the advantages of neoliberalism, meaning free markets, trade and financial liberalization and privatization of public enterprises. These policies were at the same time becoming increasingly influential within governments in the developed and developing countries, international financial institutions and academic institutions.[14] Neoliberals in Mexico criticized the economic model which had been pursued over the last two *sexenios*, and which, they claimed, was responsible for an excessively large and indebted state.[15] They argued that the state must cut back its public spending and administrative responsibilities, and re-establish its relationship with the private business sector.

From the middle of the 1980s, then, the Mexican government embarked on a rapid programme to open up its economy. At the beginning of the decade, all imports were subject to licensing requirements, the cost of which accounted on average for 30 per cent of the product's value,[16] but in 1985, the licensing requirements that affected 60 per cent of imports were replaced by tariffs.[17] The next year, the government signed a bilateral accord with the US government under which it agreed to phase out export subsidies; it designed an export promotion programme so that exporters could import merchandise up to 30 per cent of the value of their exports without requiring licensing or prior authorization; and it announced that it would apply to join the GATT.[18] Finally, the government pledged to reduce its public expenditure by reducing the size of the state, and to this end a reform of the entire public sector commenced including the restructuring, selling off, merging and liquidation of state-owned firms.

The reform of the public sector

During the three decades following the Second World War, the size of the state in the majority of countries, including the Latin American countries, increased.[19] States grew to the extent that they owned and managed public service utilities in key sectors such as railroads, power generation and telecommunications, as well as basic industries especially steel, metallurgical and petrochemical companies. One of the primary justifications for state control of public service utilities was the natural monopoly argument. The logic of this argument was based on the theory of economies of scale: since the services required large capital investment, it was more economic to have only one firm, a monopoly, providing that service. It was argued that the marginal cost of expanding the service was minimal. Domestic or foreign private firms did not in general have the necessary investments or the technical capacity to invest in projects of such a huge scale with long payback periods so the state took control of the enterprises.[20] In the case of most Latin American countries, a nationalist vision of the role of the state also played an important part in nationalization of foreign-owned industries.[21]

However, economic crises during the 1970s and 1980s contributed significantly to the decline in the dynamism and efficiency of public sector firms across Latin America, and many of them became liabilities to governments.[22] During the 1980s, many Latin American governments began to use state enterprises as macroeconomic stabilization instruments since, by holding down the price of telephone, electricity, steel and transportation rates, the government could attempt to control the general increase in prices.[23] By 1982, approximately 1155 firms were controlled by the Mexican state and these accounted for 18.5 per cent of GDP and employed around one million workers.[24]

During the De la Madrid administration around half of these public enterprises were divested.[25] Most of these were small or medium-sized,[26] and in general they were in non-priority areas where it was difficult to defend government ownership. Of the total enterprises divested, 294 were closed down, 204 sold, 72 merged and 25 transferred.[27] The majority of those that were sold operated in competitive markets and were profitable, so that a major adjustment of their financial situation and regulation was not necessary. Even though half of the state-owned enterprises were divested, there was little impact on government finances or government participation in the economy during this period. Revenue generated by sales between 1982 and 1988 amounted to US$500 million[28] and the average annual price gained for each enterprise ranged from a low of US$1.2 million in 1984 to a high of US$20.2 million in 1983.[29] The contribution of the sales totalled only 0.01 per cent of GDP in 1985 and 1986, increased to 0.1 per cent of GDP in 1987 and rose further to 0.2 per cent in 1988 and 1989. It thus had a minimal macroeconomic impact.[30] Moreover, the overall number of workers employed by public enterprises actually *increased* from around one million in 1983 to 1.017 million in 1988 since, as public enterprises were being divested, others in the private sector were being incorporated. It was not until 1990, with the sale of the large public enterprises, that jobs in the public sector underwent sharp cuts.[31]

In 1988, the last year of the De la Madrid administration, the privatization of a small number of the large public companies including Aeroméxico and Mexicana (Mexico's two national airlines) was begun. The government had intentionally started with a cautious privatization programme in order to gain experience before attempting to sell off larger companies.[32] This gave the government time to implement restructuring of the larger firms, 'cleaning them up' prior to their sale so that profit would be maximized. This strategy also allowed the government time to try to persuade Mexican society of the virtues of the policy.[33]

In many comparative studies of privatization in Latin America and the developing world, Mexico is often singled out for its relatively orderly and well-planned approach.[34] It is important to stress that the Mexican government's pursuit of privatization was slow throughout the De la Madrid administration, but not principally because, as some analysts claimed, there was internal division in the cabinet over the project.[35] On examining the process of privatization in conjunction with reform of the public sector, discussed below, it is clear that many steps were being taken by the De la Madrid cabinet to clean up firms in order to maximize profits before they were sold. The steady pursuit of privatization in Mexico therefore stands in marked contrast to the rapid way in which privatization policies were implemented in Chile during the 1970s which have since been criticized as resulting in a concentration of ownership, over-indebtedness and finally, the return of several of the firms to the government.[36] The Argentinian government's rush to privatize once Menem came to power in 1989 has also been blamed for being one of the main reasons that so many *debacles* occurred.[37] In particular, after 1986, the De la Madrid administration undertook the reform of some of the larger public enterprises. In the case of large loss-making firms, the intention was to lessen the financial burden that they placed on the state and, in the case of large profit-making firms, the aim was to increase their efficiency and productivity. Reform included financial restructuring of companies, which sometimes included the government absorbing their debts, productivity–efficiency agreements, streamlining of firms' activities, and introduction of measures to reduce price distortions particularly those which resulted in cross-subsidization.[38] In retrospect, in most of the cases, including the case of TELMEX, this reform could be seen as a pre-privatization measure since clearly a financially sound firm would attract higher offers than an indebted one. Not all the firms that were reformed were put up for sale, however, such as the electricity utility CFE and the national railroad company, Ferronales. Thus the reform must be interpreted primarily as a means to reduce the role of the state, both financially and administratively, in the public sector, whether or not privatization occurred later. During the De la Madrid administration, government subsidies and transfers to the parastatal sector fell from 12.7 per cent of GDP in 1982 to 3.42 per cent of GDP in 1988.[39]

The consequences of economic reform for organized labour

As part of the stabilization measures implemented by the De la Madrid administration, wages experienced sharp falls between 1981 and 1987. Wage cuts were typical for all Latin American economies during this period, but in comparative terms, the reductions were particularly severe in Mexico.[40] As discussed in the previous chapter, the minimum wage in Mexico between 1963 and 1979 had risen steadily. However, between 1980 and 1989, it was cut by 47 per cent.[41] Worse still, more workers came to depend on the minimum wage. Statistics show that in 1981, 47 per cent of families earned less than two minimum wages, and by 1987 this jumped to some 60 per cent of families.[42] Though contractual wage cuts varied depending on the sector, in the first few years of stabilization, the decline was fairly well spread since wages were reduced across the board by between 33 per cent and 40 per cent.[43] Two of the main reasons for cutting wages were first, that

Mexican workers would become more competitive in the global market[44] and second, that dramatic salary cuts to some extent eased the need to create mass unemployment.[45] Official statistics show that there was a rise in employment from 4.2 per cent in 1982 to 6.1 per cent in 1983, but that this then fell in succeeding years reaching a low of 2.8 per cent in 1990.[46] At the same time the informal sector employment grew by 6 per cent annually.[47] In addition to smaller salaries, workers found that their benefits were also declining. Government policies to cut social spending, relax price controls on many basic commodities, and reduce or eliminate government subsidies for mass transportation, electricity, natural gas and petrol also negatively affected workers.[48]

Government policy towards labour throughout the *sexenio* was severe, in particular when it wished to modify labour contracts, or privatize or even close down companies. In the worst cases, the government showed that it was willing to stoop to the crudest tactics to achieve its objectives. In May 1986, when workers at the Fundidora de Hierro y Acero de Monterrey went on strike in protest at plans to 'modernize' the company, the government declared the company bankrupt and all the workers were sacked.[49] On other occasions, the government used a similar tactic in order to roll back gains made by unions over the previous few decades by annulling their collective contract and designing new ones that enforced labour flexibility and mobility.[50] This new contract could be imposed on greatly reduced permanent workforces. The government accomplished this first, by declaring the company bankrupt and firing the workers, and second, by reopening the company under a new name and rehiring a percentage of the original workforce under a new contract that included the flexibility of labour. This strategy was used in July 1987, when the workers at the Ford plant in Cuautitlán went on strike to protest that they had not received the 23 per cent emergency national wage increase recently authorized by the government which other Ford workers in Chihuahua and Hermosillo had received. Ford was typical of many automobile companies in Mexico that, in the 1980s, had opened new plants in the north since labour was cheaper than in Central Mexico. The older plants were less competitive than the new ones. Ford management reasoned that the Cuautitlán workers could not expect an emergency pay increase since their wages had to be brought into line with their northern companies. In protest, the workers went on strike but, after 61 days, the entire labour force at Ford-Cuautitlán was fired. The plant was temporarily closed, to be reopened later with 2500 of the original workers rehired under a new collective contract that included labour flexibility.[51] The unions belonging to Sicartsa, AHMSA, Volkswagen and Cananea received similar treatment.[52]

Organized labour proved unable to halt the erosion of their wages and jobs.[53] Partly this was because of harsh government repression of the strikes organized by the unions mentioned above.[54] The government also undermined the CTM's power. In 1982, the CTM announced that it would back the De la Madrid administration's stabilization plan which called for wage restraints.[55] However, in 1983, when the CTM threatened to organize a strike against economic austerity due to the rising pressure from its members, the government responded by favouring other labour confederations such as the CROC and the CROM.[56] In return for this preferential treatment, these confederations rejected the CTM's call for a general strike.[57] By 1985, the CTM had returned to a conciliatory position by withdrawing outright opposition to the austerity measures and by making 'acceptable' demands on the government such as the improvement of social welfare conditions.[58] In the face of the collapse of the Mexican stock market in November 1987, an annual inflation rate of 160 per cent and the devaluation of the peso, the CT and the CTM agreed to help to support the government to combat the crisis by signing the *Pacto de Solidaridad Económica* (PSE) on 4 December 1987 which would introduce wage and price controls.[59] The government claimed that the 46 per cent wage rise that workers had demanded would put the country at the brink of disaster and therefore offered them a package of a 15 per cent wage rise and 20 per cent increase on the minimum salary effective from January 1988.[60] As mentioned in the last chapter, the CTM, afraid to lose the benefits it had accrued over the decades,[61] failed to change its negotiating tactics or approach and continued to use its traditional style of inter-élite bargaining as opposed to open confrontation with the government.[62]

TELMEX and the 'communications revolution'

In parallel with and as a complement to the government's policy to open up the economy and reform the public sector, there was a notable change in its attitude towards TELMEX, in particular after mid-1987. However, the change in the government's policy towards TELMEX did not solely arise as a result of its overall policy to reform public enterprises. There were profound changes in the telecommunications sector world-wide which made it rather different from the other sectors. One of the principal causes underpinning a change in the approach towards the telecommunications sector in the 1980s of many governments world-wide, including the Mexican government, was the so-called 'communications revolution'.[63] Governments of developed and developing countries alike were simultaneously reconsidering the future of communications in their country during the 1980s. The 'communications revolution' refers to the new opportunities brought about by the convergence of computer and telecommunications technologies and the transition from analogue to digital transmission techniques. The conversion of a range of diverse types of information into '1s' and '0s' digits meant that sound, image, text and graphics can be combined and transmitted through the same delivery channel, whether this be satellite, fibre optic cables, coaxial cable or even copper wire. Some analysts argued that new technology was breaking down the rationale that telecommunications were a natural monopoly since, they claimed, technological advances were rapidly reducing the cost of producing, installing and operating transmission and switching equipment.[64] In addition, diverse telecommunications and television companies sought to form international partnerships and mergers in order to expand their markets.

Another implication of this technological change was that communications were becoming an increasingly important factor facilitating the insertion of countries into the world economy. Throughout the developed world, the ascendancy of service and information activities has produced a structural change in the composition of the economy. In the mid-1980s, the output of the international information economy, which included mass media, electronic services, communication equipment and components, was worth US$1.185 trillion, which constituted almost 9 per cent of the world's economic output.[65] This technology has changed the way in which business is conducted and a company's or a country's provision of information to potential business partners has become increasingly important.

Technological change has important implications also for developing countries. New developments in communications throughout business and agriculture and the importance of being able to supply vast quantities of information to prospective investors have meant that information has come to be regarded as one of the main engines of growth in the economy. Since the beginning of the 1980s, international institutions, such as the World Bank, have recommended that an efficient communications system has become increasingly crucial for developing countries,[66] and it warned that countries which did not have access to communication technologies would be excluded from becoming incorporated into the increasingly integrated world economy.[67] Governments therefore should make the modernization of their communications systems one of their top priorities.[68]

TELMEX before privatization

In conjunction with the decision to open up the economy, and in the face of these technological changes, the Mexican government accepted that telecommunications were an area which must receive a high priority. Mexican trade and business depended heavily on the US, one of the world's leaders in telecommunications development and technology, and this dependence would become even more intimate during the next few years once the NAFTA Treaty had been signed. In the early 1980s, telephone calls between Mexico and the US constituted the world's second most frequent international route (after the US–Canada route). However, the volume of calls was asymmetrical, with around 70 per cent of the calls being made from the US, since the rates for calls made from the US to Mexico were cheaper than those made from Mexico to the US.[69]

During the 1980s, TELMEX came in for bitter criticism for the services it provided. Many Mexicans, including politicians, leaders of business federations, the public at large and the president himself, publicly criticized TELMEX for being a highly inefficient company. Often, they blamed its poor service on the workforce which they claimed was controlled by a corrupt union.[70] These criticisms must be interpreted with some care. While some were voicing their honest opinions, others may have had ulterior motives for attacking TELMEX and the STRM. As in most countries, the question whether a company should be privately or publicly owned and run is often a highly contentious one. Some of TELMEX's critics were quite simply interested in promoting TELMEX's privatization. By criticizing TELMEX for its inefficiency they were strengthening the case for its privatization, since they argued that it would be more efficiently run once private. Others aimed specifically to attack the union. Although the TELMEX board, whose criticism of the union was particularly vociferous, had already agreed in numerous private meetings that there were multiple problems which weakened TELMEX's performance, it publicly blamed the workers' attitude for being chiefly responsible for the company's low levels of labour productivity.[71] In private, Muñoz Izquierdo admitted that he was doing this on purpose to provoke the workers.[72] Many believed that the corrupt practices of the telephone workers were the reason for TELMEX's lack of efficiency, for example, the director of the Chamber of Commerce in Culiacán complained that 70 per cent of TELMEX customers in Sinloa were negatively affected by union corruption.[73] Spokespeople from business such as the *Cámara Nacional de Industria de la Transformación* (CANACINTRA)[74] and from labour confederations such as the CROC[75] claimed that TELMEX's problems were due to the corrupt mafia operating inside the STRM. The attack on the telephone workers for obstructing the company's success presented a significant danger to this union, given the hostile climate for labour relations.

In the analyses of TELMEX's pre-privatization performance published by diverse institutions, there is also evidence of political and ideological influences. World Bank-sponsored research tended in general to stress the low performance rates achieved by TELMEX prior to its sale. For Galal *et al.*, TELMEX 'was a moribund, poorly performing public enterprise until 1987',[76] but after its initial reform in 1987, and subsequent privatization in 1990, TELMEX became highly successful, profitable and more productive. On the other hand, Ruprah, writing on behalf of the *Comisión Económica para América Latina* (CEPAL), emphasized that TELMEX was a profitable and relatively efficient company even during the debt crisis, and was an important source of government revenue.[77] The contradictory nature of these analyses is not confined to the case under study here but it underlies one of the problems in the literature on recent economic policy. Fitzgerald has pin-pointed the problem: 'The "Washington view" (e.g. the World Bank) is that the New Trade Regime has been an almost unqualified success on both criteria, while the "view from Santiago" (i.e. from CEPAL) is almost the diametrical opposite'.[78] Toye stated that many of the analyses of policy reforms in developing countries were influenced by the New Political Economy school, and one of the results was a 'contamination (from a scientific point of view) by the very rhetorical success with which the NPE [New Political Economy] theorists have achieved in underwriting international action in support of liberalising reform'.[79]

In the academic literature there is also little consensus regarding the efficiency of TELMEX and the causes of the company's problems prior to its privatization. Ramamurti stressed that TELMEX was an attractive, profitable and relatively efficient company, particularly when it was *compared with other telephone companies in the developing world*.[80] In contrast, Heller argued that rent-seeking practices, particularly those operated by different state agencies, but also by management, were to blame for many of TELMEX's weaknesses, and that these must be considered alongside the damage done to the company by the debt crisis, the earthquake and problems in labour–management relations.[81] He argued that TELMEX's technological underdevelopment was not caused purely by a lack of investment, but also arose because the Ministry of Communications and Transport (SCT) blocked awarding TELMEX the concession which was necessary for gaining entry into data transmission services so that the ministry's own high-speed data system suffered no competition. Heller's account coincides with estimates made by Cowhey and Aronson that TELMEX was used as a 'cash-cow' by the government, since it was 'milked' of its profits, which provided 1 per cent of total government revenues and were used to subsidize other of the state's loss-making public enterprises.[82]

These variations in the analyses and opinions about the level of efficiency in TELMEX before its privatization and the principal causes of its inefficiencies stem from ideological bias, diverse approaches, and the use of different methodologies. Given these discrepancies, and, in an attempt to depoliticize the issue of TELMEX's performance, it is necessary to attempt a brief analysis of the company using primary sources, mainly from the company, for the period leading up to its sale.

An independent analysis of TELMEX in the 1980s: finances, investment and productivity

Between 1983 and 1987, reported investment in TELMEX grew incrementally and the value of its property, plant and equipment increased by around 8 per cent annually (see Table 3.1). Throughout the same period, TELMEX's long-term debt, as a percentage of total assets, remained at around 40 per cent, while its equity as a percentage of total assets was declining; in 1984 this was nearly 59 per cent and by 1987 this had dropped to 42 per cent.

Like many other public enterprises in Mexico, TELMEX was affected negatively by the debt crisis of 1982. Investment in the company was not sufficient to upgrade antiquated telephone equipment and the lack of funds stalled management plans to digitalize the plant. The board had originally decided to digitalize the telephone network in 1970, however, in practice, by 1985, only a small quantity of digital equipment had actually been installed.[83] TELMEX thus became increasingly incapable of serving the needs of the country's large and powerful users. It could not install high-tech network services for business users

Table 3.1 TELMEX: Analysis of the Structure, Debt and Capitalization, 1983–94

	1983	1984	1985	1986	1987	1988	1989	1990	1991	1992	1993	1994
Property, plant & equipment (PPE)												
in current values	312	536	839	2121	5835	9 447	12 642	18 300	22 874	27 103	30 726	46 827
constant values 1994	15 714	15 714	16 208	19 913	21 137	22 590	25 254	28 136	29 605	31 338	32 892	46 827
change in constant value		0	494	3705	1223	1431	2664	2882	1469	1733	1554	13 936
annual change (%)			3.1	22.9	6.1	6.8	11.8	11.4	5.2	5.9	5.0	42.4
PPE in total Assets (%)	78.2	77.9	74.2	74.0	70.8	71.1	70.2	67.4	66.0	63.6	59.2	63.3
Long-term Debt (LTD) in total Assets (%)	39.5	32.4	41.0	41.6	36.5	21.9	18.9	19.9	15.9	12.3	10.8	11.4
Ratio LTD/PPE	0.50	0.42	0.55	0.56	0.52	0.31	0.27	0.29	0.24	0.19	0.18	0.18
Equity in total Assets (%)	51.1	58.6	47.8	46.6	42.2	55.1	58.6	57.4	64.1	72.6	71.3	74.7
Ratio Equity/PPE	0.65	0.75	0.64	0.63	0.60	0.78	0.83	0.85	0.97	1.14	1.21	1.18
LTD & Equity in total Assets (%)	90.6	90.9	88.9	88.2	78.7	77.1	77.5	77.3	80.1	84.9	82.1	86.1
Reported Investment (millions of pesos)												
Non-consolidated (current values)	41	80	134	271	621	1497	2332	4830	5653	7327	7087	8455
Consolidated (current values)								5397	6040			
Non-consolidated (constant values 1994)	2045	2356	2596	2548	2250	3579	4658	7426	7317	8472	7587	8455
Consolidated (constant values 1994)								8297	7818			

Sources: Own elaboration based on TELMEX annual reports 1983–94.

and, left without another alternative, many of them, including some of Mexico's largest banks and private industries,[84] built their own private networks without TELMEX's help (based on Very Small Aperture Terminal technology).[85] In addition, many *maquiladoras* bypassed the TELMEX infrastructure and illegally installed advanced point to point international links. In the case that TELMEX did not provide the telephone services required, increasingly it seemed that the blackmarket would fill the gap.

Since TELMEX became a state-owed entity in 1972, the rates for its service were decided jointly between the Ministry of Finance and Public Credit (SHCP) and the SCT, and the government had the right to appoint the majority of its executive board and to subject the company to multiple regulatory regimes and taxes.[86] Between 1980 and 1987, local and national telephone rates declined in real terms and these were subsidized by international calls. Although the company's overall profits and revenues stagnated from 1981 to 1987, the government continued to extract revenue from the company, particularly through indirect taxes. Between 1982 and 1989 the government received around one-third of TELMEX's total revenue.[87]

The need to invest in new equipment was exacerbated by the severe earthquake of September 1985.[88] Severe damage was wrought on many of TELMEX's buildings, the worst of which was the Victoria operator centre where 11 workers were crushed to death.[89] Enormous damage was also done to the most important operator centre, San Juan, where radio and multiplex equipment was damaged beyond repair. Two other long-distance operator centres, with a capacity of 6500 lines, were totally destroyed, partial damage was done to another three centres and 50 microwave radios were seriously damaged.[90] Immediate consequences were that all services, including operator information, national and international operator calls and 12 500 local telephone lines had to be suspended.[91] For days after the earthquake, it was virtually impossible to make a long-distance call, and in compensation, all local calls (for those who could obtain a line) were provided free of charge from telephone booths in Mexico City.

The scale of damage done to TELMEX buildings and equipment in the capital, and the urgent need for reconstruction, meant that the question of digitalizing the network within the capital was forced on to the agenda. Some of the damaged equipment was replaced with digital equipment, but, by the end of 1986, only 5 per cent of TELMEX's 4.1 million lines had been digitalized. Digitalization was naturally concentrated in the operator centres that had been most severely damaged; in the first step digital equipment was installed in 25 per cent of long-distance operator centres, and the digital centres in Morales, Vallejo, San Juan and Estrella were linked digitally, in order to promote the decentralization of the long-distance network in the capital.[92]

TELMEX management had accused telephone workers of being responsible for dramatic falls in labour productivity during the decade.[93] Management had calculated labour productivity using one method: the number of lines installed annually per TELMEX worker. Measured in this way, the number of lines installed annually per worker dropped from a 12 per cent yearly increase in 1976 and 1977 to an 8 per cent increase in 1979, 10 per cent in 1980 and 8 per cent in 1981. In the year of the debt crisis, 1982, the increase in the number of lines had been 5.6 per cent, and it remained at around this level for the next five years. Management used this data as the basis of their claim that labour productivity had fallen dramatically. It would be more accurate, however, to state that labour productivity had in fact increased every year, albeit not so fast as the growth rate during the 1970s.

An examination of the actual number of telephone lines installed annually per worker shows that, in fact, over the 1980s, this had been more or less constant, which explains why the percentage increases fell over the years (Figure 3.1). This suggests that labour productivity was roughly constant throughout the 1980s. The year 1988 marked a turning point in labour productivity measured in this way since the percentage increases started to grow again, to nearly 7 per cent in this year and 10 per cent in 1989 (see Figure 3.1).

Another method of measuring labour productivity (which management did not use) would be to examine the number of calls handled per worker. The number of calls increased annually by around 15 per cent in the late 1970s and in 1980, but this percentage increase was reduced to 7 per cent and 3 per cent in 1981 and 1982. Between 1983 and 1988 the number of calls per worker was stagnant with percentage growth rates ranging between –3 and 1 per cent. In 1989 the calls/worker ratio improved considerably, reaching 17 per cent (see Figure 3.2). The overall conclusion that can be derived is that labour productivity did not decline dramatically between 1982 and 1988, but it was stagnant.

One of the first visible changes in the government's policy towards TELMEX occurred when, on 26 June 1987, De la Madrid removed Emilio Carrillo Gamboa from the post of General-Director of TELMEX which he

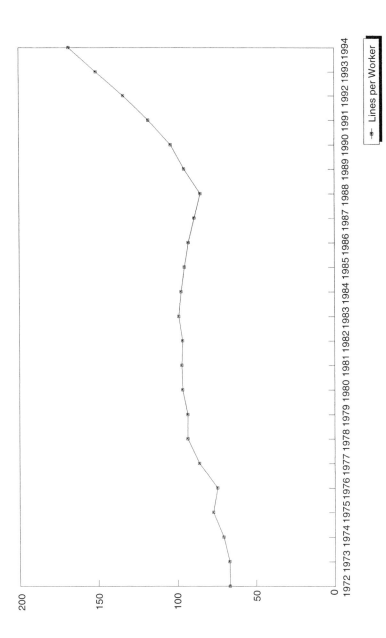

Figure 3.1 Labour Productivity in TELMEX Measured by Lines/Worker 1972–94
Source: TELMEX Annual Reports.

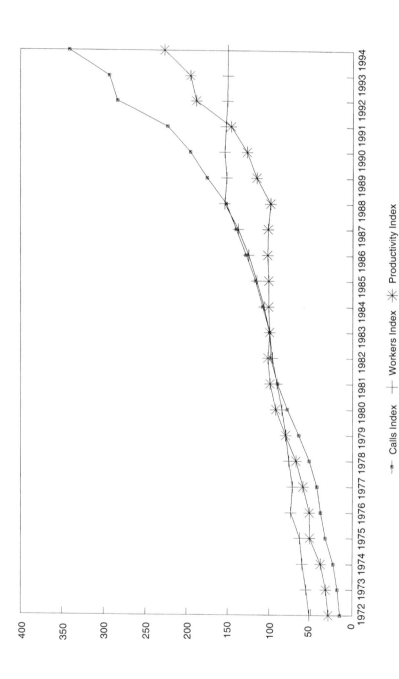

Figure 3.2 Index Calls and Worker Productivity. 1983 = 100
Source: TELMEX Annual Reports.

had held for the previous 13 years (almost the entire period that TELMEX had been a state-owned enterprise) and appointed in his place Joaquín Muñoz Izquierdo.[94] Muñoz Izquierdo had already worked in TELMEX as Director of Finance from 1972 to 1982, and then as Subdirector of Finance at PEMEX from 1982 to 1987. The president's replacement of Carrillo Gamboa, who was a graduate in law,[95] with Muñoz Izquierdo, who was a Doctor in Business Administration, showed that the government desired to see a change in management mentality towards greater efficiency and a high degree of professionalism.[96] An examination of internal TELMEX documents after Muñoz Izquierdo became company Director shows that management started more earnestly and urgently to tackle TELMEX's problems.[97] Within months, a new aggressive policy was introduced to improve the standard of the telephone service by increasing labour productivity and by introducing new technology. In addition, modifications were made to TELMEX's financial structure which helped make it more attractive.

At the end of September 1987, the TELMEX executive held its most important annual meeting in private.[98] In this frank discussion, executives showed that they were genuinely anxious about the government's future plans and the possible privatization of TELMEX.[99] Muñoz Izquierdo stated that TELMEX was undergoing the worst crisis of its history, and that radical reform was urgent. Competition in telecommunications had already arrived in Mexico,[100] and the era of the telephone monopoly was over.[101] He criticized TELMEX's sluggish rates of telephone installation and the 1.5 million telephone applications pending,[102] and stated that labour productivity must be increased in the short term.[103] He pointed out that the company had not altered its services since the 1960s and that its major source of income still came from the basic services.[104] Due to the lack of new technology, TELMEX was losing out on new, profitable areas of communications such as private switching and mobile phones. It appeared possible that the first mobile phone would not be produced by TELMEX but by another Mexican company, SOS.[105] Foreign competition, particularly the entrance of American carriers into the Mexican market, was imminent since Mexico was now a GATT member. Accepting that TELMEX was no longer a monopoly, the director maintained that it was necessary for the company to modify its cross-subsidization pricing policy in the medium term so that its international calls would become more competitive. In 1987, the cross-subsidization policy had resulted in a situation in which the local service, which represented 51.5 per cent of costs, accounted for only 15 per cent of income.[106]

The year 1988 was a turning point for TELMEX in many ways.[107] In financial terms, the price of calls was increased in real terms in January 1988 for the first time since the beginning of the decade, with the aim of generating income to fund an investment programme to improve the service.[108] Investment in the company increased substantially from 1988 to 1990.[109] Long-term debt as a percentage of total assets dropped to 22 per cent in 1988, that is, nearly half the figure of 1986. Furthermore, the figure continued to decline annually until 1994, with the exception of 1990 when it increased slightly. The year 1988 also marked a turning point in the fall of the percentage of equity as a percentage of total assets. This jumped from 42 per cent in 1987 to 55 per cent in 1988 and continued to increase every year until 1994, again with the exception of 1990 when it fell slightly.

A brief conclusion to this section underlines three salient points. A lack of investment in TELMEX during the 1980s severely restricted the firm's capacity to grow, while the availability of new technology created a different and profitable market which TELMEX simply was not able to exploit. Nevertheless, despite investment restrictions and huge damage done to TELMEX installations in Mexico City, labour productivity had not fallen but had stagnated. Finally, management introduced real changes in 1988, two years before privatization, which are directly connected to the government's decision to replace the Director-General and its adoption of a new attitude towards the telecommunications sector.

The emergence of the STRM's new strategy

For telephone workers world-wide privatization is usually perceived as a threat to job stability and so workers attempt to block it. Between 1980 and 1985, the number of operators employed by telephone companies was reduced by 20 per cent in Sweden, 48 per cent in Canada, and 35 per cent by AT&T in North America.[110] In Latin America union responses to telecoms privatization has been varied. The first instance of telecoms privatization in the region took place in Chile under the authoritarian regime of Pinochet, in which unions and other organized groups were banned, so clearly civil society imposed no impediment to the process. The most typical union response by telephone workers' unions in Latin America to the threat of privatization is resistance; however, this strategy has worked only in a few countries such as Colombia and Uruguay where union opposition to privatization was one of the reasons to stall privatization. More usually the strategy of resistance has resulted in failure.[111] In Argentina, in the early years of privatization, resistance from organized labour, including the telephone workers' unions, with the support of the Peronist party, was an important reason for the failures of privatization attempts during the Alfonsín administration. However, the Menem administration, which came to power in 1989, was determined from the start to marginalize organized labour from the process. With the aim of privatizing the national telecommunication company ENTel, the general strike launched by telephone workers in August 1990 was vigorously repressed by the government and over 400 workers were fired.[112] The government also succeeded in dividing the unity of the telephone workers' movement by recruiting one of its leaders as Secretary of Communication. While some groups supported this appointment, others did not, seeing this as the cooptation of their leadership. Through these tactics of repression and division, the power of the telephone workers' unions was largely broken.

In the face of privatization, the telephone workers' union in Mexico developed an interesting strategy which distinguished it from most other unions of the same kind in Latin America faced with similar prospects. In the case of the STRM the main difference was the decision by leaders to play the government's game and maximize benefits while so doing. From the early 1980s, STRM leaders and workers became increasingly unsettled. They feared that the impact of new technologies, in particular digital equipment, could bring about mass redundancy of thousands of workers as had happened in many other telephone companies abroad. The apprehension shown by telephone workers, particularly operators, who worked in the capital was exacerbated by the damage done to TELMEX equipment and installations in September 1985 which had left around 4000 of them without a workplace and thus even more vulnerable to the threat of redundancy. Large groups of operators demonstrated in Mexico City against the possibility of losing their jobs and also in protest at the severe discipline imposed on them by TELMEX's *personal de confianza*, who had been sent to work centres all over the city to supervise work under the rather chaotic conditions, and their protests resulted in ugly, bloody clashes with TELMEX security guards.[113] Union leaders quickly reproached the operators for their behaviour and blamed them for weakening the union's power during the negotiation of the collective contract in 1986.[114]

After the earthquake, TELMEX management assured workers that it had no plans to axe jobs[115] and the sub-secretary of the SCT publicly dismissed rumours of redundancies, claiming that fears of this kind were unfounded.[116] However, the distrust that the workers felt for the government created a highly charged and tense relationship. STRM leader, Hernández Juárez, knew that huge job cuts could unleash a rebellion within the union against him and finally jeopardize his control. Worst of all, the group of workers most likely to be sacked were the operators, his most reliable pillar of support, but also the most potentially volatile section of the union.[117] Virtually all operators were women, and they had constituted the most militant section of the STRM since the 1970s. Though during the 1970s women had rarely participated in STRM politics as union leaders, they had been important as a mass force within the union.[118] In the 1980s, the role of women in the higher echelons of the union increased slightly, since a small number were elected to powerful positions such as Secretary of Labour. Once elected to such positions, they then became visible to Hernández Juárez and some were later recruited to be *comisionadas*.[119]

One of the features of digitalization was that one operator could handle up to ten times more calls per hour than before, so, assuming the number of calls remained the same, less operators would be needed. In addition, digitalization implied that an increasing number of calls would be made automatically, without the intervention of the operator. Finally, computer-simulation to answer callers' enquiries would replace the use of the human voice. Operator redundancies would generate concern in the rest of the workers who would see their own future foreshadowed by the fate of the operators.

In response to the threat of job losses through modernization, and the possible loss of control over the union, Hernández Juárez developed a clever, innovative and well-thought-out strategy which made the telephone union distinct from most other Mexican unions facing similar challenges of higher efficiency, new technology and possible job cuts. One of the main features which distinguished this strategy from that offered by most other unions was the *acceptance* of modernization, technological change and the globalization of markets as an *inevitable* process in the development of Mexico. Union leaders argued that these changes must be embraced, not confronted. They argued that once workers accepted this, they could work towards gaining a positive role in the changes, particularly through participating more in the project of modernization via the union. These tactics, which emerged around the mid-1980s, were the roots of the 'new unionism' which would flourish during the privatization of TELMEX. The STRM leaders' tactics can be divided into two main types. First, they strove to control the behaviour of the rank and file and, in particular, to discourage them from mobilization. This would facilitate negotiation and win them the confidence of management. The new, conciliatory rhetoric used by the STRM leaders from the mid-1980s was based on the argument that, after ten years of 'democratic' class struggle, the union was now mature, and that a calm and respectful manner of conducting collective bargaining had in their experience proved to be the most successful. In particular, they argued that the strike weapon was a relatively useless tool in labour relations, particularly for unions of strategic industries such as theirs, since the government responded to a strike with the *requisa*. Workers could better participate in the process of change once they adopted a conciliatory attitude. The term the leaders used was '*concertación*' which can be roughly translated as 'harmonization' or 'reconciliation'. The second, and related, plan was to expand the traditional arena of collective bargaining – namely salaries, working conditions and jobs – to include the negotiation of wider issues which centred around the union's participation in the introduction of new technology and modernization. The new conciliatory strategy conceived by the STRM leaders had important effects on the telephone union itself, particularly during the privatization of TELMEX. It also had a limited impact on organized labour as a whole, especially after January 1987, when Hernández Juárez became president of the CT.

Tempering organized labour

During 1987 the political climate in Mexico became tense due to the emergence of the *tendencia democrática* led by Cárdenas from within the PRI. The left-wing current was mobilizing labour, peasant groups and non-party organizations with the promise of greater democracy and strong attacks on the privatization process. This period which led up to the presidential elections in 1988 became one where trade union leaders were forced to align themselves with the PRI, or take a risk and support the newly emerging current. Hernández Juárez decided to support the PRI as the left-wing challenge was emerging, and during the same period, he significantly changed his rhetoric and strategy.

Once president, Hernández Juárez advised all CT member unions to follow STRM tactics: workers must accept the 'modernization' of their industry or firm as part of the next inevitable stage in Mexico's development. Instead of fighting against changes, unions should channel their energies to maximize union power by seeking an active role in these changes.[120] In addition, in mid-August 1987, the electricity and telephone workers revitalized a pact of mutual aid that had begun in 1962 (during the first period of 'democratic' leadership in the STRM). They jointly agreed to reject a modernization plan imposed 'top–down' on to the workforce which destroyed workers' rights and union power, since they warned that this could lead to social explosion. Instead, they insisted that unions must become involved in the restructuring of their company. As the company was restructured, so must the union adapt too, particularly by becoming more democratic, by which was meant that more workers would participate in the changes under way in the company.[121] This cooperation sparked an alliance which nurtured the seeds of the *Federación de Sindicatos de Empresas de Bienes y Servicios* (FESEBES), the labour confederation that Hernández Juárez was shortly to establish, and which is discussed in Chapter 5.

In many ways, 1987 was a culmination of Hernández Juárez's efforts to bring the STRM into an increasingly close relationship with the PRI and Fidel Velázquez. His efforts had started after the 1984 strike when insurgence from within the union against him had made the leader realize the extent to which he needed powerful allies to help him keep control. Since then, the union leader sought to promote himself within the labour movement as its 'modern', young labour leader. Hernández Juárez found an opportunity to strengthen his relationship with the PRI in 1987. The year 1987 was also a key moment for the PRI. During this period it sought to recruit as many supporters as possible with a view to the presidential elections the next year. The PRI's priorities were not just to recruit organized labour in general but particularly to recruit unions from the dynamic industries which would be key to the deepening of the privatization and 'modernization' process. Thus in 1987 Hernández Juárez's profile increased through his becoming the president of the CT, the first leader of the STRM to do so since Salustio Salgado in 1974. In the same year, he announced he had joined the PRI, thus demonstrating clearly his loyalty to the PRI at a key moment and his rejection of the emerging left-wing current, the FDN. In strategic terms, the prospect of Salinas offered much more hope to the STRM leaders than Cárdenas. Hernández Juárez tried to go even further and proposed that the entire union should join the PRI. This would have been a significant turning point in the union's history but feeling among union members was so strong that this was rejected.[122] In

September 1987, in reward for this loyalty, the STRM delegates voted to accept two seats in the Chamber of Deputies which were offered to them by the government, and which would be reserved for members other than Hernández Juárez and members of the CEN.[123] This was a significant change of union tactics. Since the arrival of the 'democratic' leaders in 1976, the union had prided itself on rejecting the corrupt, *charro* practices such as enjoying the privilege of positions in the government. Hernández Juárez was overtly returning to the values he had called '*charro*' in 1976 such as benefiting from alliances with the PRI. Furthermore, in December 1987, union leadership voiced its full support for the PSE.

As Secretary of the CT, Hernández Juárez was in charge of coordinating a strike of member unions at the beginning of 1987 in demand of a 23 per cent emergency wage increase in the face of record inflation levels. The strike has been presented in a misleading way in much of the literature, where it is stated that the wave of strikes coordinated by the CT was brutally repressed by the government.[124] In fact, Hernández Juárez – divided in his aim to keep the STRM out of trouble and to restrain the unions of the CT while allowing them to vent some anger – skilfully manipulated the coordination of the strike so as to weaken its overall impact. The STRM had voted to go on strike in March 1987 to coincide with strike of the electricity workers' union, the SME. As the deadline approached, Hernández Juárez decided to postpone the STRM strike by arguing that it was premature to strike before the other members of the CT were ready. Thus he effectively abandoned the SME, leaving it to strike alone. He managed to postpone the STRM strike three times more until it finally took place on 8 April 1987.[125]

The plan was that the telephone workers would start striking at midday, and would be joined at midnight by the pilots', cargo-handlers' and trolley bus workers' unions. However, once the STRM's strike began, the other unions quickly signed contracts with respective managements. Four hours before the strike began, TELMEX was taken over by the government.[126] (The government had traditionally used the *requisa* after, not before, strikes began.) Twenty minutes after the strike officially began, workers returned to work, as had been previously agreed in the union assembly. This strike was crucially different from others in the past. The idea behind it was to cause a brief interruption in TELMEX's service in order to irritate management and the government, but not to cause serious provocation. Indeed, Hernández Juárez referred to it as a *huelga de derecho* (a strike for the right to strike) as opposed to a *huelga de hecho* (a real strike).[127] He complained that the telephone workers did not actually enjoy the right to strike, since when they did, TELMEX was seized immediately and put under the control of the government's army. Under the terms of the *requisa*, workers lose their rights as the collective contract becomes legally invalid.

Hernández Juárez was quick to point out to the press that the service had hardly been affected.[128] Instead of striking properly, telephone workers were instead encouraged to vent their frustrations by organizing meetings, erecting red and black flags outside their work centres, refusing to work overtime, and working in *tortuguismo* style[129] (to work exceedingly slowly at tortoise pace). Workers were told to wear red and black on Mondays and green on Fridays. Green symbolizes Hernández Juárez since his 'plan' was named the Green Plan. A small group of workers refused to return to work after 20 minutes, and waited a few hours before returning,[130] while others dismantled automatic equipment (which, according to the labour contract, should never be tampered with even in periods of a strike).[131] In general, the orchestration and control by union leaders of the strike were impressive.

Only one week after the outbreak of the strike, Hernández Juárez announced it was over, and he justified his attitude on the grounds that he needed to concentrate on the revision of the collective contract, which had to be finalized that month. The following day, union leaders renounced their demand for a 23 per cent emergency salary rise and called off the strike, even before the JCA had given a verdict on its legality.[132] Lasting only eight days, this was the shortest conflict in the history of the telephone workers since 1976.[133] The union accepted an 18 per cent wage rise plus a 2 per cent increase in benefits. There were two reasons for the strike. First, as president of the CT, Hernández Juárez was under particular pressure to do something in the face of record inflation, and the strike served to vent the frustration of the workers who experienced a severe loss of purchasing power that year due to record inflation. The second outcome of the strike was to demonstrate loudly and clearly to the government and management the level of control that was exerted over the union by its leaders, and at the same time, prove that they were powerful and useful allies. This was crucial in the politicized environment leading up to the presidential elections.

Confronting new technology

After 1985, STRM leaders broadened their emphasis on collective bargaining to include the topics of workers' rights, and issues relating to health and training in the introduction and use of new technology. In order to achieve this, union leaders developed a well-informed, even expert rhetoric, about the significance of new technology and how developments in the telecommunications sector could affect labour. In order to do this, they had increasingly to seek help from specialists. A lecturer from the Department of Sociology of Labour was hired as the union's permanent adviser. Union discourse became more sophisticated in technical terms so that it would be capable of answering management back on its own terms. This strategy contrasts strikingly with that of most other unions in the period which rejected modernization, such as the unions of Aeroméxico and Fundidora de Monterrey.

Union leaders tried to demonstrate that they were more ambitious even than management with their ideas. A few months before the 1986 STRM collective contract was due for renewal, Hernández Juárez presented TELMEX management with 45 suggested modifications to the existing collective contract. Apart from the more traditional demands (such as salary increases and better terms for retirement), he introduced a new set of issues which concerned the effects that modernization might have on workers. Among the most important proposals were that the introduction of new technology did not imply redundancies and that the union would have an active role in the introduction of new technology through the creation of working groups comprising members of the government, management and the union. He also proposed that adequate training be given to workers in order to operate the new equipment (leaders complained that management trained the *personal de confianza* and not unionized workers) and that research would be done on how to treat professional illnesses that might result from the use of new technology. Finally, he requested that workers be rewarded financially for intensified work practices and increased productivity.[134]

The collective contract was signed but management only accepted a few of the union's proposals.[135] First, management guaranteed workers that there would be no redundancies as a result of modernization. Second, they agreed to give the union advance notice before new technology was introduced to the company, and moreover, that each time new equipment was introduced to the company, adequate training would be provided to all STRM workers involved. Third, and most importantly, they agreed that a mixed commission be made up of government, union and company representatives in order to define labour-related needs caused by new technology such as training, hygiene and security, and to agree on a method of measuring productivity.[136] The mixed commission of modernization was established on 26 April 1986, and comprised five members each from the union, the TELMEX board and the SCT. All these promises relating to the introduction of technology were contained in a new clause, 193. The telephone workers were also awarded a 38 per cent wage increase. Delighted, the STRM leaders claimed that they were the first union in Mexico that had negotiated the introduction of new technology in the collective contract on terms favourable to workers.[137] This was the first major step in its new strategy to include issues of modernization and new technology in their collective contract. At the end of the year, STRM leaders claimed that negotiations with management had been the best experienced in the union's history since 1976, and union–management relations were entering a new phase of peace.[138]

The PIMES

Between 1987 and 1988 union leaders continued to make considerable progress in their scheme to increase the profile of the union in the decision-making process at TELMEX. In the middle of August 1987, the new director announced a plan to modernize the company with the aim of increasing labour productivity both in the short and medium term and resolving the delays experienced in the upgrading of TELMEX's equipment. This plan was known as the '*Programa para la inmediata mejoramiento del servicio*' (PIMES). Controversially, it laid most of the blame for TELMEX's inefficiency at the feet of the workers and was not surprisingly unpopular with the rank and file.[139] In the effort to implement the plan, management and union leaders collaborated intimately as never before. Top union *comisionado* Lejarza informed TELMEX's Director of Labour Relations and Arsenio Farell, the Secretary of Labour, in a private meeting, that union leaders would ensure there would be no strikes during the implementation of the programme, since the leaders, for the first time, genuinely wanted to resolve the problems of TELMEX, including the quality of service and productivity.[140]

PIMES consisted of two main parts. The first outlined management's identification of the main problems in the company, and the second set out the new targets which would overcome them. It concluded that TELMEX's service would be improved only when there was a change in worker attitude.[141] The operators were singled out in particular for having a very low level of productivity and there was a veiled threat that digitalization would reduce the company's need for them,[142] as had occurred in many telephone companies world-wide, although redundancy plans were not specifically mentioned.[143] Management's decision to blame the workers was aimed at provoking a response from them,[144] for they did not genuinely believe that workers were really the main problem.[145] Indeed, the grounds on which they blamed the workers were based on the manipulated results of a survey they had commissioned on TELMEX's performance.[146]

In the second section of PIMES, management plans to reform TELMEX were outlined. Some 59 projects were to be implemented, of which 28 would be put into action within three months. It would take one year before the results of the other 31 were apparent.[147] In order to gain short- and medium-term improvements, a special team of *personal de confianza* would strictly supervise the workers.[148] Its year-long plan included the introduction of a system[149] which would automatically calculate the time taken for calls to be answered, thus eliminating the need for human supervision.[150] It was planned that, by the year 2000, TELMEX would increase its telephone network from 7 to 30 million telephones. Digitalization would be accelerated so that the current percentage of digitalized lines would increase from 8 per cent to 70 per cent by 2000. A programme to build a digital network in 40 industrial parks was already under way, and this would particularly service the *maquiladora* industry. It also proposed progressing with the projects of LADATEL and TRIPLEX throughout the country.[151]

Management was aware that the successful implementation of the programme required not only planning and investment, but also a stable, obedient and cooperative workforce. Muñoz Izquierdo feared that resistance from the workers, and at worst, a strike, would damage the success of the programme. In particular he warned that the operators, the group of workers who were most vulnerable to the changes, should be handled with caution since they remained one of the most militant sections of the union.[152] In order to facilitate labour relations, a position of Director of Labour Relations was created in February 1987. Management saw Hernández Juárez as their main guarantor that the workers would be well controlled. Elections for the STRM secretary-general were coming up in February 1988 and they were keen to see his re-election.[153]

Ensuring rank and file quiescence

Hernández Juárez's task was to introduce an unpopular programme to the workforce while at the same time organizing and executing his victory by being re-elected as secretary-general in the elections which were scheduled for mid-1988. The strategy of union leaders was two-fold: to control any dissidence from the members, and to increase the weight of the union in the introduction of changes in the company through the creation of more mixed commissions.

Union members had already made clear that they opposed the PIMES. They had voted to refuse the option of voluntary redundancies should the government try to impose this.[154] Even the telephone operators in Mexico City – traditionally Hernández Juárez's most reliable supporters – were infuriated by the PIMES, and they spoke out to journalists claiming that management was falsely blaming the workers for the poor quality of the service. They refused to take the blame and claimed that the real problems were that many TELMEX buildings damaged in 1985 still had not been repaired, and that they were working in provisional offices without bathrooms, restrooms and dining halls.[155] They insisted that thousands of calls could not be connected because many of the trunk lines were still awaiting repair.[156]

The most serious threat to Hernández Juárez's authority from within the union came in September 1987 as a referendum was held on whether he could stand for re-election as secretary-general. According to official STRM calculations, of the 100 union bases outside the capital, 11 rejected him, and of the 170 departments in the capital, 41 rejected him.[157] The most significant dissidence came from the union base in Puebla, the third largest union branch in the country with around 4000 members. Since 1976, the telephone workers in Puebla had constituted a hotbed of dissidence against Hernández Juárez since they had more radical leftist tendencies and they perceived him as an opportunist who had violated the terms of union democracy which emerged in the late 1950s. In previous years they had demonstrated their independence from union headquarters. They had organized 'unofficial' conferences on the effects that new technology would bring to TELMEX in conjunction with academics from the *Universidad Autonoma de Puebla* (some of whom were ex-telephone workers expelled for their opposition to Hernández Juárez).[158] The STRM leaders at Mexico City headquarters wanted to be the only ones who raised issues of new technology and they were angered by this display of independence.

The Puebla executive went further in September 1987 when they announced that they would hold an 'independent' election on whether or not to accept the Hernández Juárez-led Programme of the Workers, whether to ratify the delegates at the National Convention, and whether to accept the *comisionados* chosen by the CEN at the end of August.[159] One of the major reasons for their dissidence was their disgust at the central leadership's support of the PRI and they held meetings demonstrating their wish to back the left-wing current led by Cárdenas. For this outright defiance of central authority, the entire executive committee, which had been elected by the workers in Puebla, was ousted by STRM leaders in September 1987.[160] TELMEX management cooperated overtly with this repression by refusing to deal with the 'dissidents' in any matter.[161] STRM headquarters named a new union executive which would immediately replace the old one. There was also opposition to Hernández Juárez in Sonora. His appeal for re-election was rejected in three union bases, and many ballots were scrawled with obscenities against the him. However, this opposition was quickly smothered when its ringleader, Arturo Figueroa, was 'removed' to work in another state.[162]

After the destruction of Hernández Juárez's opposition in Puebla and Sonora, the preparations to guarantee his re-election as secretary-general in 1988 went fairly smoothly. The Twelfth Annual Ordinary Convention of Telephone Workers, which began on 17 September and lasted nearly a month, was used to consolidate a double victory. First, the majority of workers had conceded in the referendum (the mechanisms of which were discussed in the last chapter) that Hernández Juárez would be allowed to run again in the elections for secretary-general for the period 1988–92.[163] In addition, union delegates agreed temporarily to modify the statutes so that the election for the secretary-general, which was set for mid-1988, could be brought forward to February 1988.[164] One reason for this was the recognition that Hernández Juárez's popularity within the union could be strained further by the negotiation of the collective contract due in April 1988. So the aim of bringing the elections forward was to guarantee his role as secretary-general in case the situation of the union worsened. A related reason was the need to guarantee that one of Mexico's most important unions would be headed by a loyal supporter of the PRI presidential candidate. This was of utmost concern to TELMEX management as well as to PRI members. Hernández Juárez was elected secretary-general in February 1987 with 25 936 votes (over 75 per cent of total votes cast) against the leader of the opposition team, the Orange Programme, which gained 8429 votes.[165] The Orange Programme had fought against him since he came to power, in protest at his violations of the statutes and anti-democratic control of the union. In 1988, they protested about the possible job losses, the STRM's recent warming to the PRI, and the STRM's support of the economic solidarity pact.[166]

Union-management truce

The STRM leader's response to change, modernization and threats from management was in marked contrast to that exhibited by leaders of most other unions. Instead of reacting against PIMES, Hernández Juárez and two of his *comisionados*[167] modified the original version, not as regards the fundamental issues of productivity increases or new technology, but as regards the role that the union would play in this process.[168] Their main proposal (which had first emerged in the revision of the 1986 collective contract) was that another commission should be formed of government, TELMEX and STRM representatives, which would be charged with improving productivity. In this way, union leaders believed they would gain direct involvement in the analysis and decisions about productivity in TELMEX. The Ministry of Labour (STPS) and management accepted the STRM's suggestion, and they created a Mixed Commission of Productivity on 24 September, headed by the Secretary of Labour, Arsenio Farell, Hernández Juárez and Muñoz Izquierdo and Guillermo del Hoyo, TELMEX's Director of Labour Relations.[169]

The PIMES document was rewritten by management embodying the new idea of the Mixed Commission of Productivity while carefully avoiding blaming the workers for TELMEX's problems. At the same time, management and STRM leaders agreed that if the union accepted PIMES, which included more flexibility in relocating workers geographically and also moving workers from one department to another, TELMEX would in return give some concessions. These included that there would be no redundancies, that workers would be retrained and relocated, and that they would be awarded a 25 per cent salary increase backdated to the beginning of October.[170] At first, the reports by the mixed commission were optimistic,[171] but as time wore on, and problems were not resolved, meetings became more tense to the point that management refused to attend.[172] Some members of the TELMEX executive were extremely wary of the STRM's intentions, and believed that they were seeking co-management in TELMEX.[173] The collective contract negotiated in April 1988 showed the union's determination to further extend the mixed commissions. In addition to being granted a 25 per cent wage increase, union leaders advanced in their aim to increase the STRM's profile in restructuring. Two more mixed committees were created: the committee for security and hygiene, which would examine the risks new technology brought to labour and seek preventative and corrective measures,[174] and the mixed commission of training, which comprised nine members from the union and nine from TELMEX and which would determine and develop the requirements for training and evaluate results. TELMEX added that when new work was introduced, it would undertake the provision of relevant courses for unionized workers.[175] Management also promised that when they decided to introduce new technology, the training commission would be briefed, so that it could prepare an examination of the kinds of training that would be required.[176]

It was ironic but telling that the signing of the STRM contract took place days before the entire workforce of Aeroméxico were sacked. The two union experiences could hardly have been more different.[177] Protests by Aeroméxico's workforce were supported by Cárdenas but these were ignored by management and the PRI alike. The PRI's presidential candidate Salinas' attention turned elsewhere to congratulate the STRM leaders' conciliatory strategy when he attended the contract signing. Salinas used the occasion to make his first important public overture to the telephone workers. He praised them for representing an exceptional, modern and mature union, and for their openness to technological change and for its defence of their members. He struck a deal with them in public that, if he became the next president, he would ensure that the modernization of TELMEX would be carried out with the participation of the workers.[178] His promise was rather vague but there was a hint that he would treat the telephone workers better in the event that TELMEX was privatized than the De la Madrid administration had treated workers.[179]

Salinas had, however, already held private meetings with Hernández Juárez and other STRM leaders on the subject of modernization at the end of 1987.[180] The promise he made to the telephone workers was only the public face of a private accord made between Salinas and Hernández Juárez which provided that, assuming Salinas became president, the union would receive presidential protection if it cooperated with the privatization plans Salinas envisaged.

The threat of privatization

In 1988 the De la Madrid administration started to privatize some of the larger public enterprises, beginning with Mexico's two national airlines, Aeroméxico and Mexicana.[181] The government's labour policy during the first large privatization was typical of the *sexenio*. Aeroméxico had been controlled by the state since 1959, and, apart from 1979–81 it had been a consistent loss-maker.[182] When, on 12 April 1988, ground workers at Aeroméxico went on strike in protest against unacceptable wages and working conditions proposed by management for the new collective contract, the Aeroméxico executive used the strike as an excuse to declare the company bankrupt. This happened six days after the strike and, immediately, all the workers were dismissed. In May, Aeroméxico reopened under the name of Aerovías, and one-third of its original work force were re-hired under a new labour contract.[183] On 11 September, the government announced its intention to sell the company and the next month it sold 65 per cent of its shares to a consortium of investors named Dictum.[184] Essentially, the sale of the airline was a liquidation of its assets. Galal *et al.* concluded that the government did not receive revenues from the sale, since the money was used to pay off the airline's liabilities so that the new owners would gain a clean balance sheet. However, the company's drain on the treasury was halted.[185]

In the delicate weeks leading up to the presidential elections in July 1988, rumours that TELMEX was next on the list for privatization intensified. Some saw the acceleration of the privatization programme as inevitable if Salinas came into power.[186] Cárdenas defended this in nationalist terms and claimed that privatization must be resisted. The rumours about the imminent sale of TELMEX were fuelled when management made public for the first time its estimate that an investment of $9.5 billion would be required over the next six years in order to pay for upgrading of the company.[187] This figure was beyond the capacity of the state to fund, so speculation focused on where the money would come from, and whether this implied the sale of TELMEX. Many TELMEX functionaries, including the Director of Strategic planning, Carlos Casasús, and principal shareholders spoke out in favour of the need for private capital.[188] Members of the business community were also in favour of the privatization.[189] Parties reportedly interested in acquiring TELMEX were listed in the press including international telephone companies such as Ericsson and Alcatel, and also Mexico's television company Televisa.

The STRM's response to these rumours was to call an emergency assembly of all delegates on 4 June. The rhetoric used by the leader showed a distinct change from the previous months. Hernández Juárez had never wholeheartedly opposed privatization, but he had usually insisted on the need for state control of strategic industries, including telecommunications. In this emergency meeting, he used a rather different argument. He warned that the TELMEX management was seeking to provoke the union, and wanted an excuse to annul its collective contract, as had happened in the case of the Aeroméxico workers. He argued that if the union went on strike in the face of rumours of privatization or uncertainty, management would have a perfect excuse to claim that the union was an obstacle to its restructuring programme. The leader drew attention away from the question whether privatization was a good or bad thing in itself, and treated it as a tool with which TELMEX management hoped to trick the union into mobilization, which would then be used as evidence that the union was anachronistic and an obstacle to progress. He warned that if the union went on strike, or resisted in any other way in the face of mounting rumours about the privatization of TELMEX, the union would be destroyed in the same way as that of Aeroméxico had been crushed.[190] The key decision taken at the meeting was that, from now on, negotiations between the union and TELMEX should be intensified and *fully centralized* in the Modernization Committee to the exclusion of other bodies. The centralization of negotiations was justified on the grounds that the STRM required a full-time, professional team in order to maximize its chances in the negotiations with TELMEX. A streamlined negotiating team was necessary, it was argued, in order to focus on being well informed about the complex subject of global telecommunications.

In the days between the presidential elections and the official disclosure of the results, union leaders published an important circular which was distributed to all workers instructing them how they should think and behave. Workers were told that they must fully support the project to modernize TELMEX and demonstrate this in any way they could, whether this meant painting their vehicles or workplaces, designing posters with pro-modernization slogans, or organizing demonstrations in their free time.[191] It also explained to the workers that union–management negotiation would be streamlined and coordinated by the Commission of Modernization. Negotiations would temporarily be more secretive, in particular because Hernández Juárez wished to avoid making any comments to the press, in order to prevent further fuelling of speculation about privatization. The secretary-general and his *comisionados* travelled to various STRM regional headquarters to enforce the message.

Conclusion

By 1988, a change in the politics of the STRM leaders had emerged. This paralleled political developments at the highest level as the PRI was seriously challenged by the Cárdenas-led coalition. The change in union strategy, which had its origins in the threat of new technology on jobs and the fear of privatization, was dramatically accelerated on the eve of Salinas' electoral victory. Union leaders decided to 'professionalize' and monopolize negotiations, and asked the rank and file to limit their action to the 'local' level (their work centre), leaving the newly appointed commission members to conduct the 'high' level negotiations with TELMEX and the government.[192] The STRM leaders' decision to centralize and concentrate negotiations served to please the TELMEX executive which had, since January 1988, planned that labour negotiations should be more centralized, since they thought dispersed agreements were delaying decision-making.[193] It also pleased the PRI presidential candidate who saw one of the country's most important unions unambiguously on his side.

Herein lies one of the paradoxes of union democracy and autonomy in the STRM. From the mid-1980s the STRM leaders adopted an increasingly cooperative attitude towards management in the belief that, in this way, they could facilitate dialogue, and, at the same time, extract the maximum benefits from the opportunities brought about by change in the company. Their aim was to obtain material benefits (salary increases, job security, training and advance knowledge about new equipment) for the union. They sought to achieve this by centralizing negotiations with management while tightly controlling workers, sometimes violently, as in the case of Puebla. The error of the Aeroméxico workers had been to oppose modernization plans, and, fatally, to strike. They cut themselves off from the possibility of dialogue and made their own collective contract vulnerable. The STRM leaders refused to risk their collective contract by behaving in this way. In their efforts to organize a rapid, informed response to the changes facing them, the STRM developed a new structure of union government composed of specialized committees. The structure was pyramidal, having at its apex the Modernization Committee which would coordinate the five sub-committees of productivity, new technology, hygiene and security, training, and worker culture. This new structure would be *superimposed* on the previous 'semi-democratic' structure of union government since the Modernization Committee would act as a coordinating organ of the CEN in all negotiations that were linked to collective bargaining.

What was not clear, as this new structure of power emerged within the union, was the impact that it would have on union democracy. If representatives of the committees were elected fairly, it would be possible that worker participation would increase significantly in the union since many new posts were created. However, if the representatives were not elected fairly, this might bring about a diminution of union democracy. In the next chapter, the way in which the union's strategy of conciliation developed, and the consequences this had on union democracy, are examined.

4
The Politics of Industrial Restructuring and Privatization

Once the Salinas administration came to power in December 1988, it took dramatic steps to deepen and extend the opening up of the economy. In 1989 the financial system was liberalized and foreign investment restrictions were overhauled enabling new areas of the economy to be opened up to foreigners and, in some circumstances, 100 per cent foreign ownership to be automatically approved.[1] As part and parcel of the overall acceleration and deepening of these policies, an ambitious programme was launched to sell off the majority of Mexico's largest public enterprises. In 1990, a divestiture unit was set up within the SHCP which helped to speed up and professionalize the privatization process.[2] Between 1989 and 1994, state-owned companies were sold off rapidly including TELMEX, the national airline Mexicana, steel mills including Altos Hornos (AHMSA) and Sicartsa, dozens of sugar mills, the insurer ASEMEX, automobile companies including Dina, branches of CONASUPO, mines including Cananea and all 18 of Mexico's commercial banks.[3] The public sector consequently shrank from 1155 firms in 1982 to around 220 by 1994.[4]

Many governments have justified privatization programmes in economic terms, such as claiming that it will promote competition and efficiency. Most of the literature published on privatization in Mexico has tended to focus on financial and business aspects.[5] Only a small proportion has been concerned with the *politics* of privatization.[6] In the 'business' analysis, the political dynamics and consequences of privatization are usually ignored. Similarly, most political analysts have not integrated the consideration of economic or financial factors into their accounts. It is, however, important to take economic and financial aspects of privatization into consideration when explaining

116

the politics of the privatization, in order to investigate how economic factors influenced political decisions and vice versa.[7]

In this chapter, the politics of industrial restructuring and privatization of the Salinas administration are analysed, with particular attention to the primary role – financial and political – played by TELMEX and the telephone workers' union in this process. An attempt is made to disentangle political factors from financial aspects, but in practice this is not always possible since they are often tightly intertwined. In addition, although industrial restructuring and privatization are distinct policies, many companies were restructured prior to being sold in Mexico, and thus restructuring policies must be interpreted as being directly linked to the privatization programme.[8]

The sale of TELMEX in itself was the most important single instance of privatization in Mexico for two principal reasons. First, the revenue generated by the sale for the Mexican Treasury – which totalled around US$6 billion – was easily the largest sum obtained from the sale of any single firm, and constituted around 30 per cent of all privatization revenues during the Salinas *sexenio*, which totalled US$20 billion. In comparison with privatization during the De la Madrid administration, the sale of TELMEX alone generated four times the revenue raised by the totality of public enterprise sales in that *sexenio*.[9] Second, TELMEX was chosen by Salinas as the 'launching pad' from which the rest of the sales were carried out.[10] Salinas believed that a successful sale would set an upbeat tone for the other privatizations that would follow. The sale of TELMEX was used to send a loud and clear message to potential investors both at home and abroad that the privatization programme in Mexico was changing in both qualitative and quantitative terms, and that the government was serious about its plan to sell off large, profitable and attractive firms.

The sale of TELMEX in December 1990 was used to further important political ends. In the run up to, and throughout the process of, privatizing TELMEX, the government made a special alliance with the telephone workers' union. Principally, Salinas offered presidential protection to the union if it agreed fully to cooperate with the restructuring (or the 'modernization' as it was called in Mexico at the time) of its labour contract, which was signed in April 1989, and with the privatization of TELMEX, which took place from December 1990. The way in which the STRM cooperated with the restructuring of the labour contract distinguished it from the previous pattern of union behaviour which had been to resist change, often by calling strikes, such as the cases of Aeroméxico and Cananea. The cooperation of the

STRM leaders was not passive; they participated in the restructuring of the labour contract by drawing up alternative plans which were just as complex and serious as those presented by management. On occasions, the leaders' proposals were accepted by management and government representatives and included in the new labour contract. As a result of pursuing this strategy, the union was heralded by Salinas as the leader of a new labour culture which was called '*nuevo sindicalismo*', which the president claimed was bringing about a permanent change in the relationship between the state and organized labour. Many observers considered that the STRM had made a breakthrough in labour relations in Mexico.[11] Both the Salinas administration and the union leaders proclaimed that the STRM was a model union whose example should be emulated by all other unions. The reasons for the government's nurturing of a '*nuevo sindicalismo*' are explained in this chapter. In addition, the extent to which this in reality represented something new in labour relations in Mexico, and its consequences for union democracy and worker participation, is discussed.

Labour policy and industrial restructuring

From 1988 there were some signs of recovery in the labour market which lasted until 1992. The real industrial wage grew around 4 per cent annually. However, wages did not reach their pre-crisis levels; the average wage in 1992 was worth only 80 per cent of that of 1981.[12] The recovery was largely due to the control of inflation and faster economic growth. In the same period, employment in the formal sector increased by around 3 per cent annually. Within this sector, there were sharp declines in the industrial employment, which were compensated for by the dramatic growth of job creation in the *maquiladora* industry. Employment in the informal sector continued to increase sharply.

One of the main labour policies pursued by the government during this period was, as part of the wider effort to open up the Mexican economy during the 1980s, its effort to increase labour market flexibility.[13] This meant that a significant programme of industrial restructuring was needed and this implied six principal changes. First, it meant that labour had to become more 'flexible' in terms of working hours and schedules. This also implied more use of third parties and increased employment of temporary workers. Second, labour needed to become more mobile. Existing restrictions on mobility had to be eliminated, so that workers could be easily moved from one job to another, from one work centre to another, or from one state to another. Third, it was necessary for the excess labour resulting from overstaffing, particularly during the 1970s, to be shed. Fourth, the workforce had to increase its level of productivity so that the Mexican economy could become more competitive on an international scale. This would involve providing new training to workers. Fifth, since trade unions were usually seen as being obstacles to obtaining greater labour 'flexibility', their power needed to be dismantled or reduced.[14] Finally, workers would have to be rewarded on the basis of merit rather than on seniority.[15] In many cases, the restructuring of the labour contract, which was an important step in the process of restructuring the entire company, was intimately connected to the goal of privatizing the company, since restructuring would render a company much more attractive to potential buyers.

During the De la Madrid *sexenio*, most attempts by the government to make labour contracts more flexible had been met with resistance, labour mobilization and strikes. In the end, this dissidence seemed futile, since the government imposed its will, sometimes following an ugly clash between the military and workers. The Salinas administration sought to continue with this policy of making the labour market more flexible. For a mixture of political and financial reasons, the administration sought to encourage an alternative model of unionism which would choose to cooperate with, and not to oppose, the policy of making Mexico's labour force more flexible and competitive in international terms. Labour cooperation with the government would help to improve state–labour relations and, at the same time, could be used by the PRI to recover some of support which had been lost from the labour sector in the 1988 presidential elections. Writ large, this might also serve to improve state–society relations, particularly if labour restructuring was accepted as a legitimate policy by the workers and other citizens. In financial terms, an alliance between labour and the state in the face of restructuring would help to lay down a smooth path for privatization. It would also ensure that potential investors would not be put off by the prospect of union militancy, and that revenues generated by the sales would not be sacrificed.

For many reasons, explained below, Salinas chose the telephone workers' union to lead this alternative, 'new' model of labour relations. He invested personal energy into ensuring that the union's collective contract was restructured with the cooperation of union leaders in April 1989. Afterwards, he promoted this negotiation as an example of modern labour relations which could and should be emulated by other unions. This preferential treatment given to the STRM by the president was not random or coincidental, but was intimately connected to the crucial political and financial role that the sale of TELMEX played in the overall process of privatization.

The logic of privatization

Since privatization is a phenomenon which has been practised by many governments world-wide there are clearly many common driving forces behind each national effort to sell off the public sector. During the 1980s a pro-privatization consensus was consolidated among the industrialized countries and, by the late 1980s, most of the OECD governments had espoused privatization to some degree.[16] In these countries, it was argued that public ownership had resulted in serious shortcomings in efficiency and investments, since firms had been operating outside of the market and had been subject to excessive governmental intervention. The academic foundation for these beliefs was the school of the 'new political economy' which based its assumptions on neo-classical microeconomics.[17]

Some analysts claimed that the reasons which explained privatization in the industrialized countries were 'positive' in comparison with the 'negative' reasons which motivated governments of developing countries. In the case of developing countries, an important international influence was the policy advice emanating from institutions such as the World Bank and the IMF.[18] Both of the organizations criticized the public sectors in developing countries for being inefficient, and recommended privatization as the solution to their problems.[19] However, in most cases in Latin America, loans were attached to the pursuit of economic liberalization generally but not to privatization specifically.[20] Revenue generated from privatization was often used by governments to pay off part of their domestic debt.

A general definition of privatization is the process of transferring a business, or an activity, into the private sector. However, this can be effected in several ways; for example, by selling the controlling stake in a firm to a private interest or by offering company shares to the public. Alternatively, services previously provided by local or central government can be contracted out to private companies. A related question is what methods of payment will be accepted (cash only, or bonds), and to whom can these firms be sold, a particularly sensitive issue for countries such as Mexico where forms of foreign ownership have been legally prohibited.

Despite the fact that there is a common drive to implement privatization in developing countries, individual governments have pursued privatization policies in diverse styles, at different paces, and with distinct objectives. In Latin America, privatization in Argentina was pursued at a rapid rate once President Menem assumed office in 1989 and,[21] largely due to this speed, there was insufficient time to restructure many Argentine companies prior to privatization.[22] The Brazilian government, on the other hand, took a much more cautious and gradual approach. Each government that embarks on a privatization programme must decide how much and which parts of the public sector it wishes to sell. This decision is influenced by the priority placed by that government on considerations such as the origins of the public sector and the importance of nationalist and ideological concerns, and on the government's concern for the control of economic resources and its need for foreign exchange.[23]

Another important question is the timing and speed of privatization. There are no hard and fast rules about how rapidly a privatization programme should be pursued, but there *is* a consensus that it should not be so fast that firms are not restructured prior to the sale, nor should it be so slow that potential investors perceive the government as indecisive and decide simply to invest elsewhere. An additional consideration when designing a programme is 'sequencing', in other words, in what order should the various firms be sold? Some advisers, including the World Bank, recommend that small and medium sized companies should be sold first, so that the government can gain experience in selling, and thus avoid making mistakes when it comes to privatizing the large and important companies such as banks and monopolies where the sale may involve significant sums of money and complex decisions about regulation.

Privatization usually provokes opposition from some sectors of society, particularly from workers and unions, since it is often accompanied by the shedding of labour. The public may also be suspicious as they tend to associate private profit-seeking firms with higher prices. In Britain, the privatization polices pursued by the Conservative Party have been associated with the launching of an assault on trade union power in the 1980s.[24] Avoiding, or at least reducing, political opposition to privatization from these different interest groups is extremely important if the government wishes to avoid disruption to its privatization programme, or, as in the case of Uruguay, complete abandonment.[25] In other cases, such as that of Mexico, privatization may present the government with the dilemma of having to make labour more flexible and unions less powerful, while at the same time trying to maintain the political support of labour on which it historically depended. In particular, in developing countries, governments must balance political and economic considerations at home with the external pressure placed upon them by international agencies and institutions which may attach new loans to commitments to privatize.[26]

Privatization in Mexico

The timing, pace and sequencing which characterized the privatization programme in Mexico have been praised by many analysts undertaking comparative studies in Latin America.[27] In terms of timing, once the Salinas administration entered office, it did not rush immediately into privatizing large public enterprises, but continued during the first year to restructure many public sector firms, including TELMEX, in order to make them more attractive propositions. The government chose to wait for an opportune moment when the economy was picking up and there were signs of price stability before announcing that some of Mexico's large state enterprises were to be sold.[28] The Salinas administration benefited at the end of 1988 from the completion of the negotiation of the *Pacto para la Estabilidad y el Crecimiento Económico* (PECE) which involved the partial freezing of wages and public sector prices and the use of the exchange rate as the nominal anchor. By the end of 1989, the success of the pact was becoming apparent. The inflation rate fell dramatically and there was a positive growth of per capita product.[29] Annual inflation during 1988 was 114 per cent but by 1989 this had been reduced dramatically to only 20 per cent, after which it became relatively stable, rising to 27 per cent in 1990 then falling again to 23 per cent in 1991 and 16 per cent in 1992. Economic growth rose from 1.2 per cent in 1988 to 3.5 per cent, 4.4 per cent, 3.6 per cent and 2.6 per cent in 1989, 1990, 1991 and 1992 respectively.[30]

There was another real improvement in the economic situation in March 1989. The end of the Cold War brought about a change in the political climate in the United States. Although it was clear that the Baker Plan was failing in its goal of achieving sustained growth in major debtor countries, the Reagan administration had stubbornly insisted in pressing on with the plan and opposed any form of debt relief, despite pressure from European countries, Japan, the IMF and the World Bank.[31] However, the new Bush administration softened US policy concerning debt repayment, and, by March 1989, it announced a new scheme called the Brady Plan. The major difference was that this plan recognized implicitly that full repayment of the debt was no longer a reasonable goal. Instead, it put pressure on commercial banks to concede some degree of debt relief, and it also called for an expansion in secondary market transactions aimed at debt reduction so that foreign investors could buy discounted debt and then sell it to the Banco de México.[32] Mexico was the first test case to emerge from this new plan. In July 1989 the Mexican government made an agreement which was finalized in February 1990 and which helped it set a climate of greater optimism for investors.[33] Interestingly, in March 1989, in the same month that the Brady Plan was negotiated, the government decided that it would sell TELMEX, and the necessary preparations began, though officials continued to deny in public statements that the privatization of TELMEX was being considered.

The pace of privatization in Mexico was rapid after 1989. One of the key differences between the speedy privatization programmes in both Argentina and Mexico after 1989 was that a large number of the Mexican companies had already undergone significant restructuring. The dramatic acceleration of the privatization programme in Mexico is clear when revenues are examined. Privatization proceeds really became significant only in 1990. Between 1983 and 1988, total revenue from privatization was US$950 million. In the single year 1989, however, revenue totalled US$730 million; in 1990 this jumped to US$3.2 billion and in 1991 to US$10.55 billion.[34] Privatization revenue accounted for nearly 0.2 per cent of GDP in 1989, 1.2 per cent in 1990 and 3.8 per cent in 1991. This rise had come not only from the increase in the number of sales but also the higher degree of success experienced in the process. The average dollar price of companies sold in 1989 was US$29.3 million; in 1990 this nearly doubled to US$54.2 million and in 1991 increased almost six times to US$292.3 million.[35] In total, between 1989 and 1994, the privatization programme raised US$20 billion for the Mexican Treasury.[36]

As for sequencing, as stated in Chapter 3, privatization during the De la Madrid *sexenio* was pursued cautiously with the initial sale of small and medium sized companies, only in 1988 did the privatization of larger companies begin. The Salinas administration sought to propel this 'second round' of privatization by opening with a successful sale that would attract the attention of investors world-wide.[37]

The political economy of the privatization of TELMEX

There were specific reasons which made TELMEX a good candidate to launch the 'second round' of privatization. It would be an extremely attractive proposition as TELMEX had been profitable, even in the years of economic contraction. It enjoyed a monopoly of providing basic telecommunications services across the country, and its growth potential was huge, since telephone density in Mexico (the number of telephones per one hundred inhabitants) was low (5 per cent in 1989 compared with around 40 per cent in European countries). Furthermore, TELMEX had new and highly profitable markets in which it had potential to grow, principally in cellular phones and private networks.

It was unlikely that the sale of TELMEX would be highly controversial among the public nor would it stir nationalistic passions. The tele-communications sector had never been included in Articles 25 or 28 of the Mexican Constitution (which define the 'strategic' sectors of the economy controlled by the government which include oil, hydrocarbons, basic petrochemicals, satellite telecommunications, railways, electricity and radioactive materials). An attempt to sell the jewel in the Mexican nationalist crown, PEMEX, could have incurred mass resistance to the entire process. Moreover, such a proposed modification of the Constitution might not even pass the Chamber of Deputies in which opposition parties controlled 240 of the 500 seats.[38] However, it would not be necessary to alter the Constitution before TELMEX's sale. Public opinion would probably not oppose the sale of TELMEX, since it had been criticized in recent years for its inefficiency and the corrupt union practices. For these reasons, the sale of TELMEX looked promising. One businessman summed up the reasoning succinctly: 'When we were selling TELMEX, we were selling Mexico as well!'[39] If the sale was success-ful, this would send a clear message to investors at home and abroad that the Mexican government was serious in its attempt to reform the economy, and wanted to bridge the gap that had been opened between the government and the private sector.[40] As Ramamurti put it:

First, it had to be loud, so that it would register above the din of international news. Second, it had to be quick, so that the economic turnaround could begin early in his term. And third, it had to show that the Mexican government was willing to let private investors earn high rates of return on their investments. The last condition required that the firm targeted for early privatization be a 'plum' rather than a 'lemon'.[41]

The tactic of launching privatization by first selling the national telecom-munications monopoly was not unique to Mexico. In Britain, one of the first large public utilities that was privatized was British Telecom in 1984. In Latin America, governments in Argentina, Jamaica and, to a lesser extent, Venezuela also launched their privatization programmes by selling their telephone companies.[42] In all of these cases, governments believed that the sale of the telecommunications monopoly would set an upbeat tone for the rest of their programmes. Telephone companies in general were particularly attractive to investors due to their monopoly of the market, their potential for future expansion, and the fact that there was commonly no legal or constitutional obstacle to transferring control over telecommunications companies to the private sector. Moreover, although most of the telephone companies were overstaffed, massive lay-offs could in general be avoided by absorbing excess staff through future growth.[43] In all cases, due to severe shortages of investment, governments as owners had been unable satisfactorily to upgrade the companies, still less enter new dynamic markets brought about by technological advances in the field.

Forging a privatization consensus

In many of the comparative analyses which treat the successes and failures of privatization in diverse Latin American countries, Mexico is singled out as being the country in which there was the least political opposition to privatization.[44] Most of the writers who make this observation are financial or business specialists with little interest in labour relations or Latin American politics, and their observations must be qualified by considering how political opposition can be measured, and whether different forms of mobilization in various countries, each of which has a distinct relationship between the state and organized labour, are in fact comparable in the way the authors believe. Nevertheless, one of the principal explanations for the relatively smooth privatization programme and for the control of inflation was the signing and periodic renewal of the 'solidarity' pact, first signed in December 1987 as the *Pacto de Solidaridad Económica*, and then renamed the *Pacto de Estabilidad y Crecimiento Económico* (PECE).[45]

In order fully to understand the politics of the privatization strategy pursued by the Salinas administration, it is crucial to remember the precarious position in which Salinas found himself as he entered office in December 1988. On 14 July 1988, the official results of the presidential election that had taken place one week earlier were finally released. The official outcome of the election was that Salinas had gained 50.36 per cent of the votes, the FDN 31.12 per cent, and the right-wing party PAN just over 17 per cent. However, the election results had been delayed for seven days due to a 'breakdown' in the computer system, and there was popular feeling that the results were fraudulent.[46] The leaders of the FDN protested that they had in fact won.[47] Many peasant-based and non-party groups rallied behind the FDN and refused to accept the PRI's victory. The elections also provoked demonstrations by organized labour in support for Cárdenas. Even unions like the STRM and SME whose leaders staunchly and unambiguously supported Salinas could not prevent dissident groups from within their unions rallying behind Cárdenas. Not only did the result create the lowest victory ever recorded for the PRI,[48] but also the abstention rate was the highest (around 50 per cent), thus the actual number of voters who supported Salinas has been estimated to be between only 25 per cent and 30 per cent.[49] Moreover, for the first time, the PRI did not have the required majority in Congress to alter the Constitution.[50] Salinas himself admitted that the elections meant the end of one-party rule in Mexico.[51]

Many analysts interpreted the election results of 1988 as a sign that the old model of representation was severely declining, and that the PRI was in danger of losing its control over the political system and its legitimacy in the eyes of Mexican people.[52] According to a privately commissioned survey, nearly 60 per cent of the Mexican population believed that there had been widespread fraud during the 1988 elections, and 26 per cent thought there had been some degree of fraud.[53] In the same survey, only 18 per cent said they trusted the PRI, while 40 per cent trusted them a bit and 42 per cent did not trust them at all.[54] As has been well documented, one of the most significant novelties in the 1988 elections was the emergence of a centre-left party, the FDN, as the most significant political challenge to the PRI, replacing the right-wing PAN as the PRI's main opposition party.[55] As already mentioned,[56] in the aftermath of the 1988 elections, the PRI, in order to strengthen the party, strove to rebuild the links between the state and society which were so clearly breaking down by 1988.[57]

One of the most important sectors which had failed to back Salinas was organized labour. This was not surprising given the fall in wages and benefits, and the destruction of many unions during the previous *sexenio*.[58] Organized labour's relationship with the newly inaugurated Mexican president was strained by the fact that 30 of the 101 candidates representing the CT had failed to be elected.[59] Many workers had preferred another PRI candidate, Alfredo del Mazo, who had previously worked in the Ministry of Energy of Mines, and who was broadly perceived to be more likely to defend the state sector. More dangerous to the PRI, however, was organized labour's support for the FDN. Jonguitud Barrios, leader of the teachers' union, had promised Salinas to turn out eight million votes for the PRI but a great number of the members of Mexico's largest union defected to the FDN.[60] Moreover, one of the most powerful labour leaders, Joaquín Hernández Galicia, known as 'La Quina', head of the wealthy and influential oil workers' union, the STPRM, had dared to provide financial backing to the opposition candidate, Cárdenas. La Quina was also known to be against the restructuring and privatization of PEMEX.[61]

In view of this widespread labour dissent, the government decided to place a high priority on reforging its links with labour. This was one of the main reasons which led to the government's promotion of a reputedly new kind of union model known as '*nuevo sindicalismo*'. Salinas largely nurtured and managed the promotion of this 'new unionism' himself, and the personal style he used was comparable to the way in which he promoted his other, more wide-reaching project, PRONASOL. Both projects were implemented in a highly personalistic style designed to leapfrog over the heads of the relevant government bureaucracies and undertake the cultivation and publicity of the projects as his own. This effort to forge a new alliance between the government and sectors of the labour movement can be understood in the light of the literature which refers to the way in which the PRI strove, after 1988, to renew its clientelistic links with society. However, unlike the PRI's attempts to rekindle support from society at large, its efforts to woo organized labour were highly selective and precisely targeted. Although the rhetoric of '*nuevo sindicalismo*' claimed that *any* union could renew itself, in fact the model was difficult, if not impossible to emulate. Moreover, the PRI was more interested in cooperation with the dynamic unions which would play an important role in its future economic policies. The creation of '*nuevo sindicalismo*' had another role of at least equal importance to the one of establishing links between the state and labour. This was its contribution to smoothing out the path for privatization in Mexico.

The rhetoric of neoliberalism

> The crisis showed us that a larger state is not necessarily a stronger state; the fact that the state owns more no longer means that it is more just. The reality is that, in Mexico, the bigger the state, the less capacity the state has to respond to the social demands made upon it by our own citizens, and, in the end, this leads to the weakening of the state. While the public sector grew, the government failed to pay attention to problems such as drinking water, health, investment in rural areas and food, housing, the environment and justice. The state got bigger while welfare deteriorated.[62]
>
> (President Salinas' First Speech to the Nation, 1989)

In the official speeches made in the first three years of the Salinas administration, the president and his cabinet took pains to emphasize that neoliberal economic policies *would not violate* the principles of the Mexican Constitution of 1917. Salinas did not want to present himself at the outset as a counter-revolutionary president with his programme of industrial restructuring, 'modernization' and privatization.[63] This was partly to avoid generating resistance from the Mexican public and also to reduce criticisms from Cárdenas who attacked the privatization programme for being against the Constitution while he argued that he was the real inheritor of the Mexican revolution. The administration justified neoliberal policies using factors similar to those used by many governments world-wide which were implementing 'neoliberal' reforms, though it infused this logic with a Mexican flavour. At the most basic level, politicians argued that market forces should replace the state as the key motor of the economy. They argued that the Mexican state had become weighed down with too many inefficient parastatals, particularly throughout the 1970s. The state had become 'obese' due to the burdens of excessive financial and managerial responsibilities. Worse still, so their argument went, the state had become unable to fulfil its original and fundamental revolutionary responsibilities, and was no longer able to act on behalf of Mexicans who most needed its support, that is, the peasants, workers, small business owners and the middle class. A 'fat' state resulted in the maintenance of a *status quo* which made life comfortable for the more privileged sections in society.[64] As a consequence, opposing the modernization programme was tantamount to supporting the élite or of being anti-patriotic and even anti-revolutionary.[65]

In order to regain its health, the state must prune its excess functions, and become again 'fit' and 'slim'.[66] The trimming of excess functions would liberate new-found energy that would be directed at social pro-grammes, such as PRONASOL, which was launched by Salinas when he gave his first speech to the nation on 1 December 1988. The logic was that the state would do away with indiscriminatory state subsidies on transport, food and other basic goods, and channel its resources, via PRONASOL, to the poorest members of society. The novelty of the programme was that, since the state would reduce its paternalism, citizens would have to participate actively in, and even take responsibility in running, the social development projects.

In order to 'ease' in the introduction of neoliberal policies without incurring the opposition of society and 'statist' politicians, PRI politicians promised that the privatization programme would not violate the Mexican Constitution. Salinas stressed in 1989, during his first report to the nation as the privatization programme was accelerating, that only the 'excess' state sectors would be privatized, and the state would remain '*rector*' of the 'core' activities outlined in Article 25.[67] At the time, these included petrochemicals, radioactive mining, nuclear energy, railways, post, satellite communication and CONASUPO. However, by the end of the administration, most of the 'core' activities had been removed from Article 25 and sold, apart from the core areas of PEMEX and the railways.

Privatization was an essential component within the overall project of reducing the size of the state. Interestingly, the government was rather uncomfortable with the word *privatización*, preferring instead *desincorporación* or *enajenación*.[68] *Desincorporación* and *enajenación* both refer to the fact that enterprises are being transferred away from the state, but they do not explain where they are going. They are therefore perceived to be more neutral than the word *privatización*. The government claimed that some of the profits from privatization would be directed at PRONASOL. It also stated that privatized companies would be required to contribute to the PRONASOL project in an appropriate way (for example by providing telephones, water, electricity in deprived rural areas). This argument constituted the bud that would flower in 1992 under the name of 'Social Liberalism'.

Salinas insisted, in many of his principal speeches, including annual reports to the nation, that economic reform was bringing about political change in Mexico. Neoliberal reform in Mexico would be 'nationalistic, popular and democratic'.[69] It would be nationalistic, he stated, since it would enable the state to return to implementing policies in order to realize the ideals of the Mexican Revolution such as more equal income distribution. It would be popular and democratic, he continued, because it was being introduced via '*concertación*'. This term, by which was meant decision-making brought about by a pact made between all societal agents including citizens, organizations, parties and sectors, instead of a top–down command, became a buzzword during this *sexenio*.[70]

Organized labour was an important case in point. Privatization was not necessarily against the interests of organized labour, Salinas argued, since the government would ensure that collective contracts were respected and jobs, wherever possible, would be maintained. Moreover, he continued, workers had the option of acquiring shares in the newly privatized company, and this financial participation meant that they were participating in the ownership of the company and its 'modernization'.[71] According to the discourse, unions could take advantage of the 'modernization' of Mexico and of privatization by 'modernizing' and democratizing their unions. To give substance to this rhetoric, the telephone workers' union was promoted as the leader of a *'nuevo sindicalismo'*, and an example to the rest of the unions that privatization could be good for workers. As will be shown in this chapter and the next, the rhetoric about *'nuevo sindicalismo'* developed and unfolded over time, responding to events, rather than being defined clearly from the beginning.

Neoliberalism, labour policy and union response

Privatization is perceived generally to be against the interests of workers and trade unions, since it is often accompanied by job cuts, the 'flexibilization' of labour, and the weakening of trade union power. An important motivation behind the privatization experience in the UK was the Conservative government's ambition to curtail the power of the public sector unions. These unions, so the government believed, exploited their position as workers of monopoly industries, and, once on strike, they held the country to ransom.[72] Privatization would introduce a non-governmental management team driven by profit-maximizing objectives which would be able to take a tougher line towards unions, and implement job losses and often, wage reductions.

Privatization during the De la Madrid administration had been associated with ruthless repressive tactics by the government, as described in Chapter 3. The fate of the Aeroméxico workers in particular hung like a spectre over other unions in a similar position. Salinas' decision to retain Arsenio Farrell as Secretary of Labour, known and hated as a 'man of iron' by unions, who had also served in the same post during the past *sexenio*, showed that the new president wished to continue with a harsh policy towards labour.[73] However, Salinas had a different mandate from that of De la Madrid, which was Salinas' task to privatize huge and complex firms. He also entered office with a low level of legitimacy after the PRI had been challenged by the FDN. If labour conflicts continued to accompany every privatization, this might generate general opposition to privatization and to the government, and it would also reduce the value of firms sold and the interest of investors in Mexico.

Just as the Salinas administration attempted a limited reform of the popular sector, and used PRONASOL to rebuild support among the poor, so it also sought to promote a new kind of unionism among organized labour. Principally, the government wished to demonstrate that the restructuring and privatization of companies could be conflict-free and advantageous for workers if they agreed to cooperate with government plans. This model of *'nuevo sindicalismo'* should not be interpreted, however, as indicating a softer labour policy, and it was made clear that, if unions did not follow this model of more collaborative labour relations, they should expect no mercy. Labour policy adopted by the government during the Salinas *sexenio* was one of sharp contrasts: the carrots were quite rewarding but the sticks were large. The president's careful, personal nurturing of relations with the STRM, and at times, his sugary praise of its leaders, stood in stark contrast to the raid and imprisonment of La Quina and the forced resignation of Jonguitud Barrios, head of the teachers' union in the first few months of his administration.

Though the government's treatment of the STPRM leaders in January 1989 was justified on the grounds of the leaders' corruption, it was clearly motivated by wishes to cut the labour force, reduce the power of the union, and facilitate the government's plan to privatize secondary petrochemical products which PEMEX controlled. It was also motivated by political and personal reasons, and the events in this month resulted partly from the culmination of a private vendetta between La Quina and Salinas. In 1984, as Secretary of Planning and Budgeting, Salinas had reduced the STPRM's power by cutting from 50 to 2 per cent the union's automatic quota of the construction contracts received by PEMEX. La Quina had responded by criticizing Salinas, both for his policies and also in personal terms. Later, when Salinas was announced as the PRI candidate, La Quina waited 15 days before voicing his support.[74] La Quina had also spoken out against privatization of PEMEX and threatened a strike if the new president attempted to carry this out.[75]

In a pre-dawn raid, the maverick leader and some of his union cronies were arrested. La Quina was imprisoned under charges of illegal possession of arms, and, a few days later, he was accused of involvement in homicide.[76] The justification of this government aggression that the union was being 'cleansed' rang hollow, since one *cacique* was forcibly removed and another, more amenable to job cuts and privatization, was imposed in his place.[77] The government's action became immediately known in popular parlance as the *'quinazo'.*[78] Such labour policy was in effect nothing less than a return to *charrazo* policies of the 1940s, although this time it was a *charrazo* of the *charro par excellence*. On 19

January, the Labour Secretary announced the appointment of a new leader for the union, Sebastián Guzmán Cabrera, a friend of the president, even though this violated the union statutes.[79] Under this new pliable leadership, the government would find it easier to implement organizational changes in PEMEX, dividing it into several subsidiary enterprises, making significant modifications to the labour contract and introducing massive job cuts.[80] The government gained international credit and, on 13 January 1989, George Bush, president-elect of the United States, praised Salinas for his brave measures to fight union 'corruption'.[81]

Another demonstration of the government's labour policy whereby it secured the changes it desired – though this time the changes were connected not to privatization but to decentralization – came in April 1989, when, taking advantage of rank and file dissidence within the teachers' union, the government engineered the replacement of Carlos Jonguitud Barrios, leader of the teachers' union, the SNTE, since 1972, by Elba Esther Gordillo Morales.[82] The new union secretary-general[83] later facilitated the government's scheme to decentralize the public education system, long resisted by Jonguitud Barrios, since it implied a weakening of the national union's bargaining power by forcing individual union branches to negotiate directly with state governments over wages and working conditions.[84]

Organized labour has been accused of being a heavy and inert body throughout the 1980s, since it continued to follow traditional methods of negotiating with the government and offered little effective resistance to government policy. However, this resistance to change constituted organized labour's last vestige of strength since it managed to prevent the reform of the LFT during both *sexenios* of De la Madrid and Salinas. Since the signing of the PSE, the debate about the need to reform this law had become more urgent.[85]

One of the ways in which neoliberal reform could be implemented peacefully, and in one fell swoop, would have been to obtain a nation-wide agreement with labour leaders about the reform of the LFT. Business groups and associations such as the *Confederación Patronal de la República Mexicana* (COPARMEX) pressurized the government to push this reform through.[86] However, CTM leader, Fidel Velázquez, actively blocked any reform, and the labour movement was divided on the issue. Instead of bringing about a nation-wide reform, the Salinas administration thus was forced to modify thousands of collective contracts on an individual basis. Finally, in the last year of Salinas' *sexenio*, when the PRI looked again to organized labour for support, the momentum of reform faded.

The birth of the STRM's 'new unionism'

At the same time that the Salinas administration was inflicting *charrazos* on the oilworkers' union and the teachers' union, the president was encouraging an entirely different relationship with what was becoming his 'pet' union, the STRM. On the one hand, the government resorted to a form of illegal crude repression to remove entrenched union leaders from their posts, and replace them with new more amenable leaders. On the other hand, the government, rather ironically, spoke of 'modernization', privatization and the prospects for a progressive, modern union democracy.

The telephone workers' union was selected by the government to lead this 'new unionism'. The president had already had direct dealings with Hernández Juárez in his capacity as Secretary of Planning and Budgeting during the previous *sexenio*, and it was clear that, since they had clashed during the 1984 strike, the labour leader had controlled the union well and had generally avoided strikes. Since this year, Hernández Juárez had moved gradually towards a more moderate political position, culminating in 1987 when he swore allegiance to the PRI and became the president of the CT. Salinas found in Hernández Juárez a new-generation labour leader, young, relatively well educated and intelligent, and who had already shown his malleability in the face of flattery and power.

The president wished to use the STRM as a positive example of how workers and unions could benefit from restructuring, 'modernization' and privatization if they cooperated with government plans. So-called 'new unionism' marked a departure from the existing types of unions in Mexico. 'New unionism' referred to a model of a union that would consider proposals to introduce greater labour flexibility or higher worker productivity, instead of opposing any kind of change, as the unions of Aeroméxico and Cananea had. This did not mean that they would be passive in the face of restructuring. They were not to become so-called 'white unions', due to their close ties with their companies, as many unions had been known in Monterrey. These white unions accepted the principle of reducing the workforce, and changes and industrial restructuring were adopted unilaterally without the participation of the unions.[87] A 'new union' would approach collective bargaining in a conciliatory and cooperative way, accepting demands for increased labour flexibilization and the introduction of new norms regarding productivity and changes to the workforce. At the same time, the union would seek to maximize advantages during the negotiations, and would actively propose alternative plans, better suited to the union, rather than reject outright management's suggestions. The principal way in which this was to be demonstrated was through the successful and non-conflictive modification of the telephone workers' collective contract. This would provide a model which other unions could emulate. It might even be a precedent for an attempt to modify the LFT itself in terms of introducing worker flexibility and productivity targets into the workplace. Hernández Juárez was outspoken on the issue of the need to the reform the LFT.[88]

The way in which the STRM came to represent the model of *'nuevo sindicalismo'* was through the signing, in April 1989, of its modified collective contract, which opened the way for a radical restructuring and later for the privatization of TELMEX. By the time Salinas came to power, the union leader had accepted implicitly that TELMEX was to be privatized by accepting management's estimate that TELMEX needed an investment of at least US$14 billion and that this would not come from state funds.[89] However, he avoided continually the topic of privatization when speaking with the STRM rank and file and the press. In February, the union leader called a meeting of STRM delegates and announced that, although renewal of their collective contract was not due for another year, it would be renewed under special circumstances within two months and that this would be the most important labour negotiation in the history of the union.[90] He promised that there would be no job losses as a result of the agreement if the negotiations were carried out without conflict. His approach was completely pragmatic and conservative: he claimed that in the end what was important was jobs and workers' rights, and not union rhetoric about its independence, autonomy or nationalism. He did not discuss privatization in connection with the contract. He also told the workers that the union had been selected by President Salinas to negotiate this new labour contract without conflicts in order to demonstrate to the rest of the labour movement that this was possible.[91]

At the end of February, increasingly intense negotiations began behind closed doors between the STRM's negotiating team and TELMEX management. Hernández Juárez avoided conversations with journalists about the content of negotiations and denied that privatization was being discussed, while he stressed that he was trying to avoid job losses. The STRM put into practice its *'nuevo sindicalismo'* by presenting to management a sophisticated negotiating team, which, instead of rejecting changes, proposed alternatives to the changes planned by management, which were more in the interests of the union.

Negotiating a 'flexible' collective contract

In February 1989, a national forum on Communications and Transport was held in order to analyse the state of the country's communications network, and one of the main issues under discussion was whether TELMEX should be privatized. The presidents of the *Confederación de Camaras Industriales* (CONCAMIN) and the CANACINTRA, and the Subsecretary of the General Controller of the Federation, Enrique del Val, pushed for the privatization of TELMEX. The STRM was attacked by Bortoni, president of CONCAMIN, for being an obstacle to TELMEX's performance.[92] The forum was concluded by the Secretary of Communications and Transport, Caso Lombardo, who emphasized the desperate need for private investment in TELMEX, and for an urgent renewal and 'modernization' of the labour contract.[93] Early in March 1989, the government finally took the decision in private that TELMEX would be privatized, and it renewed pressure on management to modify the STRM labour contract.

As early as October 1988, the STPS had sent an internal message to the TELMEX board instructing them urgently to renew the labour contract of the STRM.[94] Negotiations between management and the union were slow at first and eventually came unstuck during the first two months of 1989. Union leaders accused management of not informing the union about future plans for the 14 000 operators who would be affected by digitalization, nor of advising the union about its plans to introduce new technology, as it had promised in the 1988 collective contract.[95]

Management had three main objectives during its negotiation with the union of the labour contract revision.[96] First, it wanted to make the labour force more 'flexible'. In the existing collective contract there was a vast and complex hierarchy of job descriptions (there were 585 different job descriptions and salary bands) which made moving a worker from one job to another, or from one work centre to another, an extremely complicated and conflictive task. Principally, management wanted to reduce the job description categories so that these rigidities could be removed. Second, it wanted to simplify and centralize the process of collective bargaining. At the time, collective bargaining was conducted at two levels. The main negotiation related to the labour contract. This was carried out at the national level between union leaders, TELMEX's Director of Labour Relations and the STPS every two years. In addition, there were 57 other *convenios* which had to be negotiated between management and a particular sub-group of workers at the regional and workcentre level.[97]

Until the late 1980s, the advantages of the *convenio* had outweighed its disadvantages for management. Management had found that it was easier and quicker to negotiate the introduction of new equipment at a local level with a particular department than by negotiating this in the central labour contract. These individual *convenios* undermined the power of union leaders since not all negotiations were centralized in the collective contract. Moreover, *convenios* exacerbated differences of interest within the union, since it was unlikely that the entire union would support the demands of a small department. The disadvantage of the *convenios* for management was that different departments vied to pact a better agreement than the one most recently signed, and this became a vicious circle for management.[98] In addition, the negotiation of a *convenio* could take anything from a few months to a few years and bargaining was a protracted, messy and decentralized process. Management came to the conclusion that the only way in which new technology could be negotiated with the union was through a centralization of collective bargaining.[99] Management's third objective therefore was the complete withdrawal of the union's privileges which had been included in the labour contracts in 1986 and 1988 regarding their right to access information about plans to introduce new technology and restructuring the company.[100] Quite simply, management wanted the monopoly over administrative control, and resented the union's attempts to become more involved which it saw as an amateur effort to co-manage TELMEX.[101] If the union accepted management's conditions, management promised it would not make redundancies.

By early March, union leaders had agreed to centralize collective bargaining and to simplify the job descriptions.[102] However, the union refused to accept the loss of its rights to be involved in the introduction of new technology and restructuring of the company.[103] Since management's demands had not been accepted, management stated that it could no longer guarantee there would be no job cuts. On 21 March, TELMEX's director, the Secretary of Labour, the Secretary of Communications and the union leader met in an attempt to resolve this conflict.[104] No agreement was reached, and the following day management announced that it was cancelling all the agreements achieved so far, and warned that redundancies would be necessary, without mentioning how many.[105] In order to provoke further the union leaders, it sacked three STRM regional union leaders.[106] By 24 March, negotiations had been totally suspended.

In response to the deadlock, the STRM's Commission of Modernization speedily drew up an alternative plan. The main implications of their proposal were that they were prepared to accept most of management's demands, but they flatly refused to accept job cuts. They proposed a novel scheme whereby the *convenios* would be replaced by so-called *perfiles de puestos*. This would allow management to obtain much greater degrees of labour flexibilization and mobilization, while at the same time, the commission argued, the simplification of job descriptions would not reduce workers' rights.[107] The *perfiles de puestos* would be included in the main collective contract, thus collective bargaining would be centralized. It would become much easier for management to move workers around in different departments, areas or even states. The union requested only that management give the union notice in the event that it required a worker to move, and that suitable training would be provided for that worker. Second, albeit very reluctantly, the leaders acknowledged they would accept the withdrawal of some of the clauses recently gained which guaranteed their right to be involved in the introduction of new technology. The Commission of Modernization presented their proposal at an extraordinary assembly attended by 3000 union delegates, and the majority voted to support it.[108] Once the union leaders' proposal had been accepted by delegates, they presented it to management. The fact that the STRM had backed down on almost all their demands when job losses were threatened was pleasing for management. By 4 April, TELMEX and the STRM were almost ready to sign an agreement. The next week, the majority of telephone workers throughout Mexico voted to accept. Finally, on 14 April, the new labour contract was signed by management, government representatives and union leaders. The principal aims of the *convenio* were declared jointly by management and union to be the restructuring of TELMEX, including the digitalization of the network, without redundancies or a loss of union rights.[109]

One of the outcomes of the *convenio* was that it became easier for management to substitute absent workers with other workers.[110] It also became easier to move workers from one work centre to another, or from one state to another. Thus the union lost considerable power over its control of labour flexibility and mobility. Previously, no worker could be moved without the permission of both management and union. After April 1989, however, a worker was obliged to move once management required this, and if that worker did not want to move, the union was responsible for finding a suitable replacement who would move.[111] Collective bargaining would be conducted as a single, centralized and simplified negotiation for the entire workforce.

The union lost its newly acquired right to participate and intervene in modernization programmes and the introduction of new equipment, and the Mixed Commission of New Technology, which had been created to permit discussion between government officials, management and the union, was disbanded. Management thus reasserted its monopoly over the issue of new technology,[112] and was obliged to inform the union if it was going to implement modernization and new technology only when it considered that training would be needed to support the planned change. In this case, it agreed that it would pass on the information to the Mixed Committee for Training. The latter suffered a setback as the original plan to have training teams in every workplace was replaced by one which restricted them to only the capital and 17 regional centres.[113] Moreover, *personal de confianza* would be responsible for designating and supervising the training which was deemed appropriate by management, and not by unionized workers as union leaders had demanded. The other Mixed Commissions would continue to function. Finally, TELMEX workers were granted a 12 per cent wage increase plus 3 per cent in benefits.

Although the STRM collective contract was considerably weakened in April 1989, it was nevertheless not as severely weakened as were most other labour contracts undergoing modification at the time. Many had been drastically diluted, if not completely rewritten to the requirements of management, and there had been significant numbers of redundancies. So, the STRM had shown that it was possible to modify – without conflict – a labour contract which would make the workforce more suitable for the needs of restructuring (and later, privatization). This had been accomplished without job losses. Furthermore, the union had participated actively in the negotiation of the labour contract, in particular, by designing alternatives to management plans, which had been accepted in the overall agreement, namely the STRM Commission of Modernization's design of the *perfiles de puestos*. For many analysts, this was something new in Mexico, and they believed the STRM represented the vanguard of 'new unionism' in Mexico.[114] Certain analysts were convinced that the negotiations were 'bilateral', that is, that the union was participating in a way which was on a par with management.[115] Others expected that the signing of the so-called 'modernization agreement' was the beginning of a more peaceful way of collective bargaining, which could be used as a model for future changes in labour law on a national scale.[116]

A new conciliatory model for labour relations?

After the new labour contract was signed, Salinas repeatedly cited the agreement as a new model which unions must emulate as their companies were restructured,[117] and he claimed that the growth of participation by unions was bringing about greater industrial democracy in Mexico.[118] Hernández Juárez echoed precisely the same principle by claiming that a new stage in labour relations had been reached, and in his numerous speeches to the press he addressed the president indirectly by sending him messages that he should consider this a new stage in labour relations, which would represent a model to be emulated in the solution of other labour negotiations.[119] Hernández Juárez had accomplished his 'mission' and by leading the telephone workers' union throughout the negotiations, he gained authority to advise other unions on how to respond to the challenges of restructuring and privatization. Journalists, trade unionists and other observers regarded Hernández Juárez universally as the leader of 'new unionism'.

To celebrate the agreement, STRM leaders and TELMEX executives met the president in Los Pinos. Salinas lavished praise on the union leadership, calling it mature and talented, and he congratulated Hernández Juárez in particular for being an exceptional labour leader who understood the way in which the world economy was changing, and the way in which Mexico had to adapt.[120] TELMEX executives looked on rather perplexed when Salinas started to hug Hernández Juárez and called him '*mi viejo amigo, Pancho*'.[121] Salinas stated that the pact was a precedent in attaining agreement pacifically (through *concertación*) and said that the relationship between the state and workers had been restrengthened.[122]

The experience of the STRM in 1989 was presented as a model to be emulated by all other unions. However, I argue that this model was extremely difficult, if not impossible, to replicate with the same degree of success in other cases. The key to the lack of conflict had been the guarantee that there would be no redundancies. Both management and the Secretary of Labour had wished to dismiss workers, but had been persuaded by the president and the Secretary of Communications to avoid this.[123] Since telecommunications was such a dynamic sector with a huge growth potential, management was forced to accept that it could afford to keep and retrain the entire workforce.[124] The crucial role of TELMEX in the privatization process ensured that the president intervened to facilitate a smooth contract renewal.

The first major union to follow this 'model' set by the STRM was the SME. Like the STRM, the SME was a dynamic union and had a reputation for being more democratic than most unions.[125] From 1984, the management of the *Compañía de Luz y Fuerza* had tried to introduce the 'flexibilization' of labour into the collective contract while attempting to reduce the power of the union in the running of work centres.[126] The response of the SME had been continually to resist any changes, but finally, in March 1989, it agreed to cooperate with management plans and allow more 'flexibilization' of labour. In exchange management withdrew its plan to merge the SME with the SUTERM. Shortly afterwards, in 1990, the SME proposed the creation of two joint consultative committees, comprising members of the union, management and the STPS, to discuss and resolve new problems brought about by the changes including the introduction of productivity targets. Management accepted this proposal in 1990.

Thus by 1990, the STRM and SME provided the two blueprints as the main references of a so-called '*nuevo sindicalismo*'. At the time, it was not clear how influential this model would become for labour relations, and whether it was applicable to other cases or whether it might prove to be an anomaly. Simultaneously, the path towards the privatization of TELMEX, and the 'second round' of sales, had been partly cleared.

The strategies used by the Mexican government towards the STRM in order to facilitate the negotiation of a 'new' kind of labour contract in 1989 actually bore many resemblances with labour policy in past *sexenios*. First, there was an overt exchange of rewards from the president to the union leaders for their political support. Two days after the agreement was signed, Salinas inaugurated an extension of STRM headquarters in Parque Vía which doubled its original size. Union leaders were rewarded financially. One piece of evidence was the dramatic upgrading of the union magazine *Restaurador*, which, after April 1989, was transformed from a black and white, simple production to a glossy one complete with graphic design and colour. The production team doubled from five in April 1989 to ten in November 1989.[127]

Hernández Juárez was also rewarded personally by Salinas. His prize was the presidential nod to go ahead with the establishment and leadership of a new labour confederation.[128] A group of unions, including the SME, the pilots' and cinema workers' unions met in July 1989. They called themselves – rather ironically in the light of the privatization programme which was to follow months later – the *Federación de Sindicatos del Sector Público*. Although, from the beginning, this federation stated it would remain in the CT, it was perceived as a rival by Fidel Velázquez, leader of the CTM and 'moral' leader of the CT. The career of Hernández Juárez as Mexico's 'modern' labour leader was launched, and he was used by Salinas to accompany him on trips abroad in the negotiation of the

NAFTA. In journals and magazines, Hernández Juárez was cited as being Mexico's new, modern trade union leader who understood productivity, the need for labour flexibility, competition and cooperation with management.[129] Salinas' conferment on Hernández Juárez of the right to establish a new labour confederation was a clear move to provoke Velázquez and to divide and weaken the labour movement by creating rivalry. Despite the rhetoric of the 'newness' of this model of labour relations, there was nothing new in the way in which the party interacted with the union; in other words, the mechanisms of corporatism and clientelism were perfectly compatible with the so-called 'modernization' of the labour contract.

However, if there were no great changes at the level of government–union relations, there were consequences for the democracy within the union. The negotiation of the new labour contract was conducted without significant conflict. Since the STRM leaders were in favour of this, their cooperation with the government and management came as no surprise. However, there was also little protest from the rank and file. One of the more interesting changes within the union during this period was that there was a significant shift in the location and balance of power. First, the influence of the *'comisionados'* grew to the extent that they totally dominated the elected union representatives. Second, the gap between rank and file and those in control of the union widened considerably. Usually, when the STRM collective contract was negotiated the entire CEN team, around 40 elected representatives, were involved in the decision-making process, and finally, the entire team became the union's official signatories.[130]

In contrast, the renewal of the labour contract in 1989 was 'voluntary' – it was not due for renewal in 1989 – and different rules were followed during the negotiations. The elected CEN was excluded from the negotiation of the contract, and the recently formed Commission of Modernization, which comprised union representatives selected by the union leader, was solely responsible for conducting talks with the government and management. Little of the contents of the talks was passed on to telephone workers or to the press. When the contract was signed, only six union signatories were present, and these included Hernández Juárez and five of his *comisionados*.[131] Decision-making in the union became centralized, more controlled by the union leader and less democratic. In centralizing decision-making, union leaders were also pleasing management, since management had requested at the beginning of 1988 that decision-making be centralized.[132]

In theory, the creation of commissions within the union to discuss many of the new issues and problems brought about by restructuring, and the formation of teams charged with meeting management and government officials, could have led to a greater degree of worker participation at the level of national union strategy since new posts of responsibility were established in the union. In the literature on industrial democracy, the presence of mixed committees is generally accepted as a key indicator of industrial democracy.[133] During the 1980s, the STRM increased the union's role in negotiations with management through committees, although this increase was not lineal, and there was a loss of power in April 1989. Paradoxically, however, the growth of joint consultative committees resulted in a decline in worker participation in the union. The final outcome, therefore, was the emergence of a new hierarchical power structure imposed on top of the existing power structure (whose democratic possibilities were already compromised by the system of *comisionados*). Thus the net effect of the creation of joint consultative commissions was to remove the last vestiges of power enjoyed by elected union members. By April 1989, control by the *comisionados* had been consolidated over the union. Opportunities of increasing worker participation at the national level of union strategy had been eliminated. This shift of power was the most important and enduring reason which isolated rank and file from those in control of the union.

Another reason for the telephone workers' complicity with the '*convenio*' was that the environment around them was in general hostile to organized labour, and they were well aware that they were receiving presidential protection. Many of the workers, even active opponents of Hernández Juárez, were genuinely proud or excited about the fact that they had been chosen to show an example to the nation.[134] The alternative was the prospect of redundancies, and, throughout the negotiations, telephone workers mobilized primarily in defence of their jobs.[135] Furthermore, their cooperation with the negotiations was encouraged by management's policy of dismissing workers who tried to disrupt the negotiations and at least 200 workers were fired between February and April 1989.[136] The elimination of '*convenios*' and the centralization of collective bargaining also meant a concentration of power in the union leaders, and less autonomy on the part of local leaders.

I discuss more fully the impact on worker participation at the shop-floor level in the Appendix where survey results on shop-floor politics are analysed. However, an indicator that worker participation did not increase at the lower level is that, in accordance with a stipulation of the *'convenio'*, a so-called 'improvement plan' was implemented in work centres of 56 cities which covered 80 per cent of TELMEX's network. In reality, this 'improvement plan' was a euphemism for increased supervision of workers by around 900 bureaucrats[137] and its principal function was to prevent telephone workers from organizing in protest at the new labour contract.

Conclusion

At the beginning of the Salinas administration, the government strove to promote a 'new unionism' for two main reasons. The first, largely political in intent, was to improve state–labour relations which proved to have deteriorated significantly by the 1988 elections. The second, which had an underlying financial rationale, was to try to encourage unions to cooperate with the government's policy of privatization. The STRM was central to this government policy. This chapter analysed the origins of 'new unionism' and showed that there were certain characteristics about the alliance between the principal actors which made 'new unionism' possible. In Mexico, the 'new unionism' of the 1980s was born thanks to a series of creative and opportunistic agreements and exchanges between government, management and union officials. This kind of labour relations would seem to resemble more closely the traditional mechanisms of corporatism rather than signifying a breakdown of the logic of corporatism which some labour analysts had predicted would be the outcome of the introduction of modern labour practices and neoliberal economic reform. This question is more fully examined in the next chapter in the light of the way that 'new unionism' developed.

5
Privatizing TELMEX and Crafting a 'New Unionism'

According to analysts such as Rubio, Baer, Bizberg and Berins Collier, economic liberalization was fundamentally incompatible with the functioning of the historical pact between the state and labour in Mexico, principally because the corporate system was unsustainable in an era of competition and free markets.[1] Moreover, they claimed that the tradition whereby the government gave unions rewards in exchange for their political support was incompatible with a new regime of international competitiveness and free markets. In this chapter it is argued that the analysis of the privatization of TELMEX and the forging of a *'nuevo sindicalismo'* challenges these analysts' views in two main ways.

First, while it is undeniable that organized labour *in general* became much weaker vis-à-vis the state during the 1980s and 1990s (in terms of the number of unionized workers, the decline in working conditions, the dramatic drop in salaries, and the decreasing influence of the CTM in negotiations with the government), *certain sectors of organized labour were much more severely affected than others.* Even when Teichman argued, rather abruptly, that during the 1980s, the Mexican government decided to reorganize the political base of its coalition by shedding those elements it deemed less important – namely labour and small business – and replacing them with large business, she qualified her argument by admitting that the government had tried to renew its alliances with specific sectors of the labour movement, principally with the workers of the telecommunications and electricity sectors.[2] However, it is crucial to remember that 'organized labour' – and the economy – should not be analysed as homogeneous blocs. Instead, organized labour should be analysed as a heterogeneous body composed of many different kinds of unions and labour confederations each with distinct organizational characteristics. Each union is tied to a sector of the economy which may be dynamic or in decline, and which may be profitable or loss-making. Other important considerations when analysing unions are whether the industry or service with which they are associated is large or small and whether it is capital-intensive or labour-intensive. A particularly important question post-1982, is whether that sector is exposed to or protected from international competition.

There were many occasions during the Salinas administration when the government decided to discard labour by literally closing down industries, for example, in the mining or manufacturing sectors. At the same time, however, the government strove to renew its relationship with an 'élite' of unions, attached to the dynamic and profitable sectors, whose development was central to Mexico's insertion into the world economy. The central point here is that there was not *one* set of labour policies implemented by the government as a result of economic liberalizations as the analysts cited above suggested. Rather, the government's labour policies were discriminatory, and varied according to the kind of industrial sector and union in question. This argument insists that there is a connection between economic and political factors, but one which is more complex and less deterministic than that proposed by the analysts mentioned at the beginning of this chapter. The government's policy towards the STRM during the Salinas *sexenio*, as discussed in this chapter, was the prototypical example of an attempt to reforge links between the state and an élite labour organization.

Second, influenced by rent-seeking theory, these analysts argued that economic liberalization was inherently incompatible with the state–labour corporatist relationship.[3] The results of this research reject their argument. Instead, they concur with those analysts who found that, in many cases, economic liberalization and privatization generated *new* sources of finance which could be used to lubricate corporatist relations.[4] In contrast to Baer's claim that economic liberalization would mean that unions would become less dependent on favours and hand-outs from the state, this research shows that deals and transactions were commonplace during privatization.

In this chapter it is argued that the emergence of a *'nuevo sindicalismo'* must be understood in parallel with the privatization of TELMEX, since privatization generated key resources and opportunities which made the construction of this 'new unionism' possible. In order to do this, the major developments of the privatization of TELMEX are analysed, starting from September 1989, when the Mexican government announced officially that TELMEX was to be privatized, through 1989–90, when the government implemented reforms to prepare the company for the sale, to December 1990, when the controlling share was sold to the Grupo Carso. The evolution of *'nuevo sindicalismo'* is examined as it manifested itself in two principal stages. First, after TELMEX was privatized, Salinas pronounced that the STRM was the official leader of the movement. Second, in order to promote this 'new' kind of unionism to other unions, Salinas gave Hernández Juárez permission to establish a new labour federation, the FESEBES. Government officials and STRM leaders touted both organizations as a break with the old state–labour alliance, and as the embodiment of a new state–labour relationship. The final section of this chapter questions to what extent this relationship was actually new, and evaluates its significance for the historical state–labour relationship in general.

Negotiating and announcing the sale of TELMEX

In order for TELMEX to be privatized smoothly, with minimal conflicts, it was important that the major interests – government officials, TELMEX management, business groups, the general public, and the union – all agreed on the conditions of the sale. The government sought to ensure that the union supported the sale so that the privatization would be carried out without labour conflict. The government also considered that, in order to promote a 'new' unionism which accepted the 'challenges' of restructuring the workforce and privatizing the company, it was crucial that TELMEX was privatized with the cooperation and support of STRM leaders. Once this was achieved, a *'nuevo sindicalismo'* could be held up as the model for all other unions to emulate. In the following section, the ways in which the various interests were encouraged to cooperate with privatization are analysed.

Convincing the public

As argued in the previous chapter, TELMEX was a good candidate to launch the second round of privatization since its sale would be unlikely to rouse nationalistic passions. Moreover, the public were dissatisfied with its service and some believed that privatization would make the company more efficient. In practice, opposition from Mexican society to its privatization proved to be weak. Salinas justified the privatization programme in general by claiming that the state needed to eliminate inefficient and loss-making companies so that they could again become efficient and effective. Those who opposed the sale of TELMEX, including Fidel Velázquez, rightly pointed out that it had never been a drain on state resources; indeed, the government had used it as an important source of revenue since the 1970s.[5] Salinas overrode this objection by using a different logic which appealed to social conscience and business pragmatism, and which he had used on other occasions, for example when he had justified the sale of Mexicana airlines.[6] He claimed:

> Gentlemen, the ten billion dollars that I have, which would satisfy TELMEX's investment needs, would also be adequate to modernize the education system across the country. I want to make it perfectly clear that I would prefer to dedicate the money to the latter project, knowing that TELMEX will not go short of money since there are many interested in investing in the company.[7]

This argument was echoed by Hernández Juárez when asked by the press why he had agreed to the privatization. Increasingly, he became a spokesman for the government by wholeheartedly embracing and repeating the rhetoric about the reform of the state. The government and union officials also sought to bring about a consensus about the privatization by insisting that the government would not abandon telecommunications to the free market but would design an effective regulatory framework. Though privatization was ostensibly a means of making TELMEX more competitive in the international arena, the promise of state protection suggested a degree of immunity from the chill of international competition.

Forging a business consensus

It proved relatively easy for TELMEX management and the private sector to arrive at a consensus, since all were broadly in favour of privatization and the main debates centred around the speed and price at which TELMEX should be sold, and the question of how much of the government's share should be sold. After April 1989, once the *Convenio de Modernización* had been settled, government officials and TELMEX executives started to negotiate intensely about the terms of the TELMEX privatization,[8] although all such discussions were firmly denied in public. Internal documents show that the government had three main objectives which were: to extract the maximum revenue by selling some of its TELMEX stock; to ensure that foreigners with knowledge of telecommunications technology would be among the buyers;

and to retain a controlling stake for itself. Of the three points, only the last was not realized.[9] Another of the government's aims was to ensure that the team which would control TELMEX would comprise Mexican citizens. This was a general aim of the government during the privatization period and 98 per cent of the public enterprises sold between 1987 and 1991 ended up being controlled by Mexicans.[10]

During the summer of 1989, pressure to privatize the company was mounted on the government by the private sector, including the director of the *Cámara Nacional de la Industría Electrónica y de Comunicaciones Electricas*, Eduardo Guajardo, and in particular, the TELMEX board itself.[11] TELMEX's General Director complained that all of TELMEX's plans regarding the construction of an Integrated Services Digital Network (ISDN) for Mexico's eight major cities[12] and entry to the mobile telephones market were being held back by government indecision.[13] By September, the conditions for the sale of the controlling stock in TELMEX were prepared.

By hook or by crook: 'persuading' the STRM

As could be expected, it proved more difficult to persuade STRM's rank and file to cooperate with – or at least not oppose – the privatization of TELMEX. The cooperation of the STRM was important not only to facilitate a sale without labour problems. If the rank and file could be brought around to cooperating with the privatization, the government could use their example in order to promote the 'new' unionism which they claimed was emerging in Mexico. The rank and file finally consented to privatization after union leaders, management and the government took a joint series of measures during 1989 and 1990. These measures were of two types. On the one hand, management, supported by union leaders, took a repressive attitude in the face of resistance from the rank and file to privatization. On the other hand, the government offered the union a range of sweeteners in order to make privatization as palatable as possible.

One of the clauses of the labour contract signed in April 1989 was that a so-called '45-day improvement plan' would be implemented in TELMEX work centres in 56 cities where 80 per cent of the country's lines were concentrated. The stated objectives of the plan were to increase performance targets in 20 different areas of the service, such as the minimum time within which operators had to answer calls from the public and the minimum repair time for residential and business telephones. It was demonstrated in Chapter 3 that, after a decade of stagnancy, labour productivity started to improve in 1988 and the improvement continued during 1989. The most probable reason for the improvement was the implementation of this plan.

However, there was another dimension to the programme which was to prevent potential opposition from the rank and file to the recently signed labour contract or to privatization of TELMEX during the tense period leading up to the official announcement.[14] During the implementation, workers were supervised by an unprecedented number of inspectors from the SCT.[15] Although it was first decided that the improvement plan would be implemented for only 45 days, it was later decided to extend it over the entire six-month period leading up to the privatization of TELMEX. Under its rules, workers were forbidden to hold meetings during work hours and those who resisted, or who demonstrated opposition to privatization, were fired. In the six-month period, some 200 were sacked, including 20 STRM delegates and local leaders who had challenged both the privatization and Hernández Juárez's overall strategy.[16] Hernández Juárez was entirely unsympathetic with these disillusioned telephone workers and he repeatedly warned them that they would be sacked if they did not cooperate.[17] In interviews with the press, he showed an overtly pro-government and pro-management stance by stating that, in most cases, the sackings had been deserved.[18] In an article written for the union magazine, the leader warned workers to comply with the plan, or else, in his typical 'union-speak' style of discourse, they would be in danger of 'crossing the line'.[19]

This hard-line approach by management and union leaders soon generated anger among many workers who complained that they were working under conditions similar to a *requisa*.[20] Banned from holding meetings, telephone workers soon found minor ways to transgress. One of the 'rules of the game' of the union was that, in the case that a union member had a problem or query, he/she must first approach the immediate union representative superior for advice. Only in the last resort, if union supervisors failed to solve the problem, could a *personal de confianza* consulted.[21] Workers started to defy the union by seeking help from *personal de confianza*, instead of their STRM superiors. Some also refused to attend union assemblies which were obligatory. During this period, however, there was no strong united opposition. This was partly because of the government's extremely hostile policies towards many unions in the rest of the country, evidenced in the way the workers of Cananea and Ford had been treated. Nevertheless, if the telephone workers were not entirely happy with their lot, they knew that they were among the most privileged unions in the country.[22] In addition, the opposition to Hernández Juárez was divided, and when elections were held to vote for a new CEN in 1990, many newly formed groups including the blue, white, transparent and gold groups, challenged his green plan. But these groups did not unify to challenge him at the national level.[23] One of the reasons for the opposition's lack of coordination was the dearth of information that workers received. Many complained that there was a veil of secrecy surrounding the privatization negotiations as well as an increased concentration of power within the union which frustrated effective worker organization.[24]

Until August, Hernández Juárez continually skirted around the issue of privatization in public and in the press, neither embracing nor opposing it, but instead repeatedly referring to Salinas' promise that the state would remain *rector* of telecommunications.[25] As rumours of the imminent announcement of TELMEX's privatization gained strength in August, he took a more overtly pro-privatization stance. He then attempted, during various assemblies, to convince union delegates that privatization would be advantageous for the workers. This did not prove easy, and the bad-tempered leader walked out of assemblies since the majority of representatives did not favour privatization.[26] By mid-September, still without a pro-privatization consensus, Hernández Juárez decided to hold a referendum throughout the union. The referendum was skilfully designed to avoid giving the workers a real choice. If the referendum had enquired whether workers did or did not support the privatization of TELMEX, it was likely that the response would have been negative. Instead, the question put to the workers was, in the event that TELMEX was to be privatized, were the workers in favour of taking a share in the capital of the privatized company and of keeping their collective contract.[27] The referendum was a perfect example of Pateman's pseudo-participation.[28] Rather unsurprisingly, the workers voted in the affirmative.[29]

Salinas took an unusual step when he personally announced the privatization of TELMEX to the telephone workers at their annual convention in September 1989 before the financial community or general public had been informed.[30] He softened the blow by wrapping it up with six promises, the most important one for the telephone workers being that their labour rights would be respected, they would all be able to keep their jobs, and they would all be rewarded with shares of the newly privatized company.[31] Salinas also promised that the state would remain '*rector*' of telecommunications, and that the new controller of TELMEX would be a Mexican. In addition, state regulation would ensure that the telephone service would improve dramatically and that scientific and technological research would be strengthened.[32] Those present at the assembly were clearly delighted by this news and gave the president a standing ovation every time he mentioned his promises.[33] Even long-standing union dissidents could not help but feel euphoric with the attention showered on them.[34] Afterwards, Hernández Juárez declared that the union would try to find the funds necessary to buy 12.5 per cent of TELMEX's capital, which was valued at US$350 million, which would ensure that the union had representatives on the board.[35]

The way that the president flattered the telephone workers contrasted profoundly with the way in which the government was treating other unions in the same period. In August, miners at Cananea had rejected management plans to change their labour contract drastically, and after going on strike, they had been informed that Cananea was bankrupt and that all 3000 of them had been sacked. A similar experience had been shared by the workers at the steel plant Lázaro Cárdenas-Las Truchas (Sicartsa) when all 5400 were sacked in September 1989. Labour relations at Ford's plant in Cuautitlán had not improved much since they had lost many labour rights and had their wages cut in 1987,[36] and in January 1990, one worker was killed and nine were injured when gangs of CTM strike-breakers forced an entry into the plant to oust the dissident workers.[37]

On 20 September 1989, Caso Lombardo, accompanied by Hernández Juárez, announced the terms under which TELMEX would be privatized.[38] Caso Lombardo justified the privatization on the grounds of TELMEX's inefficiency and the need for capital investment. He stated that TELMEX would be sold as a monopoly telephone company with sole rights to provide basic telephone services (local, domestic and international) in the country. Without going into details about the percentage of shares that the government would keep for itself, he said that foreign ownership would be restricted to 49 per cent, thus the majority of capital would remain in Mexican hands. Once the company was sold, the state would 'withdraw' from the telecommunications sector since the SCT would be removed from the position of company Chairman but would enjoy a seat on the board.[39] TELMEX would not be abandoned, however, since the state would remain its *'rector'*. The way that officials insisted on this notion of *'rector'* was connected to their slight unease at the use of the word *'privatización'* and preference for *'desincorporación'*. The verb *'privar'* in Spanish means to deprive, and the word *'privatización'* also has this negative connotation. The insistence that the state would be a *'rector'* signified the state would continue guiding or supervising the telecommunications sector. The notion behind the '*rector*' was that the state would design a regulatory framework in order to ensure that TELMEX's infrastructure was developed by setting growth and productivity targets. This guarantee of continued state intervention was used by the government to argue that although TELMEX would be privately run, the state would avoid its behaving as a private monopoly by controlling price increases and promoting the growth of the network in unprofitable areas.

By September 1989, therefore, the first stage in the establishment of the '*nuevo sindicalismo*' had been achieved. After the announcement of privatization, Hernández Juárez was challenged by sections of the union. For instance, in Mexico City, groups of operators and administrators demonstrated in protest that they would lose their jobs once TELMEX was privatized since the network would be completely digitalized.[40] In Guadalajara, more operators also took action in October for the same reasons.[41] Most of these operators mobilized in order to send a signal to union leaders that they would actively defend their jobs if these were threatened, but their efforts did not in fact represent a fundamental threat.[42]

Selling TELMEX

Between the announcement of the sale of TELMEX in September 1989, and the sale of its controlling stock in December 1990, various changes, including a new regulatory framework, significant adjustments to tariffs, and a modification of capital structure, were implemented. Most privatization advisers agree that it is important that the restructuring of a public enterprise is carried out *prior* to privatization, since the failure to restructure and regulate companies beforehand often negatively affects their sale price. In addition, the implementation of these policies after privatization often proves much more complex and, indeed, may not happen at all.

Regulatory measures

The question of regulation is a delicate one since, when governments decide to privatize a monopoly, they need, on the one hand, to balance a wish to maximize the revenue they could obtain by selling the monopoly and, on the other, the desire to commit the new owners to standards which may be undesirable or unprofitable. This latter objective could be accomplished by introducing regulation prior to the sale of the company, but each government knows that unpopular and unprofitable regulations, such as rural development plans and universal telephone service, often make the company less attractive to prospective investors.[43] Beyond this question, it is important to decide on the identity of the regulator, and whether the country in question has the required institutions to implement effective regulation.

It was not necessarily standard practice to establish regulatory measures prior to the sale of large monopolies in Latin America. For instance, in Argentina, there was no attempt by the government to develop a new regulatory framework prior to the sale of the national telecommunications company ENTEL. The main change was that the company was divided into two regional operating entities, one in the north and the other in the south, splitting Buenos Aires in two. Although the Argentinian government claimed that competition would be created, since each company would try to be more efficient than the other, in effect a duopoly was created. The only way in which the companies could be deemed competitive was that, if a *porteño* living in the north of the city moved to live in the south or vice versa! One of the main reasons for the failure to implement regulatory measures was the speed at which the government sold the company.[44] Finally ENTEL was transferred to private owners in 1990 on the vague condition, laid down by presidential decree, that a variety of expansion and quality goals would be met by the new private owners.

In previous cases of privatization in Mexico the issue of regulation had been largely neglected by the government. For instance, the regulatory framework implemented prior to the sale of the two main airlines, Aeroméxico and Mexicana, was far from adequate. After both were sold, the companies were merged, so that the new company enjoyed 71 per cent of the total domestic market for air travel and virtual control over many of the most heavily used routes. It was only four months after the merger that anti-trust legislation was introduced which could have prevented the merger.[45] However, in the case of the privatization of TELMEX the regulatory framework was implemented *prior* to the sale. Regulation was managed by the SCT, in fulfilment of the government's promise that, if it withdrew as TELMEX's owner and manager, it would remain on the side-lines and protect the firm by acting as its *'rector'*.[46] In December 1990, the SCT published the modifications to the concession it had made to TELMEX in 1976.

Although the SCT had considered regionalizing TELMEX along the lines of AT&T, Rogozinski, the government official mainly responsible for the sale, decided that TELMEX would be more attractive to investors as a single company. The regulations guaranteed TELMEX a monopoly on national and international telephone services until August 1996, but stipulated that in 1997 TELMEX must allow other carriers to connect to its network in order to compete in long-distance and international services. Local services would remain a TELMEX monopoly until 2026. Other telecommunication services such as the supply of cellular telephones, private circuits, and yellow pages would be opened up to competition immediately. TELMEX would no longer be restricted to buying its equipment from two suppliers, Ericsson or Alcatel, as in the past, but would be at liberty to acquire equipment from any company.[47]

The regulations also set out a series of development and quality targets and price controls which TELMEX was obliged to respect once sold. When the regulatory conditions placed upon ENTEL and TELMEX are compared it is clear that those in Argentina were extremely lax. For instance, TELMEX was required to develop its network at a rate of 12 per cent annually, while the two Argentinian telephone companies were required to expand at only 6.5 per cent a year, and, after 1995, only 2.8 per cent a year.[48] Paradoxically, the telephone companies in Argentina were much less efficient than in Mexico prior to privatization: for instance it was notorious that it could be necessary to wait up to 22 years for a telephone installation.[49] TELMEX would also be responsible for providing public telephones to all villages with over 500 residents and a basic telephone with automatic service in all towns with more than 5000 inhabitants. By 1995, the waiting time for installation of a telephone was required to be no more than six months, reducing to one month by the year 2000. Regulation also contained service quality targets. These required TELMEX to install a reliable measurement system for quality control and to establish a system for receiving service complaints.[50] Finally, price controls were imposed, which allowed telephone charges to rise at the same rate as the consumer price index minus a factor of productivity increase set by the regulators. For the period up to 1996, this was set at zero, rising to 3 per cent during 1996–7.

The SCT had already, towards the end of 1989, announced the deregulation of the cellular telephone market by inviting interested parties to apply for concessions to operate mobile phone services. Previously, two companies, DIPSA and *Servicio Organizado Secretarial* (SOS), subsidiaries of TELMEX and Grupo IUSACELL respectively, held licences to operate car telephones, but licences to provide mobile phone services had not been granted to any company. The SCT divided the country into nine regions. In any region, only two companies would be granted permission to provide cellular telephones, and it guaranteed that DIPSA would be one of them.[51] DIPSA was quickly awarded a concession to provide mobile telephones in Tijuana[52] and one month later, IUSACELL was authorized to provide mobile telephone services in Region IX which consisted of Mexico City, Toluca and Cuernavaca.[53] By allowing the TELMEX subsidiary a nation-wide presence this gave the company a competitive advantage. Concessions to the other regions were finalized during the course of 1990.

Tariff and tax reform

Between October 1989 and January 1990 various management changes were implemented in accordance to the requirements of privatization. In October 1989, the Finance Secretary Aspe Armella took over the position of President of TELMEX from the Secretary of Communications and Transport Caso Lombardo. In addition, TELMEX's Director-General, Muñoz Izquierdo, was replaced by Alfredo Baranda García, ex-governor of the State of Mexico and former Mexican Ambassador to Spain, who was to serve in the brief transition period until TELMEX was privatized.[54] The entire board of directors was changed.[55]

At the end of December 1989, TELMEX announced a major restructuring of its tariff and tax structure which would come into effect in January 1990. The tariff structure was complex but can be broken down into five main areas: fixed charges for installation; basic rent; 'measured service' (which is the charge placed on local calls after the fixed number of free calls allocated to each user has been used up); national long distance; and international long distance. As a government-owned company, TELMEX's tariffs had been set in consultation with the SHCP, the Ministry of Planning and Budgeting (SPP) and the SCT and TELMEX executives.[56]

As briefly discussed in Chapter 3, an analysis of TELMEX's pricing policy throughout the 1980s shows that, although in general nominal tariffs were increased every year, telephone rates for local and national calls declined in real terms during most of the decade. TELMEX could afford to provide relatively cheap local and national calls since they were cross-subsidized by the profits made from international calls, which were among the most expensive in the world. The logic behind the cross-subsidy policy was that TELMEX would generate revenue at the same time as implementing an income redistribution mechanism.[57] Since it was mostly the rich who made international calls, this sector would subsidize the cost of installation and calls within Mexico.[58]

As Figure 5.1 indicates, TELMEX started to reverse its cross-subsidy policy in 1988. In this year, the costs of local and national calls started to rise in real terms, while the prices of international calls began to fall. While this change was important, it did not have a dramatic effect on the composition of TELMEX's operating revenue. The source of TELMEX's revenues can be divided into four main categories: local services (including installation, rent and measured service); national long distance; international long distance; and other telephone services including directories, cellular services and sales. In 1988, international calls continued to be proportionally the most significant source of income, as they had been for the earlier part of the decade.

However, in January 1990, the restructuring of tariffs was dramatic, as the price of local and national long-distance calls was increased radically and at the same time the price of international calls was significantly reduced. The rebalancing of tariffs in 1990 had a profound effect on the relative importance of these categories. From 1989 to 1990, the proportion of revenue TELMEX derived from international calls fell from over 40 to 29 per cent while that obtained from local calls rose from 20 to 31 per cent. These pre-privatization measures were implemented so that TELMEX's charges would be brought into line with international prices.

At the same time, the special indirect telephone tax was eliminated and replaced by a new direct tax. Before 1990, TELMEX was used by the government as a source of cash since the company had to hand over direct (35 per cent) and indirect taxes. These indirect taxes made a big difference between the amount collected for calls and the amount due to TELMEX. In 1989, local calls were subjected to a 60 per cent indirect tax, national long distance to around 40 per cent and international calls to 22 per cent.[59] The new direct tax was applied at the rate of 29 per cent to selected areas of TELMEX's revenue. However, 65 per cent of the amount due could be offset if TELMEX invested an equivalent amount in network growth from 1991 to 1996. After 1996 both the telephone tax and the investment offset were to be eliminated. The main implication behind the change in taxation meant that the government would impose a fiscal penalty if TELMEX's capital for investment fell in a given year, so that *TELMEX was effectively compelled to invest* with a specified amount every year until 1996.[60]

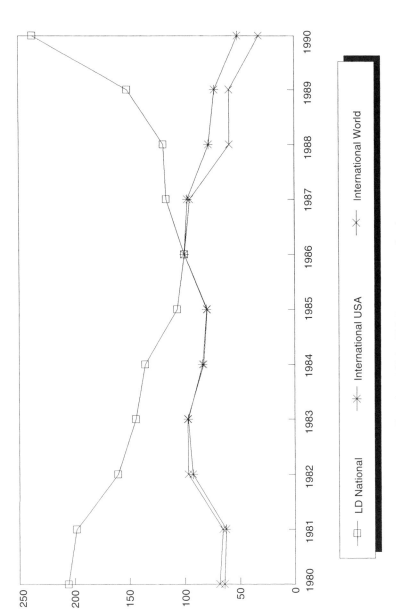

Figure 5.1 TELMEX's Average Tariffs Index. 1986 = 100 (in constant values)
Source: TELMEX Annual Reports.

The sale

From June 1990, the government modified TELMEX's ownership in an innovative way.[61] The aim of the reform was to ensure that, once sold, TELMEX would remain in Mexican hands, but that the sale price was low enough for Mexican buyers to afford. It also would encourage more bidders to put forward their offers. Before June 1990, the government held 56 per cent of shares (which represented 100 per cent of full-voting shares, or type 'AA') while 18 per cent were held by the Mexican private sector (share type 'A' were open only to Mexicans) and the remaining 26 per cent of shares were held by other capital including foreigners ('ADS' type shares were unrestricted) (see Figure 5.2). In the first stage, the government converted 5 per cent of its 'AA' shares to 'A' shares so that the government was left with 51 per cent of shares. Then, it decided that 'AA' shares, which previously could only be held by the government, could also be held by Mexican private capital. Next, TELMEX shares were 'diluted' as the government created a new series of 'L' shares (it created 1.5 L shares for every 'A' or 'AA' share).

In August 1990 the Secretary of Finance and Public Credit announced the public sale of the 'AA' shares or 20.4 per cent of TELMEX capital. The criteria used to pre-select potential buyers included financial solvency, expertise in telecommunications and Mexican control. In addition, it was stipulated that the winning consortium must be prepared to remain the managers of TELMEX over the following six years. The formal date for privatization of TELMEX was December 1990 and sealed envelope bids had to be presented by mid-November. There were only three formal offers: Gentor, Acciones and Valores and Grupo Carso.[62] After an evaluation of the bidders by a special sub-group called the *Comisión Inter-secretarial de Gasto y Financiamiento* (CIGF), which was composed of Aspe, Serra Puche, Vázquez Nava, Zedillo, Farell, Mancerra and Chirinos,[63] it was announced on 9 December 1990 that the controlling 20.4 per cent share of TELMEX would be sold to the consortium, led by the Grupo Carso, for US$1757.6 million. The Mexican conglomerate Grupo Carso owned by Carlos Slim bought 10.4 per cent of total capital stock (26 per cent of voting stock and 51 per cent of 'AA' shares).[64] The other two partners were Southwestern Bell and France Telecom, each of which bought 5 per cent of shares. On the same day, the STRM was awarded 4.4 per cent of 'A' shares for US$325 million with an eight-year low interest loan from *Nacional Financiera* and the promise of the creation of a training centre for workers.[65] At the time, the government retained 26 per cent of shares which were the 'L' type.[66]

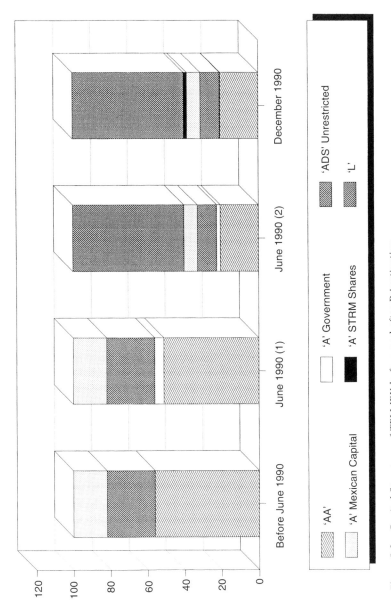

Figure 5.2 Capital Structure of TELMEX before and after Privatization
Source: TELMEX Annual Reports.

The politics of the sale

The government's aim to maximize the price gained for the controlling stock of TELMEX was partially compromised for other important objectives. First, TELMEX would be controlled by Mexicans with only 10.4 per cent of total stock. The new TELMEX managers were prohibited from selling their shares until December 1995 which meant that they should be interested in running the company, not in speculative ventures. Second, the foreign partners were both companies with expertise in telecommunications, so this alliance would bring technological know-how into the management team. There was a second advantage with the alliance with Southwestern Bell, since this company serviced Texas, and the Texas–Mexican border telephone traffic was the key area of US–Mexican service. Third, the decision to award the STRM 4.4 per cent of TELMEX's capital meant that the government could boast that it was promoting 'workers' capitalism', and government officials and union leaders claimed that this was further evidence of a '*nuevo sindicalismo*'.[67]

The objectives behind the Mexican government's sale of TELMEX contrasted sharply with the sale of the Compañía de Teléfonos de Chile (CTC) by the Chilean military dictatorship. The CTC was sold in January 1988 to the highest bidder, Alan Bond, a businessman from Australia, who had no previous experience of telecommunications or interest in managing the telephone company in the medium term. The priority of the regime was clearly to maximize fiscal revenue in the short term since it did not impose conditions about technological expertise or commitment to management. Two years later, Bond sold his CTC stock to Telefónica of Spain which caused regulatory complications since Telefónica was involved in the other Chilean telephone company too.[68]

The Mexican government also successfully maximized revenue by retaining shares to sell after the principal sale. Taking advantage of the dramatic rise in share values after the sale (TELMEX's stock value increased by four times in the first 18 months after privatization),[69] and between 1991 and 1992 it sold the remainder of its 'L' shares in tranches. TELMEX passed from a public to a private monopoly which would last until 1997. Liberalization was introduced in certain areas, and the long-distance service would be opened up in 1997. Tariff and tax reforms before privatization were highly favourable to TELMEX's new owners. In 1990, company profits were higher than those of any other Mexican company, and the business newspaper *Expansión* nominated TELMEX the 'Company of the Year'. This enormous jump in profit was not connected to privatization but the price reforms made in January 1990.[70] The new management's right to increase prices was lenient and, shortly after privatization, consumers' bills rose sharply which led to an outcry from the public and members of Congress. In 1990, Pérez Simon, one of Slim's oldest business partners was appointed TELMEX's General Director, and Slim became President.[71] The new board contained 12 Mexican investors from the Grupo Carso, four from Southwestern Bell and three from France Telecom. Communications Secretary Caso Lombardo was moved as company President but remained on the board.[72]

Since the Salinas *sexenio* ended in an explosion of murder scandals and accusations of corruption, the privatization programme in general has come under greater scrutiny. For instance, many observers have criticized the programme for creating a concentration of capital in a tiny élite, many of whom were friends of the president or other high-up government officials.[73] Investigators and politicians have criticized the way in which the commercial banks were privatized, and claimed that the so-called 'white books' in which all the details of privatization should be recorded are obscure and omit vital details. These 'white books' are still not available for public inspection.[74]

This book is not primarily concerned with the levels of personal corruption apparent during the privatization programme. However, since it would also be foolhardy to ignore the possible political and economic motivations of politicians in any country during privatization programmes, it is worth pointing to a few of the fundamental characteristics of the sale of TELMEX. It is well known that Slim, the new TELMEX owner, was a friend of Salinas, and reputedly backed him financially before the 1988 presidential elections.[75] It is rumoured that Slim acted as a straw man for Salinas, and that Salinas reaped the benefits of the sale of TELMEX since he became its new owner. Rodríguez Castañeda claimed that the process of selling TELMEX was far from transparent and that the Grupo Carso was favoured by the government.[76]

As argued in the last two chapters, TELMEX was an exceedingly attractive company for investors. It was sold as a private monopoly in the most dynamic of sectors and promised excellent growth potential. As Bazdresch has said, TELMEX was a generous package and was probably undersold.[77] The new management board included foreign telephone companies which guaranteed TELMEX technological know-how. The government had 'cleaned up' the company financially prior to its sale and thus many of the potential risks had been eliminated. Moreover, the union leaders cooperated fully with plans for future development on the condition that the promise that there would be no redundancies was respected. The government insisted that Slim acknowledge publicly that he understood this condition. STRM leaders were therefore satisfied with the new management and stated that the union would fully cooperate with it. Some TELMEX managers favoured sacking thousands of telephone workers, principally the operators, in order to avoid funding extensive retraining and relocations programmes after privatization.[78] This did not happen and, even in the face of the introduction of competition in 1997, TELMEX management insisted it would not cut the workforce. Accordingly, this has not grown since 1990.[79] TELMEX was sold at a 'bargain' price since, *with only 10.4 per cent of stock, full control by a Mexican owner was guaranteed.* The financial results after privatization speak for themselves. The value of TELMEX's stocks leaped from around US$1 billion in 1988 to US$30 billion in 1991.[80] By 1993, the *Forbes* magazine estimated Slim's fortune at US$3.7 billion, making him the 35th richest person in the world.[81]

Post-privatization results show that, in many categories, TELMEX surpassed the conditions imposed in the regulatory framework. For instance, between 1990 and 1994 the number of lines installed was, on average, above the 12 per cent annual target.[82] By 1994, a total of 8.4 million lines had been installed, so telephone density increased from 6.6 in 1990 to 9.4 lines in 1994. In the same year, TELMEX finished the construction of a national fibre optic system linking Mexico's 56 main cities. Worker productivity, measured by lines per worker, increased from 104.2 lines/employee in 1990 to 151.5 in 1993. This was mainly due to the ban on recruitment since 1989. TELMEX's weakest point continued to be quality of service, in particular, delays in repairs, failing lines, and the service offered by the operators.[83]

On the 'newness' of 'new unionism'

The STRM's role as the leader of the *'nuevo sindicalismo'* was consummated simultaneously with the sale of the majority stake in TELMEX. In the New Year of 1991, Salinas invited STRM leaders to Los Pinos to celebrate and he praised them for being at the vanguard of changes in Mexican society.[84] He encouraged the STRM leaders present to act as a model which unions across the country could follow.[85] From 1991, the union leadership responded actively to their challenge of promoting a 'new unionism'. In his capacity as founder, leader and spokesman of 'new' unionism, Hernández Juárez substantially increased his profile in politics and in the media.[86] He toured other Latin American countries and addressed telephone workers' unions on the subject of developing a strategy in the face of privatization.[87] His personal relationship with Salinas strengthened when he was invited to accompany the president on trips abroad to promote Mexican interests during the negotiations of the NAFTA. On these trips, he principally served the purpose of embodying the young, pro-'modernization' face of labour in Mexico.[88] He was also invited regularly to participate in the PRI-sponsored forum, the *Insituto de Estudios Políticos, Económicos y Sociales*, where current issues were debated by influential spokespeople.[89]

The rest of this chapter analyses the content of *'nuevo sindicalismo'* and, particularly, the extent to which it was something new. The analysis will be broken into two areas. First, the ways in which the STRM changed after privatization will be examined as will what this model of 'new' unionism signified. Second, the creation by Hernández Juárez of the FESEBES, which was touted by government officials as the embodiment of a 'new' unionism, will be discussed.

The STRM emerged from the privatization experience in a relatively strong position in comparison to most of the other unions which confronted privatization in Mexico. Their labour contract had been weakened to the extent that management gained considerable leverage in controlling labour mobility and flexibility in areas in which the union formerly had more influence. However, the union had advanced by securing its role in the introduction of new technology, training and means of measuring labour productivity. The promise that there would be no redundancies was honoured; union membership of around 50 000 has not declined nor grown since privatization. Workers who had been recruited since 1990 have been absorbed by TELMEX subsidiary companies which provide new services such as the mobile telephone company DIPSA, and the construction and maintenance of the ISDN network, for example, *Construcciones y Canalizaciones* (CYCSA) and *Construcciones Telefónicas Mexicanas* (CONTELMEX). Although on average about 70 per cent of workers in these subsidiary companies are members of individual unions representing their companies (but *not* of the STRM), some companies such as CONTELMEX have a workforce which is composed of over 85 per cent *personal de confianza*, and others are not unionized at all.[90] In terms of wages after privatization, telephone workers could be satisfied since, in 1995, the average salary of the telephone worker in 1995 was among the best in Mexico.[91]

The consequences of privatization for union democracy in the STRM

Hernández Juárez stressed repeatedly that unions were obliged to have democratic structures – like the STRM – if they were to respond success-fully to the challenges of industrial restructuring and privatization.[92] This was because he claimed that unions should respond to initiatives from workers and adopt a flexible approach. He stated that traditional unions with rigid structures could not achieve this kind of response.

In parallel with the privatization, STRM *comisionados* designed a new model of unionism which would guide STRM strategy in the post-privatization era.[93] First, they claimed that the union must become more decentralized in a similar fashion to the way in which TELMEX management had reorganized itself into regional profit centres since 1988. This would be achieved by dismantling the existing rigid union hierarchies which in the past had meant that workers' problems could be resolved only after consultation had taken place with the higher echelons of the STRM. Decentralization of the union would mean that more workers' problems would be resolved at the local level. Second, they claimed that opportunities were opening up for more union members to participate actively in union affairs. Principally, this was because there were fresh concerns such as pro-ductivity, quality standards and changing work conditions which had to be debated internally by the union, and discussed with the government and management. Worker participation would also be improved through greater communication between union leaders and rank and file.[94] Third, they argued that the union must continue with its strategy of presenting counter-proposals to challenge those made by management. This would be achieved by training the CEN in aspects of technology such as satellites, digital systems, fibre optics, cables, switching, networks and ISDN, as well ensuring they were up-to-date with the situation in telephone workers' unions in other countries.[95]

The proposal to decentralize the union was rather ironic in the light of the fact that, prior to privatization, union power had been consolidated and centralized as never before by the *comisionados*, as argued in the previous chapter. These *comisionados* performed all the negotiations on behalf of the union with management and the government. As shown in this chapter, the way in which the telephone workers were persuaded to accept privatization involved limiting the information passed on to them, and repressing and firing troublesome workers. With the monopoly of the top jobs held by *comisionados*, the likelihood that other workers would obtain important union jobs was reduced, thus, opportunities for new leaders to emerge narrowed considerably. Pateman claimed that worker participation at the 'low' level was important training ground for future leaders and for experience in democratic union practice. Thus, opportunities for increased worker participation were *substantially reduced* by 1990.[96]

A clear sign that union democracy took a step *backwards* with privatization was seen in 1991 during the elections for the STRM Secretary-General. As usual, Hernández Juárez had arranged for a referendum throughout the union to gain permission to stand again as its leader.[97] He also arranged for the elections to be brought forward from 1992 to August 1991. In this month, Hernández Juárez was voted the STRM's Secretary-General for 1992–6. For the first time since the period of the '*charro*' leadership in the 1960s and 1970s, he faced no opponent. According to the STRM's official vote counting, Hernández Juárez received a remarkable 90.3 per cent of the total votes cast.[98] Of the 45 000 members, around 37 000 voted.[99] In the elections for secretary-general in 1984 and 1988 Hernández Juárez had received around 70 per cent of the votes and he had been challenged on each occasion by at least one other candidate. Hernández Juárez interpreted the 1991 results as demonstrating that he was now more popular in the union than he had been in 1976 when he first came to power. He claimed that in the union there was 'in fact only one plan, not because of any restrictions, but because our plan is so good that even our former enemies have decided to join up with us'.[100] My first hypothesis on union democracy stated that effective opposition groups should exist for a union to be democratic. Thus, in the post-privatization period, since opposition was not effective, this showed a *net loss of union democracy*. Furthermore, the leaders' comments demonstrated a rather worrying attitude towards the meaning of union democracy.

The main beneficiaries of privatization among the workers were the *comisionados* whose dominance over the STRM was completed during the course of 1990. The strengthening of the union leaders vis-à-vis management came at the expense of the relationship of the rank and file vis-à-vis union leaders. Interviews with members of the opposition in 1995 confirmed this pattern of an increasing 'one-party' approach to union politics. As it became increasingly difficult for dissidents to organize effective opposition to the green party led by Hernández Juárez, because of the reform to electoral practices in 1983 and the way that the *comisionados* had monopolized union power,[101] they changed their tactics and, instead of trying to attack Hernández Juárez and his supporters from the outside, they strove to get themselves elected to his team, in order to make an impact from within.[102] This inevitably started to cause tensions and signs of disobedience became increasingly manifest at the highest level, particularly between the leader, his *comisionados*, and the elected CEN team.

According to Pateman, financial participation schemes, such as share ownership, may deepen worker participation, particularly when the dividends are distributed in an egalitarian way regardless of individual workers' wages.[103] The way in which the STRM's shares were managed was a clear indication of the way in which new resources created by privatization were used by union leaders to exert greater control over and repression within the union. In 1991, TELMEX shares were handed over to the union, helped by a loan by the Nacional Financiera, the dividends to be distributed equally among workers periodically. The union agreed to pay back the loan to Nacional Financiera within eight years. Hernández Juárez openly stated that he wanted to accumulate 10 per cent of TELMEX shares so that the STRM could gain a seat on the management board. However, in 1990 many telephone workers, mistrustful of the union leaders' management of the shares, started to demand that the shares be distributed to each worker. By June 1992, the CEN bowed to pressure from the workers and requested Hernández Juárez to hold a convention to address the problem.

Hernández Juárez wanted to keep all the shares in a central trust managed by union leaders. He arranged a special scheme with Nacional Financiera whereby the bank would provide special loans for houses or cars exclusively for telephone workers who kept their shares in the trust.[104] At the convention in June 1992 the leader told the delegates that the workers had two choices. The first was to keep their shares in the trust and benefit from this new arrangement with the bank. The second was to receive their shares but risk making grave errors since, the leader rather patronizingly warned, workers had no experience in handling shares. The second option was not clear-cut since, over the next few years, the union leaders used the share distribution as blackmail and made it difficult for workers who proved uncooperative with the changes at TELMEX to receive them. This particularly affected a group of around 200 maintenance workers who claimed that their jobs had been given to TELMEX subsidiaries CONTELMEX and CYCSA.[105] Thus to 1994, these workers' shares were denied them until they withdrew complaints about the loss of their jobs. Clearly, this was not an example which could fit Pateman's analysis of financial participation schemes that deepened worker participation. On the contrary, it was a new means by which the STRM leaders could effect control over rank and file.

The creation of the FESEBES

After privatization, the strategy of the STRM *comisionados* was ambitious and fiercely expansionist. First, they openly criticized the CT for its anachronistic structure, its inability to respond to industrial restructuring and privatization, and for having a labour culture steeped in clientelism. Hernández Juárez had for many years urged the need to reform the LFT, advocating in particular, the addition of a chapter to Article 123 so that productivity levels, training standards, work conditions, new technology, and the role that workers could play in the participation of newly privatized companies could be included in the law.[106] Second, STRM *comisionados* made an alliance in 1991 with the Communications Workers of Canada and America. However, the key activity of the *comisionados* was to promote a new labour confederation, the FESEBES, which they claimed would be a sign of the new state–labour relationship.

From July 1989, Hernández Juárez started to promote the creation of this new labour confederation, incorporating the *Asociación Sindical de Pilotos Aviadores* (ASPA), *Asociación Sindical de Sobrecargos de Aviación* (ASSA), *Sindicato Mexicano de Electricistas* (SME), *Alianza de Tranviarios de Mexico* (ATM) and the *Sindicato de Técnicos y Manuales de la Industria Cinematográfica* (STIC). By the end of March 1990 these six unions agreed to create the FESEBES.[107]

The next month, the statutes to underpin FESEBES were written and agreed by all representatives of the member unions. First, the FESEBES was to represent a new alliance of workers which would prioritize the modernization of the relationship between the state and labour. As one organization the unions would confront together the challenges of modernization and industrial restructuring.[108] Second, this new labour confederation would remain in the CT. Delegates elected its founder, Hernández Juárez, as the first secretary-general. According to the statutes, there would be no re-election for this post, which would be rotated every two years so that every member union would be represented.[109] Other FESEBES representatives would be elected from representatives of member unions who already had posts in their union. Another of the FESEBES' stated aims was to remain ideologically and politically independent by remaining outside of the PRI.

STRM *comisionados* and leaders of the other member unions touted the FESEBES as a new interlocutor for organized labour and the embodiment of a new state–labour relationship.[110] Like the STRM, it promoted a supposedly new labour culture which accepted that the Mexican workforce had to respond to the challenges of globalization by improving productivity and quality. It also promoted the need to reform the LFT. A new worker culture had to be accompanied by increased worker participation in the union and workplace. Hernández Juárez claimed that the FESEBES had broken away from the mould of traditional unionism, and in particular, would be a more transparent form of unionism which would genuinely represent workers. He claimed that it would reject the clientelism which permeated traditional unionism.[111] He insisted that the FESEBES would stay inside the CT, and claimed that, in this way, the CT could be transformed from the inside. He repeatedly explained: 'to break away is to be born, not to destroy'.[112]

From its establishment, Velázquez made clear his total opposition to the FESEBES. The main criticism he made was that it would cause a split in the CT and therefore weaken it.[113] It was clear that part of the government's logic of encouraging the FESEBES was its wish to weaken the CT, and the government was already showing a preferential treatment of the CROC while often rejecting CTM proposals.[114] Perhaps another of Velázquez's fears was exposed in the 'Freudian slip' he made when explaining his reasons for opposing it: 'We are opposed to the formation of this company, sorry, I mean, this federation, because it is an organisation which is parallel to the CT and will cause tensions because it will divide the labour movement'.[115] The FESEBES was a business-oriented project that was selective in the kinds of unions that it wanted to attract. It threatened to attract all the unions from the more dynamic economic sectors, thus constituting an important rival for the CT. To intimidate the FESEBES unions Velázquez threatened to expel its members from the CT.

Throughout the rest of the *sexenio*, personal tension between Hernández Juárez and Velázquez grew. On Labour Day, 1 May 1990, Salinas proposed that a 'new unionism' should be encouraged in Mexico. Paradoxically, neither Velázquez, representative of 'traditional' unionism, nor Hernández Juárez, the leader of 'new' unionism, attended the official ceremony. Velázquez arrived late with the excuse of a cramp, and Hernández Juárez did not go at all, claiming he was ill.[116] Their absences reflected the tensions and the wish to avoid direct confrontation. When Velázquez arrived, he concentrated on attacking the recently formed FESEBES, and was backed by the new CT president Lorenzo Duarte.

In June 1990, Hernández Juárez applied to the STPS for the official registration of FESEBES. However, on 5 December 1990, only days before the results of the bidding process to buy TELMEX were announced, the STPS informed FESEBES officials that their application for registration had been unsuccessful, due to 'irregularities' in the statutes.[117] The delay in the registration of the FESEBES was largely due to the fierce opposition which had been raised by Velázquez and other prominent labour leaders.[118] The press exacerbated the existing tensions by stating that the young leader wanted the job of the 90-year-old. Certainly, Hernández Juárez's career prospects had never been brighter.

The FESEBES was finally registered officially two years later in December 1992, and this was a clear example of how tightly political and economic decisions were intertwined.[119] Its registration was a direct reward to Hernández Juárez for his role in helping to put an end to the conflict at Volkswagen between July and August 1992.[120] Volkswagen was peculiar among automobile companies in Mexico because it was the only one that had not geographically dispersed its production facilities. The result was that the union had considerable influence in hiring and promotion decisions, and the movement of workers among different production areas in the plant.[121]

In July 1992, the secretary-general of the *Sindicato Independiente de Trabajadores de la Industria Automotriz de Volkswagen* (SITIAVW) signed a *convenio* behind the workers' backs significantly redefining labour conditions at the plant. An overwhelming majority of workers decided to reject this contract, and during the months of July and August a group of dissidents led a revolt against the secretary-general.[122] Volkwagen management responded in August by firing all 14 200 workers. In August management selectively rehired some of the workers and introduced a new labour contract. Workers suffered wage reductions and the loss of fringe benefits and other rights, while at the same time managerial control over the production process was enhanced. The SITIAVW leader called in Hernández Juárez to resolve the crisis. In particular, Hernández Juárez was involved in the writing of a new labour contract as well as the revised union statutes. Among the main changes made to the union statutes were that the secretary-general would gain more power by staying in that position longer and having more power over union matters. As argued in Chapter 2, Hernández Juárez was already an expert in manipulating union statutes in order to concentrate all power in the secretary-general. The FESEBES brought together the six original unions which constituted around 100 000 workers. In addition, in gratitude for Hernández Juárez's help, the SITIAVW leader decided that his union would also join.

On the 'newness' of the FESEBES

One of the few novelties of the FESEBES was that it added a new dimension to labour by organizing a small and select group of unions from dynamic sectors. The decision by the government to permit the registration of the FESEBES showed a change of heart. In the past, any alliance between the STRM and the SME had been prohibited as potentially too dangerous to the government.[123] The FESEBES not only united the STRM and the SME, but some of the other dynamic and powerful unions in Mexico.

However, in aspects such as its internal organizational structure, the FESEBES failed to signify anything new. Since it was the brainchild of Hernández Juárez, it should not be surprising that many of the characteristics of union organization in the STRM are mirrored and amplified in that of the FESEBES. According to the FESEBES statutes, the secretary-general would be voted by delegates and would remain in the post for two years and consecutive re-election would not be permitted.[124] The post would be rotated so that each member union would be represented in turn. After being voted by delegates as the first FESEBES secretary-general in 1990, Hernández Juárez managed to convince delegates to allow him to stand, on a one-off basis, for the post of secretary-general from 1992 to 1994. From this moment he became the 'permanent' secretary-general of the FESEBES, using exactly the same tactics which had made him 'permanent' secretary-general of the STRM since 1976.

In other organizational respects, the FESEBES did not offer greater opportunities for the participation of union members in its affairs. At the top of the hierarchy of the confederation was the secretary-general. He was responsible for a group of five commissions in charge of modernization, training, political affairs, strategy and labour affairs. One of the conditions necessary for election as a FESEBES representative was that the candidate already hold an important position in his or her own union. In the case of the STRM representatives in these committees, all were STRM *comisionados*, with the key posts filled by Hernández Juárez's college cronies.[125] By 1992, not only had STRM *comisionados* consolidated their power over their own union, they had also infiltrated all the key positions in the FESEBES.

In the FESEBES' declared aims, the confederation would be independent from the PRI, and member unions were not required to be PRI members. At the same time, it was clear that, by promoting a 'new' labour culture of cooperation with the government's privatization programme, the FESEBES was far from 'independent' from the government.

Conclusion

Although the STRM was promoted by government officials and STRM leaders as a model of 'new unionism' to be emulated by all unions in Mexico, to a large extent, the experience of the STRM was peculiar in Mexico. Few other unions succeeded in creating mixed committees where the union was *effectively* represented and involved in modernization agreements with management and the government. Hernández Juárez's intervention in the conflict at Volkswagen, which ended in the dismissal of the company's entire workforce and the subsequent rehiring of a reduced number of workers under a new labour contract which was less favourable to workers, showed that even the leader of '*nuevo sindicalismo*' could not simply transpose the experience of the telephone workers on to another case. The key point which differentiated the telecommunications sector from most others was its dynamism and dramatic growth potential. Although some of TELMEX management were unhappy with the political agreement made by the president and the new owner that there would be no staff redundancies, this sacrifice was more than offset by the attractiveness of the new privatized monopoly. These financial and political arrangements were the foundations upon which it was possible to persuade the telephone workers to accept the privatization of TELMEX and thus constituted the 'glue' of '*nuevo sindicalismo*'.

Despite the rhetoric used by STRM leaders about the democratic tendencies of 'new unionism', its evolution – which accompanied privatization – resulted in the consolidation of an unelected élite within the union over rank and file. The process of privatization generated new opportunities such as personal attention from the president in the form of protection, favouritism, and gifts to the union, which union *comisionados* used to maximize their gains. The introduction of new technology, work culture and training which required negotiation between the government, the union and management, were used as opportunities by union leaders to reorganize and dominate the structure of power within the union. Even the TELMEX shares bought by the STRM were captured by the union *comisionados* and used to the end of better controlling union members.

Conclusions

The principal aim of my research was to investigate the nature of the relationship between economic and political change in the case of Mexico. I questioned in particular whether the policies of economic liberalization pursued by the Mexican government since the mid-1980s would prove to be *fundamentally incompatible* with the corporatist system and might, in turn, bring about a democratization of the relationship between state and society, as has been argued by the 'rent-seekers' and those influenced by the modernization school, such as Berins Collier, Bizberg, Baer, Morici, Roett and Rubio.[1] In order to do this, a detailed study was made of the privatization of TELMEX, which was the first large public enterprise to be sold in Mexico, and the single most lucrative instance of privatization in that country.[2] The questions asked were important in regard to the political system for two principal reasons. First, the arrangement of society into a corporatist system, dating from the administration of Lázaro Cárdenas (1934–40), has been interpreted broadly as one of the major keys to the PRI's stability. Thus, if economic reform threatened to unravel the corporatist system, this would have serious consequences for the continuity of the regime. Second, if the corporatist system was dismantled or loosened, this would render society less dependent upon the state, and at the same time, more autonomous and thus democratic.

One of the assumptions of the rent-seekers was that privatization implied a significant, if not complete, withdrawal of the state from its traditional role of managing the economy and protecting individual firms and sectors. In the case of the privatization of TELMEX, however, the Mexican state managed to avoid or postpone its loss of influence over the telecommunications sector in important ways. First, the state continued to have the right to intervene since the new regulating body created in 1990 was put in charge of the SCT. Thus, if the new owners failed to comply with the agreed expansion, price and quality targets, the state had the right to intervene. Second, at the time of the sale of TELMEX, the president enforced upon the new owners the condition that there would be no job losses as a result of privatization and there have been no mass redundancy programmes up to 1999. In this way, the president extended his influence over the private company's labour relations policy during his administration.

This research highlighted the political implications and consequences of the privatization of TELMEX. One of the overriding arguments made was that a combination of factors made it a highly attractive company to privatize and its sale was used by Salinas as a launch pad for his 'second round' of privatization. Thus, the privatization of TELMEX, crucial as it was in raising US$6 billion (just less than one-third of the total profits derived from privatization during the administration of Salinas), should not be considered *solely* in terms of its short-term financial contribution to the treasury. It must also be understood within the political dynamics which guided the privatization programme in general after 1989.

In contradiction to the expectations of those analysts who predicted that the corporatist relationship between the state and labour was *inherently incongruent* with economic liberalization and privatization, this research showed that corporatist relations after privatization functioned *perfectly well* – if not better – than they had previously. Resources generated by the sale of TELMEX were used by the government to lubricate a clientelistic relationship with the STRM. The president and STRM leaders exchanged promises, perhaps the most important of which was that the former had rewarded the union with the guarantee of no redundancies resulting from privatization, in return for the latter providing assurance that the rank and file would be controlled and prevented from opposing the 'flexibility' of their labour contract in April 1989 (shortly before the announcement that TELMEX was to be privatized). Once this was accomplished, the STRM was rewarded by the president with gifts including financial aid to develop the union's infrastructure (including building extensions and funds for union propaganda). After the privatization was completed without significant labour conflict, the union was awarded 4.4 per cent of company shares, which was promoted by government and union officials as evidence of an enhancement of the workers' participation in the company.

The alliance between the president and union leaders transcended the question of the privatization of TELMEX itself, since, after the sale,

Salinas strove to use Hernández Juárez to lead a 'new unionism' which would encourage other unions to follow a cooperative stance in the face of the privatization of their firms. There were a series of personal exchanges between the president and the labour leader which made this possible. In the first major step, Salinas rewarded Hernández Juárez for his loyalty during the privatization of TELMEX with the guarantee that he could establish an alternative labour federation, the FESEBES. The second step was when Hernández Juárez was finally granted the official recognition by the government of the confederation after he sucessfully intervened and helped resolve the labour conflict at Volkswagen in 1992. Government and STRM officials proclaimed that the experience of the STRM during the privatization of TELMEX, and the subsequent emergence of FESEBES, was proof that a 'new unionism' was taking root in Mexico. According to this discourse, unions could cooperate with modernization and privatization projects, and involve rank and file in the participation of these changes, while at the same time democratizing their unions.

One of the aims of this research was to assess the nature of 'new unionism' which emerged in Mexico at the end of the 1980s and to examine whether and to what extent it represented the end of corporatist relations between the state and labour, and whether it implied a more democratic model of labour relations. By rejecting the tradition of labelling unions by using binary labels and by insisting on examining the STRM's internal union practices as well as its external behaviour, I showed how the STRM presented itself as a democratic union while retaining at its core an oligarchic internal union structure after 1976. Moreover, at certain junctures in its history, such as in 1983, the union took important steps away from union democracy. In the second chapter I outlined various hypotheses which I used to assess how union democracy in the STRM changed during the privatization process.[3] My overall conclusion was that the privatization of TELMEX in 1990 was another instance of the union becoming *less democratic*. According to the STRM's rhetoric, it embodied the prototype of 'new unionism', but, rather paradoxically, the process by which the STRM leaders came to establish this model of 'new unionism' was accomplished at the cost of a *net reduction of internal union democracy*. First, the STRM did not gain a higher degree of autonomy from the state during privatization. On the contrary its leaders were involved in a joint alliance with government and management throughout the process. Second, while the STRM increased its power within the body of organized labour, principally in its role as founder of the FESEBES, this did not bring about more democracy for union members since the internal power structure of the FESEBES replicated the oligarchic organization of the STRM.

In order to assess whether the government and organization of the STRM became more democratic during privatization I used three main hypotheses which I extracted from the literature on union democracy.[4] For each of the hypotheses, my conclusion was negative, meaning that union democracy decreased in the period. One sign of union democracy is the existence of effective opposition parties. However, I noted the trend after privatization that former dissidents chose to infiltrate Hernández Juárez's party and work from the inside since their opportunities as members of opposition parties had declined. Another signal of union democracy is that elections for all executive posts are contested. In the year after privatization, Hernández Juárez was not challenged in the elections for secretary-general by any other contender for the first time in his career.[5] The regular turnover of leaders is a further sign of union democracy. As I showed in Chapter 2, leader turnover in all positions but the secretary-general is regular in the STRM. However, this should *not* be interpreted therefore as evidence of union democracy. In the fourth and fifth chapters I explained how privatization brought about the consolidation of a group of unelected *comisionados* over the union. When this group assumed power, the role of the elected union representatives was severely weakened.

This process was facilitated by the privatization of TELMEX which generated the required financial resources to facilitate an agreement between government and union officials. The privatization of TELMEX produced a political consensus, on the part of the government, management and union leaders, to ensure control of the rank and file during such a delicate business transaction. Both these resources and political consensus facilitated the consolidation of unelected union 'leaders' over the control of the union. Rank and file and elected union leaders were excluded from the new opportunities for power which had been opened up by privatization at the 'high' level of union politics such as negotiation with management about new technology and privatization.[6] This rather dramatic decline in union democracy was accompanied by a concomitant increase in corruption in the form of the abuse of power by individuals within the union. One clear example of this was the way that the TELMEX shares, which had been intended to be distributed equally among all telephone workers, were monopolized in a central 'trust' by the *comisionados* and used to blackmail workers by threatening those who refused to conform to union rules that their shares would be forfeited.

In order to analyse the consequences of privatization on telephone workers more closely, I conducted a survey and interviews with a sub-group of telephone workers, namely, the telephone operators in Mexico City. My results, which are included in the Appendix, showed that privatization brought about a mix of advantages and disadvantages for these female workers. The most important advantage was that, although this group was the one most threatened by technological change, there were no job cuts. However, thousands of operators had to accept retraining and relocation to other areas of the company. The biggest disadvantage of this relocation programme was a dramatic reduction in the political power of women within the union. The operators, who constituted the largest and most geographically concentrated sub-group within the STRM, had participated actively in union politics and, since initiating the STRM strikes in 1976 through to 1979, had continued to consitute a significant force within the union. Through unified mobilization, these women had gained significant concessions from management including their own labour *convenio* in 1979, better work conditions and higher wages. However, the introduction of digital equipment from the end of the 1980s resulted in the relocation of former operators to many other jobs in diverse geographical areas of the country. This implied the subsequent loss of this sub-group's strength within the union. The Appendix adds to the overall conclusions of the research by providing a gendered approach to the question of union democracy, since the results were specifically relevant for women.

While it would be an exaggeration to state that the characteristics of the telecommunications sector – such as its dynamism, growth potential and rapid technological change – are unique and lack parallel in other dynamic industries, this sector *is* a special one, and has been labelled as the new 'juggernaut' of the economy in the 1980s and 1990s.[7] These qualities made feasible the project of 'new unionism' in Mexico, since the guarantee that there would be no redundancies, which was at its heart, became possible only because this sacrifice made by the new owners was more than compensated for by the fact they would enjoy a six-year monopoly of telecommunications. As mentioned at the beginning of the Appendix, a guarantee that in order to satisfy a political aim of the government there would be no job cuts was also given in Malaysia during the privatization of the national telephone company.[8] Due to the particular characteristics of this case, the model of 'new unionism' proved to be a difficult one for unions in other sectors to emulate. When Hernández Juárez intervened, on behalf of the government, to attempt to resolve the labour conflict at Volkswagen in 1992, it became clear to union members and other observers that he had failed to construct another 'new' union, and was unable to avoid mass layoffs.

As a final conclusion, I underline that, in contradiction to those who argued that a corporatist model of labour relations, as found in Mexico, would be inherently incompatible with privatization, market liberalization and competition, this research showed that, in the case of the telecommunications sector, corporate labour relations were able to function effectively. The chief importance of this study lies in the demonstration that the policies of economic liberalization and privatization *were not fundamentally incompatible with the corporatist system per se.* The privatization of TELMEX was the essential ingredient which created resources to feed the creation of a 'new' (but not necessarily different) corporatist relation, so-called *'nuevo sindicalismo'*, linking the state and labour, and which was used to promote a non-conflictive model of labour relations in the wake of privatization. I have argued that the corporatist relations between the state and the STRM were actually *consummated* during the privatization due to the generation of material resources and heightened interest on the part of union, government and business interest in the trajectory of TELMEX.

I thus reject the view that economic liberalization will *necessarily* bring about a political liberalization or democratization. It may do so, but the relationship between economic and political change is not deterministic or unilinear. I showed how political and economic change interacted as the Salinas administration implemented the policy to promote a 'new unionism' for political and economic reasons: first, to improve state–labour relations and to try to encourage other unions to cooperate with the government's policy; second, to maximize the success and profitability of the privatization programme. My results thus concur with those analysts who have argued that economic liberalization in general, and privatization in particular, have been capable of creating new resources to maintain or create certain political arrangements such as a corporatist system. In my view, economic policy does not dictate political reform, nor does political change determine economic reform. In the case of Mexico, political and economic reform are primarily brought about because the government has sufficient political consensus to do so.

Appendix: a 'Bottom-Up' Approach to the Impact of Privatization on Telephone Workers using Survey and Interview Techniques

The central focus of this book was the relationship between economic liberalization, in particular, the policy of privatization, and its consequences for union democratization. As stressed previously, privatization is not to be confused with liberalization, though it may lead to liberalization.[1] The privatization of TELMEX triggered a limited degree of liberalization of the telecommunications sector, principally in the deregulation of the provision of mobile phones and terminal equipment. However, for the most part, liberalization tended to be postponed, since TELMEX was allowed to continue functioning as a monopoly with a right to provide basic national and international telephone services to the Mexican population until 1997. As the government opened up the sector to international competition from 1997, it will be possible in future years to analyse the effects of liberalization on labour relations in the longer term. For these reasons, it is rather premature to present a comprehensive comparative analysis of the effects of liberalization on labour relations before and after privatization. While the privatization of TELMEX was implemented relatively quickly, the process of liberalizing the telephone market is a process that gradually evolves. Therefore the impact of liberalization upon labour relations will also be a process that unfolds.

One of the main changes brought about by privatization has been technological upgrading, funded by national and international finance. The introduction of new technology has had – and will continue to have – a profound impact on the restructuring of large sections of TELMEX's workforce. Although the telephone workers were promised that there would be no job losses as a result of privatization, there is no future guarantee that, as international competition erodes TELMEX's former monopoly, this promise will be renewed. Instead, the telephone workers were forced to accept the possibility of being retrained and relocated to other parts of the company in different areas of the country. The group of workers who were most dramatically affected by new technology in the first few years after privatization were the operators.[2] The replacement of analogue by digital equipment meant that the number of calls connected by each operator would increase around ten-fold. The first major change in the restructuring of this sector was the agreement in May 1992, between TELMEX management and the STRM, that the 5000 operators who would initially be displaced by digital equipment would be relocated.[3]

As I have stressed throughout this book, particularly in the second chapter, one of the problems with literature on organized labour in Mexico is the tendency for unions to be labelled in binary terms, and for their internal practice to be largely ignored.[4] One of the aims of my research on the STRM was to ensure that the internal workings of the union were analysed and contrasted with the union's outward behaviour. In this book, my analysis of the links between economic and political change has been guided by a 'top-down' approach. My examination of the emergence of a *'nuevo sindicalismo'* focused on modifications to collective contracts and changes in the internal organizational structure of the union and the analysis of the impact of privatization on labour relations examined the main political and financial negotiations made by key decision-makers, including members of the Salinas administration, the TELMEX executive, union leaders and national and international investors.

In my analysis of the STRM I have found it useful to consider two main parts: the union leadership and the rank and file. However, the rank and file is constituted of different sub-groups of telephone workers with particular characteristics and interests. In this appendix, I include the results of a survey and interviews which I carried out on the effects of the introduction of new technology upon a specific sub-group of telephone workers at the shop-floor level.[5] In this way, I was able to assess the political and social consequences of privatization upon workers from a closer range. Unfortunately, due to the way in which all my activities with workers were carefully supervised and censored by union officials, it was not possible to ask workers direct questions about union democracy. Instead, I focused on new technology and working practices which were far more neutral subjects. I chose to concentrate on examining the case of the impact of new technology on the telephone operators for the following three main reasons.

First, TELMEX operators were the sub-group of telephone workers to be most severely affected by technological change. This is a world-wide trend since, in other telephone companies including BT, the move from analogue equipment to digital computers (that is, digitalization) rendered thousands of operators redundant.[6] There were no redundancies created when TELMEX was privatized. This was unusual, but not unique, in international terms. Ng Choon Sim and Yong argued that, in the case of the privatization of the telephone company in Malaysia, TELMEL, the Malaysian government decided to avoid sacking telephone workers for primarily political reasons. The authors claimed that this decision was taken partly due to the strength of the union and partly because the government feared laying off Malays would mean a sharp decline in the support upon which they depended.[7] Instead of being made redundant, TELMEX operators were offered retraining and relocation after 1992 to enable them to work in other departments such as administration, telemarketing and maintenance. Those who continued to work as operators experienced a dramatically different working practice with the introduction of digitalization. The changes included the requirement that they achieve productivity targets, the introduction of a new concept of the customer and a wider range of services that were to be provided, use (for many the first) of a personal computer and mandatory participation in intensive training courses. New technology changed the operators' day-to-day work, the relationship which they had with management and their autonomy in getting on with the job.

Second, I chose the operators for my case study because of the potential impact which the changes could have on the future balance of power and political stability in the union. One of the original sources of the operators' power in the late 1970s was their numerical strength, since they constituted over one-third of union members.[8] Since then, the percentage of operators in the union has slowly diminished to just under 30 per cent by the end of the 1980s.[9] The number of operators has been severely hit by privatization. By 1993, they constituted only one-quarter of the union, leaving the exterior plant workers constituting the largest sub-group of the union (32 per cent).[10] Once the telephone network has been fully digitalized, there will only be a need for a maximum of 5000 operators, which represents less than an eighth of unionized workers. As argued previously, the operators have historically formed the most loyal pillar of support for Hernández Juárez. Even as privatization proceeded, the operators figured as an important consideration for Hernández Juárez and they continued to be the most important supporting faction within the union. They were the chief beneficiaries of the promise of job security when TELMEX was privatized. However, it is logical that, as operators were relocated, they were less useful as a political ally for Hernández Juárez.

Third, the operators were chosen because the nature of their job lends itself to easy analysis and they could readily be surveyed. Each operator performs a single task of connecting calls, either local or long distance. All operators do the same tasks, and the job does not change from day to day. Moreover, all operators share a common experience: all have used the old analogue equipment, and all have been retrained to use the digital system.[11] Geographically, they are concentrated in operating centres where they work all day. Other sub-groups within the STRM, such as the technicians, have highly mobile jobs. Each repair and maintenance job is different. In the case of those employed in the exterior plant, the section responsible for the installation of telephones, workers are again mobile, and jobs range from the installation of a telephone in a house to installing a network for a firm and connecting underground cables. The impact of new technology would thus be more complex to evaluate in any of these cases.

Before presenting the survey methodology and results it is worth mentioning briefly some points about the way in which I gained permission to carry out the survey and details of the organization inside the new work centres. It proved far from easy to gain permission to enter TELMEX operator centres and conduct interviews and a survey with operators. However, perhaps due to the leaders' pride in their union's 'democratic' reputation and because they see themselves at the vanguard of technology, they are more open to outsiders than many other unions in Mexico. Interestingly, at no point was I instructed to approach TELMEX management for permission to carry out my work, a fact which sheds some light on the extent to which the union controls the workplace. In order to carry out my survey I had to gain permission from union leaders at the highest level. The first step was to meet Lejarza, Hernández Juarez's 'right-hand man', and ask him for permission. All STRM leaders are highly elusive and they believe that this makes them seem more important, so it took four months after I requested an interview to finally meet with him. He gave me the go-ahead on the condition that the head operator *comisionada*, Yolanda Rendón, also agreed.

Rendón is one of the most powerful women in the union and, due to her glamorous, confident appearance, she is known as '*reinita*', the 'little queen', by the other operators. After a few unsuccessful attempts, I met with her and, some weeks later, I received a call saying that I had finally been granted permission to conduct my survey in Lindavista, one of the two new operating centres inaugurated in Mexico City in 1990. This was a calculated decision on the part of the STRM since my original request had been to conduct a survey with the operators of the old operating centre, San Juan, which had been severely affected by the 1985 earthquake. Lindavista was sparkling new and more impressive to an outsider. Moreover, it had gained the reputation of being an ardent centre of support for Hernández Juárez.[12]

Despite the fact that I had gained permission from Lejarza, and that Rendón had announced my project during meetings, my presence in the TELMEX workplaces generated both excitement and suspicion among the operators. From the start, my visits were closely coordinated by the head delegate of Lindavista, who, fortunately for my research, was extremely cooperative and open-minded. Having her contact name was crucial for entry to the sites since all TELMEX's operator centres are tightly guarded by security and entry is impossible without prior arrangement. The head delegate gave me a tour of Lindavista, even allowing me into the rooms where operators work, which Rendón had forbidden. She also presented me to the *personal de confianza* to inform them that I was doing research. The clear but unavoidable disadvantage of my links with operator delegates is that operators would associate me with representatives from Hernández Juárez's faction. Even though I had official support, some of the junior delegates were uncooperative towards me and clearly my 'meddling' presence was unwelcome. The operators themselves greeted me with different degrees of enthusiasm. The majority I approached seemed to feel they had some kind of 'duty' to cooperate with my questionnaire, and readily spent their 10- to 15-minute coffee break with me. Others – usually those who were unhappy with or disobedient to the union – wanted to chat with me at great length outside the premises, and some simply didn't want to talk with me at all.

Over the next two months I conducted my survey in Lindavista and, once I had gained the confidence of the head delegate, I was also invited to visit Rojo Gómez in order to extend my survey and interviews. Fortunately, however, I soon found that I was effectively sampling operators from all operating centres in Mexico City since all the operators had at some time worked previously at San Juan or Victoria, the older operator centres, many of them for several years.[13] Many of operators to whom I spoke were not usually based at the centre at which I met them. This is because the nature of the operator's job is mobile (she can operate at any operating station) and is organized into three eight-hour shifts in a 24-hour period. Operators are frequently moved from one centre to another, and from one shift to another. In order to maximize the representative accuracy of the survey, and to give all operators an equal chance of participating, I appeared on different days of the week, and during each of the three eight-hour working shifts. It was important to survey the operators working on night shifts since, in some cases, operator supervisors punish troublesome operators by forcing them to work at night.

It was crucial that the operators should consider their replies to my interview questions and survey as confidential. The operators, like all STRM members, have learnt through bitter experience that their workplace is not an arena of 'free speech'. Moreover, they are accustomed to two kinds of voting: voting for STRM local representatives, when they are not required to put their names on the slip, and voting for union leaders, when they are. I installed a ballot box in the lobby so that their replies could be folded and inserted by each respondent. I handed the questionnaire out personally to the operators, and was available to answer any questions they might have. I made it clear that I did not want them to write their name and operator codes on the sheets (although some did). I also put my telephone number on the top of the sheet so that I could be contacted if an operator had any queries or doubts about the questions. The operator centres are organized into three separate operating rooms, one each for international, national and information. By positioning myself alternately near the doors of the national and international operators' rooms I obtained a representative sample of both.

For these reasons, the results of the survey which I conducted are representative of the experiences of TELMEX operators in Mexico City. Furthermore, my sample of operators in Mexico is representative of operators working within the Republic. Below, I contrast the profile of my operator sample with a census of all telephone workers which was conducted by INTTELMEX.

The environment in the new operator centres is dominated by two strong power structures, one run by TELMEX, the other by the STRM. This hierarchy is most immediately striking in the way in which company and union representatives are dressed. TELMEX's *personal de confianza* wear electric blue or red uniforms depending on their seniority. Their job is to supervise operators on behalf of TELMEX. In the rooms of national, international and information operators, in each of which approximately 50 operators work, three or four *personal de confianza* check that the operators are working by walking around the room, and also by listening in at random through earphones which they have in glass booths at the sides of the operating rooms. TELMEX staff must ensure that operators are using correctly the official TELMEX phraseology when dealing with clients and that the operators are speaking in a polite and pleasant way to clients. Many operators to whom I spoke told me they had at some time been reprehended for failing to use the right tone of voice. The *personal de confianza* and the unionized workers do not mix, either during work or breaks.

In parallel with company hierarchy, the union asserts its own hierarchy over the operators. In both operator centres there is a small team of union supervisors who represent the international operators and the national operators. In both Rojo Gómez and Lindavista there is one head operator supervisor who is in charge of both these teams. The uniform of union supervisors is less formal than the *personal de confianza* and tends to be normal clothes including jeans, but tops and jackets must be dark brown or navy. While operator supervisors are elected they do not work as operators but as full-time union representatives and they have their own offices.[14] There are many factors at play which influence political relations between employees in these work centres, and the fact that there is a female-only environment influences the way in which politics are played. Operators do not wear uniforms, and after the restrictions of the past in terms of dress code, it was apparent to me that they could wear almost anything they wanted since their work wardrobe ranges from American-style track suits to immaculate and daring outfits. There is a strong element of competition in the style of dress and make-up among many employees, and compliments are the order of the day. One operator gains popularity by selling jewellery to colleagues and to supervisors, and in so doing builds up relations through an intimate female market. Employees enjoyed gossiping about each other; union supervisors enjoyed scandals and blurred the distinctions between labour-related problems and personal problems in their dealing with the operators. If an operator wanted to secure good relations with union supervisors and vice versa, the rules of the game must be played along the lines of a complex network of female vanities, rivalries and egos. One of the more formal rules of the power game played between the union and TELMEX was that operators must approach first the union supervisor in the event that she has a problem or a work or domestic query. Only if the supervisors failed to solve the problem could the operator consult a *personal de confianza*.

There is a division among the operators since international operators earn more than their national counterparts, principally because they can speak English.[15] This tends to create a certain amount of friction between the two groups.[16] The difference between the operators is reinforced since there are separate rest rooms and offices for international and national operators, so that members of one group tend not to know the others.

Women and technological change

All TELMEX operators are women. Authors including Martin (1991), Norwood (1990) and Borderías (1993) have accounted for the reasons why, at the turn of the century, this job shifted from being one that was largely the responsibility of males to being one where females were in charge.[17] From the 1970s, this phenomenon of feminization of the job of an operator has been reversed in some companies such as AT&T within the broader context of a reorganization of the entire company, since management was forced to implement 'affirmative action' recruitment plans to address accusations of discrimination in gender, ethnicity and age.[18] However, in most Latin American countries including Mexico, this transition has not taken place.

The relationship between women and technology has become a hotly debated issue in recent decades. Some analysts such as Braverman argued that female workers have been particularly vulnerable to the effects of labour de-skilling brought about by technological change.[19] Greve concurred with Braverman by stating that technological displacement – or the loss of jobs to machines – which has brought about mass unemployment has particularly affected women workers.[20] Other analysts have pointed out the errors (and dangers) of making a generalized statement about the relationship between technology and women. These authors show that, in some cases, technological change has been positive for women workers since it has brought about new opportunities for employment.[21]

It is important to consider the relationship between women and technology within specific industries or services. A cursory glance at the gender of staff working in the telecommunications sector shows that many companies such as AT&T, Northwestern Bell, TELMEX and Telefónica of Spain have witnessed dramatic drops in female employment and increases in male employment resulting from technological change, in particular since the 1940s.[22] The principal reason for this decline in women workers has been that technological change has tended to erode the need for the human operator. The first major shift in operator technology had been from manual to analogue equipment, and the second change was from analogue to digital systems.

TELMEX operators' working environment

In 1990, the Lindavista and Rojo Gómez telephone operator centres were inaugurated in Mexico City. They constitute TELMEX's state-of-the-art operating technology. In total the centres hold around 700 operators, which include '02' operators (national long distance) and '09' (international long distance). In addition, there are some '04' operators (information to the client) who are being trained to work as national long-distance operators. Both centres were designed identically and operators work on the same equipment which was supplied by Northern Telecom, Canada. The installation of digital technology in the centres was completed in 1992. My survey results indicated that all the operators had been working more than five years in TELMEX, so that they had all therefore experienced the transition from analogue to digital technology.[23]

Previously, when operators had used analogue systems they had to connect calls manually with small switches, and were seated in a row of 11 others. Each row was supervised by one union supervisor and one company *personal de confianza*. Many of the older operators told me that the job was an uncomfortable one, since the headset was heavy and awkward and the seats uncomfortable. One of the most repeated complaints of these operators was that it was extremely difficult to take even a natural break, since the supervisor gave permission to leave to only one operator at a time. Many operators told me that in the past the *personal de confianza* (most of whom were former operators) were extremely strict, forbade any talking among the operators, and referred to them by their work number not their name. They instructed operators to dress smartly and banned mini-skirts and trousers. According to the operators, the attitude of the *personal de confianza* relaxed gradually throughout the 1980s in terms of dress codes, and to the extent that many learned the operators' names. Contact between them, however, is still minimal and limited to working matters.

The change to digital equipment was dramatic in terms of work practice. Digital equipment consists of a computer and keyboard on a wooden surface which can be raised or lowered so that the operator can choose to work from either a standing or sitting position. The headset is much lighter than the cumbersome equipment used previously. When starting work, the operator attaches her headset and then keys in her worker identification number. After the connection has been made, she waits for the number of a caller to appear on the screen, then asks the caller which service they require and the telephone number desired. The operator then processes the call and immediately turns her attention to other calls which the equipment automatically places in a queue for her. The work of the operator can be continuous as there is usually a queue of work waiting for her to process. There are four computers positioned on the corner of each table with high wooden screens around each computer. The operators' work has therefore become more isolated since they cannot see or hear each other, as they had been able to when using analogue equipment. Operators do not have to ask permission to take a break since they are automatically entitled to a ten-minute rest every hour.

The survey presented in this chapter analysed the specific ways in which the introduction of digitalization affected labour practices and the operators' relations with union and company representatives. The change in technology is of course very important, but I was not only interested in the effects of the change for the individual operator; I tried to use the introduction of digitalization, the training course, the problems encountered with the system as a way of observing labour relations between TELMEX *personal de confianza*, operators and union supervisors.

The survey

The sample

The population which I targeted was the TELMEX operators within the Mexican Republic. In theory, the optimum way of getting a random sample of operators would have been to mail a questionnaire to names selected at random. The problem with this research method is that the response would probably have either been low or non-existent since for many operators the idea of a survey is a novelty. More importantly, due to the great amount of hostility shown towards outsiders asking for information about work practices in the company, the operators probably would have been too suspicious to reply. I believed that it was extremely important to have personal contact with them in order to explain my project and my interest. I thus chose to conduct my survey in person, and I limited my sample to the operators in Mexico City, which comprised the operators working in the centres of San Juan, Lindavista and Rojo Gómez, since the capital represented the greatest concentration of operators.[24]

The questionnaire

In order to compile a list of questions for use in the survey I first conducted exploratory interviews with about 50 operators. Both Lindavista and Rojo Gómez have a large central lobby where the operators congregate during their ten-minute breaks to which they are entitled every hour. I interviewed operators in this area, unless they expressed a wish to go for lunch or a coffee outside the centre, and I also conducted my survey in the lobby. Rather appropriately, there was an old analogue switchboard cased inside a glass box in the centre of the lobby which served as my main prop so I could nod in its direction every time I asked operators about the change from analogue to digital equipment.

Most individual interviews lasted between ten and 20 minutes while some lasted a few hours. The sample interviewed included both national and international operators and represented all ages, seniority and educational ranges. These interviews helped me to phrase my questions in an unambiguous way. I did not fundamentally change my original questions but added two more (questions 10 and 11 of the questionnaire, see Figure A.2). I also decided to make my questionnaire extremely brief so that the operators would be able to answer it during their ten-minute break. I believed that if the questions required too much time the majority of operators would simply not reply.

Once my questions were ready, I had to send them for inspection and possible censorship to Rendón, the head operator *comisionada*. Knowing that a sensitive question could jeopardize my chance to conduct the survey, I worded each one carefully to avoid displeasing her. She passed my survey without making any changes. Afterwards I had to circulate the questions among all the trade union officials in Lindavista for their comments. I received none and was allowed to start the survey. The questions were closed and only required that the respondent circle the appropriate reply.

The first five questions in the survey (A–E) sought to classify the sample of operators by age, seniority, education, languages spoken and whether they worked in the national or international division. These data characterized the sample, and allowed comparison with INTTELMEX's census on the STRM in order to ensure that my sample was representative. These classifications were also used to disaggregate the responses to questions 1 to 12 to enquire whether they were sensitive to age, education, seniority and so on.

The numbered questions (1–12) aimed to assess the changes in labour practice and labour relations which had taken place due to the introduction of digital equipment. Questions 1 to 3 enquired about the ease or difficulty associated with the shift from analogue to digital technology and addressed the advantages of the new system compared with the old one. Question 4 asked whether the use of digital equipment implied that the operator had more autonomy to make her own decisions in her day-to-day work, or whether she had to ask union supervisors for help. Questions 5, 6 and 8 considered the flexibility of labour practice with digital equipment. Operators were asked whether the vocabulary they used with digital equipment was more extensive than before, and whether it was now easier or more difficult to take a break or change shift when they wished. Again, the intent was to assess whether using digital technology had brought about more or less discipline in the workplace; whether the operator was more autonomous to take decisions about when she needed a rest, or change her shift; how much autonomy she had to deal with a caller, and to what extent she was restricted by the official phrases which she had to use when speaking to callers.

Question 7 assessed whether the respondent had genuinely changed her attitude in line with the ideas of liberalization and competition. The aim of this question was to try to assess how successful the campaign promoted by TELMEX and the STRM had been in educating workers about the changing nature of the telecommunications sector and promoting a new, more competitive, work culture. Question 9 tested Hernández Juárez's declaration that workers had benefited from privatization since they had received more training. Questions 10 and 11 enquired about the efficiency and the limitations of the new equipment. After exploratory interviews with some operators it was clear that the new digital equipment was far from being perceived as the ultimate in technology in their eyes; moreover, in the interviews many were extremely critical of the new technology. The national operators believed that in the past they provided a public service, and that one of their most important functions was to help callers, particularly when they handled emergency calls. They seemed frustrated that the new digital equipment did not improve their ability to help callers, and some said it lessened their capacity to help when they received emergency calls. Question 11 was added after many international operators told me they still had difficulty in connecting calls to remote countries, and that they often called AT&T in order to connect the caller. They did this in secret since supervisors would punish this behaviour because AT&T, and not TELMEX, obtained the profit for connecting the call. Finally, question 12 sought to discover whether, since modernization, operators had participated more in the union. The question was worded quantitatively, as it was apparent during my interviews that, when an operator was asked if she participated in the union, on many occasions she keenly responded in the positive, but when I followed this with a question about *how* she participated, there was blankness or confusion. This final question tested Hernández Juárez's assertion that privatization has brought with it increased worker participation in the union.[25] All the questions hinged around a clear turning point – the change of equipment from analogue to digital. This change was used as a reference point in order to analyse how the introduction of new technology affected labour relations at the shop-floor level in terms of relations between operators and auxiliaries; between operators and trusted employees and between union supervisors and *personal de confianza*, and to assess whether the operator worked in a more autonomous way in her day-to-day activities.

A profile of the operators

The sample of operators

A total of 300 questionnaires were handed out, and there were 138 replies. The response rate was thus slightly under 50 per cent. One possible reason that some operators did not respond was an unwillingness to use their break time to fill in the survey due to simple lack of interest. Others avoided the survey because they were suspicious that it could be used by a rival telephone company to damage TELMEX, even though the head operator delegate had announced that my research was being carried out in support of a doctoral qualification. A small group of operators were actively advising others not to cooperate with me, as they believed I was a spy from an American telephone company![26] Moreover, hostility towards me was increased since the work centre was busy preparing for the election of new STRM supervisors, and also, because of my perceived connection to the current head supervisor, her adversaries regarded me with suspicion.

Responses broke down into 108 from national operators and 30 from international operators. This ratio was in line with that of the actual number of national to international operators working in Mexico City which was around 4:1. Some 3 per cent of the operators sampled were under 25, 13 per cent were between 26 and 30, over a half were aged between 31 and 40, around 20 per cent were between 41 and 45, and only a small percentage were over 46 (Figure A.1). Over 60 per cent of the operators had worked in TELMEX for between 11 and 20 years (Figure A.2). The bulk of these workers were aged between 31 and 40 (Figure A.3). Among the national operators, seniority was spread quite equally. However, for international operators, the number who had worked less than ten years was low (3.3 per cent) while 40 per cent had worked for 11–15 years, and 30 per cent between 21 and 25 years.

For the operators generally, 3 per cent had received only primary education, 40 per cent had only completed secondary studies, 45 per cent had finished their education with preparatory studies and 12 per cent had obtained a degree

(Figure A.4). Comparing national and international operators, primary education only was low among national operators (nearly 4 per cent) and non-existent in the case of international operators. International operators had achieved higher levels than national operators for degree and preparatory education (16.7 per cent compared to 10.2 per cent and 56.7 per cent compared to 42.6 per cent respectively). While all the international operators spoke English, and a third spoke three or more languages, only one-fifth of national operators claimed to be English-speakers.

The degree to which the survey is representative

The INTTELMEX census was realized over the two-year period, between December 1991 and October 1992. There was therefore a three-to-four year gap between the INTTELMEX census and my survey. Some 10 627 operators were included in the 1993 INTTELMEX census, which could be broken down into 8539 (80 per cent) national operators and 2088 (20 per cent) international operators. Proportionally, the responses to my survey, 108 (78 per cent) national and 30 (22 per cent) international operators, corresponded closely to the balance throughout the republic.[27]

In the census, the average number of years worked by a national operator was 13 with a standard deviation of 6.5, and for the international operator 13.8 years with standard deviation 6.7.[28] In my survey, the average seniority of the national operator was 15.8 years with standard deviation 5.6, while the average years worked by an international operator was 17.5 with standard deviation 4.8. The differences in seniority between the census and my survey could be explained by the three- to four-year time period between the studies, and the fact that the operators have increased their seniority, since a negligible degree of new recruitment of operators took place after 1989. The average age of operators in the census was 34 years and 4 months for the national operator (standard deviation 7.1) and 35 years 3 months for the international operator.[29] My survey showed that the average age of the national operator was 35 years 7 months (standard deviation 6.3) and 35 years and 2 months for the international operators (standard deviation 5.5).

The census did not disaggregate information about workers' education levels by speciality. However, one TELMEX source did contain data on the maximum levels of education among operators.[30] This showed that 19.24 per cent of operators had secondary education; nearly 10 per cent held a technical career certificate; 24 per cent had preparatory studies; 29 per cent had commercial studies, and 13 per cent held a degree. However, my other educational categories of primary, secondary and preparatory were broader than those used by TELMEX, making exact comparisons difficult.

The results

Replies to questions 1–12 were analysed for all operators then disaggregated according to categories A–E. Operators were distinguished first by whether they worked for national or international services, since the nature of the job has some important differences for these groups. Second, they were distinguished by seniority, since this category inherently provides information about what kind of equipment that operator has used and for how long. I did not dis-aggregate the operators by age since some of their answers were unreliable – if they had been telling the truth about both age and seniority it would imply in some cases that they started working before they were ten years old!

The shift from analogue to digital technology

New labour practices brought about by digitalization were in general easily assimilated by the TELMEX operators. For the majority of both national (61 per cent) and international (53 per cent) operators, their use of digital equipment was the first contact they had with a computer (Figure A.5). Nevertheless, the majority (62 per cent) of all operators claimed that the switch to digital technology was either very easy or easy, with international operators in particular (76 per cent) finding the change an easy one. Approximately one-third of all operators found the change slightly difficult, while a small percentage claimed it was too difficult for them to master. The longer an operator had worked in TELMEX the more likely she was to state that digitalization was the first time she had used a computer (Figure A.6). The only exception to this trend was the most senior category of operators with 21–25 years of experience who had been more exposed to computers since many of them had been recruited to work as operator super-visors and trainers, for which they had received training courses involving com-puting skills and who therefore considered the transition to have been easy. Operators who had worked the least time in TELMEX (6–15 years) found the transition to digital technology particularly easy (65 per cent said it was either easy or very easy). Again, those in the next category (16–20) found the transition more difficult, since 54 per cent replied that the change was very easy while 46 per cent said it was slightly hard or too hard.

The ease with which the transition from analogue to digital technology was made was facilitated by training programmes jointly organized by the STRM and TELMEX. The overwhelming majority of all operators (88 per cent) claimed that they had received more training than they had previously experienced in order to operate the new equipment. This opinion was shared by both international and national operators as well as operators of all ranges of seniority.

The impact of digitalization on work practices

Operators generally agreed that digitalization made their work more com-fortable (98 per cent) and easier (93 per cent).[31] At the same time, both national and international operators thought that digitalization caused their work to become more repetitive, and the international operators felt even more strongly about this (83 per cent compared to 66 per cent, Figure A.7). By seniority, there were no significant discrepancies among the categories since in each section the overwhelming majority agreed that the task was easier, more comfortable but more repetitive. However, 70 per cent of those in the category of having 16–20 years experience admitted that the work was more tiring. It is reasonable to assume that this applied to the category with the lowest percentage of computer literacy.

One interesting outcome of digitalization is that a wedge has been driven between the national and international operators. While the majority of national operators stated that their work was *less* tiring than before (65 per cent), the majority of international operators (71 per cent) stated the opposite, they were more tired than before (Figure A.7). This is an important result which can be explained by TELMEX's pricing policy since 1990. The price of international calls dropped dramatically as cross-subsidization policies were phased out in order that local calls should become self-financing and the price of international calls could become competitive in world markets. Increased international traffic has generated much more work for international operators. The results from question 6 reinforced these conclusions since they revealed that the international operators are working harder than before (Figure A.8). While most national operators (74 per cent) claimed that their breaks had not changed, some 43 per cent of international operators claimed that they had less breaks than before. The survey also revealed that over half of all operators who had been working for a longer time in TELMEX (21–25 years) thought that they had less breaks than in the past, while those who have worked less years (6–10) claimed their breaks had not changed which implies a gradual increase of the workload over the years.

Another indication of a widening gap between national and international operators was the situation with regard to work flexibility. After digitalization, over half of the international operators (53 per cent) claimed that it was more difficult to change their shifts while 40 per cent said it was the same as before. Thus only 7 per cent of international operators believed it had become easier to change their shift. In contrast, 56 per cent of national operators claimed it had become easier to change their shift (Figure A.9). This question was not sensitive to a breakdown in terms of seniority which suggested that the national–international categories override the fact that operators with a greater seniority are often given special privileges (flexibility) to alter their shifts. The international operators' claims that they were working harder than before, enjoyed fewer breaks, and found it more complicated to change their shift than before was logical in the light of the growth of international traffic.

The majority of operators (64 per cent) agreed that using digital equipment meant that they needed to consult their supervisors less frequently (Figure A.10). The proportion of international operators was higher (73 per cent) than that of national operators (62 per cent). Most of the rest claimed that the degree of consultation with their supervisor remained as before. By seniority there were no significant differences, two-thirds saying that consultation with the supervisor was less than before, one-third saying that it was the same. Over half (52 per cent) of all operators claimed that they enjoyed more freedom in their use of official vocabulary when using the digital system in comparison with the analogue equipment. The international section felt more strongly about this (60 per cent) than the national (50 per cent) due to the fact that TELMEX had introduced many new international services which had to be explained to the caller.[32] Around 28 per cent thought the vocabulary used was the same as before, and 20 per cent that it had become more restricted. Disaggregating the information by seniority shows homogeneity among all categories.

The changing role of the operator

The responses of the national operators to question 10 shed light on a significant change in the nature of the operator's function. I added this question to my original list after exploratory interviews with national operators. One of the more interesting criticisms they made was that digital equipment and new working practices made it more difficult for them to provide a satisfactory service in the case that they received an emergency call. Many of them believed that their central role was to assist callers, particularly for emergency calls, and perceived their role as a kind of social service and they were passionate about this issue. Changes introduced with digitalization, including productivity drives to set targets for the number of calls which must be connected per hour, caused the operators' service to emergency callers to be sacrificed. In the survey, some 56 per cent claimed that it had become more difficult than before to connect a national emergency call and only 15 per cent said that there was no difference (Figure A.11). Contrasting the responses by seniority (Figure A.11), those who had worked longer for the company felt more strongly that handling an emergency call had become more difficult, perhaps because these operators had spent longer at the service of emergency callers and were more deeply engrained into the culture of providing a public service.

Instead of perceiving themselves as providers of a public service, operators have become more worried about the vulnerability of their jobs in the face of international competition in the telecommunications sector. Over one-third expressed serious concern about this and one-half stated they were slightly worried. These anxieties were shared by national and international operators in broadly equal proportions. Interestingly, those who had worked for TELMEX for the shortest time tended to be the most worried (48 per cent). At the other end of the scale, those in the most senior range (21–25) were the second largest group to express significant concern. The most confident group about the changes in the telecommunications sector lay in the range of 11–20 years' experience, some 60 per cent of whom expressed that they were confident or only slightly worried. Job insecurity was feared most by those with the lowest seniority ('last in first out') and those approaching retirement (Figure A.12).

Operator participation in and attitudes towards the STRM

Since my survey was scrutinized by union *comisionados* before I was given permission to carry it out, I felt a sensitive question about operators' attitudes towards the union would be enough to have my survey refused. The information on this topic was gleaned from individual interviews and is therefore qualitative rather than quantitative. Of all the survey questions, the last one regarding whether workers participated more in the union after privatization, as Hernández Juárez claimed, was potentially the most sensitive. After all, I had promoted my survey as a study of the impact of technology on workers, not as a study of union practice. During my exploratory interviews with operators, a high percentage stated that they participated more actively in the union, but when I asked them how, there were no convincing replies. I therefore decided to formulate the question in a strictly quantitative way.

The result was that 60 per cent of the operators claimed that their participation in the STRM remained unchanged, about 29 per cent claimed they participated more and around 10 per cent said they participated less. The national–international distinction was not sensitive to these results. By seniority, there was a stable 25 per cent across the board who claimed they now participated more. Only in the category of the most senior was the claim of greater participation particularly high (67 per cent). This is the smallest group of the sample (six workers). These results are not surprising because those workers who continue after 25 years are usually recruited to positions as union officials. The largest groups to claim that they now participate in the union less are those with fewest years in TELMEX (20 per cent in the 6–10 range and 16 per cent in the 11–15 range). The majority of those in the middle ranges claimed their participation was unchanged (72 per cent in the 16–20 range and 67 per cent in the 21–25 range). These results do not throw much light on details about operators' participation in the union. Participation is a complex topic and it is likely that it meant different things to different operators. Those who stated that their participation had not changed in the union included a mixed bag of those who vehemently opposed it and avoided contact with it at all costs; those who used their maternal duties as an excuse to avoid participation; and those who passively did what they had to do but no more. Perhaps there is one tentative conclusion that can be drawn from these results. The sector which claimed that it participated more was spread equally among all operators, but those who claimed that they participated less was firmly in the younger categories. Since the group of operators is ageing (recruitment has been negligible since 1989) it is logical to suppose that, as the older generation operators retire, the newer operators, less interested in the union, will become a more significant proportion of the operator sub-group.

Operators' attitude towards the union leadership could only be gleaned through interviews. It was hardly surprising that the operators who were prepared to spend whole afternoons talking to me were disgruntled and, often, active dissidents. Overall, even those operators most critical of Hernández Juárez could do no more than accept his success through TELMEX's privatization and his privileged relationship with the president.[33] They laughed about the way in which Hernández Juárez was totally open to union members about his closeness with Salinas, and his habit of arriving seven hours late to meetings with the excuse of having been with the president. Anecdotes told by Hernández Juárez's enemies included union members teasing him by demanding a photograph of him in a tuxedo when he was invited to an international dinner dance in the company of Salinas and Thatcher.[34] Thus although Hernández Juárez and his cronies have many enemies, in general, his enemies regard him with respect and they themselves admit that Lejarza is 'muy culto'.[35] Many assume that Salinas has become the new owner of TELMEX even though they know this has not been proved but is a strong rumour.

Conclusion

The introduction of digitalization in TELMEX has fundamentally transformed the nature of the operators' job. For the national operator, the job has changed from one of providing a social service to the public to one in which the speed of making the maximum number of connections is crucial. For the international operator, the dramatically increased workload has translated into more tiring and repetitive work with fewer opportunities to rest. In both cases, there is a profit-making drive behind the changes, which reflects clearly the motivations of the new management team.

In terms of the way that relations between operators and their supervisors changed, the operators claimed that they now consulted their supervisors less when working could have been interpreted to mean that they therefore became more autonomous in their work. However, it should be noted that one of the characteristics of the introduction of digital equipment is that supervision of operators changed from being a job performed by humans to one accomplished largely by machines. Each call, and the number of seconds taken to connect it, is recorded by the digital equipment and assigned to the operator. In this way, at the end of the day or week, the supervisor can calculate each individual operator's productivity performance by referring to the computer. The supervision of the operator has been largely transferred from humans to machines. Now, the supervisors have access to much simpler and more accurate tools by which they can assess the performance of each operator at the push of a button.

The logic is that as the use of new technology increases the number of operators will inevitably continue to fall. As this happens, they will become a much less valuable tool to Hernández Juárez as a central bloc of political support. Previously, it had been relatively easy for union leaders to target benefits to the operators in exchange for their mass support, such as in 1979, when they were awarded a *convenio*, and after the 1985 earthquake, when the government announced they were not going to be sacked. Even after privatization, the operators had continued to exert a considerable influence over union leaders. When, in 1992, management and union leaders had agreed on the relocation of 5000 operators, the operators had refused to accept that they would uproot themselves from wherever they worked. By 1993, management was forced to agree that operators would be moved to different jobs but within the same geographical area.

However, once former operators are dispersed to other jobs such as telemarketing and administration, they will make different demands upon union leaders and it will be more complex to satisfy them. Women in the STRM benefited by being the largest sub-group of workers until the late 1980s. Restructuring means that this bargaining power they enjoyed vis-à-vis union leaders will become much weaker, and they will find it increasingly difficult to attain their demands. One of the net effects of labour restructuring is thus a weakening of women's position as a political force inside the STRM. The introduction of new technology in TELMEX did not lead to mass redundancy of women, as in the worst scenario painted by Braverman, since new work opportunities were created for them. Thus, it will be increasingly difficult for operators to rectify newly emerging labour problems such as the way that the international operators are being increasingly overworked which was highlighted in the survey responses.

Table A.1. Questionnaire to Operators of Teléfonos de México (English translation)

Thank you for your cooperation in filling in this questionnaire in order to help me conclude my doctoral thesis on the operators of TELMEX. Please call me if you have any questions.

Personal information

A. You are a national (02) or international (09) operator.
B. You have worked for TELMEX for the following years:
   0–5; 6–10; 11–15; 16–20; 21–25; OVER 25.
C. Your age range is:
   20 OR LESS; 21–25; 26–30; 31–35; 36–40; 41–45; 46–50; OVER 50.
D. Your maximum level of education has been:
   Primary; Secondary; Preparatory; Degree.
E. Languages: English; Others.

What is your opinion about the change from analogue to digital equipment undertaken by TELMEX?

1. The change from analogue to digital for you was at first: Very easy; Easy; A bit Hard; Too hard.
2. Was your contact with digital equipment the first time you had used a computer? Yes/No.
3. How would you describe your work with the new digital equipment?
   More/less difficult than before; More/less comfortable than before; More/less monotonous than before; More/less tiring than before.
4. Your work with digital equipment means that you consult your auxiliary: More times than before; The same as before; Less times than before.
5. The phraseology that you use with digital equipment is:
   Broader than before; The same as before; More restricted than before.
6. Your chances to take a break during working hours are:
   Better than before; The same; Less than before.
7. How do you feel about international competition in the world of communications after 1997?
   Confident; A bit worried; Very worried; Indifferent.
8. To change your workshift is:
   Harder than before; The same; Easier than before.
9. Since the introduction of digital equipment have you participated in more training courses? Yes/No.
10. For national operators: In order to provide services for an emergency caller it is now:
    Easier than before; The same as before; Harder than before.
11. For international operators: In order to call a distant country (like Cuba or Nigeria) it is now:
    Easier than before; The same as before; Harder than before.
12. Since the modernization of TELMEX, your participation in the STRM has been:
    More frequent than before; The same as before; Less frequent than before.

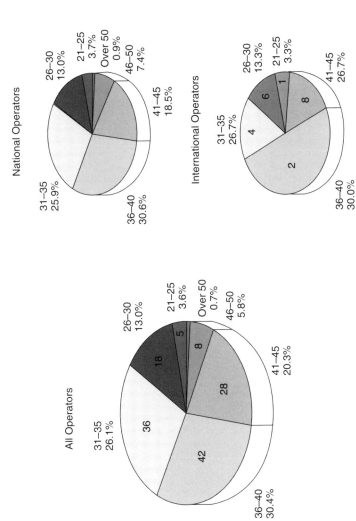

Figure A.1   Age of the Sample of TELMEX Operators
Source: TELMEX Survey (June 1995).

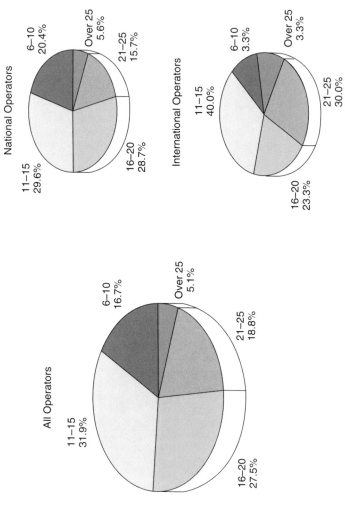

Figure A.2 Years that Sample of Operators Worked in TELMEX
Source: TELMEX Survey (June 1995).

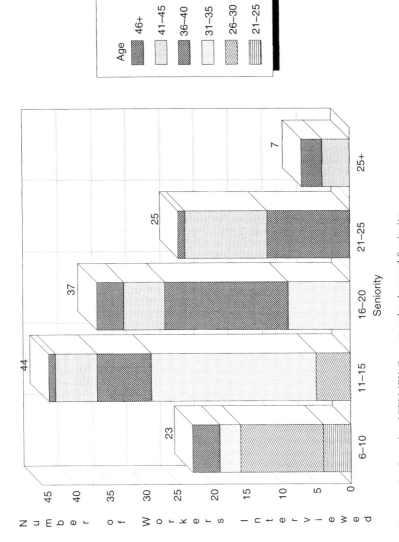

Figure A.3 Sample of TELMEX Operators by Age and Seniority
Source: TELMEX Survey (June 1995).

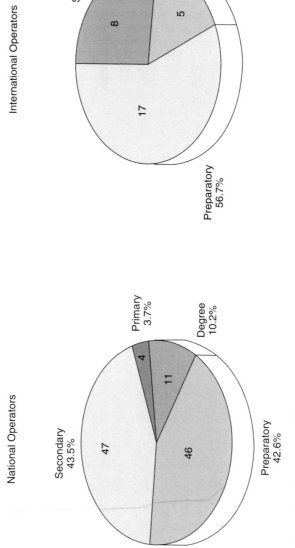

Figure A.4 Education of Sample of TELMEX Operators
Source: TELMEX Survey (June 1995).

199

'Was this the first time you
had contact with a computer?'

International

Yes
53%

16

14

No
47%

National

Yes
61%

66

42

No
39%

Figure A.5   Computer use of TELMEX Operators
Source: TELMEX Survey (June 1995).

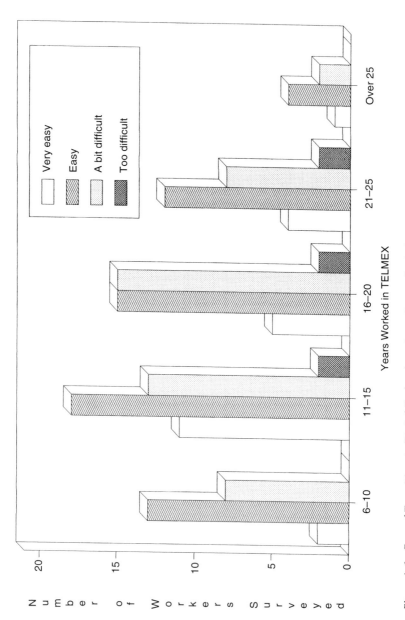

Figure A.6 Ease of Transition to Digital Technology According to Seniority
Source: TELMEX Survey (June 1995).

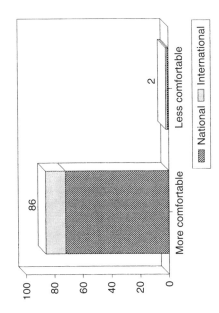

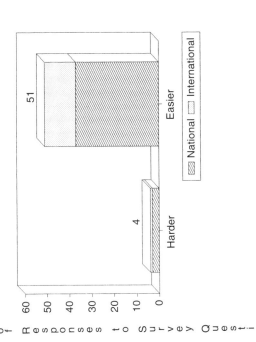

Figure A.7   Operators' Views on Digital Technology
Source: TELMEX Survey (June 1995).

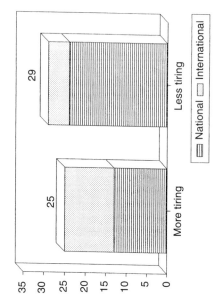

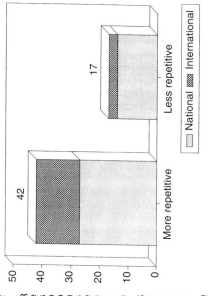

Figure A.7 (continued)

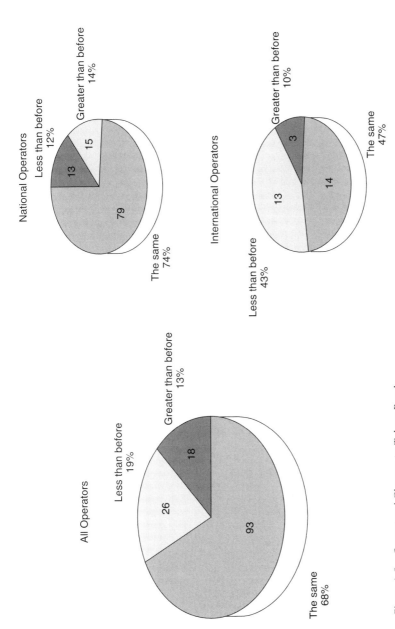

Figure A.8 Operators' Chance to Take a Break
Source: TELMEX Survey (June 1995).

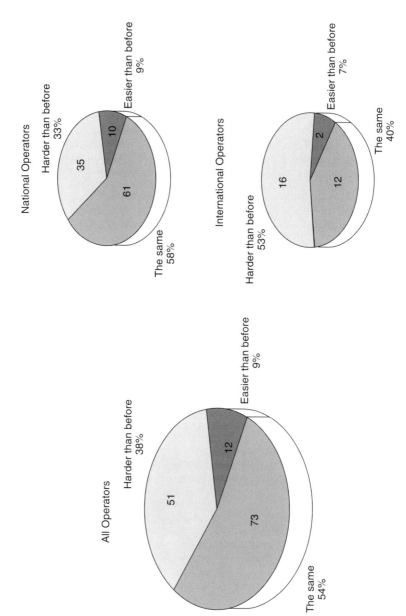

Figure A.9 Changing Shifts of All Operators
Source: TELMEX Survey (June 1995).

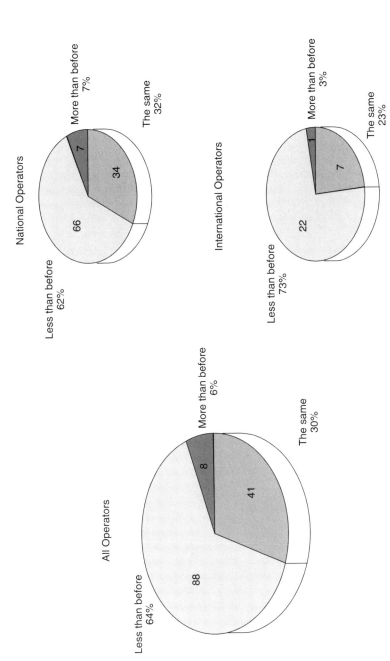

Figure A.10 Need to Consult Supervisor (All Operators)
Source: TELMEX Survey (June 1995).

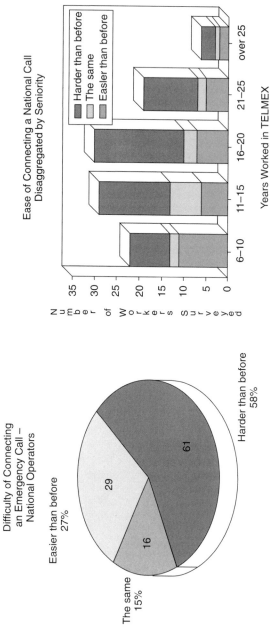

Figure A.11   Connecting Calls
Source: TELMEX Survey (June 1995).

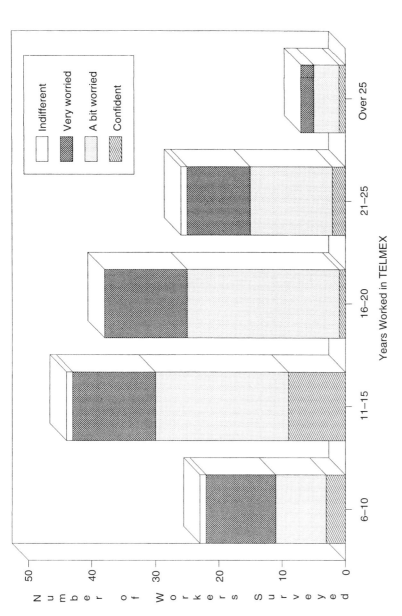

Figure A.12   Anxiety in the Face of International Competition
Source: TELMEX Survey (June 1995).

Notes

Introduction

1. Diamond *et al.* (1989), O'Brien and Cammack (1985), O'Donnell *et al.* (1986) and Diamond *et al.* (1993).
2. Diamond *et al.* (1989), p. xiii and O'Brien and Cammack (1985).
3. Huntington in Diamond and Plattner (1993), p. x, and Huntington (1991).
4. McGowan in (ed.) Clarke (1994), p. 29.
5. Clarke (ed.) (1994), p. 2.
6. For an analysis of the history of the key concepts and thinkers on this theme, see Whitehead, 'Some Insights from Western Social Theory' (1993) and Lal, 'Participation, Markets and Democracy' in (eds) Lundahl and Ndulu (1996).
7. Events were so dramatic that Fukuyama's *The End of History and the Last Man* (1992) which postulated that the world had arrived at its final point, liberal democracy, became a best-seller.
8. The volume edited by Roett (1993) which includes chapters by Delal Baer, Roett and Rubio has an underlying tone of optimism for the future of democracy in Mexico. In addition see Weintraub (1990), Morici (February 1993) and Weintraub and Delal Baer (Spring 1992).
9. In many comparative analyses of the political systems in Latin American countries, Mexico has continually defied attempts to classify the systems neatly, such as in Diamond *et al.* (eds) 1989 and Diamond *et al.* (eds) 1990. Regardless of the fact that Mexico is one of the largest and most important Latin American countries, analysts have often resorted to treating it largely in the footnotes of comparative works including in Rueschemeyer *et al.* (1992).
10. Cornelius *et al.* (1989), pp. 1 and 30.
11. Roett (1993), p. 11, Rubio in (ed.) Roett (1993), p. 37 and Delal Baer in (ed.) Roett (1993), p. 53.
12. The central argument regarding the formation of a political élite made by Centeno (1995) was also accepted by many other analysts including Teichman (1995) and Heredia (1993).
13. Craske (1994), Heredia (1993) and Samstad and Berins Collier (1995).
14. Middlebrook (1995).
15. Chapter 1 sets out in more detail the reasons why this approach was rejected.
16. The reasons why the sale of TELMEX was the most important instance of privatization in Mexico are provided in Chapter 4.
17. See (eds) Harriss-White and White (1996) and Manzetti and Blake (1996).
18. See Toye for a critique of the New Political Economy in (eds) Colclough and Manor (1991).
19. Puebla has historically been a hot-bed for telephone worker dissidents, so it was also worth doing some fieldwork there to become acquainted with STRM union dissidents.

20. Roxborough (1981) and interview with Middlebrook, June 1997, Oxford.
21. Interestingly, in the case of TELMEX, I was required to seek the union but not management permission to conduct my research.
22. Roxborough (1981) and (1984).
23. There are relatively few works which treat internal union practice in any great depth. Some of the main exceptions are Roxborough (1984) and Foweraker (1993).
24. Roxborough's criticism of the weaknesses in the analyses of organized labour published in 1981 is still applicable to much contemporary literature.
25. However, I was often mistaken for being a *'gringa'* which was not to my advantage since some of the Mexican telephone workers were worried that I was a spy from AT&T.
26. Fitzgerald summarized the dilemma succinctly: ´The "Washington View" (e.g. the World Bank) is that the New Trade Regime has been an almost unqualified success on both criteria, while the "view from Santiago" (i.e. from CEPAL) is almost the diametrical opposite´. Fitzgerald in Bulmer-Thomas (ed.) (1996), pp. 29–30.

1   Continuity and Rupture in the Mexican Political System

1. The origin of the PRI is in the establishment of the *Partido Nacional Revolucionario* by President Calles in 1929. The party was consolidated by President Lázaro Cárdenas in 1938 and given a new name, the *Partido de la Revolución Mexicana*. Finally, in 1946, it was re-named the *Partido Revolucionario Institucional*. To avoid confusion I will refer to the ruling party as the PRI in this chapter.
2. Whitehead (1981), p. 29.
3. Stevens (1974), pp. 1–15 and Whitehead (1981).
4. Vargas Llosa recently confirmed he still thought the PRI was the 'perfect dictatorship' even when the party lost a significant number of its seats in the Congress to the PAN and the PRD in July 1997. *El País*, 14 July 1997.
5. See chapter by Cornelius in (ed.) Gentleman (1987).
6. Cosío Villegas (1972), p. 31.
7. Middlebrook (1995), p. 30.
8. Whitehead (1994), p. 13.
9. The obvious exception to this was the splintering off by Cuauhtémoc Cárdenas to form the *Frente Democrático Nacional* in 1988, which mounted one of the most significant political challenges to the PRI in its history. Previously, in 1952, Henríquez Guzmán had also led a dissident faction within the PRI, but this was quickly disbanded and repressed.
10. The term 'Revolutionary Family', first coined by Brandenburg (1964), refers to those biological and political descendants of the group who assumed power during the Mexican Revolution and who continue to rule to this day. See Knight in Higley and Gunther (1995), p. 121.
11. For example, the Mexican government's insistence that the armed peasants in Chiapas had been trained by Guatemalan, and later, by Cuban guerillas was a strategy to avoid admitting there was an endogenous problem in Mexico, that is, a Mexican problem.

12. Fagen and Tuohy (1972), p. 30 painted a picture of a government apparatus in Jalapa which constantly sought to recruit potentially threatening, often talented, candidates into the PRI apparatus. Once inside the system, the government distributed welfare benefits and other patronage in exchange for continued political support. See also Morris (1991), p. 31 and Adler Hellman (1988), Chapter 5.

13. Middlebrook (1995).

14. Knight (1996a), p. 22.

15. Smith (1984), p. 19.

16. Tucker (1957), pp. 42–3, Bailey (1988), p. 14.

17. Camp (1993), p. 115.

18. Among those who point out that President Cárdenas refused to allow peasants and workers to form a single corporatist organization, Trejo Delarbre (1976) is perhaps the most critical.

19. The word *charro* (cowboy) first became a term used to describe an aspect of the labour movement when the government intervened in the railworkers' union by ousting the incumbent elected leader Gómez Z with a government supporter, Díaz de Leon. This character was known as '*el charro*' due to his passion for sporting cowboy-like clothes. After this, every leader imposed by the government as leader of a union would be known as a *charro*. See Stevens (1974), p. 105.

20. As Scott (1959), p. 155–96 had believed in the 1950s.

21. When I refer to the 'state' I coincide with Whitehead's minimalist description of its 'three essential and inter-related characteristics – territoriality, administration, and command over resources'. See Whitehead in (ed.) Bethell (1994), p. 11. The problem for political scientists analysing the case of Mexico is that the PRI is intimately bound up with the state. For instance, it is often the case in Mexico that one of the requirements before being hired in public administration is PRI membership. Throughout this book I use 'state' to refer to the features mentioned above, and PRI when meaning the party, however, in reality both institutions are tightly interwoven.

22. Hansen (1971), p. 107.

23. In terms of literature on organized labour, Roxborough argued that the conventional image presented by many authors of the state–labour pact as conflict-free golden age was oversimplified and misleading: it had always been a conflictual pact. Roxborough (1984).

24. For example, Anderson wrote in 1967 that the PRI was one of the 'living museums' in Latin America. See Cornelius *et al.* (1989), p. 1.

25. Camp claimed that the events in Tlatelolco in 1968 were of fundamental significance in challenging the legitimacy of the system which had been secured after 1930. See Camp in (ed.) Rodríguez (1993), p. 246. The period after 1968 was described by Newell and Rubio (1984), p. 264 as one whereby the regime used material incentives to massage areas in society which had been injured.

26. Newell and Rubio (1984), p. 264.

27. See the chapters by Clarke, Knight and Pansters in (ed.) Aitken *et al.* (1996) and Roxborough (1984).

28. Pansters in (eds) Aitken *et al.* (1996), p. 244.

29. Rubin cited by Knight in (eds) Foweraker and Craig (1990), p. 95.

30. Roxborough (1984) argued that the depiction of a PRI controlling labour throughout the period of economic growth is oversimplified.
31. Chapter by Rubin in (eds) Foweraker and Craig (1990), p. 260.
32. Roxborough (1984), pp. 1–35.
33. See Knight in (eds) Foweraker and Craig (1990), p. 79.
34. Smith in (ed.) Bethell (1991), p. 321.
35. For recent examples of the application of regression techniques applied to studies on Mexico see Chapter 5 of Middlebrook (1995). See also Molinar Horcasitas and Weldon's use of regression techniques applied to data on PRONASOL spending in 'Electoral Determinants and Consequences of National Solidarity' and Gershberg, 'Distributing Resources in the Education Sector: Solidarity's Escuela Digna Program' in (eds) Cornelius *et al.* (1994).
36. See (eds) Clarke and Pitelis (1993).
37. Fishlow (1987) argued that one of the reasons for blaming Latin America's failures on ISI is because the region has been compared with the more liberal outward-growing economies of Asian countries, particularly Korea and Taiwan, which switched from ISI to export orientation in the 1960s.
38. See (ed.) Ramamurti (1996), p. 5.
39. See Whitehead (1993) and Lal in (eds) Lundahl and Ndulu (1996).
40. See (eds) Cornelius *et al.* (1989), pp. 1 and 30.
41. They were not resurrecting O'Donnell's theory of an 'elective affinity' between Bureaucratic Authoritarian regimes and a particular stage in capitalist development. See O'Donnell (1977).
42. Craske in (eds) Aitken *et al.* (1996), p. 78.
43. Calvocoressi (1991), p. 65.
44. Weintraub and Delal Baer (1992).
45. Camp's interview with Salinas appeared as 'A New Hope for the Hemisphere?', *New Perspective Quarterly*, Vol. 8, No. 1, Winter 1991 and was quoted in Smith (1992), p. 6.
46. Lipset (1959), p. 83.
47. Roett (1993), p. 11.
48. Rubio in (ed.) Roett (1993), p. 37.
49. As set out by Krueger (1974) in her classic article.
50. Morici (1992), p. 50 and Delal Baer in (ed.) Roett (1993), p. 51.
51. Weintraub (1990), p. 62.
52. Delal Baer in (ed.) Roett (1993), p. 53–5.
53. This is one of the conclusions reached by Qadir *et al.* (1993), p. 420.
54. Weintraub (1990), p. 203.
55. To counter the complacent view that advanced industrial countries are free from entrenched corruption, Harriss-White and White point out the recent revelations of corruption scandals in Japan, Belgium, Italy, France, Spain and the United Kingdom (and the United States) to remind readers that corruption is not only a characteristic of underdeveloped and authoritarian countries. See (eds) Harriss-White and White (1996), p. 2.
56. Morici (1993), p. 53 and Weintraub and Delal Baer (1992), p. 193.
57. Morici (1993), p. 53.
58. Bizberg in (ed.) Harvey (1993), p. 305 and Berins Collier (1992), p. 156.
59. Bizberg in (ed.) Harvey (1993), p. 309 and p. 312.
60. He did not specify which modern labour techniques he had in mind.

61. Rubio in (ed.) Roett (1993), pp. 41–53.
62. Rubio in (ed.) Roett (1993), p. 40.
63. O'Donnell (1973) criticized modernization theory's assumptions but went on to assert that there was an 'elective affinity' between the 'difficult' state of ISI and bureaucratic authoritarianism. As is usual, the case of Mexico, since it does not fit into the general pattern proposed by O'Donnell, is footnoted and the Revolution is used to explain its differences.
64. Fishlow (1990), pp. 64–5.
65. Fishlow (1990), p. 65.
66. Streeten (1993), pp. 1284–92.
67. See (eds) Harriss-White and White (1996).
68. That there is no mechanical causal link between economic and political reform was one of the conclusions reached in (ed.) Collier (1979).
69. Gourevitch (1993), p. 1272.
70. Whitehead (1993b), p. 1372.
71. Hamilton and Kim (1993), p. 129.
72. Gourevitch (1993), p. 1271 and Philip (1993), p. 560.
73. See chapter by Cornelius in (ed.) Gentleman (1987).
74. Cornelius argued that political liberalization is often undertaken by the PRI in order to stabilize the regime and restore the effectiveness of the party. Cornelius in (ed.) Gentlemen (1987), p. 16.
75. Whitehead (1993b), p. 1373.
76. Bailey attempted to consider political reform in terms of the way 'democracy' was understood by the PRI. See the chapter by Bailey in (ed.) Gentleman (1987). See also Hamilton and Mee Kim (1993).
77. Smith (1992).
78. Dresser (1992), p. 26.
79. The editors preferred not to make an inevitable connection between political and economic change in (eds) Cornelius *et al.* (1989).
80. Camp in Roett (1993), p. 28.
81. Coppedge in (ed.) Roett (1993), p. 128.
82. Smith (1992), p. 19.
83. Smith (1992), p. 6.
84. Whitehead (1994), p. 24.
85. Smith (1992), p. 19.
86. Weintraub (1990), p. 6.
87. However, the PRI did not need to manipulate as much in 1991 as they did in 1988 since PRI support was much improved. See Delal Baer and Weintraub (1992), p. 195.
88. Stansfield in Aitken *et al.* (1996), p. 136 discusses some of the assassinations of FDN leaders and the way in which the PRI wooed some of the FDN back into the PRI using the PRONASOL project.
89. Morici (1993), p. 53.
90. See (eds) Aitken *et al.* (1996); Cornelius (1996); (eds) Cornelius *et al.* (1994), Middlebrook (1995) and Centeno (1995).
91. On the topic of human rights, a report by Amnesty International (1995) claims that the budding of many, diverse human rights organizations during the Salinas *sexenio* did not necessarily mean a reduction in claims of human rights abuses. On the subject of electoral reform, Knight

observes that the PRI still uses a high degree of discretion when 'recognizing' opposition victories. See Aitken *et al.* (1996), p. 8.
92. See (eds) Aitken *et al.* (1996) and Centeno (1995).
93. Centeno (1995) opened his argument enquiring into the connection between economic and political reform but admitted that the scope of his answer was confined to a political and state-centred approach. Heredia (1993) was more explicit: she claimed that much of the recent literature on Mexico suffered from concentrating too much on the potential of economic change to transform: she decidedly reverted to the 'primary of the political'.
94. These categories are not my impositions, since most of the authors defined their work in these terms. Middlebrook (1995, p. 29), rightly emphasized that a state-centred analysis was not enough in itself, and claimed that a society-centred approach should also be considered. Centeno (1995) admitted his argument was limited to the 'walls' around the state.
95. Centeno (1995).
96. Teichman (1995), pp. 24, 198.
97. Teichman (1995), pp. 24, 191–2.
98. Middlebrook (1989).
99. Stansfield in (eds) Aitken *et al.* (1996).
100. See (eds) Cornelius *et al.* (1994), p. 6.
101. See (eds) Cornelius *et al.* (1994), p. 161.
102. See the chapter by Dresser in (eds) Cornelius *et al.* (1994).
103. Varley noted that it was complex to reveal the political intentions behind PRONASOL due to the heterogeneity of projects involved and geographical spread of its reach. See Varley in (eds) Aitken *et al.* (1996), p. 208.
104. In (eds) Cornelius *et al.* (1994), pp. 123–41, Horcasitas and Weldon showed, by correlating electoral patterns and Solidarity spending in 31 Mexican states, how Solidarity funds had specifically been targeted to areas where the PRD had previously been strong, a plan devised to decouple mass support and the left.
105. See (eds) Cornelius *et al.* (1994), p. 13.
106. Bailey in (eds) Cornelius *et al.* (1994), p. 117.
107. Knight in (eds) Cornelius *et al.* (1994), p. 44.
108. Bailey in (eds) Cornelius *et al.* (1994), p. 107.
109. Knight in (eds) Higley and Gunther ([1992], 1995).
110. Brachet-Marquez (1994).
111. Craske (1994).
112. My translation of a direct quotation in Craske (1994), p. 34.
113. Heredia (1993), p. 266.
114. Heredia (1993), p. 288.
115. Heredia (1993), p. 277.
116. Cornelius (1996), p. 82.
117. Zapata's main evidence was that Salinas did not want rid of the economic solidarity pact since he renewed it ten times during the *sexenio*, and failed to reform the *Ley Federal de Trabajo*. See Zapata (1996).
118. Middlebrook (1995).
119. Unfortunately, Middlebrook's analysis (1995) of organized labour in the Salinas administration is brief.

120. Middlebrook (1995), p. 3.
121. Middlebrook (1995), pp 266–8.
122. Middlebrook (1995), pp. 298–305.
123. Middlebrook (1995), pp. 265, 297.
124. See the chapters by Varley and Craske in (eds) Aitken *et al.* (1996).
125. Stansfield in (eds) Aitken *et al.* (1996).
126. Knight in (eds) Aitken *et al.* (1996), p. 9.
127. Dresser in (eds) Cornelius *et al.* (1994).
128. Jones (p. 79) and Craske (pp. 197–8) both in (eds) Aitken *et al.* (1996).
129. See (eds) R. Aitken *et al.* (1996).
130. Jones in (eds) Aitken *et al.* (1996), p. 195, demonstrated the contradictions of *ejido* reform within Article 27. Craske argued that the *Movimiento Urbano Popular Territorial* (MT) was also a disguised attempt to reincorporate the 'black sheep' back into the PRI fold. The 'reform' of the CNOP was U-turned so that at the end of the *sexenio*, the newly named *Federación Nacional de Organizaciones y Ciudadanos* (FNOC) was just about all that was new about it; it had returned to the same structure as before. See Craske in (eds) Aitken *et al.* (1996), pp. 79, 86. Rodríguez (1993) concluded that the De la Madrid administration's plan to decentralize via 'federalization' was blocked by the lack of political will.
131. Knight in (eds) Foweraker and Craig (1990), p. 97.
132. Knight pointed to the major failed reforms of the socialist education programme of the 1930s, including Madrazo's efforts to democratize the party in the 1960s and De la Madrid's attempt to introduce electoral reform in Mexico City in the mid-1980s. See Knight in (eds) Aitken *et al.* (1996), p. 15.
133. Davies (1994) showed how demands from Mexico City citizens to vote for their own Mayor rather than having one imposed top–down by the PRI were defeated by politicians, bureaucrats and others afraid of losing their entrenched economic and political privileges in addition to a lack of political will. Cornelius in (ed.) Gentleman (1987, p. 30) analysed the resistance by local party members to giving up their positions to the PAN.
134. North in (eds) Harris *et al.* (1995), p. 25.
135. See (eds) Harriss-White and White (1996).
136. Manzetti and Blake (1996), pp. 662–95.
137. See (eds) Harriss-White and White (1996).
138. Vickers and Yarrow (1988).

2 State–Labour Relations in Mexico: Opening up the Black Box

1. See Zapata (1995).
2. Hernández Juárez and Xelhuantzi López (1993).
3. Ramamurti (1996), p. 72.
4. Ramamurti (1996), p. 73, claimed that the privatization of TELMEX was 'at the heart of Salinas' $20-billion privatization program'.
5. Membership of the STRM is obligatory for all TELMEX workers.
6. Camacho (1977), pp. 187–8.
7. Smith in (ed.) Bethell (1991), p. 371.

8. Such as Middlebrook (1995) and Brachet-Marquez (1994).
9. Roxborough (1981).
10. Article 123 included clauses on limiting the working day to eight hours, six days a week, restricting labour of women and children under 16, set a minimum wage in cash (as opposed to the 'tokens' which many employers used for payment that could only be spent in *tiendas de rayas* (company shops)), and recognized workers' right to strike and organize. Importantly, it also made the state the official arbiter of conflicts between labour and capital. See Carr (1976), Chapter 3.
11. Ashby (1967), p. 10.
12. Hamilton (1982), pp. 110–11.
13. Knight (1984), p. 78.
14. Carr (1976), p. 86.
15. Middlebrook (1995), pp. 48, 51.
16. Gruening (1928), p. 357.
17. Hamilton (1982), p. 92.
18. Carr (1976).
19. Handleman (1979); Bethell and Roxborough (1992); Hamilton (1982).
20. For an analysis of different approaches see Knight (1994).
21. In addition, the number of unionized workers tripled in the decade after 1930, from 294 000 (5.6 per cent of the active workforce) to 878 000 (15.4 per cent of the active workforce). Handleman (1979), p. 3.
22. Leal and Woldenburg (1976), p. 50.
23. Hamilton (1982), p. 161.
24. Ashby (1982), p. 193.
25. Ashby (1982), p. 89.
26. Trejo Delarbre (1976), p. 144 and Ashby (1982), p. 96.
27. Ashby (1982), p. 287.
28. Hamilton (1982), p. 270.
29. Handleman (1979), p. 4; Trejo Delarbre (1976); Kofas (1992), p. 34.
30. Bethell and Roxborough (1992); Middlebrook (1995), pp. 209–10; Zapata (1989), p. 173.
31. See (ed.) Dietz (1995), p. 9.
32. Cardoso and Fishlow (1992), p. 199.
33. Roxborough (1994), p. 250.
34. Cardoso and Fishlow (1992), p. 212.
35. Bethell and Roxborough (1992), p. 195.
36. Bethell and Roxborough (1992), p. 13.
37. Middlebrook (1995), pp. 109–11.
38. Middlebrook (1995), p. 117.
39. Smith (1991), p. 343.
40. Middlebrook (1995), p. 116.
41. Talavera and Leal (1977), Table 2, p. 1260.
42. See Chapter 1, Note 19.
43. Smith (1991), p. 343.
44. Middlebrook (1995), p. 150.
45. Roxborough in (eds) Bethell and Roxborough (1992), p. 214.
46. Roxborough in (eds) Bethell and Roxborough (1992), p. 190; Handleman (1979), p. 5; Middlebrook (1995), p. 210 and Roxborough (1984), p. 24.
47. Bethell and Roxborough (1992); Middlebrook (1995), p. 110.

48. Talavera and Leal (1977), Table 3, p. 1261.
49. Talavera and Leal (1977), Table 4.
50. Middlebrook (1995), p. 150.
51. Zapata (1989), p. 190; Zapata (1986) pp. 113–14; Adler Hellman (1988), p. 42.
52. Middlebrook (1995), Chapter 5.
53. Middlebrook (1995), p. 220.
54. Bortz (1988), Table 2.2, p. 266.
55. Middlebrook (1995), p. 220.
56. Smith (1991), p. 349.
57. Handleman (1979), p. 7.
58. Smith (1991), p. 352. Stevens (1974) detailed the major strikes during the 1960s which were in non-industrial sectors, namely the doctors and the students.
59. Foweraker (1993), p. 28.
60. Smith (1991), p. 367.
61. Smith (1991), p. 371.
62. Smith (1991), p. 370.
63. For instance research on organized labour has been based on the automobile unions in Roxborough (1984) and Middlebrook (1995).
64. Middlebrook (1995), Table 6.4, p. 231.
65. Middlebrook (1995), p. 226.
66. In 1960 VAM employed 450 workers and by 1975 this had increased to 1892. See Middlebrook (1995), p. 231.
67. Middlebrook (1995).
68. Roxborough (1984), p. 1.
69. Since then publication of monographs has included two important series: *La Clase Obrera en la Historia de Mexico* and *La Revolución Mexicana*.
70. Roxborough (1984), p. 26.
71. Roxborough (1981), p. 85.
72. Roxborough (1981), p. 87.
73. Roxborough (1984), p. 108.
74. Roxborough (1984) pp. 113, 160.
75. Middlebrook (1989); Roxborough (1989).
76. Davies and Coleman (1989) are among the authors who have continued to probe descriptions and assumptions about 'official' and 'independent' unions.
77. There are, of course, exceptions, for example Foweraker (1993); Roxborough (1984).
78. Gómez Tagle (1980), p. 215.
79. Conversation with Middlebrook, July 1996, Oxford.
80. Thompson and Roxborough (1982), p. 201.
81. Some of the leading labour analysts in Mexico are refused help in their research by STRM leaders since they have criticized the way in which the union is run.
82. The results of my analysis of shop-floor union politics are contained in the Appendix.
83. I am most grateful to Professor F. Zapata of El Colegio de México, for his help, among other things, for putting me in contact with Dr J. Sandoval, one of the intellectual *comisionados* of the STRM.

84. Middlebrook (1995); Brachet-Marquez (1994); Roxborough (1984).
85. Bethell and Roxborough (1992).
86. Smith (1991), p. 371.
87. Middlebrook (1995).
88. See (ed.) Roberts (1996).
89. Brachet-Marquez (1994).
90. Lipset *et al.* (1956), p. iii.
91. Jackson (1991), pp. 98–9; Michels (1979).
92. Handelman (1977), p. 206.
93. Handleman (1977), pp. 207–8.
94. Handleman drew on the work of Dahl and Sartori in his article. See Handleman (1977), p. 206. See also Lipset *et al.* (1956).
95. Thompson and Roxborough (1982), p. 204 .
96. Thompson and Roxborough (1982), p. 203.
97. Pateman (1989), p. 90.
98. Pateman's *Participation and Democratic Theory* was first published in 1970 and has been reprinted virtually every year since. This work is cited as the main work in a recent textbook on the subject of industrial democracy and worker participation: see Jackson (1991), p. 197.
99. Jackson (1991), p. 197.
100. Pateman (1989), p. 5.
101. Pateman (1989), p. 78.
102. Pateman (1989), p. 58.
103. Pateman (1989), p. 69.
104. Pateman (1989), p. 70.
105. Jackson (1991), pp. 200–3.
106. As Pateman (1989), p. 77, revealed in a study of the profit-sharing scheme in John Lewis of the United Kingdom.
107. Zazueta and de la Peña (1984), p. 179, and Article 52, STRM (1983) and interview by author with E. Torres, STRM Press Secretary and *comisionado*, March 1995, Mexico City.
108. Ruprah (1994a), p. 9.
109. Various copies between 1970–75 of *1o de Agosto*, the STRM magazine before 1976.
110. There was a short interlude between these *charro* leaders which is discussed below.
111. Luis Reyna and Trejo Delarbre (1988), pp. 126–8.
112. The *requisa* was initially introduced during the war on the grounds that a strike could seriously damage the national interest. However, since then, it has been used regularly by the government to repress an unwanted strike.
113. Luis Reyna and Trejo Delarbre (1988), pp. 168–72, and STRM (1998a), p. 12.
114. Luis Reyna and Trejo Delarbre (1988), p. 173 and interviews by author with telephone workers.
115. Luis Reyna and Trejo Delarbre (1988), p. 173.
116. Various copies of STRM, *1o de Agosto* (between 1965 and 1975).
117. An examination of the curriculum of the CEN and CNV from 1970 to 1975 shows they were active in union positions. STRM, *1o de Agosto* (1970–5).

118. Valle Sánchez (1978), p. 124.
119. Basurto (1984), p. 173 and interviews by author with telephone workers, May 1995.
120. The precise way in which Hernández Juárez came to be the new leader of the STRM is not clear in the scarce primary sources written about the union.
121. Xelhuantzi López (1988), p. 34.
122. Norwood (1990), p. 82.
123. STRM, *Restaurador*, July 1976, p. 12.
124. Lavrin in (ed.) Bethell (1994), pp. 500–2.
125. Serrano Vallejo in (ed.) Cooper (1989), p. 532.
126. There were strict rules for operators wishing to take breaks to the bathroom; they had to indicate when they wanted to go and continue working, sometimes for up to one hour, before they were given permission. Interviews by author with operators in Mexico City, June 1995.
127. STRM, *Restaurador* (issues in 1976 and 1977).
128. Lipset *et al.* (1956).
129. Basurto (1984), p. 176, obtained this electoral data from the newspaper *Excelsior*.
130. STRM, *Restaurador*, July 1976, p. 7.
131. STRM (1983), Article 86.
132. STRM, *Restaurador*, July 1976, p. 24.
133. STRM (1976), Article 55.
134. The newly created Article 88 in Chapter 29 declared that the National Electoral Commission would register planillas submitted for elections, observe the electoral procedure, verify electoral results and resolve post-electoral problems. STRM, *Restaurador*, November 1976 , p. 29.
135. Interviews by author with STRM leaders and telephone workers, May 1995.
136. STRM (1983), Article 45.
137. Pateman (1970), p. 69.
138. Basurto (1984), pp. 178–9.
139. STRM, *Restaurador*, July 1976, p. 12.
140. Basurto (1984), p. 179.
141. Basurto (1984), p. 179.
142. *Unomásuno* (1980), p. 14.
143. *Unomásuno* (1980), p. 68.
144. *Unomásuno* (1980), p. 184.
145. STRM, *Restaurador*, March–April 1983, p. 21. See also Millan *et al.* (1986), p. 107, who cited STRM sources claiming that there were 8600 votes for extending the incumbent leaders' time in power and 2400 votes against.
146. *Unomásuno* (1980), p. 35.
147. Translation by author, cited in *Unomásuno* (1980), p. 198.
148. Sánchez Daza (1991), p. 67.
149. This information is based on interviews by the author with dozens of rank-and-file union members including operators and technicians, who are either normal workers or union delegates. Mexico City, between May and July 1995.
150. Interviews with telephone workers (operators, delegates and technicians) in Puebla and Mexico City, between May and July 1995.

151. Hernández Juárez was reinstalled as secretary-general; Saturnino Morales was moved from second Labour Secretary (1976) to Secretary of Organization (1980); Adolfo Maldonado from Secretary of Relations (1976) to Secretary of Ajustes (1980); Juan Luis Montero was Secretary of Sport (1976) and Secretary of Labour (1980), Patricia Alemán Villa was partly responsible for Press (1976) and made Secretary of the Interior (1980) and Rodolfo Villareal Chávez was CNV President (1976) and made first Secretary of Social Benefits (1980). See STRM, *Restaurador* between 1976 and 1977.

152. There are a small number of exceptions to this rule: Francisco Orozco Calderón appeared in the executive twice: as first Secretary of Conflicts (1980–4) and as first Secretary of Ajustes (1992–6). Irma Monge served in the executive committee (1980) then as Coordinator of the House of Culture (1988). According to union statutes, this is legal, since there was more than a four-year period in between posts.

153. Arnaut (1992), p. 30.

154. Interview by the author with E. Torres, STRM Head of Press and *comisionado*, March 1995, Mexico City.

155. STRM (1983, Article 58d). It is an open fact that the secretary-general, in consultation with the Secretary of the Interior, has the right to select the *comisionados*.

156. Interview with E. Torres, Mexico City, March 1995.

157. The *cacique* was the Indian chief who was paid by the Spanish colonizers to keep a defined group of people subservient.

158. Interviews by author with telephone workers.

159. Interviews with TELMEX operator delegates, Mexico City, May and June 1995. See Chapter 5 for the repeated use of union *comisionados* during the process of privatization.

160. Interview with E. Torres, Head of Press and Union *comisionado*, March 1995. STRM Press Office, Mexico City.

161. Camp (1995), p. 24 and p. 237.

162. Camp's definition of a *camarilla* is based on a mentor–disciple relationship, which could be founded on a similar ideology, personal qualities, kinship or educational companionship. Most *camarillas* are fluid, and loyalty is not exclusive to one mentor, indeed, many *camarillas* are overlapping, and it is acceptable to shift your loyalties from one mentor to another if the 'upward ascendancy of your political mentor is congelado' (frozen). Camp (1990), pp. 106–7.

163. Ruíz García was a political activist/writer, Spanish exile, and also used the names Hernando Pacheco and J. María Alponte. See Xelhuantzi López (1988), pp. 158, 387.

164. Interview with Luis Hernández, Mexico City, November 1995.

165. Interview with Pilar Vázquez, Mexico City, December 1994.

166. Interview with Hernández Juárez published in Xelhuantzi López (1988) and interview by author with Luis Hernández, November 1994 in Mexico City. See also (ed.) Anaya Rosique *et al.* (1983), p. 23.

167. Xelhuantzi López (1988), p. 147.

168. Xelhuantzi López (1988), p. 158.

169. For example, the following were important comisionados in 1995: J. Castillo Magaña served as Labour Secretary (1988–92); M. Heredia Figuero

as Labour Secretary (1984–8); C. Bustos as First Secretary of Labour (1988–92) and Y. Rendón as Second Secretary of Conflicts (1984–8).
170. Top-level 'intellectuals' include M. Xelhuantzi López who was a student who completed her undergraduate thesis on the STRM at the UNAM: and J. Sandoval, a professor of Sociology at UAM.
171. STRM, *Restaurador*, January 1984, p. 48.
172. Sánchez Daza (1991), p. 62.
173. Xelhuantzi López (1988), p. 34.
174. She continues to challenge him to this day for usurping her right to be secretary-general.
175. See (eds) Millan *et al.* (1986), p. 103. The *cláusula de exclusión* basically refers to the fact that any TELMEX worker is obliged to be a member of the STRM. Thus if a worker is ejected from the STRM he or she inevitably loses the job.
176. In 1982, a group with links to the PCM (*Partido Comunista Mexicano*) formed the Orange Slate, and may have gained up to 5000 out of 15 000 votes. See Aguilar (1989), p. 20.
177. Sánchez Daza (1991), p. 75.
178. STRM, *Restaurador*, March–April 1983, p. 20 and November–December 1982, p. 8.
179. See (ed.) Aguilar (1989), pp. 16–26.
180. See (ed.) Aguilar (1989), p. 26.
181. In 1982, there were 10 000 operators out of a total union membership of 27 000, which constituted by far the largest sub-group. See (ed.) Aguilar (1989), p. 26.
182. STRM, *Restaurador*, November–December 1982, p. 7.
183. See (ed.) Aguilar (1989), p. 33.
184. See (ed.) Aguilar (1989), p. 36.
185. STRM, *Restaurador*, March–April 1983, p. 1 and also (ed.) Aguilar (1989), p. 42.
186. STRM, *Restaurador*, March–April 1983.
187. STRM (1983), Article 90.
188. Interview with E. Torres, STRM Head of Press and *comisionado*, March 1995, Mexico City.
189. STRM, *Restaurador*, January 1984 and (ed.) Aguilar (1989), p. 43.
190. STRM *Restaurador*, March–April 1983, p. 1.
191. See (ed.) Aguilar (1989), p. 38.
192. STRM, *Restaurador*, March–April 1983, p. 3 and (ed.) Aguilar (1989), pp. 39, 53.

3   Neoliberal Economic Reform, Unions, and the Anomaly of the STRM

1. Inward-looking policies were characterized by protectionism, ISI, financial restrictions in the movement of capital, regulation and state control of the strategic sectors of the economy.
2. Díaz Fuentes (1994) and Dietz in (ed.) Dietz (1995), p. 9.
3. Such as the opening of international trade, privatization, deregulation and social security reforms. See Edwards (1995), p. vii.

4. When the government expressed its wish to 'modernize' a company it generally meant two things: a modification of the labour contract in order to introduce labour flexibility and a reduction of the workforce.
5. Bulmer-Thomas (1994), pp. 360–5; Teichman (1988).
6. Feinberg in (ed.) Diehl (1997), pp. 217–32; Dietz in (ed.) Dietz (1995), p. 14.
7. The term 'Washington Consensus' is described in Williamson (1990).
8. IADB (1986), p. 315.
9. Bulmer-Thomas (1994), p. 373.
10. The Baker Plan called for a $30 billion increase in new lending to the 15 most heavily indebted countries, but it was soon clear that this sum was insufficient to reverse negative transfers from Latin America. See Bulmer-Thomas (1994), p. 374.
11. Teichman (1995), p. 82.
12. Ruprah (1994b), p. 7.
13. Bazdresch and Elizondo in (eds) Baer and Conroy (1993), p. 47.
14. See Biersteker (1995) for an explanation about how 'neoliberal' ideas became popular with policy-makers around the world during the 1990s.
15. See for instance Aspe's explanation of the excesses of the public sector in Mexico in Aspe (1993).
16. García (1993), p. 175.
17. Tariffs were deemed more transparent than licensing requirements and were therefore essential in the shift towards trade liberalization. IADB (1986), p. 317.
18. IADB (1986), p. 317.
19. Maddison (1995), p. 68.
20. Edwards and Baer (1993), p. 11 and (ed.) Ramamurti (1996), p. 3.
21. Clarke (1994), p. 27.
22. Ruprah's estimation of labour productivity in public enterprises during the 1980s shows that it fell continuously from 1983 to 1986, after which it recovered slightly to 1989 and then rose significantly. Ruprah (1994b), Figure 6, p. 31.
23. Edwards and Baer in (eds) Baer and Conroy (1993), pp. 12–13.
24. Aspe (1993), p. 154.
25. Aspe estimates 595 were divested in the period. Aspe (1993), Table IV.5, p. 184.
26. For a chronological list of firms divested see Ruprah (1994b), pp. 45–55.
27. Aspe (1993), Table IV.5, p. 184. See also Vera Ferrer in (ed.) Glade (1991) which shows discrepancies in the sources, including different estimations within the same government report.
28. Aspe (1993), p. 182.
29. Galal *et al.* (1994), Table 18.2, p. 410.
30. Ruprah (1994b), Table 11, p. 66; Aspe (1993), Table IV.7, p. 185.
31. Ruprah (1994b), Table 8, p. 64.
32. Aspe (1993), p. 172.
33. Aspe (1993), p. 173 claimed that the political task of education and persuasion used the argument that resources freed by divesting inefficient firms would be destined for education, infrastructure, and health programmes. This was the way that privatization was defended during the Salinas administration as will be discussed later.

34. The privatization programme in Mexico was praised by Ruprah (1994b), p. 37.
35. Teichman (1995) argued that the principal obstacle to privatization during the De la Madrid administration was internal division in the cabinet and the main reason for the acceleration of privatization during the Salinas administration was the cohesion of cabinet members. I argue that cabinet cohesion is one useful factor to explain the speed of privatization, but there are many other important factors including international pressure and the economic situation of the country which should also be considered. Moreover, the author tends to overlook the extent to which restructuring took place between 1982 and 1988 which helped prepare companies for privatization in the next *sexenio*.
36. Galal *et al.* (1994), p. 189.
37. Manzetti in (eds) Baer and Conroy (1993), p. 68.
38. Ruprah (1994b), p. 20.
39. Aspe (1993), Table IV.8, p. 187.
40. Sheanan (1991), Table 2, p. 10 claimed that this represented a decline twice as steep as the average decline in all Latin American countries, and was the biggest decline of all Latin American countries except Peru. García (1993), p. 200, concurred with Sheanan in his analysis that wage decreases in Mexico were particularly sharp in the period.
41. Middlebrook (1995), p. 257.
42. Sheanan (1991), p. 12.
43. World Bank (1995), p. 100.
44. Escobar Latapí and Roberts in (eds) González de la Rocha and Escobar Latapí (1991), p. 104.
45. García (1933), p. 229.
46. García (1993), Table 3, p. 201; World Bank (1995), Table 15.2, p. 99.
47. García (1993), p. 202.
48. Middlebrook (1995), p. 255.
49. Under Mexican law, workers are protected from being fired by their collective contract, but if a company is declared bankrupt, the collective contract is void.
50. Zamora (1990), p. 127.
51. Middlebrook (1995), p. 277.
52. Zapata (1995), p. 114; (eds) Sánchez and Corona (1993), p. 125.
53. Middlebrook (1995).
54. Strike petitions made to the JCA jumped from 6589 in 1981 to 16 095 in 1982, after which they fell steadily to 8754 in 1985, then jumped again to 16 141 in 1987. However, only a small percentage of these (1.8 per cent) were recognized officially. See Middlebrook (1995), Chapter 5 for fuller details on strikes during the 1980s.
55. Middlebrook (1995), p. 259.
56. Roxborough in (eds) Stalling and Kaufman (1989), p. 103.
57. Middlebrook (1995), p. 177.
58. Middlebrook (1995), p. 262.
59. Middlebrook (1995), p. 263; Roxborough (1992).
60. *La Jornada*, 15 December 1987, p. 1.
61. The CTM refused to cooperate with the revision of the LFT. See Zapata (1995), pp. 121–36.

62. Middlebrook (1989), p. 208; Middlebrook (1995), p. 265.
63. Freeman and Soete (1994), p. 39.
64. Ambrose *et al.* (1990), pp. 5–6.
65. Comor in (ed.) Comor (1996, [1994]), p. 2.
66. Some economists in the 1960s went as far as to plot the relationship between a country's GDP against the number of telephones installed per 100 inhabitants (or a country's telephone density) and concluded that in order for developing countries to 'catch up' and grow it was important that their communications system be modernized. See Saunders *et al.* (1994), p. 86.
67. Saunders *et al.* (1994), p. 305.
68. Saunders *et al.* (1994), p. 199.
69. A large proportion of callers from Mexico used a 'call-back' facility so that they could pay rates at American prices. In order to keep up with the integration of trade, business and other relations, the government decided that modernization of Mexico's telecommunications system was vital. *Financial Times Supplement: International Telecommunications*, 3 October 1995, p. 23.
70. In his fifth speech to the nation in 1987 President De la Madrid had openly criticized the quality of the service provided by TELMEX.
71. TELMEX (1987b).
72. In a private meeting, Muñoz Izquierdo admitted his intention was to infuriate STRM leaders. TELMEX (1987a), p. 366.
73. *La Jornada*, 17 October 1987, p. 5.
74. *La Jornada*, 8 August 1987, p. 3.
75. *La Jornada*, 19 October 1987, p. 11.
76. Galal *et al.* (1994), p. 436.
77. Ruprah (1994a).
78. Fitzgerald in (ed.) Bulmer-Thomas (1996), pp. 29–30.
79. The New Political Economy approach has been characterized as being founded on a neo-classical microeconomic model with firm beliefs in methodological individualism and rational utility maximization. See Toye in (eds) Colclough and Manors (1995), pp. 321–35.
80. Ramamurti (1996), Table 3.1, p. 74 measured efficiency by the time required to wait for a telephone connection, which in Mexico was between two and three years, while in Indonesia this was eight years and in Argentina 22 years. He also calculated efficiency by the number of employees per 1000 lines, and showed that TELMEX was more efficient than the telephone companies in Argentina, Brazil, Venezuela though not as efficient as Chile's telephone company.
81. Heller in (ed.) Harvey (1993), p. 178.
82. Cowhey and Aronson in Cowhey *et al.* (1989), p. 8; Heller in (ed.) Harvey (1993), p. 178.
83. TELMEX (1986a), p. 9.
84. See Pyramid Research (1994), p. 131.
85. Very Small Aperture Terminals are small, relatively inexpensive transmitting and/or receiving stations designed to send and receive radio signals in the form of magnetic waves such as signals reflected by an orbiting communications satellite.
86. Botelho and Addis (1993), p. 5.
87. Galal *et al.* (1994), Fig 19.1, p. 421.

88. The earthquake lasted two minutes and registered eight on the Richter scale.
89. STRM, *Restaurador*, March 1986, p. 5.
90. TELMEX (1990a).
91. TELMEX (1990a).
92. TELMEX (1986a), p. 91.
93. TELMEX (1987b).
94. Since 1972, when the government had acquired 51 per cent of TELMEX shares, it reserved the right to appoint the majority of the board as well as its General-Director.
95. Carrillo Gamboa received his degree in law from UNAM in 1959. See (ed.) Camp (1982), p. 52.
96. Internal TELMEX documents show that Muñoz Izquierdo had been instructed that the government wanted TELMEX to modernize in accordance with the needs of the opening up of the Mexican economy and to professionalize its management and become more accountable and less dependent upon the state. TELMEX (1987a), p. 45.
97. TELMEX (1987a, 1987b).
98. I was fortunate enough to be given by a journalist from *La Jornada* the fascinating 500-page minutes of the principal annual meeting for TELMEX executives in 1987 in which the future strategy of the company is discussed. One of the most interesting parts of the meeting was the revelation that executives and the Secretary of Labour had met with top union leaders and had agreed to put conflict behind them, and work together towards a non-conflictive and effective modernization of the company. TELMEX (1987a).
99. TELMEX (1987a), p. 141.
100. TELMEX (1987a), p. 43.
101. Conclusions of Muñoz Izquierdo's speech during the reunion with executives. TELMEX (1987a), p. 354.
102. TELMEX (1987a), p. 112.
103. TELMEX (1987a), p. 163.
104. TELMEX (1987a), p. 50.
105. SOS already had the only concession in Mexico to install phones in vehicles.
106. TELMEX (1987a), p. 43.
107. It should be noted that many accounts of the privatization of TELMEX did not find a turning point in 1988 but concentrated on 1990. However, the analyses by Ruprah (1994a) and Galal *et al.* (1994) correctly emphasize changes in TELMEX two years prior to its privatization.
108. Ruprah (1994a), p. 16 also suggested that TELMEX received income by selling future accounts receivable.
109. Investment reached 3.6 million 1994 pesos in 1988; 4.6 million 1994 pesos in 1989 and 7.4 million 1994 pesos in 1990, which was three times the annual investment levels made between 1983 and 1987 (see Table 3.1).
110. *La Jornada*, 4 September 1987, p. 10.
111. Noam and Baur (1998) p. xiii.
112. Petrazzini (1995), p. 83.

113. When the contents of fire extinguishers were released by guards against workers some were hospitalized. Interview by author with STRM operator head delegate, June 1995, Mexico City.
114. In his annual speech to the union, the Secretary-General strongly criticized the operators for dividing and weakening the union, for failing to trust the union leaders by acting on their own initiative, and blamed them for compromising the union's position during the negotiation of its collective contract. STRM, *Restaurador*, March 1986, p. 20.
115. My examination of internal TELMEX documents from 1986 confirms the public statements by TELMEX executives that there were no plans to sack workers. For example, TELMEX's Director of Planning, Dr Alfredo Pérez de Mendoza (1986), gave a seminar to the board entitled 'Technological Change and Employment'. During the speech he outlined the benefits that digitalization would bring and claimed that redundancies would be unnecessary since workers could be relocated and retrained to perform other jobs. Moreover, he predicted that as a result of TELMEX's modernization and growth TELMEX's workforce would actually grow by the year 2000 to 75 000 employees.
116. *La Jornada*, 4 January 1987, p. 8.
117. As shown in Chapter 2 the operators initiated the strike in 1976 which led Hernández Juárez to power, and again, in 1979, the operators struck until they were granted a *convenio*.
118. The operators' role in the union conforms with Craske's analysis of the role of women in politics in Mexico when she stated that women tend to act as a 'backbone' within movements rather than as their head. Craske in (eds) Radcliffe and Westwood (1993), p. 133.
119. In a union where over one-third of workers are women, their representation in the STRM's CEN is extremely low. In 1976–80 and 1980–4 there were only two women in the STRM's CEN. The increase to three or four between 1984 and 1996 is insignificant since the overall size of the CEN increased. Between 1984 and 1988 one woman served as Secretary of Labour, and between 1988 and 1992 a woman was Secretary of Interior, both of which are leading union positions.
120. Hernández Juárez had put himself forward as a candidate for secretary-general of the CT in February 1986, but was defeated by Riva Palacio, leader of INFONAVIT. Grayson (1989), p. 45 argued that Hernández Juárez was perceived as being too aggressive and outspoken for the position, and accordingly moderated his discourse so that in the next elections he was elected.
121. *La Jornada*, 14 August 1987, p. 13.
122. Interview by author with opposition union delegate, Mexico City, May 1995.
123. STRM, *Restaurador*, November 1987, p. 103.
124. Roxborough in (eds) Stallings and Kaufman (1989), p. 105.
125. TELMEX (1990b), p. 41.
126. *El Financiero*, 9 April 1987, p. 35.
127. *La Jornada*, 9 April 1987, p. 11.
128. *La Jornada*, 10 April 1987, p. 11, 11 April 1987, p. 9; *El Financiero*, 9 April 1987, p. 35.

129. *La Jornada*, 11 April 1987, p. 9.
130. *La Jornada*, 10 April 1987, p. 11.
131. *La Jornada*, 15 April 1987, p. 11.
132. As is usual in Mexico, once a union goes on strike, the respective firm applies to the JCA in the hope that the workers' demands will be perceived as mistaken or illegal, so that the strike be declared 'inexistent'. On 11 April TELMEX management had asked that the strike be declared illegal.
133. *La Jornada*, 16 April 1987, p. 6.
134. *El Cotidiano*, No. 11, 1986, p. 60.
135. This was 2 per cent higher than the increase awarded to the electricity workers some two months before. *El Cotidiano*, No. 11, 1986, p. 60.
136. STRM-TELMEX (1986), clause 193.
137. STRM, *Restaurador*, May 1987, p. 1.
138. *El Cotidiano*, No. 11, 1986, p. 60.
139. It was also conceded that TELMEX had other problems apart from the workers' attitude, such as the debt crisis of 1982, the earthquake in September 1985, and the lack of investment which had stalled replacement and modernization of the plant. However, the drop in worker productivity was not connected to these problems and was blamed on the unwillingness and inertia of the workforce.
140. TELMEX (1987a), p. 186.
141. *La Jornada*, 31 August 1987, p. 1.
142. An internal TELMEX (1987c) document published early in 1987 was an important source for the PIMES. In this, it was claimed that automatically connected calls accounted for around 90 per cent of all calls in 1986. Manual calls were declining: between 1980 and 1985 they dropped from 342 million to 306 million (a fall of 12.6 per cent). It was calculated that there was an excess of 2500 operators.
143. *La Jornada*, 4 September 1987, p. 10.
144. During the private meeting, Muñoz Izquierdo admitted his intention was to infuriate STRM leaders. TELMEX (1987a), p. 366.
145. Even the internal executive meeting pointed out problems of lack of investment and delayed decision-making as serious obstacles to TELMEX's growth. TELMEX (1987a).
146. In 1987, TELMEX commissioned a company called BIMSA to conduct a survey about the public's view of TELMEX's service. The results of this survey were never published, but the survey results were presented in a manipulated way in the PIMES document and used as justification for blaming the telephone workers for the company's problems. For instance, it was stated that 62 per cent of 05 users (a service where callers complain about TELMEX) claimed that they were treated in a regular (standard), bad or terrible way. The merging of the three categories (regular, bad or terrible) is unhelpful and means that the public's opinion about the 05 service is not clarified. With respect to repairs, 43 per cent of customers said the service was regular, bad or terrible, again, an unhelpful way to clarify the public's opinion, and which begs the question: did the other 57 per cent think the service of repairs was good or excellent? Some 72 per cent of those surveyed claimed that the attention they received from national and international long-distance operators

was regular, bad or terrible; again, this is inconclusive. Only certain aspects of the PIMES' presentation of the survey actually made sense. For instance 27 per cent complained that they had bribed a TELMEX engineer when they needed their telephone to be fixed. TELMEX (1987b), p. 3. Additionally, 49 per cent of users complained of crossed lines and 37 per cent of background noise during a conversation. TELMEX (1987b), p. 11. Some 52 per cent said it was difficult to obtain a line at all. Apart from the first complaint, the problems were certainly not the fault of workers but of the rickety state of TELMEX's network.

147. TELMEX (1987b), p. V.
148. *La Jornada*, 31 August 1987, p. 1.
149. This system was called the *'medidor de tiempo de contestación'*. See *La Jornada*, 4 August 1987, p. 10.
150. *La Jornada*, 3 August 1987, p. 16.
151. LADATEL is a public telephone in which users can make international calls. TRIPLEX is a telephone especially designed for installation in an apartment, so that for example three families can use the telephone and receive separate bills.
152. TELMEX (1987a), p. 368.
153. The Director of Labour Relations assured them that Hernández Juárez exerted full control over the union. Muñoz Izquierdo's concluding speech claimed that Hernández Juárez was sure to be re-elected in the forthcoming elections four months ahead. TELMEX (1987a).
154. *La Jornada*, 31 August 1987, p. 6. Voting took place at the STRM National General Assembly on 27 June 1987.
155. Since operators work day and night shifts, these demands were not trivial.
156. *La Jornada*, 10 September 1987, p. 13.
157. STRM, *Restaurador*, November 1987, pp. 90–1.
158. This conference included discussions on new kinds of professional diseases such as stress, fatigue and hand paralysis that had been experienced in the Telefónica del Norte, where digital equipment had been installed on a trial basis. *El Cotidiano*, No. 11, 1986, p. 60.
159. STRM, *Restaurador*, November 1987, p. 97.
160. *La Jornada*, 12 September 1987, p 10.
161. *La Jornada*, 12 August 1987, p. 10.
162. STRM, *Restaurador*, November 1987, p. 97.
163. Some 86 sections outside the capital and 129 departments in the capital supported him. STRM, *Restaurador*, November 1987, p. 98.
164. STRM, *Restaurador*, November 1987, p. 98.
165. As explained in Chapter 2, since the reform of the STRM's electoral practices in 1983, opportunities for opposition parties to organize were severely reduced, and the result was that the margin of votes for the Green Plan led by Hernández Juárez and all other opposition plans was widened dramatically. In 1984, the Green Plan won 70 per cent of all votes cast, according to Borja and Barbosa in (ed.) Aguilar (1989), p. 42.
166. *La Jornada*, 28 February 1988, p. 13.
167. Jorge Castillo Magaña and Martha Heredia Figueroa.
168. The STRM presented their version of the PIMES to the Secretary of Labour on 21 September. STRM, *Restaurador*, November 1987, p. 11.

169. *La Jornada*, 18 August 1987, p. 8.
170. *La Jornada*, 12 October 1987, p. 11.
171. The primary step, which was a 100-day 'emergency improvement' plan, was introduced at the beginning of October 1987. During three months, the newly constituted Mixed Productivity Commission met four times. At the beginning of December, two-thirds of the way through the primary step, the Commission produced a glossy pamphlet which boasted of the progress made so far. Seven new offices had been opened in the capital and four outside it to deal with customers' payments, four-fifths of damaged ANC-11 centres had been repaired in order to avoid crossed lines, and two repair centres in Veracruz and Guaymas had been established. In addition, the number of unanswered 05 calls (made to complain about the service) had been halved through extra time worked. Nearly half of the new vehicles had been delivered and 173 000 lines had been put into place since the PIMES had started, so that a total of 350 000 were installed during 1987. TELMEX director Muñoz Izquierdo claimed that the commission was a real team and that so far the results were excellent. STRM-TELMEX (1987b), p. 9.
172. From February 1988 the programme started to run into trouble. Management criticized TELMEX workers for not meeting the productivity targets. The STRM replied that management had failed to deliver its part of the bargain such as its promise to fully rebuild before the end of 1987 all the workplaces damaged after the earthquake. *La Jornada*, 12 October 1987, p. 11. The repair of San Juan was not finished until February 1988. Other delays in finishing the reconstruction of the Victoria centre, and in building the new centres Lindavista and Rojo Gómez, meant that thousands of operators remained without a fixed workplace. The latter two centres were not inaugurated until the end of November 1988. Between February and April, the month when the collective contract had to be negotiated, union–management tensions were high and TELMEX refused to hold any meetings of the mixed productivity commission. *La Jornada*, 19 June 1988, pp. 1, 14.
173. Interview by author with H. Olavarría, TELMEX Director of Labour Relations, May 1995, Mexico City.
174. STRM-TELMEX (1988), clause 136.
175. STRM-TELMEX (1988), clause 185.
176. STRM-TELMEX (1988).
177. *La Jornada*, 25 April 1988, p. 1.
178. 'Dear telephone workers, today I am going to promise you something that I will do if you and the majority of Mexicans vote for me. I promise you that in the modernization of the telephone network and telecommunications, I will support the telephone workers' union; the modernization of TELMEX will be done with the workers, and not against them.' Translation by author, cited in STRM, *Restaurador*, June 1988, p. 21.
179. He repeated his promise in May at a PRI-sponsored meeting on Telecommunications and Information. STRM, *Restaurador*, December 1988, p. 21.
180. Salinas also met Hernández Juárez in his capacity as CT secretary-general. *La Jornada*, 22 October 1987, p. 13 and STRM, *Restaurador*, November 1987, p. 100.

181. The sale of Mexicana was actually completed during the Salinas administration.
182. Galal *et al.* (1994), p. 464.
183. In 1987 Aeroméxico employed 11 644 employees: this was reduced to 3752 in the following year. Galal *et al.* (1994), Table 20.7, p. 478.
184. Among whom Gerardo de Prevoisin Legorreta, who controlled Mexico's largest insurance company, eventually emerged in a dominant position. See Galal *et al.* (1994), p. 460.
185. Galal *et al.* (1994), p. 472.
186. *La Jornada*, 27 April 1988, p. 10.
187. The report, prepared by TELMEX assessor, Patrón Luján, claimed that the regulatory framework must be modified in order to permit increased private investment. Seven main options for funding were proposed: opening investment to private investors; reducing cross-subsidies so local calls would pay for themselves; borrowing from banks; increasing prices; and/or halting the government's filtering of TELMEX's income through telephone taxes into its own coffers. *La Jornada*, 20 June 1988, p. 1.
188. The families of Ruiz Galindo, Trouyyet, Vallina, Sendero and others, according to *La Jornada*, 20 June 1988, p. 6.
189. These included the director of the Banco Nacional de México (Banamex), José Covarrubias, General Director of Servicios para la Telecomunicación, Alejandro López Toledo, and the Director of Condumex, Luis Carcoba García. *La Jornada*, 18 June 1988, p. 8.
190. 'If we do not behave with the maturity and experience that we have on past occasions, new obstacles will be created that will favour those who do not want to see any change in TELMEX nor in the country.' Translation by author, cited in *La Jornada*, 19 June 1988, p. 14.
191. STRM, *Restaurador*, December 1988, p. 12.
192. By 'high' and 'low' I am referring to Pateman's discussion about two main ways in which workers can participate in union affairs, as discussed in Chapter 2. See Pateman (1989), Chapter 4.
193. STRM-TELMEX (1987a).

4 The Politics of Industrial Restructuring and Privatization

1. Ros (1993), p. 314.
2. Prior to the creation of this unit, firms had remained under the control of their respective ministry until they were sold, but this had resulted in delays and infighting within the ministries concerned. After 1990, once the government decided to privatize a company, the company was transferred from the ministry to which it had previously belonged to the divestiture unit in the Ministry of Finance. The divestiture unit was charged with overseeing the entire process, and of pre-screening interested parties, an intermediary between potential buyers and the government, and of appointing a bank which would write a technical and financial pre-sale prospectus and calculate a minimum sale price. Ruprah (1994b), pp. 21–2.

3. For an exhaustive list of firms divested see SHCP/SCGF/Fondo de Cultura Económica (1994).
4. Rogozinski (1997), Table 4.2, p. 111.
5. Ruprah, (1994a, 1994b); Tandon (1992, 1994); Galal *et al.* (1994); Ramamurti (1996).
6. Heller in (ed.) Harvey (1993); Teichman (1995).
7. This is one of the chief objectives of analysts of the international political economy such as Strange (1988), pp. 13–14 and Spero (1996), p. 4.
8. This can be contrasted to privatization in other countries such as Argentina where restructuring was not, in general, accomplished prior to the sale of firms.
9. See Ramamurti in (ed.) Ramamurti (1996), p. 72.
10. Devlin (1996); Tandon (1992); Galal *et al.* (1994); Ramamurti (1996); Ruprah (1994a, 1994b).
11. Such as Aguilar García (1990), p. 69; De Buen (1989); Vásquez Rubio (1989); De la Garza Toledo (1989a).
12. García (1993), pp. 210–16.
13. See Figure 1.2 in Killick in (ed.) Killick (1995), p. 8 for a diagrammatic representation of a disagregation of 'economic flexibility'.
14. Killick, p. 22 and H. Chang, p. 198, in (ed.) Killick (1995).
15. García (1993), p. 190.
16. According to McGowan, the privatization of the state sector was an idea whose 'time had come', just as nationalization had been promoted as the appropriate development strategy in the postwar period. See McGowan in (ed.) Clarke (1994), pp. 28–30.
17. Toye criticized the 'new political economy' for, among other things, its cynical, extreme and pessimistic approach to the state, as well as for analysing countries in isolation without taking into account international factors. Toye in (eds) Colclough and Manor ([1995]), pp. 321–37.
18. Bienen and Waterbury argued that in Britain and France, privatization was used to build 'popular capitalism' and boost middle-class support, while the governments reaped huge profits from the sales. See Bienen and Waterbury in (eds) Wilber and Jameson (1992), p. 376.
19. Feinberg in (ed.) Diehl (1997), p. 223.
20. In contrast, Baibai claimed that various African governments came under real pressure to privatize as a consequence of international institutions. See Baibai in (ed.) Vermon ([1995]), pp. 271–84.
21. By 1994 the list of privatized companies included two electric power companies, the national water and sewer system, the Buenos Aires subway system, other parts of the national railway system, ports and harbours, the national coal company, a giant steel company, one-half of the national oil company, and several industrial firms, including defence firms.
22. For the Argentine case see the chapters on privatization of Empresa Nacional de Telecomunicaciones and the airline Aerolíneas in (ed.) Ramamurti (1996).
23. Bienen and Waterbury in (eds) Wilber and Jameson (1992 [1973)] p. 387.
24. See the discussion about the Ridley Report in Dobek (1993), pp. 57–9 where the unions of nationalized companies are referred to as 'the enemies of the next Tory government'.

25. Edwards (1995), p. 170.
26. Bienen and Waterbury highlighted four major factors that shape privatization in less developed countries. First, the origins of the public sector; second, the nature of the state's deficit and fiscal crisis; third, the nature of coalitions with vested interests in the *status quo*; and fourth, the preoccupation of leadership for the control of economic resources and patronage. See Bienen and Waterbury in (eds) Wilber and Jameson (1992), p. 387.
27. See (ed.) Ramamurti (1996), pp. 72–107.
28. García (1993), p. 181.
29. Ruprah (1994b), p. 10.
30. Ruprah (1994b), p. 59, Table 1.
31. Spero (1996), p. 193 and Feinberg in (eds) Wilber and Jameson (1992), p. 243.
32. Krugman and Obstfeld (1994), pp. 701–5.
33. García (1993), p. 184.
34. Calculations by Devlin in (eds) Jameson and Wilber (1996), Table 25.3, p. 435.
35. Galal *et al.* (1994), p. 410.
36. See (ed.) Ramamurti (1996), p. 72.
37. In the opinion of many observers, the sale of TELMEX convinced investors that the Mexican government was honouring its commitment to privatization. See Roberto Salinas (1990), p. 4.
38. Constitutional amendments required two-thirds of votes to be passed. Székely in (eds) Cowhey *et al.* (1989), p. 85.
39. Interview by Ramamurti with a Mexican policy-maker, quoted in (ed.) Ramamurti (1996), p. 11.
40. Tandon (1994), p. 419.
41. See Ramamurti in (ed.) Ramamurti (1996), p. 77.
42. See Ramamurti (ed.) (1996), p. 11. L. González Lanuza (1992), p. 761, argued that the success or failure of the sale of Entel had implications for the credibility of the newly incumbent Menem.
43. Ramamurti in (ed.) Ramamurti (1996), p. 12.
44. Galal *et al.* (1994), p. 411. See also Edwards (1995), p. 185, who claimed that political opposition was 'very minor'.
45. Roxborough (1992); Edwards (1995), p. 192.
46. Smith in (eds) Cornelius *et al.* (1989), p. 407.
47. Carr in (eds) Carr and Ellner (1993), p. 91.
48. Amparo Casar (1995), p, 7.
49. Craske (1994), p. 1; Smith in (eds) Cornelius *et al.* (1989), p. 408.
50. Smith in (eds) Cornelius *et al.* (1989), p. 409.
51. Centeno (1995), p. 63.
52. Craske (1993), p. 1; (eds) Cornelius *et al.* (1989), pp. 1 and 30; Hernández Rodríguez (1994), p. 196; Centeno (1995), p. 63.
53. This survey was conducted by Consultores 21, a Venezuelan company owned by Emisora de Televisión of Los Angeles, California. The results of the survey are interpreted by Von Sauer (1992), Table 7, p. 269.
54. Von Sauer (1992), Table 14, p. 276.
55. The FDN was a coalition of different groups who were united in their wish to see the fall of the PRI. Its leader, Cuauhtémoc Cárdenas, son of Lázaro

Cárdenas, claimed to be a more legitimate leader than any PRI leader due to blood ties. In the pre-election campaign the FDN called for the end of presidentialism, abandonment of electoral corruption and manipulation, the rejection of many aspects of the neoliberal economic model. See Carr in (eds) Carr and Ellner (1993), p. 91; Centeno (1995), p. 63.

56. See Chapter 1.
57. See Dresser (1991) and (eds) Cornelius *et al.* (1994) on the way the PRI used PRONASOL to renew patronage links with poorer sectors of society and Craske (1994) on the party's efforts to reform and bolster the PRI's links with the popular sector.
58. Carr in (eds) Carr and Ellner (1993), p. 92; Middlebrook (1995); Smith in (eds) Cornelius *et al.* (1989), p. 387.
59. Middlebrook (1995), p. 415n.
60. Craske (1993), p. 3n.
61. Middlebrook (1995), p. 293; Russell (1995), p. 11.
62. Cited in Salinas (1994b), p. 24. Translation by author.
63. See the president's first, second and third speeches to the nation in Salinas (1994b).
64. See for example the First Report to the Nation, cited in Salinas (1994b), pp. 21–47.
65. Aitken in (eds) Aitken *et al.* (1996), p. 26, compared this pro-privatization justification in Mexico with Margaret Thatcher's infamous phrase in Britain, 'there is no alternative'.
66. This 'sporty' rhetoric was epitomized by President Salinas who liked to be photographed as he was jogging through parks wearing a 'Solidaridad' T-shirt, and his insistence that he liked light, healthy food. See for instance PRI propaganda publications like Ferraez Comunicación, 1994.
67. See C. Salinas (1994b), p. 25.
68. The titles of many government or company documents use the word *desincorporación*, while official speeches and documents are peppered with the words *desincorporación* and *enajenación*.
69. Salinas (1994b), p. 22.
70. Salinas (1994b), p. 30.
71. Salinas (1994b), p. 25.
72. Haskel and Szymanski in (eds) Bishop *et al.* (1994), pp. 337–8.
73. Arsenio Farell was the only member of the De la Madrid cabinet who was kept on by Salinas to work in the same position.
74. Russell (1995), p. 11.
75. *El Financiero*, 4 January 1989, p. 4.
76. *La Jornada*, 11 January 1989 pp. 3, 4, 7; *La Jornada*, 13 January 1989, pp. 1, 8, 19–22.
77. *La Jornada*, 16 January 1989, p. 9.
78. After La Quina was imprisoned, Velázquez was instructed to keep silent, he withdrew from his weekly press meetings and made no comments in national newspapers. Correa and Corro, *Proceso*, 13 February 1989. *La Jornada* is notable for the lack of statements by Velázquez throughout the period January to April 1989.
79. Correa and Corro, *Proceso*, 1 May 1989, p. 9.
80. Middlebrook (1995), p. 295.
81. *La Jornada*, 13 January 1989, p. 1.

82. Correa and Corro, *Proceso*, 1 May 1989, p. 11; Campa, *Proceso*, 1 May 1989, p. 16.
83. Elba Esther Gordillo had been supported by Manuel Camacho Solís. See Campa, *Proceso*, 1 May 1989, p. 14.
84. Middlebrook (1995), p. 295.
85. Zapata (1995), p. 137. As stated in Chapter 2, the LFT constitutes the centre-piece in the formal relationship between organized labour and the government. It covers fundamental rules such as how prospective unions can become registered officially, how they must formulate their internal union statutes, how many unions are allowed in different sectors, and in which circumstances the union is permitted to strike.
86. Zapata (1995), p. 126.
87. See De los Angeles Pozas (1993), p. 63.
88. Zapata (1995), p. 130.
89. *La Jornada*, 7 March 1989, p. 17.
90. *La Jornada*, 14 February 1989, p. 7.
91. *La Jornada*, 14 February 1989, p. 7.
92. *La Jornada*, 8 March 1989, p. 3.
93. *La Jornada*, 18 February 1989, p. 8.
94. TELMEX (1990b).
95. *La Jornada*, 15 January 1988, p. 7.
96. During 1990 the department of Labour Relations in TELMEX published a 250-page confidential document on the history of labour relations in the company. This document, which revealed management's policies towards labour in the 1980s, was lent to me by the Director of Labour Relations. TELMEX (1990b).
97. *Convenios* are a typical characteristic of collective bargaining in Mexico. They are created when an issue must be resolved due to political or time constraints, but for some reason they are not included in the overall collective contract, and often serve as a pragmatic short-cut to a particular labour dispute.
98. TELMEX (1990a), p. 34.
99. TELMEX (1987a), p. 163.
100. Poole (1986), p. 53, observed that management generally has no interest in sharing information with the union about new technology if the union goes on to use this as a tool in collective bargaining.
101. TELMEX (1990b), p. 38 and interview by author with H. Olavarría, Director of Labour Relations, May 1995, Mexico City.
102. *La Jornada*, 21 March 1989, p. 7.
103. *La Jornada*, 20 March 1989, p. 1.
104. *La Jornada*, 24 March 1989, p. 15.
105. *La Jornada*, 22 March 1989, p. 32; *La Jornada*, 24 March 1989, p. 15.
106. *La Jornada*, 22 March 1989, p. 10.
107. *La Jornada*, 27 March 1989, p. 3.
108. *La Jornada*, 28 March 1989, p. 3.
109. Joint declaration by management and union in STRM-TELMEX (1989b), p. 2.
110. Clause 38 of the new agreement stated that in short periods of absence management could substitute the worker with a temporary worker. In longer periods of absence, management could replace the worker by

another full-time worker who may be slightly lower in rank than the
absent worker. STRM-TELMEX (1989b), p. 4.
111. STRM-TELMEX (1989b), Clause 65. Moreover, management promised to
give a worker 15 days' notice before asking for that worker to move
temporarily (Clause 70), and 30 days' notice if that worker was to be
moved permanently (Clause 71).
112. STRM-TELMEX(1989b), Clause 193.
113. STRM-TELMEX (1989), Clause 185.
114. Aguilar García (1990), p. 69; De Buen (1989); De la Garza and Melgoza
Valdivia (1991), p. 15; Vásquez Rubio (1989).
115. De la Garza and Melgoza Valdivia (1991), p. 20.
116. De Buen (1989), pp. 59–61.
117. See Salinas' speech during his official closing of the STRM National
Assembly cited in Salinas (1994b), pp. 83–4.
118. Ferraez Comunicación (1994), p. 180.
119. Vázquez Rubio (1990b), p. 60.
120. La Jornada, 15 April 1989, p. 1.
121. Interview by author with TELMEX Director of Labour Relations, Mexico
City, May 1995.
122. See Salinas' speech during the celebrations of the negotiation of the STRM-
TELMEX collective contract cited in Salinas (1994a), pp. 196–8.
123. Interview by author with the Caso Lombardo, Secretary of
Communications and Transport (1988–94) and with Arsenio Farrell,
Labour Secretary, May 1995, Mexico City.
124. Interview by author with H. Olavarría, TELMEX's Director of Labour
Relations, May 1995, Mexico City.
125. The SME was considered a relatively democratic union in Thompson
(1970) and Thompson and Roxborough (1982).
126. De la Garza and Melgoza Valdivia (1991), p. 18.
127. STRM, Restaurador, March 1989 and November 1989.
128. STRM, Restaurador, November 1989, p. 1.
129. See for example the description of Hernández Juárez in Silverstein (1992),
p. 22.
130. This can be done by comparing signatories of labour contracts. See STRM-
TELMEX (1986), pp. 131–2, STRM-TELMEX (1988), pp. 144–5 and STRM-
TELMEX (1990), pp. 153–5.
131. The comisionados who signed the contract in April 1989 were: Jorge
Castillo Magaña, José Guadalupe Reyes Pérez, Martha Heredia Figueroa,
Yolanda Rendón Lizárraga and Amabilia Olivares Torres. STRM,
Restaurador, November 1989, p. 1 of supplement.
132. STRM-TELMEX (1987a).
133. Jackson ([1992]), p. 200; Poole (1986), p. 71.
134. Interview by author with operator delegate dissent, Mexico City, June
1995.
135. La Jornada, 28 March, 1989, p. 3.
136. STRM, Restaurador, November 1989, p. 27.
137. STRM, Restaurador, November 1989, p. 28; TELMEX (1989b), p. 6.

5 Privatizing TELMEX and Crafting a 'New Unionism'

1. In the first chapter the main arguments of these authors were outlined and the arguments were set within a broader framework of the schools of rent-seeking and modernization.
2. Teichman (1995), pp. 24, 191.
3. Some analysts such as Morici (1993) used corruption and corporatist relationships synonymously. In order to assess whether, in the case of the privatization of TELMEX, corruption increased, it will be necessary to examine whether the mechanisms guiding the reforging of the state–labour relationship changed in a significant way.
4. See (eds) Harriss-White and White (1996); Manzetti and Blake (1996), pp. 662–95.
5. *El Financiero*, 19 September 1989, p. 33.
6. When Mexicana was sold, Salinas justified this by claiming that he had chosen to invest money in the modernization of the water system in poor areas rather than buy 40 aircraft needed by the airline company. See Russell (1994), p. 186.
7. See *El Financiero*, 31 November 1989, p. 10 and *The Financial Times* 20 October 1989, p. 22. Translation by author.
8. With the benefit of hindsight, it is clear that this labour agreement constituted the most important precursor of privatization. TELMEX and government documents refer to it repeatedly as the obstacle which, once removed, made it possible to think seriously about the way in which TELMEX would be sold. Company documents which stress the primary importance of the labour agreement include: TELMEX (1989b), p. 5; TELMEX (1991a), p. 15; SCT (1990a). See also *El Financiero*, 2 October 1989, p. 72.
9. The TELMEX (1989b) document contains three different ways of privatizing the company and have in common these priorities.
10. Ruprah (1994b), p. 24.
11. *La Jornada*, 22 June 1989, p. 40.
12. This would enable banks, hotels, financial and commercial services to be interconnected to a system where voice, data and images were transmitted. See *La Jornada*, 23 August 1989, p. 31 and *La Jornada*, 24 August 1989, pp. 1, 31.
13. *La Jornada*, 25 August 1989, p. 29.
14. Once the first 45 days were over, management announced that the programme would be converted to a permanent one with progress being monitored every two months jointly by the Secretary of Communications and Transport, the Secretary of Labour, TELMEX executives and STRM leaders. See *La Jornada*, 23 June 1989, p. 33 and 7 July 1989, p. 29.
15. The plan justified the introduction of an unprecedented level of supervision in the major TELMEX work centres including 900 inspectors from the SCT who were installed in work centres across the country. STRM, *Restaurador*, November 1989, pp. 26–8; TELMEX (1989b), p. 6; *La Jornada Perfil*, 7 October 1989, p. 10.

16. A small number of them had occupied important positions in the union, including two members of the executive in Hermosillo who were laid off on 24 June. STRM, *Restaurador*, November 1989, p. 27.
17. STRM, *Restaurador*, November 1989, p. 27.
18. Interview with Hernández Juárez in *La Jornada*, 29 July 1989, p. 15.
19. STRM, *Restaurador*, November 1989, p. 7.
20. *El Financiero*, 2 October 1989, p. 72.
21. The way in which union politics work in TELMEX operator centres is explained in more detail in the Appendix.
22. Interview by author with operator delegate and union dissident, June 1995, Mexico City.
23. STRM, *Restaurador*, March 1991, pp. 35–7.
24. Anonymous STRM union opposition (1993).
25. This is evident in his statements to *La Jornada* from April to August. See especially *La Jornada*, 21 June 1989, p. 27.
26. Interview by author with Hector Olavarría, TELMEX Director of Labour Relations, May 1995, Mexico City.
27. 'We want to be actors, not just objects of privatization. That is, we do not want to be fired, and then rehired with a new collective contract without the workers' rights we now enjoy.' Author's translation of Hernández Juárez's speech from *La Jornada*, 14 September 1989, p. 11.
28. See Chapter 2.
29. *La Jornada*, 19 September 1989, p. 10.
30. Salinas (1989c), pp. 66–71.
31. *La Jornada*, 19 September 1989 pp. 1, 10; STRM, *Restaurador*, February 1990.
32. STRM, *Restaurador*, February 1990, p. 4.
33. *La Jornada*, 19 September 1989, p. 10.
34. Interview by author with operator delegate and union dissident, June 1995, Mexico City.
35. *El Financiero*, 31 October 1989, p. 10; *La Jornada*, 31 October 1989, p. 9.
36. Chapter 3 contains more details on these labour disputes.
37. Middlebrook (1995), p. 277.
38. *El Financiero*, 21 September 1989, p. 1.
39. *El Financiero*, 21 September 1989, p. 5.
40. *Proceso*, 20 November 1989, p. 9.
41. *La Jornada*, 26 October 1989, p. 8.
42. *Proceso*, 20 November 1989, p. 8.
43. Armstrong and Vickers in Bishop *et al.* (1995), p. 289.
44. See Petrazinni in (ed.) Ramamurti (1996), p. 121.
45. Hanson in (eds) Baer and Conroy (1993b), p. 200.
46. In some countries, regulation was implemented by an independent body, such as the Office for Telecommunications (OFTEL) in the United Kingdom.
47. SCT (1990d).
48. Petrazzini in (ed.) Ramamurti (1996), p. 132.
49. Ramamurti in (ed.) Ramamurti (1996), p. 74.
50. SCT (1990d).

51. The regions were Baja California, Northeast, North, Northwest, West, Central, the Gulf and South, Southeast. Foreign ownership of any company interested in providing mobile telephones would not be allowed to exceed 49 per cent. The concession to provide the service would last for 20 years, and the successful company would be obliged to present a project of expansion every five years to the Ministry of Communications. See SCT (1989e), pp. 1, 13.
52. *La Jornada*, 21 October 1989, p. 31.
53. Pyramid Research (1994), p. 98.
54. *La Jornada*, 28 October 1989, p. 29; *El Financiero*, 26 October 1989, p. 8.
55. TELMEX (1989), p. 77.
56. Ruprah (1994a), p. 11.
57. Ruprah (1994b), p. 11; (eds) Cowhey *et al.* (1989).
58. My analysis concurs with that by Pérez Escamilla who shows, in a study of TELMEX's pricing policy between 1970 and the mid-1980s, that rates for basic rent (annual rental charge) and local calls fell dramatically while access rates (cost of installation) and international rates declined the least. Using 1970 as the 100 index, he calculated that basic rent fell from 100 in 1970 to 41 in 1984 and national long-distance calls fell to 36 in the same period. Meanwhile, the cost of telephone installation decreased from 100 in 1970 to 80 in 1984 while international long-distance calls fell to 67. See Pérez Escamilla in (eds) Cowhey *et al.* (1989), pp. 101–24.
59. At first glance it may seem contradictory that rates for local calls were cheap and international calls high when indirect tax was high on local calls and lower on international calls. This is because there was no limit on the charge for calls within Mexico since clients had no option but to use TELMEX, but in the case of international callers, too high a cost would encourage Mexicans to ask the person they were calling to call them back. See Pérez Escamilla in (eds) Cowhey *et al.* (1989), p. 115.
60. Ruprah (1994a), Table 7, presented a case study comparing tax payable by TELMEX with different investment capitals and proved that TELMEX would have been penalized if investment fell below a given level.
61. The government also diluted the capital of Mexicana airlines when it was sold in August 1989 so that it also was sold for a relatively small amount (relative to the value of the company) to the Mexican private sector. See Devlin (1994), p. 214.
62. Ruprah (1994a), p. 23.
63. *Proceso*, 18 September 1995, p. 13.
64. Grupo Carso was a leading holding company involved in mining, manufacturing, tobacco and restaurants.
65. STRM-TELMEX (1993).
66. TELMEX (1991a), pp. 16–19.
67. The award of shares to unions had been relatively rare, largely because the unions could not afford to buy shares. One of the previous cases had been the Aeroméxico workers who bought 25 per cent of the company. One of the main motivations of this rather half-baked policy of 'workers' capitalism' was to smooth over potential or actual labour conflicts and its resistance to privatization.

68. Galal *et al.* (1994), p. 261.
69. Ruprah (1994a), p. 26.
70. *Expansión*, 26 June 1991, pp. 30–8.
71. *Expansión: Informe Especial*, 1 February 1991, p. 11.
72. *La Jornada*, 10 January 1991, p. 20.
73. See Teichman (1995), pp. 217–19 for a list of Mexico's new 'economic élite'.
74. *Proceso*, 18 September 1995, pp. 6–11.
75. *La Jornada: Perfil*, 1 April 1994, p. 1.
76. Rodríguez Castañeda claimed that the difference in the sale price offered by the Grupo Carso was not sufficiently higher than the second highest bidder to allow the sale to continue. Thus, he claimed that Slim said he would 'top-up' his sale price offered once he had received the first profits as the new TELMEX owner. *Proceso*, 18 September 1995, pp. 12–14.
77. Interview with Bazdresch, CIDE, Mexico City, November 1994.
78. Interview by author with H. Olavarría, TELMEX Director of Labour Relations, May 1995, Mexico City.
79. INTTELMEX (1993).
80. Bazdresch and Elizondo in (eds) Baer and Conroy (1993a), p. 59.
81. See *US–Latin Trade*, Special Issue, September 1993, p. 29.
82. SCT (1991a); (1992a); (1993a).
83. Ramamurti in (ed.) Ramamurti (1996), p. 90.
84. *La Jornada*, 10 January 1991, p. 5.
85. Hernández Juárez's speech at the 1990 annual STRM convention quoted in Xelhuantzi López (1992), p. 511.
86. In 1992, Salinas commissioned him to write a book on the topic of new unionism and the reform of the state, which was published in a series of ideological tracts by the Fondo de Cultura Económica. The series was entitled 'A Vision of Modernization in Mexico' (*'Una Visión de la Modernización de México'*). This book, co-authored with union ideologue Xelhuantzi López was called 'Unionism in the Reform of the State' (*'El Sindicalismo en la Reforma del Estado'*). See Hernández Juárez and Xelhuantzi López (1993). He was interviewed and wrote articles for magazines like *Nexos*, *El Economista* and *Expansión*.
87. For instance, he addressed Venezuelan telephone workers about privatization. STRM (1990g).
88. He was quoted and photographed as such in magazines such as *Business Mexico*. See for instance Silverstein in *Business Mexico*, December 1992, pp. 20–2.
89. *La Jornada*, 25 August 1990, p. 3.
90. INTTELMEX (1994a), p. 6.
91. Unpublished statistical data on telephone workers' salaries provided by INTTELMEX.
92. *La Jornada*, 11 September 1991, p. 15.
93. This project was first presented to an assembly of STRM executives and delegates on 10 June 1989, and its title would have been viewed with some scepticism by many of the rank and file, since union leaders were calling for a 'deepening' of the union at a time when many members felt the union had been seriously debilitated. Nevertheless, the project was

discussed and ratified as the guide for the new union strategy at the Annual Convention in September 1989. See *Restaurador*, November 1989, p. 1 and STRM (1989b). Finally, it was published by the union in September 1990 in the form of a glossy booklet.

94. STRM (1989c), pp. 13, 18.
95. STRM (1989c), p. 17.
96. See Chapter 2.
97. Of the 47 040 respondents to the referendum, 32 042 accepted Hernández Juárez's standing as Secretary-General again, while 2420 did not. *La Jornada*, 6 May 1991, p. 10.
98. *La Jornada*, 8 September 1991, p. 15.
99. *La Jornada*, 8 September 1991, p. 15.
100. *La Jornada*, 8 September 1991, p. 15.
101. As explained in Chapter 2.
102. Interviews with dissident operator delegate and member of the workers' plan, and interview with technician dissident, Mexico City, May 1995.
103. As was revealed in a study of the profit-sharing scheme in John Lewis of the United Kingdom. Pateman (1989), p. 77.
104. STRM (1992a).
105. *La Jornada*, 23 February 1993, p. 15.
106. STRM (1989d), pp. 5–6 and STRM (1989c).
107. *La Jornada*, 27 March 1990, p. 16.
108. *Restaurador*, November 1989, p. 3.
109. This was also the mechanism of the CT leadership. However, Grayson (1989) pointed out how, in the year prior to presidential elections, Velázquez always takes over.
110. Hernández Juárez and Xelhuantzi López (1993), p. 151.
111. *La Jornada*, 8 May 1990, p. 10.
112. *La Jornada*, 28 April 1990, p. 9.
113. Corro, *Proceso*, 30 April 1990, p. 26.
114. Corro, *Proceso*, 4 January 1993.
115. *La Jornada*, 28 April 1990, p. 9.
116. *La Jornada*, 8 May 1990, Back page.
117. Xelhuantzi López (1992), p. 549.
118. When FESEBES was finally authorized there had not been any significant change in the arrangement of its statutes.
119. Middlebrook (1995), p. 285.
120. Middlebrook (1995), p. 296.
121. Middlebrook (1995), p. 283.
122. Zapata (1995), p. 93.
123. See Chapter 3.
124. FESEBES statutes, April 1990.
125. Lejarza, the 'right-hand man' of Hernández Juárez was made secretary, and commissioner of modernization as well as a member of the subcommission of ideology; Marino and Xelhuantzi both gained posts as union secretaries in the strategy commission. Marino was also subcommissioner of ideology, and Xelhuantzi of information. In her thesis on the FESEBES, Xelhuantzi López lists the representatives of the first FESEBES committee. See Xelhuantzi López (1992), pp. 537–8 and pp. 587–8.

Conclusions

1. See chapters by Roett, Rubio and Baer in (ed.) Roett (1993), Weintraub (1990), Morici (1993), Weintraub and Baer (1992).
2. Ramamurti (1996).
3. See Chapter 3.
4. This is included in Chapter 2.
5. See Chapter 5.
6. Pateman (1989) and Poole (1986).
7. Freeman and Soete (1994).
8. See Appendix and also Ng Choon Sim and Yong in (eds) Mitter and Rowbotham (1995).

Appendix: a 'Bottom-Up' Approach to the Impact of Privatization on Telephone Workers using Survey and Interview Techniques

1. See Chapter 1.
2. Maintenance workers were also affected but to a lesser extent and not as quickly as the operators.
3. TELMEX (1995c).
4. The problems with this literature have been best documented by Roxborough (1981, 1984).
5. My fieldwork in operator centres in Mexico City was conducted over a period of several weeks between April and June 1995.
6. When BT was privatized, over 10 000 operators lost their jobs. Interview by author with Alan Robinson, Global Business Development Manager, BT, London, August 1995.
7. See Ng Choon Sim and Yong in (eds) Mitter and Rowbotham (1995), pp. 177–203.
8. In 1976, there were around 8000 operators, making up over 36 per cent of the union. One-quarter were based in Mexico City (either in San Juan or Victoria) and the other 6000 in the larger urban cities.
9. From 1976 to 1986, the number of operators increased from around 8000 to 11 839, while unionized workers almost doubled, from 22 078 to 40 662. See chapter by Cortés in (eds) Cooper and De Barbieri (1989).
10. In a census on the union from 1991 to 1993, INTTELMEX (1993a) calculated that unionized workers totalled 40 616. Some 26 per cent of the workers were operators (21 per cent national operators and 5 per cent international operators).
11. Since TELMEX's recruitment of new operators has been negligible since 1989, all the operators have worked at least six years in the company.
12. One of the more outspoken operators whom I spoke to told me the centre's nickname was 'Verdevista' referring to the fact that the operators in the centre support the green plan of Hernández Juárez. For this reason, I persuaded the head union supervisor to introduce me to the other new operator centre Rojo Gómez.

13. My survey showed that the minimum period for which operators had worked for TELMEX was six years, so that they had experience of San Juan (Lindavista and Rojo Gómez were inaugurated in 1990). This is easily explained since TELMEX's recruitment of operators since 1989 has been negligible.

14. Union supervisors receive their normal salary as an operator from TELMEX and in addition a salary (which is usually a minimum salary) from the STRM.

15. During my second day in Lindavista a national operator came to tell me that national operators wanted to talk to me but were afraid I had been speaking English with the international operators and that I couldn't speak Spanish. This revealed a feeling of inferiority among the national operators since I had been speaking Spanish to all the operators.

16. In June 1995, a national operator who had worked at TELMEX for 20 years, and was therefore in the second highest paid bracket, earned less than 400 pesos a week after tax, while an international operator who had worked for 14 years earned 550 pesos a week after tax.

17. Originally, during the nineteenth century, the job of an operator was perceived as being suitable for a male because it involved some understanding of technical matters, and because the main telephone users were politicians and businessmen. At the beginning of the twentieth century, in the United States and Canada, and in the following two decades in other countries including Mexico and most European countries, women started to replace men and boys as operators. According to Norwood (1990) and Martin (1991) this was for three main reasons. First, women were used due to shortages of male labour during the war. Second, it was thought that women were more polite and tactful than males. The need for tact was reinforced as telephone services diversified and the operator's job was increasingly recognized as being a kind of social service, since the operator dealt directly with the general public in order to help them to resolve problems and answer queries. Third, it was perceived that the job of the operator was similar to that of the typist, a job that women were accustomed to performing. Feminist critics Cockburn and Ormrod (1993), p. 2, argued that, in telecommunications, as in any other industry, there was a general trend whereby jobs that required a greater understanding of technology were assigned to men, and women were recruited to do the simplest and least technical work.

18. Now in AT&T, there is, in theory, no discrimination as regards gender, race and age during the recruitment of all varieties of telephone workers so men can be found in operating centres and women in management-level positions. See Hacker in (eds) Kahn-Hut *et al.* (1982), p. 249.

19. See Braverman (1974).

20. See Greve in (eds) Bamber and Lansbury (1989), pp. 200–11.

21. For a good summary of these positions see Murray in (ed.) Gattiker (1994), p. 95.

22. For statistics on the American companies see Hacker in (eds) Kahn-Hut *et al.* (1982), p. 252, and Murray in (ed.) Gattiker (1994), p. 100. For statistics on Spanish telecommunications see Borderías (1993), pp. 126–7, who showed that the number of female staff as a percentage of total staff in Telefónica dropped from 40 per cent in 1933 to 29 per cent in 1980.

23. See Figure A.2.
24. INTTELMEX's unpublished data on the distribution of operators in the republic shows that after Mexico City's 1833 operators, the second largest concentration is in Veracruz where there are 666 operators.
25. As argued by Hernández Juárez and Xelhuantzi López (1993).
26. The ringleader of this group approached me and asked whether I had obtained permission from the union leaders and which company I worked for.
27. INTTELMEX (1993a), Table 32.
28. INTTELMEX (1993a), Table 38.
29. INTTELMEX (1993a), Table 39.
30. Levels of education are not broken down by speciality in INTTELMEX (1993a). However, in INTTELMEX (1993a), p. 16, there is information about education according to worker speciality.
31. Question 3 aimed to establish whether the operators found working with new equipment more or less comfortable, easy, monotonous and tiring than before. The idea of this question was that each respondent would answer each part of the question, so that there would be four answers from every respondent. However, many respondents answered only one or two of the question's parts. For this reason, I have drawn the graph of the results labelling the *y*-axis 'number of respondents to survey question'. Disaggregated by national and international categories, there were no significant differences in responses to the first two parts of the question.
32. Interview by author with an international operator, June 1995, Mexico City.
33. Interview with head operator delegate, and ex-operator union dissident.
34. Interview with ex-operator dissident.
35. Interview with dissident technician.

Bibliography

Primary sources

1. Interviews

Carlos Kauachi Kauachi, TELMEX Director of Telephone Development, April 1995.

Gildardo Lara Palacios, TELMEX Director of Technology Transfer, May 1995.

Héctor Olavarría Huerta, TELMEX Director of Labour Relations, April and May 1995.

Jésus Barroso Ramírez, INTTELMEX Director of Market Research, June 1995.

Dr Javier Elguea, Director of INTTELMEX, March 1995.

Pilar Marmalejo, INTTELMEX Director of Training Course Design, March 1995.

Vidal Ruíz, INTTELMEX Director of Training Courses, April 1995.

John H. Atterbury, President of Southwestern Bell in Mexico, January 1995.

Bert Geyser, Northern Telecom Director of Technical Operations in Mexico, November 1994.

Alan Robinson, BT Global Business Development Manager, London, August 1995.

Andrés Caso Lombardo, Secretary of Communications and Transport 1988–94, March 1995.

Arsenio Farrell, Secretary of Labour 1988–94, April 1995.

Mateo Lejarza, STRM head *comisionado*, April 1995.

Carlos Bustos, STRM *comisionado* (salaries), January 1995.

Jorge Castillo, *comisionado* (public relations), Head of *Comision de Modernisación*, May 1995.

José Méndez, *comisionado* (organization), STRM, May 1995.

María Xelhuantzi López, STRM *comisionado* (publications), February 1995.

TELMEX Operator Head Delegate, Lindavista Operator Centre, Mexico City, June 1995.

TELMEX Opposition activist technician, May 1995, Mexico City.

TELMEX Operator Delegate, opposition activist, May 1995, Mexico City.

Former TELMEX worker opposition activist, Puebla, December 1994.

30 TELMEX operators in Mexico City.

Roberto Robledo, Senior Vice President, Lehman Brothers (formally of Banco Internacional).

Raúl Solís Wolfowitz, General Director of Engineering and Financial Services of Banco Internacional, November 1994.

Jaime del Palacio, Writer/Researcher, April 1995.

Luis Hernández, CNOC, November 1994.

Pilar Vázquez Rubio, Journalist, December 1994.

Prof. Dr Alberto Arnaut, CIDE, December 1994.

Prof. Dr Carlos Bazdresch, CIDE, November 1994.

Prof. Dr Carlos Elizondo, CIDE, December 1994.

Prof. Dr De la Garza Toledo, UNAM, February 1995.

Prof. Dr Germán Sánchez Daza, UAP, January 1995.

2.   Primary documents

2a   *Government documents*

Caso Lombardo, A., *Desincorporación de Teléfonos de México*, SCT, Mexico, 1989.

Caso Lombardo, A., *Discursos: (1989–1991)*, SCT, Mexico, 1992.

Salinas, C., Letter to Mr Iain Vallance, Chairman of BT, Mexico, 1989.

Salinas, C., *Comunicación y Transportes: Reflexiones y prononciamientos 1988–1992*, SCT, Mexico, 1992a.

Salinas, C. *Americas Telecom 92; Palabras pronunciadas por el presidente de la Republica*, Inauguration of the Foro Mundial Y Exposicion Americas Telecom, Acapulco, Mexico, 1992b.

Salinas, C., *Crónica del Gobierno del Carlos Salinas de Gortari, 1988–1994: Sintesis e indice tematico*, Presidencia de la República, Unidad de la Crónica Presidencial y Fondo de Cultura Económica, Mexico, 1994a.

Salinas, C., *Crónica del Gobierno del Carlos Salinas de Gortari, 1988–1994*, Presidencia de la República, Unidad de la Crónica Presidencial y Fondo de Cultura Económica, Mexico, 1994b.

SCT, *Seminario Latinoamericano sobre el impacto socioeconomico de la nuevas tecnologías de la comunicación*, SCT/UNESCO/CT, Mexico, 1987.

SCT, *Historia de las comunicaciones y los transportes en México*, SCT, 1988.

SCT, *Las comunicaciones y los transportes en el mundo. La regulación de las telecomunicaciones: el caso de British Telecom*, SCT, Mexico, 1989a.

SCT, *Consideraciones sobre la regulación de la telefonía celular*, SCT, Mexico, 1989b.

SCT, *Foro de consulta popular para la modernización de las comunicaciones y el transporte. Diagnóstico*, SCT, Mexico, 1989c.

SCT, *Instructivo para integrar la solicitud de concesion servicio de radiotelefonia movil celular*, SCT, Mexico, 1989d.

SCT, *Programa nacional de modernización de las telecomunicaciones 1990–1994*, SCT, Mexico, 1990a.

SCT, *Reglamento de telecomunicaciones*, SCT, Mexico, 1990b.

SCT, *History of the Telephone*, SCT, Mexico, 1990c.

SCT, *Modificación al titulo de concesión de Teléfonos de México*, SCT, Mexico, 1990d.

SCT, *Informes de labores 1989–1990*, SCT, Mexico, 1990f.

SCT, *La reforma del estado y la desincorporación de Teléfonos de México* (Version 1), SCT, Mexico, 1990g.

SCT, *Título de concesión de Teléfonos de México*, SCT, Mexico, 1990h.

SCT, *Informes de labores 1990–1991*, SCT, Mexico, 1991a.

SCT, *La reforma del estado y la desincorporación de Teléfonos de México* (Version 2) SCT, Mexico, 1991b.

SCT, *Selecciones de publicaciones nacionales e internacionales*, SCT, Mexico, 1991c.

SCT, *Informes de labores 1991–1992*, SCT, Mexico, 1992.

SCT, *Informes de labores 1992–1993*, SCT, Mexico, 1993a.

SCT, *El sector comunicaciones y transportes*, SCT, Mexico, 1993b.

SCT, *Informes de labores 1993–1994*, SCT, Mexico, 1994a.

SCT, *El sector comunicaciones y transportes*, SCT, Mexico, 1994b.

Pérez de Mendoza, A., *Seminario sobre cambio tecnológico y el empleo: El cambio tecnológico en las telecomunicaciones* (TELMEX Director of Planning), SCT, Mexico, 1986.

2b   Union and STRM-TELMEX documents

FESEBES, *Asamblea nacional constituyente*, FESEBES, Mexico, 1990a.

FESEBES, *Estatutos*, 1990b.

Hernández Juárez, F., *Privatización de empresas*, Conference presented to unions in Venezuela, STRM, Mexico, 1990.

Organo Informativo de los Trabajadores, *Telefonistas, Petroleros y Electricistas, Boletin Cardenista* (Short-lived pamphlet supporting PRD candidate Cárdenas), Organo Informativo de los Trabajadores, Mexico, 1988.

SCT-TELMEX, *Estrategía para la evolución de TELMEX*, SCT, Mexico, 1989.

SME, *Una huelga intervenida: Historias del sindicalismo mexicano*, SME, Mexico, 1988.

STRM, *1o de Agosto*, (Official STRM magazine before 1976), STRM, Mexico. Entire collection between 1970 and 75.

STRM, *Restaurador 22 de abril* (Official STRM magazine after 1976). STRM, Mexico. Entire collection 1976–95, Mexico.

STRM, *Estatutos del Sindicato de Telefonistas de la República Mexicana*. STRM, Mexico, 1976.

STRM, *Logros de la revision contractual 1978–1980. Clausulas modificadas y comentarios*. STRM, Mexico, 1978.

STRM, *Democratización sindical*, STRM, Mexico, 1979.

STRM, *Estatutos del Sindicato de Telefonistas de la República Mexicana*, STRM, Mexico, 1983a.

STRM anonymous union opposition group, *Las pretensiones de Juárez con la reforma estatutaria*, STRM, Mexico, 1983b.

STRM, *Primer congreso nacional telefonistas-electricistas*. STRM-SME, STRM, Mexico, 1987.

STRM opposition group Coordinadora Democrática de Telefonistas, *Teléfonos: la modernización privada*, Coordinadora Democrática de Telefonistas, Mexico, 1988.

STRM, *Planilla de los trabajadores verde 1988–1992*, STRM, Mexico, 1988a.

STRM, *Conceptos utiles para la negociación*, STRM, Mexico, 1988b.

STRM, *Comision de modernización, Proyecto*, STRM, Mexico, 1988c.

STRM, *Sintesis de los temas de nueva cultura sindical y laboral, de la globalización y la revolución mundial de las telecomunicaciones*, STRM, Mexico, 1988d.

STRM, *Propuesta de proyecto para la elaboración de un programa de capacitación en higiene y seguridad en el trabajo, para los representantes sindicales ante las Comisiones Mixtas de Seguridad e Higiene de Teléfonos de México*, STRM, Mexico, 1988e.

STRM, *Comisión de Modernización: Propuesto*, STRM, Mexico, 1988f.

STRM, *Proyecto ante las Comisiones Mixtas de Seguridad e Higiene de Teléfonos de México*, STRM, Mexico, 1988g.

STRM, *Movimiento 16 de marzo: El ataque a los telefonistas: un golpe mas a la clase obrera*, STRM, Mexico, 1988h.

STRM anonymous union opposition group, *A todos los telefonistas*, Mexico, 1989a.

STRM, *Productividad y Calidad, punto central en cambio. STRM 1988*, STRM, Mexico, 1989b.

STRM, *Acuerdos tomados por la XIV Convención Nacional Ordinaria Democrática*, Mexico, 1989c.

STRM, *Profundización del proyecto sindical*, STRM, Mexico, 1989d.

STRM union opposition group Intendencia, *Porqué surgen los reacomodos?*, Intendencia, Mexico, 1990.

STRM, *Estatutos del Sindicato de los telefonistas de la República Mexicana*, STRM, Mexico, 1990a.

STRM, *Reforma economica popular: Nuevos empleos, nueva productividad, nuevo sindicalismo. La transformación del CT*, STRM, Mexico, 1990b.

STRM, *Competividad, relaciones laborales y organización sindical*, STRM, Mexico, 1990c.

STRM, *Circulares informativas de la Comision de Modernización de fechas: 1 de noviembre 1990, 21 de julio de 1990, 16 de diciembre 1990, 7 de diciembre de 1989*, STRM, Mexico, 1990d.

STRM, *Profundización del proyecto sindical*, STRM, Mexico, 1990e.

STRM, *Las telecomunicaciones en Europa: (Tres casos: France Telecom, British Telecom y Telefónica Española)*, STRM, Mexico, 1990f.

STRM, *Privatización: Un diálogo necesario*, STRM, 1990g.

STRM, *Modernización de empresas: Nuevo sindicalismo y reforma del estado.* STRM, Mexico, 1991a.

STRM, *Planilla de los Trabajadores 1992–1996*, STRM, Mexico, 1992a.

STRM anonymous union opposition group, *Sindicalismo y las nuevas relaciones laborales en los 90s*, Mexico, 1993.

STRM, *XIX Convención Nacional Ordinaria Democratica de Telefonistas. Informe*, STRM, Mexico, 1994a.

STRM union opposition group Intendencia, *Porqué esconden la Cara?*, Intendencia, Mexico, 1995.

STRM, *Formación de la planilla de los trabajadores 1996–2000*, STRM, Mexico, 1996.

STRM-TELMEX, *Contrato colectivo de trabajo*, STRM-TELMEX, Mexico, 1982; 1984; 1986; 1998; 1990; 1992; 1994 and 1996.

STRM-TELMEX, *Primera Reunión Conjunta de Comunicación sobre las proyección de TELMEX*, STRM-TELMEX, Mexico, 1987a.

STRM-TELMEX, *Primera Reunión Conjunta de Comunicación Sobre la projección de TELMEX: Memoria*, STRM-TELMEX Commission of Productivity, Mexico, 1987b.

STRM-TELMEX, *Perfiles de Puesto*, STRM-TELMEX, 1989a.

STRM-TELMEX, *Concertación para la modernización de Teléfonos de México*, STRM-TELMEX, Mexico, 1989b.

STRM-TELMEX, *Participación de los trabajadores en el capital de la empresa*, STRM-TELMEX, 1990a.

STRM-TELMEX, *Participación Accionaria de los Telefonistas y Apoyos Bancarios para los que Decidan Integrar el Patrimonio Colectivo*, STRM-TELMEX, Mexico, 1992a.

STRM-TELMEX, *Programa General de Incentivos a la calidad y prod uctividad en Teléfonos de México*,STRM-TELMEX, Mexico, 1993a.

STRM-TELMEX, *Programa General de Incentivos a la calidad y productividad en Teléfonos de México, 1994–1995*, STRM-TELMEX, 1994a.

Telefonistas para la Democrácia, *Boletin Cardenista*, Mexico, 1988. (A short-lived pamphlet produced jointly by dissident telephone, electricity and petroleum workers that supported the candidacy of Cárdenas.)

2c   Company documents

INCATEL, *Proyecto del Instituto Nacional de Capacitacion Telefónica*, INCATEL/ TELMEX, Mexico, 1991.

INTTELMEX, *Balance Social 1992, Teléfonos de México*, INTTELMEX, Mexico, 1993a.

INTTELMEX, *Inventario de Recursos Humanos. Personal Sindicalizado*, INTTELMEX, Mexico, 1993b.

INTTELMEX, *Balance Social 1993*, INTTELMEX, Mexico, 1994a.

INTTELMEX, *Balance Social 1994*, INTTELMEX, Mexico, 1995a.

INTTELMEX, *Nomina de salarios pagados para personal sindicalizado por especialidad*, INTTELMEX, Mexico, 1995b.

INTTELMEX, *Proceso de reubicación: TELMEX*, INTTELMEX, Mexico, 1995c.

Kauachi, C., *Is there Life after Privatization?*, TELMEX, 1993.

TELECOMM, *Sistema de planeación estrategía*, Telecomm, Mexico, 1992.

TELMEX, *Annual Reports*, TELMEX, Mexico, 1987, 1988, 1989, 1990, 1991 1992, 1993 and 1994.

TELMEX, *Implicaciones Laborales de la introduccion de la tecnologia digital en TELMEX*, TELMEX, Mexico, 1986a.

TELMEX, *Octava Reunion de planeación corporativa. Memoria*, TELMEX, Mexico, 1987a.

TELMEX, *Programa Intensivo para el mejoramiento del servicio*, TELMEX, Mexico, 1987b.

TELMEX, *Tendencias en la evolución de trafico manual y sus implicaciones para las operadoras*, 1987c.

TELMEX, *Etapas de Modernización en el area trafico manual*, TELMEX, Mexico, 1989a.

TELMEX, *Estrategía para la evolución de TELMEX*, TELMEX, Mexico, 1989b.

TELMEX, *Plan de Modernización de TELMEX*, TELMEX, Mexico, 1989c.

TELMEX, *A Business Perspective*, TELMEX, Mexico, 1989d.

TELMEX, *El Nuevo Proceso de Planeacion*, by TELMEX's Director of Planning, Dr Alfredo Pérez de Mendoza, TELMEX, Mexico, 1989e.

TELMEX, *Consideraciones sobre la regulacion de la Telefonia celular*, TELMEX, Mexico, 1989f.

TELMEX, *Concertación para la Moderniziación de Telefonos de México*, TELMEX, Mexico, 1989g.

TELMEX, *Informe del Consejo de Administración a la Asamblea General Extraordinaria de Accionistas*, TELMEX, Mexico, 1989h.

TELMEX, *Historia de la Telefonía*, TELMEX, Mexico, 1990a.

TELMEX, *Dirección Corporativa de Relaciones Laborales y Juridico: Memoria*, TELMEX, Mexico, 1990b.

TELMEX, *Modelo de Capacitacion*, TELMEX, Mexico, 1990c.

TELMEX, *Bases para la reorganización de Telefonos de Mexico*, TELMEX, Mexico, 1990d.

TELMEX, *Modelo para el Esfuerzo de Calidad*, TELMEX, Mexico, 1990e.

TELMEX, *La Desincorporación de Teléfonos de México. TELMEX*, TELMEX, Mexico, 1991a.

TELMEX, *Programa Trianual 1991–1993*, TELMEX, Mexico, 1991b.

TELMEX, *Historia de la telefonía en México, 1878–1991*, TELMEX, 1991c.

TELMEX, *Programa General de Incentivos a la Calidad y Productividad en Teléfonos de México SA de CV*, TELMEX, Mexico, 1993a.

TELMEX, *La Revolución de la Telefonía en México 1878–1993*, TELMEX, Mexico, 1994a.

TELMEX, *Modernización de los servicios de Larga Distancia*, TELMEX, Mexico, 1995a.

TELMEX, *Resultados 1991–1994*, TELMEX, Mexico, 1995b.

TELMEX, *Proceso de Reubicación de personal de trafico*, TELMEX, Mexico, 1995c.

Voces, Official TELMEX staff magazine, Complete collection of issues between 1990 and 1995, TELMEX, Mexico.

3. Commercial newspapers and magazines

Business Mexico:
Salinas, R., 'Pushing Privatization', June 1990.
Silverstein, J., 'Labor's Laissez-Faire Economics', December 1992, pp. 20–2.

Capital:
Cabrera Martínez, J. 'Telecomunicaciones: Pilar del desarollo' in Vol. 4, No. 41, April 1991, pp. 25–7.

El Cotidiano: 1984–95.

El Financiero: 1987–94.

Expansión:
'Neocorporativismo Sindical?', 15 August 1990, pp. 324–5.
'Telecomunicaciones: Un nuevo mundos', 21 November 1990, p. 53.
'TELMEX: La Empresa del año', 26 June 1991, pp. 30–8.
'TELMEX: Más dinero por el auricular', 24 June 1992, p. 62.
'TELMEX: Buen negocio, siempre', 23 June 1993, p. 50.

Informe Especial:
'TELMEX: Informe Especial', 1 February 1991, pp. 1–37.

La Jornada: 1987–94.

Proceso: 1987–94.

The Financial Times: 1987–94.

4. Primary data

Bolsa de Valores, Reports on TELMEX, 1988–94, Bolsa de Valores, Mexico.

Economic Intelligence Unit, *EIU Country Report: Mexico*, Issues from 1986 to 1995, EIU, London.

Goldman Sachs, *Teléfonos de México*, London, 1991.

IADB, *Economic and Social Progress in Latin America*, Annual Reports for 1985–96.

INEGI, *IX Censo de Transportes y Comunicaciones*, INEGI, Mexico, 1981.

INEGI, *X Censo de Transportes y Comunicaciones*, INEGI, Mexico, 1985.

INEGI, *Mexican Bulletin of Statistical Information*, January–March 1993 (No. 7); October–December 1993 (No. 10); July–September 1994 (No. 13); October–December 1994 (No. 14).

INEGI, *Información Estatistica sobre relaciones Laborales de jurisdicción local. Tomo II and III*, INEGI, Mexico, 1994a.

INEGI, *Estadísticas Historicas de México*, Vols I and II, INEGI, Mexico, 1994b.

INEGI, *International Year Book. 1991–1994*, INEGI, Mexico, 1995.

ING Barings, *Telecommunications Valuation*, Global Sectoral Analysis, London, 1995.

Musaccio, H. (ed.), *Diccionario Enciclopedico de México ilustrado*, Editorial Andrés Leon, Mexico, 1989.

Pyramid Research, *Telecom Markets in Mexico*, Cambridge, Massachussetts, 1994.

Research Logistics, *World Telecom Fact Book 1990–91*, Telecommunications Research, West Sussex, 1992.

SHCP/SCGF/Fondo de Cultura Económica, *Desincorporación de entidades paraestatales: Información básica de los procesos del 1 de diciembre de 1988 al 31 de diciembre de 1993*, Mexico, 1994.

United Bank of Switzerland, *Telecoms in Latin America*, UBS Securities, New York, 1995.

United States Trade Center, *Market Research Summary: 1990 the Mexican Market for Telecommunications Equipment*. October 1989.

Secondary sources

1. Books

Adler Hellman, J., *Mexico in Crisis*, Holmes & Meier, New York & London (1988). First published 1978.

Aguilar García, J. (ed.), *IV: Los Sindicatos Nacionales: Educación, Telefonistas y Bancarios*, GV Editores, Mexico, 1989.

Aguilar García, J. (ed.), *Historia de la CTM (1936–1990)*, UNAM, Mexico, 1990.

Aitken, R., 'Neoliberalism and Identity: Redefining State and Society in Mexico' in (eds) R. Aitken *et al.*, *Dismantling the Mexican State?*, Macmillan Press, London, 1996.

Aitken, R. *et al.*, *Dismantling the Mexican State?*, Macmillan Press, London, 1996.

Alarcón González, D., *Changes in the Distribution of Income in Mexico and Trade Liberalization*, El Colegio de la Frontera Norte, Mexico, 1994.

Alba, V., *Politics and the Labor Movement in Latin America*, Stanford Unviersity Press, Stanford, 1968.

Alvarez Béjar, A. (ed.), *La Clase Obrera y el Sindicalismo Mexicano*, UNAM, Mexico, 1990.

Amnesty International, *Violaciones de los derechos humanos en México: El reto de los noventa*, Amnesty International, London, 1995.

Anaya Rosique, J., *et al.* (eds), *La Obrera en México*, Editorial Popular de los Trabajadores, Mexico, 1983.

Angell, A., *Politics and the Labour Movement in Chile*, Royal Institute of International Affairs/Oxford University Press, London, 1972.

Anguiano, A., *El Estado y la política obrera del cardenismo*, Era, Mexico, 1975.

Armstrong, M. and Vickers, J., 'Competition and Regulation in Telecommunications' in (eds) M. Bishop *et al.*, *The Regulatory Challenge*, Oxford University Press, New York, 1995.

Arriagada, I., 'Unequal Participation by Women in the Work Force', in (ed.) J. Dietz, *Latin America's Economic Development: Confronting Crisis*, Second Edition, Lynne Rienner Publishers, Boulder & London, 1995.

Aspe Armella, P., *El Camino mexicano de la transformación económica*, Fondo de Cultura Económica, Mexico, 1993.

Ashby, J., *Organized Labor and the Mexican Revolution under Lázaro Cárdenas*, University of North Carolina Press (1967). First published 1963.

Aziz Nassif, A., *El Estado Mexicano y la CTM*, Centro de Investigaciones y Estudios Superiores en Antropología Social, Mexico, 1989.

Baer, W. *et al.* (eds), *Latin America: the Crisis of the Eighties and the Opportunities of the Nineties*, University of Illinois, Illinois, 1991.

Baer, W. and Handelman, H. (eds), *Paying the Costs of Austerity in Latin America*, Westview Press, Boulder, San Francisco & London, 1989.

Baibai, D., 'El Banco Mundial y el FMI: apoyo o rechazo al papel del estado?' in (ed.) R. Vernon, *La Promesa de la privatización*, Fondo de Cultura Económica, Mexico (1995). First published 1988.

Bailey, J., 'Can the PRI be Reformed?' in (ed.) J. Gentleman, *Mexican Politics in Transition*, Westview Press, Boulder & London, 1987.

Bailey, J., *Governing Mexico*, St Martin's Press, New York, 1988.

Bailey, J., 'Centralism and Political Change in Mexico: the Case of the National Solidarity' in (eds) W. Cornelius *et al.*, *Transforming State–Society Relations in Mexico: The National Solidarity Strategy*, Center for US–Mexican Studies, University of California, San Diego, 1994.

Bamber, G. J. and Lansbury, R. D. (eds), *New Technology: International Perspectives on Human Resources and Industrial Relations*, Unwin Hyman, London, 1989.

Barry, T. (ed.), *Mexico: a Country Guide*, Inter-Hemispheric Education Resource Center, Albuquerque, New Mexico, 1992.

Basañez, M., *El Pulso de los Sexenios: 20 años de crisis en México*, Siglo Veintiuno Editores, Mexico, 1990.

Basurto, J., *En el régimen de Echeverría: rebelión y independencia* (Series number 14 in *La Clase Obrera en la historia de México*), UNAM, Mexico, 1983.

Basurto, J., *Del avilacamachismo al alemanismo (1940–1952)* (Series number 11 in *La Clase Obrera en la historia de México*), UNAM, Mexico, 1984.

Bateson, N., *Data Construction in Social Surveys*, George Allen & Unwin, London, 1984.

Bensusan, G. and García, C., *Estado y Sindicatos: Crisis de una relación*, Friedrich Ebert Stiftung/UAM, Mexico, 1989.

Berins Collier, R., *The Contradictory Alliance: State–Labor Relations and Regime Change in Mexico*, University of California at Berkeley, Berkeley, 1992.

Berins Collier, R. and Collier, D., *Shaping the Political Arena*, Princeton University Press, Princeton, New Jersey, 1991.

Bethell, L. (ed.), *Mexico since Independence*, University of Cambridge, Cambridge (1992). First published 1991.

Bethell, L., *The Cambridge History of Latin America. Vol VI, Part Two (Politics and Society)*, Cambridge University Press, Cambridge, 1994.

Bethell, L. and Roxborough, I., *Latin America between World War II and the Cold War 1944–1948*, Cambridge University Press, Cambridge, 1992.

Bienen, H. and Waterbury, J., 'The Political Economy of Privatization in Developing Countries' in (ed.) C. K. Wilber and K. P. Jameson, *The Political Economy of Development and Underdevelopment*, Fifth Edition, McGraw-Hill (1992). First published 1973.

Biersteker, T., 'The "Triumph" of Liberal Economic Ideas in the Developing World' in (ed.) B. Stallings, *Global Change, Regional Response: the New International Context of Development*, Cambridge University Press, Cambridge, 1995.

Bishop, M. *et al.* (eds), *Privatization and Economic Performance*, Oxford University Press, Oxford, 1994.

Bishop, M. *et al.* (eds), *The Regulatory Challenge*, Oxford University Press, Oxford, 1995.

Birch, A. H. *The Concepts and Theories of Modern Democracy*, Routledge, London, 1993. Chapter 12, 'Corporatism'.

Bird, G. and Helwege, A. (eds), *Latin America's Economic Future*, Academic Press, London & New York, 1994.

Bizberg, I., *Estado y Sindicatos en México*, El Colegio de México, Mexico, 1990.

Bizberg, I., 'Modernization and Corporatism in Government–Labour Relations' in (ed.) N. Harvey, *Mexico: Dilemmas of Transition*, ILAS, London, 1993.

Borderías, C., *Entre líneas: Trabajo e identidad feminina en la España contemporanea 1924–1980*, Icaria Editorial, Barcelona, 1993.

Borja, R. and Barbosa, F., 'El movimiento del 8 de marzo en el sindicato de telefonistas' in (ed.) J. Aguilar, *IV: Los Sindicatos Nacionales: Educación, Telefonistas y Bancarios*, GV Editores, Mexico, 1989.

Bortz, J. L., *Los salarios industriales en la ciudad de México 1939–1975*, Fondo de Cultura Económica, Mexico, 1988.

Brachet-Marquez, V., *The Dynamics of Domination: State, Class and Social Reform in Mexico, 1910–1990*, University of Pittsburgh Press, Pittsburgh & London, 1994.

Brandenburg, F., *The Making of Modern Mexico*, Prentice-Hall, Englewood Cliffs, New Jersey (1965). First published 1964.

Braverman, H., *Labour and Monopoly Capital: The Degradation of Work in the Twentieth Century*, Monthly Review Press, New York, 1974.

Budge, I. and McKay, D. (eds), *Developing Democracy*, Sage, London, 1994.

Bulmer-Thomas, V., *The Economic History of Latin America since Independence*, Cambridge University Press, Cambridge, 1994.

Bulmer-Thomas, V. (ed.), *The New Economic Model in Latin America and its Impact on Income Distribution and Poverty*, Macmillan Press, London, 1996.

Cain, M., 'Women and Technology' in (eds) R. Dauber and M. Cain, *Women and Technological Change in Developing Countries*, AAAS, Colorado, 1981.

Calvocoressi, P., *World Politics since 1945*, Longman, London & New York, 1991.

Camacho, M., 'Los nudos históricos del sistema político mexicano' in (ed.) Centro de Estudios Internacionales, *Las crisis en el sistema político mexicano (1928–1977)*, El Colegio de México, Mexico, 1977.

Camp, R. A., *Mexican Political Biographies*, Arizona Press, Arizona, 1982.

Camp, R. A., *Intellectuals and the State in Twentieth Century Mexico*, University of Texas Press, Austin, 1985.

Camp, R., 'Political Modernization in Mexico: Through a Looking Glass' in (ed.) J. O. Rodríguez, *The Evolution of the Mexican Political System*, SR Books, Wilmington, Delaware, 1993.

Camp, R., 'Political Liberalization: the Last Key to Economic Modernization in Mexico?' in (ed.) R. Roett, *Political and Economic Liberalization in Mexico: at a Critical Juncture?*, Lynne Rienner, Boulder & London, 1993.

Camp, R. A., *Politics in Mexico*, Oxford University Press, New York. First edition 1993; second edition 1996.

Camp, R. A., *Political Recruitment across Two Centuries: Mexico 1884–1991*, University of Texas Press, Austin, 1995.

Cardoso, E. and Helwege, A., *Latin America's Economy: Diversity, Trends and Conflicts*, MIT Press, Cambridge, Massachusetts & London, England, 1992.

Carr, B., *El Movimiento Obrero y la política en México 1919–1929*, Era, Mexico, 1976.

Carr, B., 'The Mexican Economic Debacle and the Labour Movement: a New Era or More of the Same?' in (ed.) D. L. Wyman, *Mexico's Economic Crisis: Challenges and Opportunities*, University of California, San Diego, 1983.

Carr, B., *Marxism and Communism in Twentieth Century Mexico*, University of Nebraska Press, Lincoln & London, 1992.

Carr, B., 'Mexico: the Perils of Unity and the Challenge of Modernization' in (eds) B. Carr and S. Ellner, *The Latin American Left: From the Fall of Allende to Perestroika*, Westview/Latin American Bureau, London, 1993.

Carr, B. and Ellner, S. (eds), *The Latin American Left: From the Fall of Allende to Perestroika*, Westview/Latin American Bureau, London, 1993.

Cawson, A., *Corporatism and Political Theory*, Basil Blackwell, Oxford & New York, 1986.

Centeno, M. A., *Government and Opposition Speak Out*, University of California, San Diego, 1991.

Centeno, M. A., *Democracy within Reason: Technocratic Revolution in Mexico*, Pennsylvania State University Press, Pennsylvania, 1994.

Chang, H., 'Explaining "Flexible Rigidities" in East Asia' in (ed.) T. Killick, *The Flexible Economy: Causes and Consequences of the Adaptability of National Economies*, Routledge, London & New York, 1995.

Clarke, T. (ed.), *International Privatization: Strategies and Practices*, Walter de Gruyer, Berlin & New York, 1994.

Clark, T. and Pitelis, C, 'The Political Economy of Privatization' in (eds) T. Clarke and C. Pitelis, *The Political Economy of Privatization*, Routledge, London & New York, 1993.

Clarke, T. and Pitelis, C. (eds), *The Political Economy of Privatization*, Routledge, London & New York, 1993.

Cockburn, C. and Ormrod, S., *Gender and Technology in the Making*, Sage, London/Thousand Oaks/New Delhi, 1993.

Cooper, J. and de Barbieri, T. (eds), *Fuerza de Trabajo: Femenina Urbana en México: Participación Economica y Politica*, Vol. 2. UNAM, Mexico, 1989.

Colclough, C. and Manor, J., *States or Markets?: Neo-liberalism and the Development Policy Debate*, IDS Development Studies Series, Clarendon Paperbacks, Oxford (1995). First published 1993.

Collier, D. (ed.), *New Authoritarianism in Latin America*, Princeton University Press, Princeton, 1979.

Colmenares, I. *et al.*, *Cien Años de Lucha de Clases en México: 1876–1976*, Vol. 1., Ediciones Quinto Sol, Mexico, 1990.

Comor, E. A. (ed.), *The Global Political Economy of Communication*, Macmillan, London (1996). First published 1994.

Cook, P. and Kirkpatrick, C. (eds), *Privatisation Policy and Performance: International Perspectives*, Prentice-Hall/Harvester Wheatsheaf, Hertfordshire, 1995.

Cooper, J. and de Barbieri, T. (eds), *Fuerza de Trabajo: Femenina Urbana en México. Participación Economica y Politica*, Vol. 2. UNAM, Mexico, 1989.

Coppedge, M., 'Mexican Democracy: You can't get there from here' in (ed.) R. Roett, *Political and Economic Liberalization in Mexico: at a Critical Juncture?*, Lynne Rienner Publishers, Boulder & London, 1993.

Cordera Campos, R. and González Tiburcio, E., 'Crisis and Transition in the Mexican Economy' in (eds) M. González de la Rocha and A. Escobar Latapí, *Social Responses to Mexico's Economic Crisis of the 1980s*, Center for US–Mexican Studies, University of California, San Diego, 1991.

Cornelius, W., 'Liberalization in an Authoritarian Regime' in (ed.) J. Gentleman, *Mexican Politics in Transition*, Westview Press, Boulder & London, 1987.

Cornelius, W. *et al.*, *Mexico's Alternative Political Futures*, Centre for US–Mexican Studies, University of California, San Diego, 1989.

Cornelius, W. *et al.*, *Transforming State–Society Relations in Mexico: the National Solidarity Strategy*, Center for US–Mexican Studies, University of California, San Diego, 1994.

Cornelius, W., *Mexican Politics in Transition: the Breakdown of a One-Party Dominant Regime*, Monograph Series 41, University of California, San Diego, 1996.

Cortés, G., 'La mujer en la fuerza de trabajo: El caso de las operadoras de TELMEX' in (eds) J. Cooper and T. de Barbieri, *Fuerza de Trabajo: Femenina Urbana en México: Participación Economica y Politica*, Vol. 2., UNAM, Mexico, 1989.

Cosío Villegas, D., *El sistema político mexicano*, Cuadernos de Joaquín Mortiz, Mexico (1973). First published 1972.

Cowhey, P. F. *et al.* (eds), *Changing Networks: Mexico's Telecommunications Options*, University of California, San Diego, 1989.

Cowhey, P. F. and Aronson, R., 'Trade in Services and Changes in the World Telecommunications Options in the World Service Market' in P. F. (eds) Cowhey *et al.*, *Changing Networks: Mexico's Telecommunications Options*, University of California, San Diego, 1989.

Craske, N., 'Women's Political Participation in Colonias Populares in Guadalajara, Mexico' in (eds) S. A. Radcliffe and S. Westwood, '*VIVA' Women and Popular Protest in Latin America*, Routledge, London & New York, 1993.

Craske, N., 'Dismantling or Retrenchment?' in (ed.) R. Aitken *et al.*, *Dismantling the Mexican State?*, Macmillan, London, 1996.

Crouch, Colin, *Industrial Relations and European State Tradition*, Clarendon Paperbacks, Oxford (1994). First published 1993.

Crozier, M., *The Bureaucratic Phenomenon*, University of Chicago, Chicago, 1964.

Cruz Cervantes, C., 'Condiciones de Trabajo en la industria Telefónica' in (ed.) A. Alvarez Béjar, *La Clase Obrera y el Sindicalismo Mexicano*, UNAM, Mexico, 1990.

Cuadernos Unomásuno, *Tres Huelgas de Telefonistas: Hacia un sindicalismo democrático*, Unomásuno, Mexico, 1980.

De la Garza Toledo, E., *Reestructuración productiva y respuesta sindical en México*, UNAM/UAM, Mexico, 1993.

Delal Baer, M., 'Mexico's Second Revolution: Pathways to Liberalization' in (ed.) R. Roett, *Political and Economic Liberalization in Mexico: at a Critical Juncture?*, Lynne Rienner, Boulder & London, 1993.

De los Angeles Pozas, M., *Industrial Restructuring in Mexico: Corporate Adaptation, Technological Innovation and Changing Patterns of Industrial Relations in Monterrey*, Monograph Series 38, Centre for US–Mexican Studies, University of California, San Diego, 1993.

Devlin, R., 'Privatization and Social Welfare in Latin America' in (eds) G. Bird and A. Helwage, *Latin America's Economic Future*, Academic Press, London & New York, 1994.

Devlin, R., 'Privatisation and Social Welfare' in (eds) K. P. Jameson and C. K. Wilber, *The Political Economy of Development and Underdevelopment*, Sixth edition, McGraw-Hill, New York (1996). First edition 1973.

Díaz-Fuentes, D., *Crisis y cambios estructurales en América Latina: Argentina, Brasil y México durante el periodo de entreguerras*, Fondo de Cultura Económica, Mexico, 1994.

Diehl, P. F., *The Politics of Global Governance: International Organizations in an Interdependent World*, Lynne Rienner, Boulder & London, 1997.

Dietz, J. L., (ed.), *Latin America's Economic Development: Confronting Crisis*, Lynne Rienner Publishers, Boulder & London, Second edition, 1995.

Dietz, J. L., 'A Brief Economic History' in (ed.) J. Dietz, *Latin America's Economic Development: Confronting Crisis*, Lynne Rienner, Boulder & London, Second edition, 1995.

Dobek, M., *The Political Logic of Privatization: Lessons from Great Britain and Poland*, Praeger, Westport, Connecticut & London, 1993.

Dresser, D., *Neopopulist Solutions to Neoliberal Problems: Mexico's National Solidarity Program*, Current Issue Brief 3, Center for US–Mexican Studies, University of California, San Diego, 1991.

Dresser, D., 'Bringing the Poor Back in: National Solidarity as a Strategy of Regime Legitimation' in (eds) W. Cornelius *et al.*, *Transforming State–Society Relations in Mexico: the National Solidarity Strategy*, Center for US–Mexican Studies, University of California, San Diego, 1994.

Duch, R., *Privatizing the Economy: Telecommunications Policy in Comparative Perspective*, University of Michigan, Ann Arbor, Michigan, 1991.

Edwards, S., *Crisis and Reform in Latin America: from Despair to Hope*, World Bank/Oxford University Press, Washington DC, 1995.

El Colegio de México (ed.), *Modernización Económica, Democracia Política y Democracia Social*, El Colegio de México, Mexico, 1993.

El Colegio de México (ed.), *Transformaciones sociales y acciones colectivas: América Latin en el contexto internacional de los noventa*, El Colegio de México, Mexico, 1994.

Elguea, J. (ed.), *Telecomunicaciones y Desarollo*, INTTELMEX, Mexico, 1994.

Epstein, E. C., *Labor Autonomy and the State in Latin America*, Unwin Hyman, Boston, 1989.

Escobar Latapí, A. and Roberts, B. R., 'Introduction' in (eds) M. González de la Rocha and A. Escobar Latapí, *Social Responses to Mexico's Economic Crisis of the 1980s*, Center for US–Mexican Studies, University of California, San Diego, 1991.

Fagen, R. and Tuohy, W. S., *Politics and Privilege in a Mexican City*, Stanford University Press, Stanford, California, 1972.

Feinberg, R. E., 'Defunding Latin America: Reverse Transfers by the Multilateral Lending Agencies' in (eds) C. K. Wilber and K. P. Jameson, *The Political Economy of Development and Underdevelopment*, McGraw-Hill, New York, 1992.

Feinberg, R., 'The Changing Relation between the World Bank and the IMF' in (ed.) P. F. Diehl, *The Politics of Global Governance: International Organizations in an Interdependent World*, Lynne Rienner Boulder & London, 1997.

Fernández Christlieb, P. and Rodríguez Araujo, O., *En el sexenio de Tlatelolco* (Series number 13 of *La Clase Obrera en la historia de México*), Siglo Veintiuno Editores/UNAM, Mexico, 1985.

Ferraez Comunicación, *Líderes Mexicanos: Carlos Salinas de Gortari*, Ferraez Comunicación, Mexico, 1994.

Fitzgerald, E. V. K., 'The New Trade Regime, Macroeconomic Behaviour and Income Distribution in Latin America' in (ed.) V. Bulmer-Thomas, *The New Economic Model in Latin America and its Impact on Income Distribution and Poverty*, Macmillan, London, 1996.

Foweraker, J. and Craig, A., (eds), *Popular Movements and Political Change in Mexico*, Lynne Rienner, Boulder & London, 1990.

Foweraker, J., *Popular Mobilization in Mexico: the Teachers' Movement 1977–1987*, Cambridge University Press, Cambridge, 1993.

Foweraker, J., 'Popular Political Organization and Democratization: a Comparison of Spain and Mexico' in (eds) I. Budge and D. McKay, *Developing Democracy*, Sage, London, 1994.

Fowler, F. J, *Survey Research Methods. Applied Social Research Methods Series*, Vol. 1, Sage Publications, London, Second edition 1993.

Freeman, C. and Soete, L., *Work for all or Mass Unemployment? Computerised Technical Change into the 21st Century*, Pinter Publishers, London & New York, 1994.

Fukayama, F., *The End of History and the Last Man*, Hamish Hamilton, London, 1992.

Galal, A. *et al.*, *Welfare Consequences of Selling Public Enterprises: an Empirical Analysis*, World Bank/Oxford University Press, New York, 1994.

Galal, A. and Shirley, M. (eds), *Does Privatization Deliver?* IBRD/World Bank, Washington DC, 1994.

García, C., 'El Sindicalismo Mexicano Frente al Modelo Neoliberal' in (eds) D. Kohler and M. Wannoftel, *Modelo Neoliberal y Sindicatos en America Latina*, Fundación Friedrich Ebert, Mexico, 1993.

García, N. E., *Ajustes, Reformas y Mercado Laboral: Costa Rica (1980–1990), Chile (1973–1992), México (1981–1991)*, ILO, Geneva, Switzerland, 1993.

Gattiker, U. E. (ed.), *Women and Technology*, Walter de Gruyter, Berlin & New York, 1994.

Gentleman, J. (ed.), *Mexican Politics in Transition*, Westview Press, Boulder & London, 1987.

Glade, W. (ed.) *Privatization of Public Enterprises in Latin America*, ICS Press, San Francisco, California, 1991.

Gómez Tagle, S., *Insurgencia y Democrácia en los sindicatos electricistas*, Jornadas 93, El Colegio de México, Mexico, 1980.

González de la Rocha, M. and Escobar Latapí, A. (eds), *Social Responses to Mexico's Economic Crisis of the 1980s*, Center for US–Mexican Studies, University of California, San Diego, 1991.

Grayson, G., *The Mexican Labor Machine*, Center for Strategic and International Studies, Washington DC, 1989.

Green, D., *The Rise of Market Economies in Latin America*, Cassell/Latin American Bureau, London, 1995.

Greve, R. M., 'Technological Change and Women Workers' in (eds) G. J. Bamber and R. D. Lansbury, *New Technology: International Perspectives on Human Resources and Industrial Relations*, Unwin Hyman, London, 1989.

Grindle, M., 'The Response to Austerity: Political and Economic Strategies of Mexico's Rural Poor' in (eds) M. González de la Rocha and A. Escobar Latapí, *Social Responses to Mexico's Economic Crisis of the 1980s*, Center for US–Mexican Studies, University of California, San Diego, 1991.

Gruening, E., *Mexico and its Heritage*, Stanley Paul and Co., New York, 1928.

Gutiérrez Garza, E. (ed.), *Reconversión industrial y lucha sindical*, Nueva Sociedad, Mexico, 1989.

Hacker, S. L., 'Sex Stratification, Technology and Organization Change: a Longitudinal Case Study of AT&T' in (eds) R. Kahn-Hut *et al.*, *Women and Work*, Oxford University Press, New York & Oxford, 1982.

Haggard, S. and Webb, S. (eds), *Voting for Reform*, World Bank/Oxford University Press, Washington DC, 1994.

Hamilton, N., *The Limits of State Autonomy: Post-Revolutionary Mexico*, Princeton University Press, New Jersey, 1982.

Hansen, R., *The Politics of Mexican Development*, The Johns Hopkins University Press, Baltimore, 1971.

Harriss, J. *et al.* (eds), *The New Institutional Economics and Third World Development*, Routledge, London & New York, 1995.

Harvey, N. (ed.), *Mexico: Dilemmas of Transition*, Institute of Latin American Studies, London & New York, 1993.

Haskel, J. and Szymanski, S., 'Privatization and the Labour Market: Facts, Theory and Evidence' in (eds) M. Bishop *et al.*, *Privatization and Economic Performance*, Oxford University Press, New York, 1994.

Heidenheiner, A. *et al.* (eds), *Political Corruption: a Handbook*, Transaction Publishers, New Brunswick & Oxford, 1989.

Held, D. and Pollitt, C., *New Forms of Democracy*, Sage Publications and Open University, London, 1986.

Held, D. (ed.), *Prospects for Democracy*, Polity Press, Oxford, 1993.

Heller, M., 'Hijacking the Public Interest – the Politics of Telecommunications Policy in Mexico' in (ed.) N. Harvey, *Dilemmas of Transition*, ILAS, University of London/British Academic Press, London & New York, 1993.

Heredia, B., 'Making Economic Reform Politically Viable: the Mexican Experience' in (eds) W. C. Smith *et al.*, *Democracy, Markets and Structural Reform in Latin America*, Transaction Publishers, New Brunswick & London, 1993.

Hérnandez Chavez, A., *Historia de la Revolución Mexicana: la Mecánica Cardenista 1934–1940*, El Colegio de México, Mexico, 1979.

Hernández Juárez, F. and Xelhuantzi López, M., *El Sindicalismo en la reforma del estado*, Fondo de Cultura Económica, Mexico, 1993.

Hernández Navarro, L. and Célis Callejas, F., 'Solidarity and the New Campesino Movements' in (eds) W. Cornelius *et al.*, *Transforming State–Society Relations in Mexico: the National Solidarity Strategy*, Center for US–Mexican Studies, University of California, San Diego, 1994.

Higley, J. and Gunther, R. (eds), *Elites and Democratic Consolidation in Latin America and South Europe*, Cambridge University Press, Cambridge (1995). First published 1992.

Horcasitas, J. M. and Weldon, J. A., 'Electoral Determinants and Consequences of National Solidarity' in (eds) W. Cornelius *et al.*, *Transforming State–Society Relations in Mexico: the National Solidarity Strategy*, Center for US–Mexican Studies, University of California, San Diego, 1994.

Huntington, S. P., *The Third Wave: Democratization in the Late Twentieth Century*, University of Oklahoma Press, 1991.

Ibarra Yunez, A. *et al.*, *Telecomunicaciones en México ante el reto de la integración*, ITESM, Mexico, 1994.

Jackson, M. P., *An Introduction to Industrial Relations*, Routledge, London & New York (1992). First published 1991.

Infante, R. and Klein, E., 'The Latin American Labor Market 1950–1990' in (ed.) J. Dietz, *Latin America's Economic Development: Confronting Crisis*, Lynne Rienner, Boulder & London, 1995. Second Edition.

Jones, G., 'Dismantling the Ejido: a Lesson in Controlled Pluralism' in (eds) R. Aitken *et al.*, *Dismantling the Mexican State?*, Macmillan Press, London, 1996.

Kahn-Hut, R. *et al.*, (eds), *Women and Work*, Oxford University Press, New York & Oxford, 1982.

Kaufman, R., 'Corporatism, Clientelism, and Partisan Conflict: a Study of Seven Latin American Countries' in (ed.) J. Malloy, *Authoritarianism and Corporatism in Latin America*, University of Pittsburgh Press, London, 1977.

Kaufman, R., Bazdresch, C. and Heredia, B., 'Mexico: Radical Reform in a Dominant Party System' in (eds) S. Haggard and S. Webb, *Voting for Reform*, World Bank/Oxford University Press, Washington DC, 1994.

Killick, T., 'Relevance, Meaning and Determinants of Flexibility' in (ed.) T. Killick, *The Flexible Economy: Causes and Consequences of the Adaptability of National Economies*, Routledge, London & New York, 1995.

Killick, T. (ed.) *The Flexible Economy: Causes and Consequences of the Adaptability of National Economies*, Routledge, London & New York, 1995.

Kiloh, M., 'Industrial Democracy' in (eds) D. Held and C. Pollitt, *New Forms of Democracy*, Sage Publications and Open University, London, 1986.

Knight, A., *The Mexican Revolution: Vol. 2. Counter-Revolution and Reconstruction*, Cambridge University Press, Cambridge, 1986.

Knight, A., 'Revolutionary Project, Recalcitrant People: Mexico 1910–1940' in J. E. Rodríguez O., *The Revolutionary Process in Mexico: Essays on Political and Social Change 1880–1940*, University of California, Los Angeles, 1990.

Knight, A., 'Historical Continuities in Social Movements' in (eds) J. Foweraker and A. Craig, *Popular Movements and Political Change in Mexico*, Lynne Rienner, Boulder & London, 1990.

Knight, A., 'Mexico's Elite Settlement: Conjuncture and Consequences' in (eds) J. Higley and R. Gunther, *Elites and Democratic Consolidation in Latin America and South Europe*, Cambridge University Press, Cambridge (1995). First published 1992.

Knight, A., 'El Abrigo de Arturo Alessandri: Populismo, Estado y Sociedad en América Latina, Siglo XX' in (ed.) El Colegio de México, *Transformaciones Sociales y Acciones Colectivas: América Latin en el contexto internacional de los noventa*, El Colegio de México, Mexico, 1994.

Knight, A., 'Solidarity: Historical Continuities and Contemporary Implications' in (eds) W. Cornelius *et al.*, *Transforming State–Society Relations in Mexico: the National Solidarity Strategy*, Center for US–Mexican Studies, University of California, San Diego, 1994.

Knight, A., 'Salinas and Social Liberalism in Historical Context' in (eds) R. Aitken *et al.*, *Dismantling the Mexican State?*, Macmillan Press, London, 1996.

Knight, A., 'Corruption in Twentieth Century Mexico' in (eds) W. Little and E. Posada-Carbó, *Political Corruption in Europe and Latin America*, ILAS, London, 1996.

Kofas, J. V., *The Struggle for Legitimacy: Latin American Labor and the United States 1930–1960*, Tempe, Center for Latin American Studies, Arizona State University, Arizona, 1992.

Kohler, D. and Wannoftel, M. (eds), *Modelo Neoliberal y Sindicatos en America Latina*, Fundación Friedrich Ebert, Mexico, 1993.

Krugman, P. and Obstfeld, M., *International Economics: Theory and Policy*, HarperCollins, New York, 1994.

La Botz, D., *Mask of Democracy: Labor Suppression in Mexico Today*, Black Rose Books, Montreal & New York, 1992.

Lal, D., 'Participation, Markets and Democracy' in (eds) M. Lundahl and B. J. Ndulu, *New Directions in Development Economics*, Routledge, London & New York, 1996.

Lavrin, A., 'Women in Twentieth Century Latin American Society' in (ed.) L. Bethell, *The Cambridge History of Latin America: Vol VI: Latin America since 1930: Politics and Society*, Cambridge University Press, Cambridge, 1994.

Lawrence, E., *Gender and Trade Unions*, Taylor & Francis, London, 1994.

León, S. and Marván, I., *En El Cardenismo (1934–1940)* (Series number 10 of *La Clase Obrera en la Historia de México*), Siglo Veintiuno Editores/UNAM, Mexico, 1985.

Levy, D. and Székely, G., *Mexico: Paradoxes of Stability and Change*, Westview Press, Boulder, Colorado (1987). First published 1982.

Lipset, S. M. *et al.*, *Union Democracy*, Free Press, New York, 1956.

Little, W. and Posada-Carbó, E. (eds), *Political Corruption in Europe and Latin America*, Macmillan/ILAS, London, 1996.

Lundahl, M. and Ndulu, B. J. (eds), *New Directions in Development Economics*, Routledge Studies in Development Economics, London & New York, 1996.

McBeth, B., *Privatisation: a Strategic Report*, Euromoney Books, Coventry, 1996.

McGowan, F., 'The Internationalisation of Privatisation' in (ed.) T. Clarke, *International Privatisation: Strategies and Practices*, Walter de Gruyer, Berlin & New York, 1994.

McLean, I., *Oxford Concise Dictionary of Politics*, Oxford University Press, Oxford & New York, 1996.

Maclean, M. and Genn, H., *Methodological Issues in Social Surveys*, Macmillan Press, London, 1979.

Maddison, A., *Monitoring the World Economy 1820–1992*, OECD, Paris, 1995.

Malloy, J. (ed.), *Authoritarianism and Corporatism in Latin America*, University of Pittsburgh Press, London, 1977.

Martin, M., *'Hello, Central?': Gender, Technology ad Culture in the Formation of Telephone Systems*, McGill Queen's University Press, Montreal, Kingston, London & Buffalo, 1991.

Martínez de Ita, M. *et al.*, *El Proceso de Reestructuración en México*, Universidad Autónoma de Puebla, Puebla, 1993.

Mercado Maldonado, A., *TELMEX-STRM: una Historia Política*, Universidad Autónoma del Estado de México, Mexico, 1994.

Merino Rocha, R., 'La participación del sindicato en la modernización de Teléfonos de México' in (ed.) E. Gutiérrez Garza, *Reconversión industrial y lucha sindical*, Nueva Sociedad, Mexico, 1989.

Michels, R., *Political Parties*, Collier Books, New York, 1962.

Middlebrook, K. (ed.), *Unions, Workers and the State in Mexico*, University of California, San Diego, 1991.

Middlebrook, K., *The Paradox of Revolution: Labor, the State, and Authoritarianism in Mexico*, Johns Hopkins University Press, Baltimore & London, 1995.

Millan, R. *et al.*, *Sindicalismo y Política en México*, Estudios Políticos/UNAM, Mexico, 1986.

Millward, N., *The New Industrial Relations?*, Policy Studies Institute, London, 1994.

Mitter, S. and Rowbotham, S. (eds), *Women Encounter Technology: Changing Patterns of Employment in the Third World*, UNU/INTECH/Routledge, London & New York, 1995.

Morris, S. D., *Corruption and Politics in Mexico*, University of Alabama Press, London, 1991.

Murray, L. W. H., 'Women in Science Occupations: Some Impacts of Technological Change' in (ed.) U. E. Gattiker, *Women and Technology*, Walter de Gruyter, Berlin & New York, 1994.

Needler, M. C. 'Problems in the Evaluation of the Mexican Political System' in (eds) J. W. Meyer *et al.*, *Contemporary Mexico: Papers of the IV International Congress of Mexican History*, University of California Press, University of California, 1976.

Newell, R. and Rubio, L., *Mexico's Dilemma: the Political Origins of Economic Crisis*, Westview Press, Boulder & London, 1984.

Ng Choon Sim, C. and Yong, C., 'Information Technology, Gender and Employment: a Case Study of the Telecommunications Industry in Malaysia' in (eds) S. Mitter and S. Rowbotham, *Women Encounter Technology: Changing Patterns of Employment in the Third World*, UNU/INTECH/Routledge, London & New York, 1995.

Noam, E. and Baur, C. *Telecommunications in Latin America*, Oxford University Press, Oxford, 1998.

North, D. C., 'The New Institutional Economics and Third World Development' in (eds) J. Harriss *et al.*, *The New Institutional Economics and Third World Development*, Routledge, London & New York, 1995.

Norwood, S. H., *Labor's Flaming Youth: Telephone Operators and Worker Militancy 1878–1923*, University of Illinois Press, Urbana & Chicago, 1990.

O'Donnell, G., *Modernization and Bureaucratic Authoritarianism*, Institute of International Studies, University of California, Berkeley, 1973.

O'Donnell, G., 'Corporatism and the Question of the State' in (ed.) J. Malloy, *Authoritarianism and Corporatism in Latin America*, University of Pittsburgh Press, London, 1977.

OECD, *Privatisation in Asia, Europe and Latin America*, OECD, Paris, 1996.

Ott, A. F. and Hartley, K., *Privatization and Economic Efficiency: a Comparative Analysis of Developed and Developing Countries*, Edward Elgar Publishers, Hants, Aldershot, 1991.

Pansters, W., 'Citizens with Dignity: Opposition and Government in San Luis Potosí 1938–1993' in (eds) R. Aitken *et al.*, *Dismantling the Mexican State?*, Macmillan, London, 1996.

Pateman, C., *Participation and Democratic Theory*, Cambridge University Press, Cambridge (1989). First published 1970.

Pérez de Mendoza, A., 'Teléfonos de México: Development and Perspectives' in (eds) P. F. Cowhey *et al.*, *Changing Networks: Mexico's Telecommunications Options*, University of California, San Diego, 1989.

Pérez Escamilla, J. R.,'Telephone Policy in Mexico: Rates and Investment' in (eds) P. Cowhey *et al.*, *Changing Networks: Mexico's Telecommunications Options*, Centre for US–Mexican Studies, University of California, San Diego, 1989.

Petrazzini, B., *The Political Economy of Telecommunications Reform in Developing Countries: Privatization and Liberalization in Comparative Perspective*, Praeger Publishers, Westport, CT, 1995.

Poole, M., *Towards a New Industrial Democracy: Workers' Participation in Industry*, Routledge and Kegan Paul, London & New York, 1986.

Powell, K., 'Neoliberalism and Nationalism' in (eds) R. Aitken *et al.*, *Dismantling the Mexican State?*, Macmillan, London, 1996.

Radcliffe, S. A. and Westwood, S. (eds), *'VIVA' Women and Popular Protest in Latin America*, Routledge, London & New York, 1993.

Ramamurti, R. (ed.), *Privatizing Monopolies: Lessons from the Telecommunications and Transport Sectors in Latin America*, The Johns Hopkins University Press, Baltimore & London, 1996.

Ramanadham, V., *Privatisation in the UK Experience and Developing Countries*, Routledge, London, 1989.

Ramírez, M. D., 'The Social and Economic Consequences of the National Austerity Program in Mexico' in (eds) H. Handleman and W. Baer, *Paying the Costs of Austerity in Latin America*, Westview Press, London, 1989.

Rangel Pérez, M., *Los Telefonistas Frente a la Crisis y la Reconversión*, Editorial Nuestro Tiempo, Mexico, 1989.

Revista Punto Crítico, *Problemas y Perspectivas del Movimiento Obrero 1970–1980*, Revista Punto Crítico, Mexico, 1983.

Reyna, J. L. and Trejo Delarbe, R., *De Adolfo Ruíz Cortines a Adolfo López Mateos (1952–1964)* (Series number 12 of *La Clase Obrera en la Historia de México*), Siglo Veintiuno Editores, Mexico (1988). First published 1981.

Roberts, B. (ed.), *New Forces in the World Economy*, The MIT Press, Cambridge, Massachusetts & London, 1996.

Rodríguez O., J. E., *The Revolutionary Process in Mexico: Essays on Political and Social Change 1880–1940*, University of California, Los Angeles, 1990.

Rodríguez O., J. E., *The Evolution of the Mexican Political System*, Scholarly Resources Books, Wilmington, Delaware, 1993.

Roett, R. (ed.), *Political and Economic Liberalization in Mexico: at a Critical Juncture?*, Lynne Rienner, Boulder & London, 1993.

Roett, R. (ed.), *The Challenge of Institutional Reform in Mexico*, Lynne Rienner, Boulder, Colorado, 1995.

Rogozinski, J., *La Privatización de Empresas Paraestatales*, Fondo de Cultura Económica, Mexico, 1993.

Rogozinski, J., *La Privatización en México: Razones e impactos*, Trillas, Mexico, 1997.

Ros, J., 'On the Political Economy of Market and State Reform in Mexico' in (eds) W. C. Smith, C. H. Acuña and E. A. Gamarra, *Democracy, Markets and Structural Reform in Latin America*, Transaction Publishers, New Brunswick, London and USA, 1993.

Roth, G., *The Private Provision of Public Services in Developing Countries*, World Bank/Oxford University Press (1988). First published 1987.

Roxborough, I., *Unions and Politics in Mexico*, Cambridge University Press, Cambridge, 1984.

Roxborough, I., 'Organized Labor: a Major Victim of the Debt Crisis' in (eds) B. Stallings and R. Kaufman, *Debt and Democracy in Latin America*, Westview Press, London, 1989.

Roxborough, I., 'Mexico' in (eds) L. Bethell and I. Roxborough, *Latin America between the Second World War and the Cold War 1944–1948*, Cambridge University Press, Cambridge, 1992.

Rubio, L., 'Economic Reform and Political Change in Mexico' in (ed.) R. Roett, *Political and Economic Liberalization in Mexico: at a Critical Juncture?*, Lynne Rienner, Boulder & London, 1993.

Roxborough, I., 'Labor Control and the Postwar Growth Model in Latin America' in (ed.) D. Rock, *Latin America in the 1940s War and Postwar Transitions*, University of California Press, Berkeley, Los Angeles & London, 1994.

Rueda Peiro, I. (ed.), *Tras las Huellas de la Privatización: El Caso de Altos Hornos de México*, Siglo Veintiuno Editores, Mexico, 1994.

Ruiz, R. E., *Labor and the Ambivalent Revolutionaries: Mexico 1911–1923*, The Johns Hopkins University Press, Baltimore, 1976.

Ruprah, I., *The Divestiture of TELMEX*, ECLAC, United Nations, Santiago de Chile, Chile, 1994a.

Ruprah, I., *Divestiture and Deregulation of Public Enterprises: the Mexican Case*, ECLAC, United Nations, Santiago de Chile, 1994b.

Ruprah, I. *The Privatization of Mexicana (CMA)*, ECLAC, United Nations, Santiago de Chile, 1995.

Russell, P., *Mexico under Salinas*, Mexican Resource Center, Austin, Texas, 1994.

Sánchez, M, and Corona, R., *Privatization in Latin America*, Centre for Research in Applied Economics, ITAM/IADB, Washington DC, 1993.

Sandoval, J., 'El sistema digital en Teléfonos de México' in (ed.) E. Gutiérrez Garza, *Reconversión industrial y lucha sindical*, Nueva Sociedad, Mexico, 1989.

Saunders, R. J. *et al.*, *Telecommunications and Economic Development*, World Bank Publications, Washington, 1994. Second Edition.

Scott, R., *Mexican Government in Transition*, University of Illinois Press, Urbana, 1959.

Serrano Vallejo, P., 'Participación Femenina en Teléfonos de México' in (eds) J. Cooper and T. de Barbieri, *Fuerza de Trabajo: Femenina Urbana en México: Participación Economica y Politica*, Vol. 2. UNAM, Mexico, 1989.

Sheanan, J., *Conflict and Change in Mexican Economic Strategy: Implications for Mexico and for Latin America*, Center for US–Mexican Studies, University of California, San Diego, Monograph Series 34, 1991.

Siller Rodríguez, R., *La Crisis del PRI*, Instituto Mexicano de Cultura, Mexico, 1976.

Smith, P. H., *Mexico: Neighbour in Transition*, Foreign Policy Association, No. 267, New York, 1984.

Smith, P. H., 'Mexico Since 1946: Dynamics of an Authoritarian Regime' in (ed.) L. Bethell, *Mexico since Independence*, Cambridge University Press, Cambridge, 1991.

Smith, W. C. *et al.* (eds), *Democracy, Markets and Structural Reform in Latin America*, Transaction Publishers, New Brunswick & London, 1993.

Southall, R. (ed.), *Trade Unions and the New Industrialisation of the Third World*, University of Ottawa Press and Zed Books, London, 1988.

Spero, J. E., *The Politics of International Economic Relations*, Routledge, London (1996). First published 1977.

Stallings, B. (ed.), *Global Change, Regional Response: the New International Context of Development*, Cambridge University Press, Cambridge, 1995.

Stansfield, D., 'The PAN: the Search for Ideological and Electoral Space' in (eds) R. Aitken *et al.*, *Dismantling the Mexican State?*, Macmillan, London, 1996.

Stevens, E., 'Mexico's PRI: the Institutionalization of Corporatism?' in (ed.) J. Malloy, *Authoritarianism and Corporatism in Latin America*, University of Pittsburgh Press, London, 1977.

Stevens, E., *Protest and Response*, MIT Press, Cambridge, Massachusetts, 1974.

Story, Dale, *The Mexican Ruling Party*, Praeger, New York/Westport/Connecticut/London, 1986.

Strange, S., *States and Markets: an Introduction to International Political Economy*, Pinter Publishers, London, 1988.

Székely, G., 'Developing a New Economic Strategy' in (eds) Cowhey *et al.*, *Changing Networks: Mexico's Telecommunications Options*, University of California, San Diego, 1989.

Székely, G. and del Palacio, J., *Teléfonos de México: una Empresa Privada*, Planeta, Mexico, 1995.

Tandon, P., *Welfare Consequences of Selling Public Enterprises. Mexico. Volume One. Background, TELMEX*, Paper presented at the World Bank Conference 11–12 June 1992.

Tandon, P., 'Mexico' in (eds) A. Galal and M. Shirley, *Does Privatization Deliver?*, IBRD/The World Bank, Washington DC, 1994.

Teichman, J., *Policymaking in Mexico: from Boom to Crisis*, Allen and Unwin, Boston, 1988.

Teichman, J., *Privatization and Political Change in Mexico*, University of Pittsburgh Press, Pittsburgh & London, 1995.

Toye, J., 'Is there a New Political Economy of Development?' in (eds) C. Colclough and J. Manor, *States or Markets?: Neo-liberalism and the Development Policy Debate*, IDS Development Studies Series, Clarendon Paperbacks, Oxford (1995). First published 1993.

Trejo Delarbre, R., 'Telefonistas: La difícil democracia' in (eds) R. Millan *et al.*, *Sindicalismo y Política en México*, UNAM, Mexico, 1986.

Trejo Delarbre, R., *Crónica del Sindicalismo en México*, Siglo Veintiuno Editores, Mexico, 1990.

Treu, T. (ed.), *Participation in Public Policy-Making: the Role of Trade Unions and Employers' Associations*, Walter de Gruyter, Berlin & New York, 1992.

Tucker, W. P., *The Mexican Government Today*, University of Minnesota, Minneapolis, 1957.

Ugalde, A., *Power and Conflict in a Mexican Community*, University of New Mexico Press, Albuquerque, 1970.

Vanhanen, T., *Prospects of Democracy: a Study of 172 Countries*, Routledge, London & New York, 1997.

Varas, A., 'Latin America: toward a New Reliance on the Market' in (ed.) B. Stallings, *Global Change, Regional Response in the New International Context of Development*, Cambridge University Press, Cambridge, 1995.

Varley, A., 'Delivering the Goods: Solidarity, Land Regularisation and Urban Services' in (eds) R. Aitken *et al.*, *Dismantling the Mexican State?*, Macmillan Press, London, 1996.

Vera Ferrer, O. H., 'The Political Economy of Privatization in Mexico' in (ed.) W. Glade, *Privatization of Public Enterprises in Latin America*, International Center for Economic Growth, San Francisco, California, 1991.

Vernon, R. (ed.), *La Promesa de la Privatización: un desafío para la política exterior de los Estados Unidos*, Fondo de Cultura Económica, Mexico (1995). First published 1988.

Vickers, J. and Yarrow, G., *Privatization: an Economic Analysis*, MIT Press, Cambridge, 1988.

Weintraub, S., *A Marriage of Convenience: Relations Between Mexico and the US*, Twentieth Century Fund Report/Oxford University Press, New York & Oxford, 1990.

Weiss, J., 'Mexico: Comparative Performance of State and Private Industrial Corporations' in (eds) P. Cook and C. Kirkpatrick, *Privatisation Policy and Performance: International Perspectives*, Prentice-Hall/Harvester Wheatsheaf, Hertfordshire, 1995.

Weiss, J., 'Economic Policy Reform in Mexico: the Liberalisation Experiment' in (eds) R. Aitken *et al.*, *Dismantling the Mexican State?*, Macmillan Press, London, 1996.

Whitehead, L., 'On Presidential Graft: the Latin American Evidence' in (eds) A. Heidenheiner *et al.*, *Political Corruption: a Handbook*, Transaction Publishers, New Brunswick and Oxford, 1989.

Whitehead, L., 'State Organisation in Latin America since 1930' in (ed.) L. Bethell, *Cambridge History of Latin America, Politics and Society*, Vol. VI, Part 2, Cambridge University Press, 1994.

Williamson, J. W., *Latin American Adjustment: How Much Has Happened?*, Institute for International Economics, Washington DC, 1990.

Wonnacott, T. H. and Wonnacott, R. J., *Introductory Statistics*, John Wiley, Canada, Parts 1.1, 11.6. Fifth Edition (1990). First published 1969.

World Bank, *World Development Report: Workers in an Integrated World*, Oxford University Press, New York, 1995.

Wyman, D. L. (ed.), *Mexico's Economic Crisis: Challenges and Opportunities*, University of California, 1983.

Xelhuantzi López, M., *Sindicato de Telefonistas de la República Mexicana: Doce Años (1976–1988)*, STRM, Mexico, 1988.

Zapata, F., *El Conflicto Sindical en América Latina*, El Colegio de México, Mexico, 1986.

Zapata, F., 'Labour and Politics: the Mexican Paradox' in (ed.) E. C. Epstein, *Labour Autonomy and the State in Latin America*, Unwin Hyman, Boston, 1989.

Zapata, F., 'Social Concertation in Mexico' in (ed.) T. Treu, *Participation in Public Policy-Making: the Role of Trade Unions and Employers' Associations*, Walter de Gruyter, Berlin & New York, 1992.

Zapata, F., *Autonomía y subordinación en el sindicalismo latinoamericano*, Fondo de Cultura Económica, Mexico, 1993.

Zapata, F. *et al.*, *La Restructuración Industrial en México: El Caso de la Industria de Autopartes*, Cuadernos del Centro de Estudios Sociologicos, El Colegio de México, Mexico, 1994.

Zapata, F., *El Sindicalismo Mexicano Frente a la Restructuración*, El Colegio de México, Mexico, 1995.

Zazueta, C. and de la Peña, R., *La Estructura del Congreso del Trabajo*, Fondo de Cultura Económica, Mexico, 1984.

2. Articles

Ades, A. and Di Tella, R., 'The Causes and Consequences of Corruption: a Review of Recent Empirical Contributions' in (eds) B. Harriss-White and G. White, *Liberalization and the New Corruption*, International Development Studies Bulletin, Sussex, Vol. 27, No. 2, 1996, pp. 6–11.

Aguilar García, J., 'Relaciones Estado–Sindicatos 1982–1990', *El Cotidiano*, No. 38, November–December 1990, pp. 67–70.

Aguilar García, J., 'El Sindicalismo mexicano ante las tendencias políticas actuales', *Trabajo y Democracia Hoy*, No. 1, 1991, pp. 32–5.

Alberto, A., 'La Federalización de la educación básica y normal (1978–1994)', *Política y Gobierno*, Vol. 1, No. 2, Second semester 1994, pp. 237–74.

Alvarez Béjar, A., 'Los sindicatos en México ante la globalización', *Revista Mexicana de Sociología*, No. 1, 1994, pp. 89–103.

Alzaga, O., 'La rivalidad sindical del sexenio: CTM v FESEBS', *Trabajo y Democracia Hoy*, No. 17, January–February 1994, pp. 62–6.

Aparicio, J., 'De la reconversión a la modernización en las relaciones laborales, 1986–1991', *El Cotidiano*, No. 46, March–April 1992, pp. 34–43.

Arroyo, A., 'Mitos o realidades: el salario real 1989–1992', *Trabajo y Democracia Hoy*, No. 11, 1993, pp. 10–13.

Ashby, J., 'The Dilemma of the Mexican Trade Union Movement', *Mexican Studies*, Vol. 1, No. 2, Summer 1985, pp. 277–301.

Baer, W. and Conroy, M. (eds), 'Latin America: Privatization, Property Rights, and Deregulation I and II', *The Quarterly Review of Economics and Finance*, Vols 33 and 34, Special Issues, 1994.

Bazdresch, C. and Elizondo, C.,'Privatization: the Mexican Case' in (eds) W. Baer and M. Conroy, *The Quarterly Review of Economics and Finance*, Vol. 33, Special Issue 1993, pp. 45–66.

Bensusan, G., 'Los sindicatos mexicanos y la legalidad laboral', *Revista Mexicana de Sociología*, No. 1, 1994, pp. 45–79.

Berins Collier, R. and Collier, D., 'Inducements versus Constraints: Disaggregating Corporatism', *American Political Science Review*, Vol. 73, No. 2, 1979, pp. 967–86.

Berntzen, E., 'Democratic Consolidation in Central America: a Qualitative Comparative Approach', *Third World Quarterly*, Vol. 14, No. 3, 1993, pp. 589–604.

Bizberg, I. and Roxborough, I., 'Union Locals in Mexico: the New 'Unionism' in Steel and Automobiles', *Journal of Latin American Studies*, Vol. 15, No. 1, 1983, pp. 117–35.

Bizberg, I., 'Política Laboral y Acción Sindical en México (1976–1982)', *Foro Internacional*, October–December 1984, pp. 166–89.

Borrego, J. and Mody, B., 'The Morelos Satellite System in Mexico', *Telecommunications Policy*, September 1989, pp. 265–89.

Bresser Pereira, L. C., 'Economic Reforms and Cycles of State Intervention', *World Development*, Vol. 21, No. 8, 1993, pp. 1337–54.

Calderón, F., 'The Trade Union System: its Background and Future Prospects', *Cepal Review*, 49, April 1993, pp. 103–15.

Camp, R. A., 'Camarillas in Mexican Politics: the Case of the Salinas Cabinet', *Mexican Studies*, Vol. 6, No. 1, Winter 1990, pp. 85–107.

Campos Ríos, G. and Sánchez Daza, G., 'Modernización: negociación y respuesta obrera en TELMEX y Ferronales', *Brecha*, No. 4, Summer 1987, pp. 13–28.

Campuzano Montoya, I., 'El impacto de la crisis en la CTM', *Revista Mexicana de Sociología*, Vol. 52, No. 3, 1990, pp. 161–90.

Cárdenas, M. and Juárez, C., 'Labor Issues in Colombia's Privatization: a Comparative Perspective' in (eds) W. Baer and M. Conroy, 'Latin America: Privatization, Property Rights, and Deregulation II', *The Quarterly Review of Economics and Finance*, Vol. 34, Special Issue, 1994, pp. 237–59.

Cardoso, E. and Fishlow, A., 'Latin American Economic Development: 1950–1980', *Journal of Latin American Studies Supplement*, Vol. 24 Quincentenary, 1992, pp. 197–218.

Carrillo, F., 'Autonomía y democracia sindical', *Trabajo y Democracia Hoy*, No. 19, 1994, pp. 13–15.

Castañeda, J. G., 'The Clouding Political Horizon', *Current History*, Vol. 92, No. 571, February 1993, pp. 59–66.

Castelar Pinherio, A. and Schneider, B., 'The Fiscal Impact of Privatization in Latin America' in (eds) W. Baer and M. Conroy, 'Latin America: Privatization, Property Rights, and Deregulation II', *The Quarterly Review of Economics and Finance*, Vol. 34, Special Issue, 1994, pp. 9–42.

Centeno, M. A. and Maxfield, S., 'The Marriage of Finance and Order: Changes in the Mexican Political Elite', *Journal of Latin American Studies*, Vol. 24, Part 1, 1992, pp. 57–85.

Chabat, J., 'Mexico: So Close to the United States, So Far from Latin America', *Current History*, Vol. 92, No. 571, February 1993, pp. 55–8.

Córdova, A., 'Modernización y democracia', *Revista Mexicana de Sociología*, No. 1, 1991, pp. 261–81.

Corro, S. and Correa, G., 'Los gritos de la protesta rompen la paz de la modernización', *Proceso*, 20 November 1989, pp. 6–9.

Corro, S. and Correa, G., 'La CTM, la CNC y la CNOP de debilitan, mientras crece el sector empresarial del PRI', *Proceso*, 18 August 1989, pp. 6–9.

Couffignal, G., 'La gran debilidad del sindicalismo mexicano', *Revista Mexicana de Sociología*, Vol. 52, No. 3, 1990, pp. 191–210.

Cruz Bencomo, M. A., 'El quinismo, una historia del charrismo petrolero', *El Cotidiano*, No. 28, March–April 1989, pp. 23–9.

Davies, C. L. and Coleman, K. M., 'Structural Determinants of Working-Class Politicization: the Role of Independent Unions in Mexico', *Mexican Studies*, Vol. 5, No. 1, Winter 1989, pp. 89–112.

Davies, D., 'Failed Democratic Reform in Contemporary Mexico: from Social Movements to the State and Back Again', *Journal of Latin American Studies*, Vol. 26, May 1994, pp. 375–408.

De Buen, N., 'El convenio de modernización en Teléfonos de México', *El Cotidiano*, 30, July–August 1989, pp. 59–61.

De la Garza Toledo, E., 'Requisa en TELMEX', *El Cotidiano*, 1984, pp. 9–19.

De la Garza Toledo, E., 'Estilos de investigación sobre la clase obrera', *Revista Mexicana de Sociología*, Vol. 50, No. 4, 1988, pp. 3–29.

De la Garza Toledo, E., 'Paraestatales y corporativismo', *El Cotidiano*, 28, March–April 1989a, pp. 3–12.

De la Garza Toledo, E., 'Quién ganó en TELMEX?', *El Cotidiano*, 32, November–December 1989b, pp. 49–56.

De la Garza Toledo, E. and Melgoza Valdivia, J., 'Telefonistas y Electricistas', *El Cotidiano*, 41, May–June 1991, pp. 14–20.

De la Garza Toledo, E., 'El Tratado de Libre Comercio y sus consecuencias en la contratación colectiva', No. 45, January–February 1992, pp. 3–12.

De la Garza Toledo, E., 'Reestructuración del corporativismo en México: siete tesis', *El Cotidiano*, No. 56, July 1993, pp. 47–53.

De la Garza Toledo, E., 'Sindicato y restructuración productiva en México', *Revista Mexicana de Sociología*, No. 1, 1994, pp. 3–43.

De la Garza Toledo, E., 'Los Sindicatos en America Latina frente a la reestructuración productiva y los ajustes neoliberales', *Trabajo y Democracia Hoy*, No. 23, January 1995, pp. 46–54.

Durand Ponte, V. M., 'Notas sobre el estado, la sociedad civil y los sindicatos', *Revista Mexicana de Sociología*, Vol. 43, No. 3, 1981, pp. 989–1023.

Durand Ponte, V. M., 'Corporativismo Obrero y Democracia', *Revista Mexicana de Sociología*, Vol. 52, No. 3, 1990, pp. 97–110.

Edwards, J. and Baer, W., 'The State and the Private Sector in Latin America: Reflections on the Past, the Present and the Future' in (eds) W. Baer and M. Conroy, 'Latin America: Privatization, Property Rights, and Deregulation I', *Quarterly Review of Economics and Finance*, Special Issue 33, 1993, pp. 9–19.

Elizondo, C., 'In Search of Revenue: Tax Reform in Mexico under the Administrations of Echeverría and Salinas', *Journal of Latin American Studies*, 1994, pp. 159–90.

Esther Ibarra, M., 'Alejo Peralta se defiende: No tengo la culpa de que TELMEX esté tan atrasado', *Proceso*, 20 November 1989, pp. 24–7.

Figueroa Saucedo, A., 'La experiencia a un año de la reprivatización de Teléfonos de México', *Trabajo y Democracia Hoy*, No. 8, July–August 1992, pp. 23–5.

Figueroa Saucedo, A. and Solís, V. 'Los dilemas de los telefonistas en el escenario de la productividad y la calidad', *Trabajo y Democracia Hoy*, No. 11, 1993, pp. 25–7.

Fishlow, A., 'The Latin American State', *Journal of Economic Perspectives*, Vol. 4, No. 3, Summer 1990, pp. 61–74.

Garavito, R. A., 'Los conflictos obrero – patronales (mayo–junio de 1985)', *El Cotidiano*, No. 6, May–June 1985, pp. 39–41.

Garavito, R. A., 'La CTM hoy', *El Cotidiano*, No. 10, 1986, pp. 3–9.

Gilly, A. 'La fundación de la CTM', *El Cotidiano*, No. 10, 1986, pp. 15–25.

Glade, W., 'Privatization in Rent-Seeking Societies', *World Development*, Vol. 1, No. 5, 1989, pp. 673–82.

González Lanuza, L, 'The Argentine Telephone Privatization', *Telecommunications Policy*, December 1992, pp. 759–63.

Gourevitch, P. A., 'Democracy and Economic Policy: Elective Affinities and Circumstantial Conjunctures', *World Development*, Vol. 21, No. 8, 1993, pp. 1271–80.

Hamilton, N. and Mee Kim, E., 'Economic and Political Liberalisation in South Korea and Mexico', *Third World Quarterly*, Vol. 14, No. 1, 1993, pp. 109–36.

Handleman, H., 'Oligarchy and Democracy in Two Mexican Labor Unions: a Test of Representation Theory', *Industrial and Labor Relations Review*, Vol. 30, No. 2, January 1977, pp. 205–18.

Hanson, G. 'Anti-Trust in Post-Privatization in Latin America' in (eds) W. Baer and M. Conroy, *The Quarterly Review of Economics and Finance*, Vol. 33, Special Issue, 1993, pp. 199–216.

Harriss-White, B., 'Liberalization and Corruption: Resolving the Paradox (A Discussion based on South Indian Material)' in (eds) B. Harriss-White and G. White, *Liberalization and the New Corruption*, International Development Studies Bulletin, Sussex, Vol. 27, No. 2, 1996, pp. 31–9.

Harriss-White, B. and White, G. (eds), *Liberalization and the New Corruption*, International Development Studies Bulletin, Sussex, Vol. 27, No. 2, 1996.

Harriss-White, B. and White, G., 'Corruption, Liberalization and Democracy' in (eds) B. Harriss-White and G. White, *Liberalization and the New Corruption*, International Development Studies Bulletin, Sussex, Vol. 27, No. 2, 1996, pp. 1–5.

Hawthorn, G., 'Liberalization and "Modern Liberty": Four Southern States', *World Development*, Vol. 21, No. 8, 1993, pp. 1299–313.

Hernández Juárez, F., 'El nuevo sindicalismo', *Nexos*, May 1991, pp. 43–9.

Hernández Rodríguez, R., 'La Difícil Transición Política en México', *Mexican Studies*, Summer 1992, Vol. 8, No. 2, pp. 237–57.

Hernández Rodríguez, R., 'Inestabilidad política y presidencialismo en México', *Mexican Studies*, Winter 1994, Vol. 10, No. 1, pp. 187–216.

Hills, J., 'The Telecommunications Rich and Poor', *Third World Quarterly*, Vol. 12, No. 2, April 1990, pp. 71–90.

ILO, *Social and Labour Bulletin*, March 1992, pp. 294–5.

Jones, C., 'The Argentine Debate' in (eds) B. Harriss-White and G. White, *Liberalization and the New Corruption*, International Development Studies Bulletin, Sussex, Vol. 27, No. 2, 1996, pp. 71–7.

Khan, M. H., 'A Typology of Corrupt Transactions in Developing Countries' in (eds) B. Harriss-White and G. White, *Liberalization and the New Corruption*, International Development Studies Bulletin, Sussex, Vol. 27, No. 2, 1996, pp. 12–21.

Kikeri, S. *et al.* (eds), 'Privatization: Lessons from Market Economies', *The World Bank Research Observer*, Vol. 9, No. 2, July 1994, pp. 241–72.

Knight, A., 'The Working Class and the Mexican Revolution, *c*. 1900–1920', *Journal of Latin American Studies*, No. 16, May 1984, pp. 51–79.

Knight, A., 'Cardenismo: Juggernaut or Jalopy', *Journal of Latin American Studies*, Vol. 26, No. 1, February 1994, pp. 73–107.

Knight, A., 'México bronco, México manso: una reflexión sobre la cultura cívica mexicana', *Política y Gobierno*, Vol. III, No. 1, 1996a, pp. 5–30.

Knight, A., 'Latin America: Political Economy and Geopolitics since 1945', *Oxford Development Studies*, Vol. 24, No. 2, 1996b, pp. 145–68.

Kok, B., 'Privatization in Telecommunications – Empty Slogan or Strategic Tool?', *Telecommunications Policy*, December 1992, pp. 699–704.

Krueger, A. O., 'The Political Economy of the Rent-Seeking Society', *The American Economic Review*, Vol. 64, No. 3, June 1974, pp. 291–303.

Krueger, L, 'Telecommunications Issues concerning the Texas–Mexico Border', *Telecommunications Policy*, August 1992, pp. 504–10.

Labastida, J., 'México: transición democrática y reforma económica', *Revista Mexicana de Sociología*, No. 2, 1991, pp. 127–39.

Laurell, A. C., 'The Role of Union Democracy in the Struggle for Workers' Health in Mexico', *International Journal of Health Services*, Vol. 19, No. 2, 1989, pp. 279–98.

Leal, J. F. and Woldenburg, J., 'El Sindicalismo Mexicano, aspectos organizativos', *Cuadernos Políticos*, No. 7, 1976, pp. 35–53.

León, S., 'Réquiem por el sindicalismo', *Revista Mexicana de Sociología*, No. 3, 1991, pp. 171–83.

Lindau, J. D., 'Schisms in the Mexican Political Elite and the Technocrat/ Politician Typology', *Mexican Studies*, Summer 1992, pp. 217–35.

Lipset, S. M., 'Some Social Requisites of Democracy: Economic Development and Political Legitimacy', *American Political Science Review*, Vol. 53, 1959, pp. 69–105.

Little, W., 'Corruption and Democracy in Latin America' in (eds) B. Harriss-White and G. White, *Liberalization and the New Corruption*, International Development Studies Bulletin, Sussex, Vol. 27, No. 2, 1996, pp. 64–70.

Lorena Cook, M., 'Mexican State–Labor Relations and the Political Implications of Free Trade', *Latin American Perspectives*, Issue 84, Vol. 22, No. 1, Winter 1995, pp. 77–94.

Lovera, S. and Vásquez, P., 'La Modernización Avanza...y los trabajadores?', *El Cotidiano*, No. 11, 1986, pp. 60–5.

Lutz, E., 'Human Rights in Mexico: Cause for Continuing Concern', *Current History*, February 1993. pp. 78–82.

McComb, R. *et al.*, 'Privatization and Performance in the Mexican Financial Services Industry' in (eds) W. Baer and M. Conroy, 'Latin America: Privatization, Property Rights, and Deregulation II', *The Quarterly Review of Economics and Finance*, Vol. 34, Special Issue, 1994, pp. 217–35.

Manzetti, L., 'The Politics of Privatization and Deregulation in Latin America' in (eds) W. Baer and M. Conroy, 'Latin America: Privatization, Property Rights, and Deregulation II', *Quarterly Review of Economics and Finance*, Special Issue 33, 1993, pp. 43–76.

Manzetti, L. and Blake, C. H., 'Market Reforms and Corruption in Latin America: New Means for Old Ways', *Review of International Political Economy*, Vol. 3, No. 4, Winter 1996, pp. 662–97.

Meller, P., 'A Review of the Chilean Privatization Experience' in (eds) W. Baer and M. Conroy, 'Latin America: Privatization, Property Rights, and Deregulation I', *The Quarterly Review of Economics and Finance*, Vol. 33, Special Issue, 1994, pp. 95–112.

Méndez, L., 'Los Conflictos obrero-patronales', *El Cotidiano*, No. 4, January–February 1985, pp. 36–9.

Méndez, L., 'Los Conflictos obrero-patronales', *El Cotidiano*, No. 5, March–April 1985, pp. 37–9.

Méndez, L., 'Conflictos obrero-patronales: enero-febrero de 1986', *El Cotidiano*, No. 10, 1986, pp. 57–60.

Méndez, L., 'En busca de un pasado que no volverá: lucha obrera en el 87', *El Cotidiano*, No. 22, March–April 1988, pp. 80–5.

Méndez, L. and Othón Quiroz, J., 'El FAT: autogestión obrero y modernidad', *El Cotidiano*, No. 40, March–April 1991, pp. 37–43.

Méndez, L. and Othón Quiroz, J., 'Respuesta obrera: los sindicatos frente a la reestructuración productiva (1983–1992)', *El Cotidiano* No. 50, September–October 1992, pp. 94–105.

Méndez, L. and Othón Quiroz, J., 'Productividad, respuesta obrera y sucesión presidencial', *El Cotidiano*, No. 58, October–November 1993, pp. 71–8.

Merquior, J. G., 'Democracy and Economic Policy: Elective Affinities and Circumstantial Conjunctures', *World Development*, Vol. 21, No. 12, 1993, pp. 1263–70.

Meyer, L., 'El presidencialismo: Del populismo al neoliberalismo', *Revista Mexicana de Sociología*, No. 2, 1993, pp. 57–81.

Middlebrook, K., 'The Sounds of Silence: Organized Labour's Response to Economic Crisis in Mexico', *Journal of Latin American Studies*, Vol. 21, No. 2, 1989, pp. 195–220.

Middlebrook, K., 'Estructuras del Estado y política de registro sindical en el México posrevolucionario', *Revista Mexicana de Sociología*, No. 4, 1992, pp. 65–92.

Moore, M. and Hamalai, L., 'Economic Liberalization, Political Pluralism and Business Associations in Developing Countries', *World Development*, Vol. 21, No. 12, 1993, pp. 1895–912.

Morici, P., 'Grasping the Benefits of NAFTA', *Current History*, Vol. 92, No. 571, February 1993, pp. 49–54.

Novelo, V., 'Las fuentes de poder de la dirigencia sindical en Pemex', *El Cotidiano*, No. 28, March–April 1989, pp. 13–22.

O'Donnell, G., 'On the State, Democratization and some Conceptual Problems: a Latin American View with Glances at some Postcommunist Countries', *World Development*, Vol. 21, No. 8, 1993, pp. 1355–70.

Ortiz, R. and García, R., 'Los caminos del cambio tecnológico y laboral en TELMEX', *Trabajo y Democracia Hoy*, No. 1, 1991, pp. 22–3.

Othón Quiroz, J. and Méndez, L. 'El conflicto de la Volkswagen: Crónica de una muerte inesperada', *El Cotidiano*, No. 51, November–December 1992, pp. 81–91.

Othón Quiroz, J. and Méndez, L., 'El Sindicalismo mexicano en los noventas: los sectores y las perspectivas', *El Cotidiano*, No. 56, July 1993, pp. 3–7.

Pereyra, C., 'Estado y Movimiento obrera', *Cuadernos Políticos*, No. 28, April–June 1981, pp. 35–42.

Petrecolla, A. *et al.*, 'Privatization in Argentina' in (eds) W. Baer and M. Conroy, 'Latin America: Privatization, Property Rights, and Deregulation I', *The Quarterly Review of Economics and Finance*, Vol. 34, Special Issue, 1994, pp. 67–93.

Philip, G., 'Mexican Politics and the Journals', *Bulletin of Latin American Research*, Vol. 5, No. 1, 1986, pp. 121–32.

Philip, G., 'The New Economic Liberalism and Democracy in Latin America: Friends or Enemies?', *Third World Quarterly*, Vol. 14, No. 3, 1993, pp. 555–71.

Qadir, S., Clapham, C. and Gils, B., 'Sustainable Democracy: Formalism vs Substance', *Third World Quarterly*, Vol. 14, No. 3, 1993, pp. 415–22.

Rodiles, J., 'Juntos, pero no revueltos', *América Economica*, April 1995, p. 52.

Rodríguez, V., 'The Politics of Decentralisation in Mexico: from Municipio Libre to Solidaridad', *Bulletin of Latin American Research*, Vol. 12, No. 2, 1993, pp. 133–45.

Rodríguez, F., 'The Mexican Privatization Programme: an Economic Analysis', *Social and Economic Studies*, Vol. 41, No. 4, 1992, pp. 149–71.

Rodríguez Castañeda, R., 'Cronología de las maniobras con que Salinas llevó a su amigo Slim a la cima mundial de la riqueza', *Proceso*, 18 September 1995, pp. 12–15.

Rojas, A., 'Congreso de Trabajo: Movimiento hacia la unidad', *El Cotidiano*, No. 10, 1986, pp. 33–48.

Romero, M. A. and Robles Berlanga, F., 'La reestructuración de las paraestatales', *El Cotidiano*, No. 14, 1987, pp. 13–15.

Romero, M. A. and Méndez, L., 'SNTE, CNTE y modernización educativa', *El Cotidiano*, No. 28, March–April 1989, pp. 40–1.

Roxborough, I., 'The Analysis of Labour Movements in Latin America: Typologies and Theories', *Bulletin of Latin American Research*, Vol. 1, No. 1, October 1981, pp. 81–95.

Roxborough, I., 'Inflation and Social Pacts in Brazil and Mexico', *Journal of Latin American Studies*, Vol. 24, No. 3, October 1992, pp. 639–64.

Roxborough, I., 'Neo-liberalism in Latin America: Limits and Alternatives', *Third World Quarterly*, Vol. 13, No. 3, 1992, pp. 421–41.

Roxborough, I., 'Las posibilidades de las prácticas sociales bajo el neoliberalismo', *Revista Mexicana de Sociología*, No. 4, 1994, pp. 73–90.

Roxborough, I. and Bizberg, I., 'Union Locals in Mexico: the "New Unionism" in Steel and Automobile Unions', *Journal of Latin American Studies*, Vol. 15, No. 1, 1983, pp. 117–35.

Rubio, R. and Veloquio, F., "La respuesta obrera a la modernización" cronología de 10 años de lucha', *El Cotidiano*, No. 12, 1987, pp. 350–2.

Sánchez Daza, G., 'La lucha sindical en TELMEX: Salarios o condiciones de trabajo?', *El Cotidiano*, No. 7, 1986, pp. 37–41.

Sánchez Daza, G., 'La modernización de las telecomunicaciones y los trabajadores', *Trabajo y Democracia Hoy*, No. 6, April–May 1992, pp. 11–13.

Sánchez Daza, G. et al., 'La digitalización en TELMEX, una transformación global', *El Cotidiano*, No. 21, January–February 1988, pp. 63–70.

Sánchez Daza, G., 'La negociación de la productividad en TELMEX: un recuento', *El Cotidiano*, September–October 1994, pp. 37–42.

Schmitter, P. C., 'Still the Century of Corporatism?', *The Review of Politics*, Vol. 36, No. 1, January 1974, pp. 85–131.

Smith, P. H., 'The Political Impact of Free Trade on Mexico', *Journal of InterAmerican Studies*, Vol. 34, No. 1, Spring 1992, pp. 1–25.

Slim, C., 'Carta de Carlos Slim', *Proceso*, 2 October 1995, pp. 36–7.

Solís, V, 'Propuestas para una alternativa sindical ante la crisis y reestructuración productiva', *Trabajo y Democracia Hoy*, No. 8, 1992, pp. 15–19.

Solís, V., 'La Modernización de Teléfonos de México', *El Cotidiano*, No. 46, March–April 1992, pp. 60–7.

Solís, V., 'Balance de la política de productividad de TELMEX', *Trabajo y Democracia Hoy*, No. 17, January–February, 1994, pp. 55–7.

Streeten, P., 'Markets and States: against Minimalism', *World Development*, Vol. 21, No. 8, 1993, pp. 1281–98.

Talavera, F. and Leal, J. F., 'Organizaciones Sindicales Obreras de México: 1948–1970. Enfoque Estadístico', *Revista Mexicana de Sociología*, Vol. 39, No. 4, October–December 1977, pp. 1251–86.

Teichman, J., 'Mexico: Economic Reform and Political Change', *Latin American Research Review*, Vol. 31, No. 2, 1996, pp. 252–62.

Teichman, J., 'The Mexican State and the Political Implications of Economic Restructuring', *Latin American Perspectives*, Vol. 19, No. 2, Spring 1992, pp. 88–104.

Thompson, M., 'Collective Bargaining in the Mexican Electrical Industry', *British Journal of Industrial Relations*, Vol. VIII, No. 1, March 1970, pp. 55–68.

Thompson, M. and Roxborough, I., 'Union Elections and Democracy in Mexico: a Comparative Perspective', *British Journal of Industrial Relations*, Vol. XX, No. 2, July 1982, pp. 201–17.

Trejo Delarbre, R., 'The Mexican Labor Movement: 1917–1975', *Latin American Perspectives*, Issue 8, Winter 1976, Vol. III, No. 1, pp. 133–53.

Trejo Delarbre, 'Disparidades y Dilemas en el sindicalismo mexicano', *Revista Mexicana de Sociología*, Vol. 47, No. 1, 1985, pp. 139–60.

Valenzuela, J. S., 'Labour Movements in Transitions to Democracy: a Framework for Analysis', *Comparative Politics*, Vol. 21, No. 4, July 1989, pp. 445–72.

Vásquez Rubio, P., 'Los telefonistas: al filo de la navaja', *El Cotidiano*, No. 25, September–October 1988, pp. 64–5.

Vásquez Rubio, P., 'Los telefonistas cruzaron el pantano: concertaron con TELMEX', *El Cotidiano*, No. 31, September–October 1989, pp. 59–60.

Vásquez Rubio, P.,'Habrá final feliz en el conflicto de la Ford?', *El Cotidiano*, No. 34, March–April 1990, pp. 61–4.

Vásquez Rubio, P., 'Conseguimos avanzar, pero esto no garantiza un triunfo: Revisión Contractual 1990 del SME', *El Cotidiano*, No. 35, May–June 1990a, pp. 72–4.

Vásquez Rubio, P., 'El telefonista sostiene su apuesta', *El Cotidiano* No. 35, May–June 1990b, pp. 66–71.

Vásquez Rubio, P., 'Por los caminos de la productividad', *El Cotidiano*, No. 38, November–December 1990c, pp. 10–14.

von Sauer, F. A., 'Measuring Legitimacy in Mexico: an Analysis of Public Opinion during the 1988 Presidential Campaign', *Mexican Studies*, Summer 1992, pp. 259–80.

Waylen, G., 'Women's Movements and Democratisation in Latin America', *Third World Quarterly*, Vol. 14, No. 3, 1993, pp. 573–87.

Weintraub, S., 'The Economy on the Eve of Free Trade', *Current History*, Vol. 92, No. 571, February 1993, pp. 67–72.

272 *Bibliography*

Weintraub, S. and Delal Baer, M., 'The Interplay between Economic and Political Opening: the Sequence in Mexico', *The Washington Quarterly*, Spring 1992, pp. 187–201.

White, G., 'Corruption and Market Reform in China' in (eds) B. Harriss-White and G. White, *Liberalization and the New Corruption*, International Development Studies Bulletin, Sussex, Vol. 27, No. 2, 1996, pp. 40–7.

Whitehead, L., 'On "Governability" in Mexico', *Bulletin of Latin American Research*, Vol. 1, No. 1, 1981, pp. 27–47.

Whitehead, L. (ed.), *World Development*, Vol. 21, No. 8, 1993. Special Issue on Economic Reform and Democratization with papers from conference held in the European Centre for the Study of Democratization, Palazzo Mangelli, Forlí campus, University of Bologna, April 1992.

Whitehead, L., 'Introduction: some Insights from Western Social Theory', *World Development*, Vol. 21, No. 8, 1993a, pp. 1245–62.

Whitehead, L., 'On "Reform of the State" and "Regulation of the Market"', *World Development*, Vol. 21, No. 8, 1993b, pp. 1371–93.

Wiarda, H. J., 'Mexico: the Unravelling of a Corporatist Regime?', *Journal of InterAmerican Studies and World Affairs*, Winter 1988–9, pp. 1–28.

Williamson, J., 'Democracy and the "Washington Consensus"', *World Development*, Vol. 21, No. 8, 1993, pp. 1329–54.

Zamora, G., 'La política laboral del Estado Mexicano: 1982–1988', *Revista Mexicana de Sociología*, Vol. 52, No. 3, 1990, pp. 111–38.

Zapata, F., 'La democracia en el sindicalismo mexicano', *El Cotidiano*, No. 15, January–February 1987, pp. 26–9.

Zapata, F., 'Towards a Latin American Sociology of Labour', *Journal of Latin American Studies*, Vol. 22, Part 1, May 1990, pp. 375–402.

Zapata, F., 'Los dilemas de la modernización', *El Cotidiano*, No. 21, January–February 1988, pp. 20–4.

Zapata, F., 'Crisis del sindicalismo en México', *Revista Mexicana de Sociología*, No. 1, 1994, pp. 79–88.

3. Working/occasional papers

Alberto, A., *La Evolución de los Grupos Hegemónicos en el SNTE*, Documentos de Trabajo 4, Estudios Políticos, CIDE, 1992.

Ambrose, W. et al., *Privatizing Telecommunications Systems*, Discussion Paper No. 10, International Finance Corporation, The World Bank, Washington, 1990.

Amparo Casar, M., 'The 1994 Mexican Presidential Elections', Occasional Papers, University of London, 1995.

Arena, E., 'Privatization and Training: the Mexican Case', Occasional Paper 19, International Labour Organisation, Switzerland, 1994.

Bizberg, I., 'Restructuración productiva y transformación del modelo de relaciones industriales: 1988–1994', Unpublished paper presented at a seminar in El Colegio de México, Mexico, 20 January 1995.

Botelho, A. and Addis, C., *Privatization of Telecommunications in Mexico: its Impact on Labour and Labour Relations*, ILO, Occasional Paper 14, November 1993.

Carr, B., 'Organised Labour and the Mexican Revolution 1915–1928', Occasional Papers, Latin American Centre, University of Oxford, 1972.

CILAS (Centro de Investigación Laboral y Asesoría Sindical), 'Estudio Económico, Financiero, Productivo, Contractual y Salarial de la Empresa Teléfonos de México', Working Document, Mexico, 1992.

Craske, N., 'Corporatism Revisited: Salinas and the Reform of the Popular Sector', Research Paper No. 37, University of London/Institute of Latin American Studies, London, 1994.

De la Garza Toledo, E. *et al.*, *Telecommunications in Mexico*: Notes from the Second Meeting of the International Telecommunications Research Network. Toronto, 15–17 June, 1994.

Dubb, S., 'Trozos de Cristal: Privatization and Union Politics at Teléfonos de México', Paper presented at the 1992 Latin American Studies Association Conference, Los Angeles, California, 24–27 September 1992.

Elizondo, C., 'The Making of a New Alliance: the Privatization of the Banks in Mexico', Documentos de Trabajo 5, Estudios Políticos, Centro de Investigación y Docencia Económicos, Mexico, 1993.

Fishlow, A., 'Some Reflections on Comparative Latin American Economic Performance and Policy', World Institute for Development Economics Research of the United Nations University, Helsinki, Finland, August 1987.

Gadsen, C. H., 'In Mexico: Everything under Control? Political Control over the Labour Force and its Organisations', Paper presented to the XIth World Congress of Sociology, New Delhi, India, 18–23 August 1986.

Haggard, S. and Webb, S., 'What do we know about the Political Economy of Economic Policy Reform?', *The World Bank Research Observer*, Vol. 8, No. 2, July 1993.

Handleman, H., *Organized Labor in Mexico: Oligarchy and Dissent*, American Universities Field Staff Reports No. 18, Hanover, New Hampshire, 1979.

Heller, M., 'From Satellite to Metropole by Satellite: Mexico's Morelos Telecommunications System', Unpublished paper, School of Oriental and African Studies, University of London (undated).

Ortíz, R. and García, R., 'La Modernización en Teléfonos de México', Paper presented at a conference: *Segundo Taller de Telefonistas sobre la privatización de TELMEX y el STRM*, Mexico, November 1991.

Sánchez Daza, G., 'Flexibilidad Laboral y Productividad del Trabajo: El Caso de Teléfonos de México', Working Document, Mexico, 1995.

Sánchez Daza, G., 'TELMEX: Una Breve Sintesis Historica', Unpublished paper, 1991.

Whitehead, L., 'The Peculiarities of "Transition" a la Mexicana', Paper presented to the Academic Workshop on Democracy, Kellogg Institute, University of Notre Dame, 30 April 1994.

Zapata, F., 'Mexican Labour and Economic Crisis', Paper presented at the Latin American Centre, University of Oxford, 26 January 1996.

4. Theses

Barrera, E., 'Telecoms and International Capital. The peripheral state: the Case of Mexico', PhD, University of Texas at Austin, 1992.

Del Valle Sanchez, M., 'El Movimiento Telefonista del 22 de abril de 1976: Alcances y Limitaciones en el Movimiento Obrero Nacional', Thesis in Sociology (Degree), UNAM, Mexico, 1978.

Heller, M., 'The Politics of Telecommunications Policy in Mexico', PhD in Political Science, University of Sussex, 1991.

Luz Ruelas, A., 'México y Estados Unidos en la Revolución Mundial de las telecomunicaciones', Thesis in History for UNAM/University of Texas at Austin, 1995.

Martínez de Ita, M. E. *et al.*, 'Explotación, Dominación y Lucha: El Caso de los telefonistas', Undated thesis in Economics, Universidad Autonoma de Puebla, Mexico.

Mondragon Pérez, Y., 'Cambio en la relación corporativa entre estado y los sindicatos: El caso del Sindicato de Telefonistas de la República Mexicana 1987–1993', Masters thesis in Politics, UNAM, 1994.

Solís Granados, V. J., 'El Cambio Estructural y la Privatización en TELMEX', UNAM Degree thesis in Economics, Mexico, 1992.

Won-ho, K., 'The Mexican Regime's Political Strategy in Implementing Economic Reform in Comparative Perspective: a Case Study of the Privatization of the Telecommunications Industry', PhD in Politics, University of Texas at Austin, 1992.

Xelhuantzi López, M., 'Reforma del estado mexicano y sindicalismo', Masters Thesis in Political Science, UNAM, 1992.

Index